DRUGS & DEMOCRACY IN RIO DE JANEIRO

Enrique Desmond Arias

DRUGS & DEMOCRACY
IN RIO DE JANEIRO

TRAFFICKING,
SOCIAL NETWORKS,
& PUBLIC SECURITY

THE UNIVERSITY OF NORTH CAROLINA PRESS   CHAPEL HILL

Designed by Heidi Perov
Set in Charter and Champion

The paper in this book meets the guidelines for permanence and durability of the Committee on Production Guidelines for Book Longevity of the Council on Library Resources.

Portions of this book have been reprinted with permission in revised form from "The
Dynamics of Criminal Governance: Networks and Social Order in Rio de Janeiro," *Journal of
Latin American Studies* 38 (May 2006); "Trouble en Route: Drug Trafficking and Clientelism
in Rio de Janeiro Shantytowns," *Qualitative Sociology* 29, no. 3 (Fall 2006); and "Faith in Our
Neighbors: Networks and Social Order in Three Brazilian Favelas," *Latin American Politics
and Society* 46 (Spring 2004).

Title page photograph by Luiz Flávio de Carvalho Costa

Library of Congress Cataloging-in-Publication Data
Arias, Enrique Desmond.
   Drugs and democracy in Rio de Janeiro : trafficking, social networks, and
public security / Enrique Desmond Arias.
      p. cm.
   Includes bibliographical references and index.
   ISBN-13: 978-0-8078-3060-4 (cloth: alk. paper)
   ISBN-10: 0-8078-3060-7 (cloth: alk. paper)
   ISBN-13: 978-0-8078-5774-8 (pbk.: alk. paper)
   ISBN-10: 0-8078-5774-2 (pbk.: alk. paper)
      1. Violence—Brazil—Rio de Janeiro. 2. Slums—Brazil—Rio de Janeiro. 3. Crime—Brazil—
Rio de Janeiro. 4. Drug traffic—Brazil—Rio de Janeiro. 5. Police corruption—Brazil—Rio de
Janeiro. 6. Community organization—Brazil—Rio de Janeiro. I. Title.
   HN290.R47V53 2006
   364.10981'53—dc22   2006013089

cloth   10 09 08 07 06   5 4 3 2 1
paper   10 09 08 07 06   5 4 3 2 1

For my parents, Catherine and Enrique

CONTENTS

Departure

Around 10:00 P.M. one rainy Friday night, a friend and I drove out of a favela (shantytown) and headed up an access ramp onto one of the major highways that runs from Rio de Janeiro's gritty working-class Zona Norte (North Zone) to the glittering seaside Zona Sul (South Zone). As we rounded the curve on the slick incline, our tires lost traction and the car spun out of control as other vehicles bore down behind us.

A few minutes earlier, we had left a notoriously crime-ridden favela where my friend, a European ex-patriot, runs a nongovernmental organization (NGO) focused on keeping at-risk adolescents out of criminal activity. He had received some substantial funding over the past year and was in the process of completing an expansion of the NGO's facilities that would allow for a dramatic increase in his group's services. As we drove to the community that evening, he had told me that he had asked me to come out there with him to serve as his guinea pig. The favela had just come through a rash of gunfights between police and the local drug gang, and my friend wanted to show his new construction to donors and other visitors who would arrive in Brazil in a few weeks. My place in all this was to see how the drug dealers who had a heavy presence on the favela's main street would react to my friend showing up with an unknown outsider on a Friday evening, a peak drug-dealing time.

We arrived in the favela around 8:00 P.M. As things go in Rio's favelas, we had to turn down our headlights so as not to provoke a hail of bullets from the traffickers who had positioned themselves at the entrance of the community. We drove down the street past the usual groups of young people and adults out enjoying their Friday night in this very busy favela. Along the way we passed the occasional *boca de fumo* (mouth of smoke, drug sales point), where a group of adolescents and young men would sit with automatic rifles and other weapons selling cocaine and marijuana.

We parked our car and walked to the NGO's facilities. As we strolled down the main street, we passed several bars playing blisteringly loud music where groups of men sat, drank beer, and somehow managed to carry on conversations. With no streetlights, much of the illumination came from bare incandescent bulbs in the many homes and shops that lined the street. As the rain misted around us, the intense lights diffused into a low-level glare above which there was only darkness spotted with lamplight from the insides of homes.

Further on, we walked calmly past a couple of groups of armed men. I had been researching favelas for nine years at this point and had walked past well-armed groups many times. My friend had brought me along for this reason. He knew that if things got dicey and police or dealers questioned us about my presence, I understood what I needed to say to get out of the situation safely.

Eventually, we made it to the building that would house his NGO. After showing me around, my friend talked for a while with some of the people working at the NGO. Eventually we noticed the time and remembering that we had agreed to meet a friend for dinner in Copacabana, a Zona Sul neighborhood, we calmly walked back up the street past the groups of armed men, got into our car, and headed out of the favela.

Happily, we survived our very minor accident. The car swerved out of control and popped itself loudly over a low curb, and the vehicles coming from behind had enough time to avoid hitting us. We succeeded in getting the car restarted and headed back off to our appointment. As we drove away, I noted with irony that we had gone to one of Rio's more notoriously dangerous favelas and the most immediate threat to our safety had come not from police, drug traffickers, or even one of the stray bullets that Rio's press reports on so frequently but, rather, from a routine traffic accident.

Danger and Fear in Rio de Janeiro

When I talk about my research with friends and colleagues, they often ask me: "How did you do this work? Wasn't it really dangerous?" Here I attempt to answer these questions.

Media outlets in both Brazil and the United States put a tremendous amount of time into reporting on certain poor urban areas as dangerous and even barbarous places that outsiders, especially from the middle and upper classes, venture into only at their own peril. In both the United States and Brazil, frightening and threatening depictions of poor urban neighborhoods have existed at least since the end of the nineteenth century.[1] Despite important efforts to show the integration of poor neighborhoods with the rest of the city, these ideas have not gone away.[2] Indeed, with growing homicide rates stemming from the narcotics and arms trades, such thoughts have become even more entrenched in both North and South America. These images are, in part, political and social tools that help to consolidate different class identities and advance particular political agendas. If you believed what people on the street tell you or pay passing attention to what appears in Rio's sensationalist newspapers, you would think that no outsider, especially not a relatively well-educated, middle-class, U.S. citizen such as me, would survive more than five minutes in one of these places. Indeed, when I first visited Rio in 1994 to study Portuguese, the upper-middle-class Carioca (Rio native) family that I lived with told me in no uncertain terms that I had to stay out of the favelas because drug gangs ran them and I would be putting myself in danger if I visited one.

Of course, this only made me more curious. After a couple of weeks in Rio, despite the horrific stories I had heard, I realized that many of the people I had contact with, be they bus drivers, waiters, or janitors, lived in these places. By some estimates, nearly a fifth of Rio's population lives in the city's more than six hundred favelas. I wondered how it could be that areas where so many people lived were no-go areas for such a substantial portion of the population. I quickly found out, however, that this was not the case. All sorts of people from better-off areas of the city and even tourists regularly go to favelas to visit friends, go to a dance such as at a samba school rehearsal or at one of the city's notorious *baile funks* (hip-hop balls), buy drugs, or do social work.[3]

What holds all of these different activities together is that outsiders visit favelas for a discernible reason that they can easily explain to the residents of the community. Further, if we exclude people visiting to buy products available in favelas, be it drugs or more legitimate forms of entertainment, virtually all other outsiders who spend any time in a favela have a direct personal connection in the community—a person who can vouch for and explain their presence. Thus, contrary to the stories of my friends, almost anyone, using reasonable caution, can go to a favela without much fear of drug trafficker violence against them, as long as they have an accepted personal or commercial reason for their visit.

When I began the process of conducting research, I sought to build individual ties that would help me gain access to favelas. During an exploratory research trip one summer, my primary challenge was gaining access to a favela. Everyone I initially talked to, usually people who taught in local universities, told me how dangerous the work was and offered little help in putting me in touch with favela residents. After a month of trying and unhappily getting nowhere, I first visited a favela with the assistance of an internship program run by the Pontifíca Universidade Católica that placed undergraduates in favelas to provide social services. Later I traveled to favelas with a candidate for city council. Neither of these efforts, however, resulted in strong contacts that could provide the basis for later research. My big break-through came when I made contact with one young program officer at Viva Rio, at the time an up-and-coming local NGO, who provided me with a long list of names and phone numbers of civic organizers in favelas around the city. I also received similar, though more focused, help through the Fundação Bento Rubião. Armed with a fairly long list of phone numbers that came from trusted references, I spent my last month in the city visiting favelas and choosing the three research sites that I discuss in this book.

In each community, I established strong connections with leaders of the local Associação de Moradores (Residents' Association, AM), the civic organization that generally mediates relations between outsiders and the community. In two of the three favelas that I studied, these men had very close ties to the local drug gang. When I started work, drug dealers often challenged me as I walked by their *bocas*. I always responded that I was visiting one of my connections in the AM, and they invariably let me in without further problems. After awhile if an inexperienced look-out stopped me, others would just say something like, "Oh, he's a friend of Josias, its cool," and let me go by. In one community, the adolescent gang member who kept watch became friendly and joked with me as I went to work.

The following event drives home the usefulness of these connections. One night I was working very late in the favela of Tubarão, one of my research sites, inter-viewing a drug addict and his girlfriend, when a dealer decided that I looked like an x-9 (undercover informant) that gang members suspected operated in the favela. If he and other traffickers decided this was true they would have brutally murdered me. The addict I had interviewed tried to explain things but did not get anywhere. Despite all of this, I was never really nervous since I had the protection of the AM president who was also the godfather of an important drug trafficker's child. On other occasions this had always worked to resolve potential problems. After I explained myself and my work, the trafficker apologized, suggested I take care and that I, perhaps, should not stay out on the street so late.

Learning

At the most basic level, a *lei do silencio* (law of silence), which informally enjoins residents from talking about issues related to drug trafficking on pain of expulsion or death, governs personal interactions in favelas. Residents, however, constantly talk about violence and crime and, in the end, honor the *lei* more in its breach than in its practice. Those same residents, nonetheless, are usually extremely wary about talking to people they do not know, especially if they purport to be writing a book.[4] Even though I had the protection of important residents, I found out shortly after arriving in each place that this in no way guaranteed me useful data. I often had a very hard time conversing about any substantive issue with residents during the first two months I spent in each community. People might not have had a problem with my presence, but they certainly had no reason to risk their lives providing me with information.

To overcome this barrier in each community, I spent considerable time building relationships with individual residents. I began this study with historical interviews of older residents. These were generally easy interviews to schedule, since retirees often have little to do, stay at home, and look forward to new company and talking about old times. These interviews mostly covered uncontroversial topics such as local settlement and the distribution of public services to the favela. On occasion, however, our conversations went deeper and provided information about contemporary conditions. Beyond this, however, just conducting interviews and spending time in the community built my credibility among residents. The longer I spent in a place, the more people trusted me. During these early days, I would buy sodas from local merchants and just sit and chat with people about mundane things like soccer, the weather, or my life in the United States. Inevitably, interesting things would happen that would, on occasion, lead to a more open conversation.

Slowly, residents would let their guard down. Sometimes this happened when a police action occurred while I was visiting a community. On several occasions, police searched me, along with other residents. This helped confirm my claims that I was just a researcher and helped residents to relax. On other occasions, something tragic, such as a murder or beating, would take place, and residents would talk about that in my presence. Gradually, I suspect that a significant number of residents realized that they had said sensitive things around me and that nothing had happened to them as a result. A few began to trust me. Over time, in each community, I developed a handful of strong relationships that, along with other supplementary conversations and observations, provided me with an understanding of what was happening in each favela.

Eventually, I began to get fairly full accountings of events from a number of residents. I then faced the not-insignificant challenge of sorting through and evaluating the quality of this information. Rumors swirl around favelas like leaves on a fall day. Sometimes people tell stories to build themselves up. Occasionally informants outright lie. Often, those lies, if you can find them, are telling. To distinguish among these stories, I regularly talked to multiple residents. Often a contact would tell me one story and then I would ask another about the incident to see what they would say. This occasionally led to two versions of the same events, which, in the context of who was telling the story, provided me with more insights into what had happened. Sometimes I had the opportunity to watch a group of residents talk after an event and watch them sort out for themselves what they thought had occurred. This helped me understand the relational and dialogic processes that build the political reality of the community. From these different perspectives, I built an account of the contemporary life of the favela.

Many of my interviews were tense, and even residents I was relatively close to openly worried about talking to me or would use euphemisms during conversations to avoid exposing themselves. To protect contacts, I recorded no interviews. To prevent data from falling into the hands of police when leaving the favela, I kept very spare outlines of notes while I was in the community. I wrote these outlines in English using my own shorthand to prevent any possibility that local police would know who had said what to me. Later, I reconstructed these notes in detail, first by hand and then on my computer. This book contains numerous quotes from residents that are all based on the detailed reconstructions that I made after I had left the community. In preparing these quotes for use in this book, I have had to change some personal pronouns so that the quotations make sense in the context I use them in. Nevertheless, the quotations in this book are my best reproduction of what residents were trying to say to me while I spoke with them.

The most substantial and real danger I faced while working on this project was that a gunfight would break out while I was visiting a favela. In these cases very little could have protected me from a stray bullet. In general, especially during the early part of the research, I reduced this risk by staying in the communities only during the day. Toward the end of my research, as I grew to know a community and as I had closer relationships with residents, I would visit the favelas at night. During a brief period at the end of my research, I lived in one of the communities.

Conducting Research in Dangerous Environments

So, as my friends and colleagues ask, how did I conduct this research and how did I deal with the danger associated with it? To a certain extent, my status as a foreigner afforded me a degree of protection. Neither traffickers nor police wanted the trouble associated with the injury or death of a graduate student from the United States. As someone who was visibly not from the community, I was stopped by the police usually only to see if I had bought drugs. I was regularly searched and politely questioned about what I was doing in the favela, but, as I speak Portuguese reasonably well, I never had any trouble explaining myself to their satisfaction.

I worked hard to manage the extent to which I exposed myself to risk during this research. I carefully chose who I associated with and how I built and expanded relationships. My most regular contacts were with men and women between the ages of thirty and sixty who had active and respected lives in the community and who personally knew many traffickers. Usually they were involved with social programs, political groups, civic organizations, and churches. These residents had a substantial knowledge of the broad politics of the community but, at the same time, were far enough removed from adolescence, the age group most at risk of physical violence, that they could feel secure in the community talking with an outsider. Their position and stature within the favela protected them to a certain extent from trafficker reprisals. I also was very aware of how I paced the growth and the development of those different relationships so that I would not arouse fear or suspicion among residents in general or among those involved in illegal activities. In the end, I controlled my exposure to risk as best I could. In practice, this is a lot easier to do than controlling the risk of a car accident on Rio's streets.

My connections to respected NGOs and community members also helped greatly. Strong positive ties to local leaders who could vouch for me made my work possible, enabled me to explain what I was doing in the communities, and provided me with the basis for building relationships with other contacts in the favelas.

Finally, the one thing that perhaps kept me the safest was my promise to virtually everyone I talked to that I would not quote them by name and that I would do my best to protect their identities. To this end, with one exception, I use pseudonyms for all the contacts referenced. In addition, in an effort to further protect their residents, I have also used pseudonyms for Tubarão and Santa Ana, two of the three communities in this study. Of the three communities that appear in this book, I use the correct name only for Vigário Geral, since telling the story of that community would not make sense without its particular history and the extensive literature associated with it.

Acknowledgments

I am indebted to numerous people and institutions, without whom this undertaking would have been much more difficult, if not impossible.

First, there are my friends and colleagues from in and around Madison, Rio de

Janeiro, Oberlin, Miami, and New York. They have provided me with support, companionship, tough questions, and good advice while I worked on this project. They include Andy Baker, Amy Chazkel, Stephen Deets, Beth Dougherty, Luke Dowdney, Ken Ehrenberg, Sergio Ferreira, John Fieno, Joshua Frielich, Anna Gade, Martha Hanson, Jay Krishnan, Ross Lippert, Vitor Lledo, Luciana Lopez Delphim, Ben Penglase, Ed Paulino, Dan Pinello, Rosane Moraes Rego, Corinne Davis Rodrigues, Aaron Seeskin, Carrie Smith, Paul Sneed, Daryle Williams, and Erica Windler.

Special thanks here go to a number of people in Brazil who provided me with profound insights into life in favelas, help in navigating Brazil's bureaucracy, or assistance in gaining access to favelas. They are Eliane Junqueira, Elizabeth Leeds, André Porto, Maria Alice Rezende de Carvalho, José Augusto Rodrigues, and Pedro Strozenberg.

In the New York area, at John Jay and around CUNY, a number of individuals and institutions have provided support and advice on this project. At John Jay, Harold Sullivan has provided me with the time and support necessary to complete revisions of this book. Jacob Marini has provided important advice on grant writing. The CUNY Faculty Publications Program group in the social sciences led by Stephen Steinberg provided helpful feedback on the manuscript, as did the Mellon Fellowship group on violence at the Humanities Center led by John Collins and Omar Dabour. My thanks to all of the colleagues who participated in these meetings and who provided comments on drafts of the project. A fellowship from the Center for Place, Culture, and Politics also provided helpful release time during the final revisions. Finally, the Bildner Center for Western Hemisphere Studies provided helpful support for this project, as well as a dynamic intellectual environment within the CUNY system to discuss issues related to Latin American politics. I am particularly grateful to Mauricio Font for his efforts to organize such a high-quality program there.

This project benefited from discussion, criticism, and comments that came from presentations made at the Bildner Center for Western Hemisphere Studies, at the Watson Institute for International Studies at Brown University, at the Brazil Faculty Seminar at Columbia University, at the Roger Thayer Stone Center at Tulane University, at the Foro Latino at Carleton College, and at the Latin American Studies Program at Cornell University.

This project profited especially from the insights and commentary of Javier Auyero, Susan Burgerman, Jerry Dávila, Robert Gay, Janice Perlman, and Mark Ungar, as well as the anonymous reviewers at the University of North Carolina Press. My editor, Elaine Maisner, has been efficient and supportive throughout this process and has helped in shaping and improving the manuscript. My thanks to her and all the other people at the University of North Carolina Press who helped bring this project to publication.

Portions of this project have previously been published in *Latin American Politics and Society*, the *Journal of Latin American Studies*, and *Qualitative Sociology*. I thank the editors and publishers of those journals for allowing me to use some portions of those articles in this book.

The research involved in this book could not have been conducted without substantial financial support from a Title VI FLAS Fellowship and a Tinker Summer Research Fellowship from the Latin American and Iberian Studies Center of the University of Wisconsin–Madison; a Scott Kloeck-Jensen International Practitioner Fellowship and a MacArthur Fellowship from the International Institute of the University of Wisconsin–Madison; a short-term research grant from Oberlin College; a grant from the PSC-CUNY research awards program; a Dorothy Danforth Compton Fellowship from the Institute for the Study of World Politics; and a Fulbright fellowship. Many thanks to all of these funding agencies. Their commitment to supporting field research is extremely important to maintaining our ongoing body of knowledge on the complex problems facing countries in the global south.

At the University of Wisconsin, I am particularly grateful to three people who have long been involved in this project. Michael Schatzberg and Richard Merelman provided extensive, helpful, and demanding commentary. Their thoughts and ideas have greatly influenced my growth as a scholar and the structure of this book. Special thanks go to Leigh Payne, who has provided support for this project from the beginning and through its many iterations—I could not have imagined more competent, thoughtful, and human advice. My profound thanks to her for her unflagging support.

I also thank my parents, Catherine and Enrique Arias, and my brother and sister, Andres and Karolina, who provided me with the immense personal support and grounding needed to undertake this venture. Without them, I, literally, wouldn't be who I am.

Finally, I want to express my deepest gratitude to Julia Busch, who has put up with research trips, long nights, and the many weekends of work that it took to finish this project. But all of this would have been impossible without the acceptance and tolerance of the residents of the three communities where I conducted research. In these places, I met some of the most courageous and remarkable people that I have known. I learned a great deal from them about life and politics in favelas—which is reflected in this book—and much more about living with dignity. I am humbled by what many of them have accomplished under what can only be described as extreme adversity. My book cannot do them or their experience justice. I can only give them my thanks.

MOGEC	Movimento de Gestão Comunitário (Movement for Community Management)
MSF	Médicos Sem Fronteiras (Doctors without Borders)
NGO	nongovernmental organization
PC	Polícia Civil (Civil Police)
PCC	Primeiro Comando do Capital (First Command of the Capitol)
PM	Polícia Militar (Military Police)
PNP	People's National Party
PRI	Partido Revolucionario Institucional (Institutional Revolutionary Party)
PT	Partido dos Trabalhadores (Workers' Party)
SDLC	Scuderie Detetive Le Cocq (The Shield of Detective Le Cocq)
SENAI	Serviço Nacional de Aprendizagem Industrial (National Service for Industrial Learning)
TC	Terceiro Comando (Third Command)
UFMG	Universidade Federal de Minas Gerais

DRUGS & DEMOCRACY IN RIO DE JANEIRO

Thinking about Social Violence in Brazil

Recently, drug traffickers based in Rio de Janeiro's favelas have attacked government buildings, bombed buses, and successfully ordered widespread business closings.[1] Over the past decade, murder rates have averaged 50 per 100,000, in line with the most violent U.S. cities, and overall rates may actually be even higher as a result of increasing rates of disappearances. In poor districts, murder rates can exceed 150 per 100,000 inhabitants.[2] Indeed, riding this wave of criminal and police violence, human rights abuse has increased in Brazil since its transition to democracy two decades ago.[3] Things have gotten so bad that an enraged press and parts of the academic establishment declare that parallel "powers," "authorities," or "states" have emerged in the city's favelas, where criminals oppose the rule of law and act as judge, jury, and executioner.[4]

Brazil is not alone in suffering high levels of ongoing social violence. More than twenty years after authoritarian regimes began to fall, the region's democracies are far from perfect.[5] Much of this growth in violence arises not from expanding systematic state abuse but, rather, comes out of burgeoning crime feeding off the world cocaine market, the expansion of the international arms trade, and the changes in state institutions in an era of globalization. In Colombia, Jamaica, Peru, and Mexico, governments have lost control of some territory to guerrilla groups or gangs of highly organized, politically connected, drug dealers.[6] Rising crime justifies repressive policing policies, corruption penetrates deep into the state, and, while the rich flee to walled communities, the poor are forced to rely on criminals and predatory police for protection.[7] Why have things gotten so bad, and what can governments and social organizations do about it?

The drug traffickers that operate in Rio's favelas are overwhelmingly impoverished, poorly educated, nonwhite adolescents and young men. They constitute collectively one of the most disempowered, discriminated against, and heavily policed populations in Brazil. How can a group with these characteristics pose such a serious threat to the city as a whole and hold such substantial power that they can establish "parallel" states in the midst of one of the most important cities in one of Latin America's most powerful nations? The answer to this question is that criminals operating in favelas effectively build links into more powerful segments of state and society to gain a degree of localized power that is able to fend off state agents trying to repress crime.

Although drugs, drug trafficking, and violence have been major policy concerns for some time, with a few notable exceptions analyses of contemporary Latin America have eschewed discussing the political impact of violent organizations on domestic governance.[8] For too long, political analyses of crime and violence have used a top-down approach that sees criminal organizations, consistent with the claims of state officials, not as political actors but rather as subjects of justly repressive public policies. This book sets out to reverse this trend through a micro-level examination of the problem of violence in three Rio de Janeiro favelas. I will argue that crime and criminality are integral components of politics in Rio. Building on academic work on trafficking and clientelism in Rio and the role of criminals in politics, I will show that the persistence of trafficker power in this city emerges out of ongoing political relations that criminals maintain with civic actors and state officials through extensive and flexible illegal networks that help them to build the support and the protection necessary to engage in long-term criminal activities. By tying themselves into existing state and social networks, traffickers avail themselves of both governmental resources and existing social capital. As we will see, these relationships undermine and co-opt state and social efforts to control drug trafficking. The dense interconnections among state officials, civic leaders, and criminals suggest that to understand drug trafficking and, indeed, the broader problem of social violence in Latin America, we need to move beyond the state-society model of politics that has dominated our perceptions of the region and develop a more nuanced basis for understanding political relationships that includes criminal groups as active, though clandestine, participants in the polity. Finally, I will show that civic mobilization, when coordinated with state action, can, over the medium term, provide a limited local-level strategy to control violence in Rio. Empirically, these claims move favelas from the periphery of Rio political life, where they are seen as marginal and violent communities somehow operating in opposition to the democratic state system, to the center, where they can be seen as integral and essential parts of a pervasively violent political system. The politics of favelas and the political operations of criminal gangs are central to any understanding of democracy and the rule of law in Rio—and in Brazil more generally.

Existing Approaches to Violence in Favelas

The study of favela violence in Rio is dominated by two schools of thought: the "divided city" approach and the neoclientelism approach. Those who suggest that Rio is a "divided city" see Rio as an urban area at war with itself. Here traffickers dominate a dangerous feudal underworld on the city's hillsides that stands dramatically apart from the life of the wealthy seashore neighborhoods of the middle and upper classes. The alternative approach, neoclientelism, elaborates a different model of state-favela relations that examines how contacts among traffickers, police, civic actors, business leaders, and favela residents contribute to the violent conflicts that make Rio one of the world's most dangerous metropolises. Building on these writings, I will suggest a third approach based on a more flexible conception of criminal organizations operating in the context of state and social networks.

The "divided city" approach argues that since the mid-1980s, favelas, as a result of varied and complex forms of state policy failure, have emerged as "feudal" bastions of criminal dominance set apart from the rest of the city.[9] Roberto Kant de Lima, an anthropologist studying security issues in Rio, states, "The bandits do not follow the same norms as the State. They create a state within a state."[10] Rubem César Fernandes, an NGO leader, argues that "organized crime is growing in these regions, imposing on them a regime of unchecked violence." For Fernandes, the "parallel power and tyrannical rule" of these organizations "is impossible to contain . . . without abolishing the division between the civilized center and the margins excluded from civil rights."[11]

Luiz Eduardo Soares, a sociologist and former national secretary for public security, writes: "The territorial control of the bandits subtracts the zones of urban poverty from the national State and creates an archipelago of independent areas, a species of clandestine feudal barony, nonetheless visible, that the rule of law cannot reach, where democratic institutions, the Constitution, and the law do not operate."[12] These observers, and many others, see Rio as a "divided city," where poor areas are separated from the polity and dominated by a premodern form of authoritarian rule. The concept of feudalism is an interesting, if incomplete, way of looking at the challenges facing Rio.

This argument builds on assumptions about the weakness of a Brazilian state bereft of the social ties necessary to effectively implement policy and that, as a result, adopts counterproductive strategies to solve the crime problem.[13] Roberto Kant de Lima suggests that poor state policymaking plays an important part in creating the conditions for this violence: "And the legal State has been absolutely disastrous, because [it functions] like an actor in that conflict with bandits, using the same weapons and ethics as the bandits, who are considered enemies. It engages in combat with them and, as a result, is transformed into an equal of the bandits."[14] The state, then, empowers criminals and legitimizes existing parallel power by responding to criminals in a reciprocally barbaric way. Soares similarly argues that the breakdown of state control stems from a collapse of internal control of the police forces within the state and their use of illegal violence. He writes: "The state itself, many years ago, became part of the problem. This happened because of the irresponsibility of governments and of sectors of public opinion that created situations in which the police corporations received a green light to act outside of legal limits."[15] Police operating violently to repress crime "became" part of the problem by engaging in a war with criminals. This gives legitimacy to traffickers by placing the state on an equal footing with them in the eyes of many citizens.

Especially in its cruder, journalistic, iterations, this approach has its historic roots in perceptions of favelas as an "other" to the modern civilized city and begins from the premise that the state is too weak to control the powerfully armed criminals who dominate poor areas the city.[16] For these writers, Rio de Janeiro is a city in danger of suffering the type of state breakdown that has occurred in Colombia.[17]

In the more complex and sophisticated scholarly variations described above, this approach suggests that the growing power of traffickers and the breakdown of state power in favelas and other poor areas of Rio emerges as a result of the failure of the state to adequately integrate the population of those areas into the wider polity and the failure of the state to adopt coherent and effective policing strategies. This variation provides significant insights into the problems with the logic of the war on drugs and provides an effective approach to understanding how people in Rio feel about the problem of violence and drug trafficking. Nevertheless, by beginning from the premise of a modern democratic state that is absent from and unable to penetrate poor communities dominated by traffickers, the "divided city" does not go far enough in examining how the deep interconnections among state officials and favela leaders contribute to the violence affecting Rio. The conflict in Rio's favelas does not occur because favelas are cut off from the state but, rather, because of the way the state is present in those communities and the relationships state actors maintain with criminals who operate in them.

The neoclientelist approach starts from a very different perspective by arguing that trafficker power is overlaid on a history of patrimonial engagement between politicians and favela leaders.[18] This formulation argues that traffickers use traditionally structured connections to officeholders to obtain resources and bolster their political position within favelas. Neoclientelism stems out of work from the 1970s onward that examines the deep interconnections between favelas and the city's political life.[19] Traffickers and other favela leaders use patronage to reproduce in favelas general forms of domination and exploitation that exist in Rio and Brazil as a whole.[20] Leeds argues that "the physical and criminal violence resulting from the drug trade is a visible and tangible form of violence used by the state and it masks a structural-institutional and more hidden violence while perpetuating neo-clentelistic political relationships."[21] Traffickers and the poor survive in an unequal democracy through a form of clientelism that opens up in the spaces left by a weakening state and that is engendered by certain types of state and social activity. For Leeds, traffickers establish direct relationships with state actors to obtain resources to strengthen their organizations.[22] Leeds uses the language of parallel power and state absence, but the thrust of her article focuses on how older modes of political connection and representation have been updated to support drug trafficking in the cities' favelas. Marcos Alvito has noted the growing similarities of the patronage relations among traffickers, politicians, and favela residents.[23] Through criminal activities and contacts with politicians, traffickers assemble the resources necessary to provide basic welfare and public services to favela residents. This support—and bribes to police—buys traffickers the security to continue operating and creates a system of state-tolerated, localized criminal dominance.[24]

Clientelist approaches begin from the premise of asymmetrical, durable, personalist relationships among individuals and groups of different status.[25] Clientelist relations are generally hierarchical, with a powerful high-status actor delivering aid to a lower-status actor in exchange for favors.[26] In clientelist relations, be they within Mexican camarillas or between legislative candidates and favela residents in Rio, status relations reflect flows of resources and lead to political networks involving patrons, clients, and brokers that reproduce themselves within certain social groups.[27] In the broader national political landscape, patrons have higher status than their clients, although clients may look on their patrons with some ambivalence.

Political relations in Rio's favelas, however, are more complex. The problem with using this model to describe traffickers' relations with politicians and favela residents is that status hierarchies in this situation are very unclear. Traffickers themselves may possess relatively high status among some favela residents, but other residents may view traffickers as a problem and see them as having lower status than respected older residents, dedicated workers, or heads of families. Further, traffickers, as a result of their criminal activities, possess extremely low status in society at large. Unlike other traditional clientelist patrons, who may very well be viewed dubiously by their poor clients, drug traffickers lie outside the pale of government even while they engage with it. State legitimacy, in fact, is partially based on the suppression of banditry.[28] Neither national nor international norms tolerate traffickers, and government leaders devote significant resources to destroying their organizations.[29] As a result, they cannot directly interact with many members of civil society or the state and need to work through actors who can confer higher degrees of status on them to undertake many activities.[30] This leads to much more complex networks than those typically described by clientelism, made up of mutually dependent and differentially equal status actors.[31] Traffickers, like militias or private armies in Africa, are a new type of political actor—part of a wider privatization of violence in Brazil—whose political position in poor communities stems from an appropriation of state power made possible by the unique ways international illegal markets have expanded into Rio and the ways their new market power allows traffickers to build contacts with civic actors and state officials.[32] Evidence I will present suggests that these newly empowered criminals deal with state and social actors through the deployment of an illegal network that brings criminals together with state and social actors to engage in a variety of political activities, including clientelism.

Violent Democracy in Latin America

The endemic social conflict, persistent human rights violations, and inequality that characterize Latin American polities twenty years after the return of democratic rule pose a major challenge to scholars studying the politics of the region. Some researchers have ascribed these disappointments to the failure of political institutions to eliminate the vestiges of authoritarian rule and penetrate retrograde sectors of state and society. But others have suggested that violence persists in Latin America not because of state weakness but, rather, because of the existence of external social forces and institutions that not only resist efforts to extend the rule of law but also engage with state actors to promote illegal activities and rights violations.

Guillermo O'Donnell, in a seminal 1993 article, argued that endemic human rights abuse in the hemisphere stemmed from the failure of public institutions. This resulted in the existence of "brown areas" where the state has a "very low or nil" presence and where power rests in private hands that work to use state resources to reproduce authoritarian practices—practices that often discriminate against the poor at local and regional levels. These "brown areas" emerged as a result of the debt crisis and the historic inability of the Latin American state to penetrate certain segments of society and the national territory.[33] Other scholars have built on this approach by ascribing the endemic conflict in the region to the failure of political institutions to force retrograde police bureaucracies to respect human rights or adequately strengthen judicial systems to eliminate official impunity and provide citizens with access to justice.[34] This trajectory is most apparent in several otherwise excellent volumes on the rule of law in Latin America, where chapters focus on the failure of the state to guarantee rights, rein in rogue police, control prison violence, and establish adequate judicial systems.[35] Not one of these volumes systematically analyzes the ongoing impact of active criminal organizations and activities on the broader political systems in Latin America.

This approach provides a vivid but incomplete picture of violence in the hemisphere. Clearly there are places in the region today where the rule of law only partially exists, and it is important to engage in police and judicial reforms if residents of these areas are to have any hope of having their rights protected. Nevertheless, if we only focus on institutional failure, we will not pay sufficient attention to the active political constellations that promote violence both inside and outside the state and resist meaningful reforms.

In *Laughter Out of Place*, a fascinating account of the ideologies of violence operating among the poor in Brazil, Donna Goldstein suggests that O'Donnell's approach could be applied to Rio's favelas when, she writes, "local gangs provide a parallel state structure and alternative rule of law" providing "housing and employment and help in times of trouble." In the context of maintaining order, she writes that "they do what the police cannot."[36] Favelas, then, lie outside the normal rule of law and are subject to a separate political order. The problems that favelas pose, in this formulation, stem from the breakdown of the state's ability to enforce order in these communities and the emergence of alternative, parallel, structures of political power.[37]

The problem with this approach is that it cannot adequately account for variations among criminal actors and the different types of relationships they maintain with state and civic actors. Goldstein acknowledges that gangs in Rio's favelas "become mediators in the face of a violent and corrupt police force" and suggests that criminality operates in Rio's favelas at least in part because of state corruption.[38] Building on a reading of Anton Blok's enthnography of the Mafia in Sicily, Goldstein argues that "parallel states" emerge in Rio's favelas as drug traffickers fill the void left by the state to provide services to the community and mediate the relationship between the community and the larger state. This, however, represents a limited reading of Blok's book, *The Mafia of a Sicilian Village*, where he is concerned not just with describing the Mafia as a mode of governance associated with the consolidating Italian state in nineteenth- and twentieth-century Sicily but also with contrasting the Mafia with bandits as two different forms of violent actors that have very different social and political roles. The Mafia, for Blok, are bandits co-opted by powerful landowners to help maintain localized order and put down peasant/bandit insurgencies in a place where bureaucratic state power is contingent, unreliable, and seen as, perhaps, not fully legitimate.[39] Reading Rio's gangs simultaneously as "Mafia" and "parallel states" obscures the critical distinction that Blok makes between the Mafia, a form of collusive organized crime that operates in the market place of private protection, and bandit uprisings, violent armed groups in direct confrontation with landowners and the state that look much more like incipient "parallel states" than either the Mafia or Rio's gangs do. If trafficker power emerges from and depends, at least in part, on state policy toward these communities and a positive participation in the support of trafficking organizations, then we need to investigate not how these groups form separate "parallel" orders but instead how state power and social forces actually help build, maintain, and extend trafficker power.[40]

This analysis reveals the weakness of the parallel state/"brown" area approach to studying favelas. If there are strong connections among criminals and the state that (may) include criminals participating in the state building process, it is very difficult to view gangs as parallel state entities that have something fundamentally in common with, for example, the Sendero Luminoso or other Maoist-influenced guerrilla groups.[41] Blok reveals that the Mafia colluded with elements of the state and local landowners to repress bandit uprisings that arose among disaffected peasants demanding justice in an extremely unequal political and economic system. Blok's discussion of bandits, actors much easier to categorize as somehow "parallel" to the state, is essential to understanding the collusive arrangements the Mafia maintained with the developing Italian state. Like the Mafia, Rio's organized criminals are well tied into the Brazilian state system, although they may, again like the Mafia, impose a rough justice at the local level. Conflating bandits and the Mafia and arguing that parallel states somehow also collude with police and other state officials obscures important elements of how criminals operate in Rio, as well as important distinctions among forms of contention in twentieth-century Sicily. All of this makes it hard to understand the differences between urban criminal gangs and actual revolutionary groups that have attempted to establish parallel states in other parts of Latin America, as occurred with the Sendero Luminoso and as occurs in more limited ways with elements of the FARC today. These are very different types of political formations, and only by discerning their differences can we understand the problems that Rio faces and disentangle urban policymaking from the logic and language of counterinsurgent warfare.

It is worth noting here that O'Donnell at no point makes use of the term "parallel state" (nor for that matter does Leeds, who prefers the more flexible term "parallel polities") when referring to "brown" areas. His recent work on "brown" areas, in fact, focuses on how state breakdown in these places is caused by connections among powerful regional and local authoritarian actors and the state. The weakness of the concept of "brown" areas, however, lies precisely in the type of misreading discussed above.[42] By looking at areas of localized nondemocratic forms of order primarily as places of state breakdown where the rule of law is absent that can be characterized as similarly "brown," this approach obscures important distinctions among different ways that law breaks down in different places and focuses insufficiently on the types of order that are built in those places. Blok suggests two different forms of order in Sicily: areas dominated by bandits and areas dominated by the Mafia. An examination of Latin America today offers a wide diversity of different types of subnational nondemocratic orders that have emerged across the region. It is important to understand these variations. To do this, we need to leave aside an analysis of violence as a breakdown of the rule of law; instead we need to look at the political constellations that lead to the creation of the varied forms of subnational orders that have emerged in violent places throughout the Americas.

Other scholars have begun to critically assess this approach by examining how actors and institutions inside and outside the state build political organizations and connections that promote ongoing conflict. Diane Davis, Anthony Pereira, and their collaborators have argued that to understand social violence, especially in a post–Cold War environment where interstate conflict appears less relevant to questions of security than do terrorism and intrastate conflict, we need to understand not just the operation and failure of formal institutions but the nature and form of irregular armed forces and how their connections to other state and social actors contribute to those conflicts.[43] The ongoing civil war in Colombia, for example, can only be understood through linkages that criminals, paramilitaries, and, to a limited extent, guerrilla groups maintain to each other and to "legitimate" sectors of state and society.[44] On a different tack, Teresa Caldeira has argued that violence in Brazil is characterized not just by authoritarian legacies in the police force but also by the ways that the wealthy have privatized urban space and created walled communities based on a principle of private security. This environment of greater inequality creates positive factors that lead to new violent actors in the guise of private security guards and persistent support among the upper classes for a police force that directs extremely high levels of repression against the poor.[45] Leigh Payne has argued that "uncivil movements," violent and exclusionary social mobilizations, can effectively organize in transitional democracies and use connections with state institutions to undermine the process of democratization and strengthen the political hand of proauthoritarian elements in the political system.[46] Finally, for some time, Martha Huggins has been suggesting that the growing activity of death squads and other forms of privatized violence in Brazil has led to changing practices of localized sovereignty that have undermined basic democratic guarantees for much of the population.[47] These approaches go beyond earlier efforts to understand violence by examining the networks of state and social actors, institutions, and interests that actively support rights abuse and conflict.

A full understanding of the violence affecting Rio's favelas can only be achieved by building on these theories to understand not just the inadequacies of the state but also the active involvement of criminals and other social groups in behavior that promotes violence and obstructs reform. Looking at the particular configuration of interactions among criminals and other actors in state and society will offer a deeper understanding of the formal and informal factors that prevent the full protection of basic rights and contribute to the ongoing conflicts affecting many parts of the region. Only by understanding how criminals and other persistently violent actors inside and outside the state work together to perpetuate violence will we appreciate the full challenges facing Latin America's democracies today.

Fitting Criminals into the Political Picture

In developing countries, violent nonstate actors operating through networks with civic and state actors play increasingly important roles in the control of space, people, and resources.[48] Evidence from Africa, Asia, and Latin America indicates that intense long-term conflicts are sustained by black markets, NGO activities, and private military contractors often working in conjunction with formal state actors.[49] These networks, which cross the criminal/state/society frontiers, engage in political and social conflict with other similar illegal networks and with constellations of state and social actors that work to control crime and violence.[50] Although most political analysis of developing areas over the past twenty-five years has overlooked these issues by focusing on state institutions and relationships among the state and legitimate civic actors, in recent years a number of scholars have suggested that organized violent nonstate actors need to be incorporated into our picture of everyday politics.[51] Building on these analyses, this book attempts to further our understandings of the challenges facing democratic government in Latin America by developing a nuanced understanding of the political role of criminals and other violent actors.

What Role Do Persistent Violent Actors Have in the Polity?

In his classic book, *The Mafia of a Sicilian Village*, Anton Blok argued that criminals played a critical role in mediating the complex and often difficult relations among landlords, rentiers, and peasants in rural Sicily. Far from arguing that this criminal-political function was a reflection of a collapsing state, incapable of enforcing order, Blok claimed that criminals played an essential role in supporting the state structure on the island by helping to repress banditry and other forms of peasant dissent that might have created broader threats to the landholding structure.[52]

Similarly, writers working on contemporary Latin America have shown a variety of state/criminal connections that have impacted politics—ranging from state domination of illegal activities in Mexico, which has helped to fund important government candidates in elections, to a partial state breakdown in the face of a narco-guerrilla uprising in Peru.[53] The political environment in urban Rio and other parts of Latin America today, however, differs greatly from that which existed in Sicily in the early twentieth century, and, as a result, the political role of criminals is markedly different from the one that Blok observed. Nevertheless, Blok's central insight that criminals play a critical, if not constitutive role, in certain political systems remains key to understanding social order in Latin America in the postauthoritarian period.

The world that we live in today is one in which sovereign state power has been substantially rearranged. The international debt crisis and structural adjustment have forced many states in the developing world to dramatically scale back services to their citizenry, and governments find themselves unable to adequately fund and train police to deal with new challenges.[54] At the same time, globalization and the growth of transnational trade have dramatically expanded illegal markets in drugs and arms, which have enabled private actors to gain access to powerful combat weapons and the money to buy them. Thus, as state resources have declined, criminals and other private violent actors have gained the clout to confront state actors and provide some, albeit very limited, social services to the population. Excluded from labor markets and old forms of state assistance in these increasingly unequal political regimes, some citizens turn to illegal markets and actors for employment and welfare. This has led to spiraling crime and, as Martha Huggins and Teresa Caldeira have observed, the formal and informal privatization of security through private security firms and death squads.[55] In the face of changing power relationships, private actors, including criminals, have created new forms of regulation, dispute resolution, and security.

As the balance of state and private power shifts, gaps open up in political systems where the needs of certain groups, formerly provided for by the state but not adequately supplied by the legitimate private sector, are generally ignored. In this environment, which is also characterized by growing limits on public funds and the state's ability to provide basic security, organized criminals, persistent violent groups that operate in violation of the law but who are not formally in the employ of state institutions, play increasingly large roles in the political system by offering access to new sources of funding and the institutional capacity to support the activities of certain state and social actors. These criminals are skilled operators in growing illegal markets and the expanding private security arena. As such, they can tap into illegal resources that other social actors cannot and, among some portions of the population, command a degree of loyalty that can be useful to politicians seeking votes and civic actors working to build public support. Further, criminals, when coordinating with powerful state or civic actors, can employ violence to help those groups achieve ends that they might not have been able to through the courts or the police. This is particularly important in an international environment in which state actors, constrained by global human rights norms, cannot directly engage in certain forms of violence and may want to employ violence by proxy through nonstate actors.[56] Criminals, in turn, work with civic actors and state officials because, despite all of these changes, they are usually weak social actors who could easily be jailed or killed if they did not have the support of powerful civic actors or the protection of state officials. Contacts with actors in other segments of the polity provide criminals with access to state services and resources as well as popular legitimacy and support, which they could not avail themselves of on their own. Understanding the nature of these connections that criminals maintain with state and civic actors is essential to any understanding of how criminals operate, the effects they have on the polity, and how state and civic actors can work to control violence.

It is important to stop for a moment and note the inevitable imprecision of the concept of criminality in this context. Nearly all of the actors I analyze are engaged in some form of illegal activity and could, in a broad definition of the term, be considered "criminals." For the purposes of this book, however, I will define criminals as actors who regularly engage in illegal activities as a primary vocation but who have no formal ties to the state. That said, I fully recognize the extent to which state and civic actors may not only engage in illegal activity but, also in the case of state actors, define criminal activities in such a way as to advance particular political and professional projects that they are engaged in. The result is that, in popular discourse, in both Brazil and the United States, the most common image of criminals is of poor, nonwhite men engaged in generally low-level, overtly violent, illegal activities rather than of the well-off powerful traffickers and corrupt officials who facilitate large-scale movements of drugs and arms.

How Criminals Interact with Other Citizens and State Officials

Despite all of the compelling reasons that criminals, state officials, and civic actors may have to work together, the illegal and, indeed, dangerous behavior of criminals makes it difficult for criminals and legitimate political actors to maintain relationships. On the one hand, criminals are often extremely wary of establishing new relationships or deepening existing ones for fear that this could cause others to learn things about them that could expose them to danger. On the other hand, civic leaders or politicians could lose their positions if their ties to criminals were exposed. Under the circumstances that exist in many parts of Latin America today, where there are compelling reasons for criminals, state officials, and civic actors to develop and maintain connections, a networked model of social interactions, which keeps relationships relatively secret and flexible so that groups can deny connections in the event of exposure and limit the amount of compromising information their partners know about them, provides important insights into how these groups interact.[57]

Networks are voluntary and flexible organizations that allow individuals and groups to collaboratively and informally work together to achieve mutual or independent goals.[58] As institutions, networks are based on flexible links among component groups pursuing often similar interests.[59] When actors need to maintain trust and cultivate long-term contacts in conditions where hierarchical connections prove disadvantageous, networks offer an effective alternative form of organization that can facilitate political activity in circumstances where collaborators lack state protection.[60] Networks enable groups to easily and effectively work with a diverse and specialized set of actors, while sharing needed data and withholding confidential information.[61] Mutual observation of member groups helps to build organizational trust and social capital, transmit norms, and transfer legitimacy.[62] As a result, networks enable criminals to establish and build positive relations with social groups they depend on for protection and build functional, mediated, and varied connections with noncriminal actors whose expertise is of value to them. By using combinations of what Mark Granovetter calls weak and strong ties, criminals can mediate contacts with outsiders, while at the same time avoiding arrest or detection.[63]

These connections help criminals, civic actors, and state officials to work together, despite repressive efforts by some state officials and broad public opprobrium.

State/civic/criminal links help to channel political resources in ways that support illegal activity and make the reduction of violence difficult. This creates an active coalition of political actors who are supportive of long-term conflict and criminality that can resist efforts to control violence. An understanding of these coalitions and how they operate at the local level will help us to understand why violence is so extensive and persistent in Rio today.

Structures of Violence in Urban Brazil

Evidence presented in this book will show that criminals operating in Rio's favelas depend on connections to state and civic actors to fend off efforts by other criminals and some law-abiding state actors to arrest, kill, or displace them from the communities where they manage the drug trade. Knowing they must retain the support of local populations, criminals provide politicians with monopoly access to favelas during elections in exchange for resources to provide limited services to residents. More often than not, these connections are mediated by local civic leaders who have the skills and the social position to negotiate and appear with public figures. These civic leaders also do the difficult job of mediating the sensitive ties that traffickers maintain with favela residents on whom they depend for protection but who also suffer the brunt of the violence of the city's drug trade. These local leaders depend on traffickers for resources, protection, and support in local decision making and conflict. This all results in an environment in which criminals, civic actors, and state officials network together to accomplish specific personal and institutional goals and collectively support conditions that lead to long-term violence.

How Can Violence Be Controlled?

Today, as a result of state/civic/criminal networking, there is no adequate solution to the problem of violence in Rio. The most popular political response is to call for more-repressive policing policies to crush drug traffickers, who are seen as threatening to the body politic and as enemies in a national war on drugs. For some in Rio, this solution involves giving the federal government more power to deploy troops in the city to repress trafficking, as happened during the 1992 Rio Eco Summit and the 1994 Operação Rio, when the federal military was deployed in the city to restore order.[64] This response is, however, counterproductive. Not only does intense repression cause law-abiding residents of the favelas that are targeted in policing operations to identify more closely with traffickers, but giving law enforcement a freer hand and more weaponry only allows the many corrupt police in Rio to demand a larger cut of the drug trade, thus intensifying already existing illegal networks.

Another solution, which has been pursued by NGOs and progressive actors in the state, is to strengthen local civil society and help those organizations develop links with the state to control violence in particular communities.[65] Some money today does flow into social projects in favelas, but these small isolated efforts seem to have relatively little effect on violence and, to make matters worse, can, in their isolation, often be co-opted by traffickers. The result then is that resources intended for social assistance actually go to trafficker efforts to build support in these communities. Indeed, poorly thought through and managed social programs and NGO actions can actually contribute to and become part of criminal networks. A far more efficacious strategy to meet residents' needs and control violence is a networked approach in which civic and state actors interested in reducing conflict work with each other to respond to illegal networks that promote crime. These efforts build institutions that can gain access to state, international, and large-scale civic resources to help meet basic needs at the local level to decrease dependence on traffickers. This strategy also places well-connected groups on the ground that can observe the behavior of police and other state officials within favelas to ensure that they perform their jobs properly. This can help to reduce police corruption and ensure effective policy implementation. The approach, which has had some success over the medium term, partially confirms observations that higher levels of social capital lead to better government.[66]

A variety of structural and institutional factors, however, interfere with the long-term success of these civic networks. Favelas are violent and dangerous places. Without extensive outside support, these groups tend to deactivate over time, and then favelas return to their "normal" level of violence as NGO workers move on to other jobs and local activists tire of constant threats or succumb to temptations from traffickers. Unfortunately, there seems to be little interest at the state or national level to commit the type of resources necessary to change this situation.[67]

At the heart of the dilemma for those working from both a repressive and civil society approach to controlling violence is the ability of criminals and their allies to co-opt their opponents. Criminals, operating through illegal networks, have already dramatically changed and weakened local representative organizations. As Leeds notes, "During the eight years in which I have monitored the relationship between drug groups and favela associations, the autonomy of these associations has gradually been eroded."[68] Through carrots and sticks, traffickers have been able to co-opt these leaders into their networks and cut off a significant amount of political debate within favelas.[69] Networks enable criminals to build contacts with groups operating in and around favelas that undermine the very types of reforms that should work to control violence. Thus, when the state devotes resources to a favela, those resources often go through the AM and end up benefiting those close to AM leaders and traffickers. If favela residents want to profit from that support, they must maintain good relationships with criminal network members. When an NGO sets up operations in a community, traffickers will work to develop a relationship with that organization. When police devote more resources to the community, traffickers will often work harder to broker an agreement with the police. By co-opting their opposition into their network, traffickers gain hold of the very resources sent to the community to break their power. Thus, in some cases, the more resources the government and NGOs throw at the problem of favela violence, the worse the problem becomes. Indeed, one could argue that under some circumstances, traffickers are able to co-opt increasing levels of local social capital in favelas to improve their political position within these communities. Strong connections to the outside can provide groups with support to avoid co-optation, but even with this support, local groups face serious challenges.

Outline of the Book

This project provides a new conceptual framework for discussing problems of violence in developing societies. Chapter 1 sets the stage by tracing the history of the politics of Rio's favelas. Chapter 2 details the book's theoretical contributions, looking at the place that criminals have in politics in a changing world and the ways they interact with other political actors and analyzes, in this context, possible ways to control violence. Chapters 3, 4, and 5 examine the political organization of the three favelas to understand how criminal networking creates conditions for ongoing violence and disrupts democratic government. Chapter 3 examines Tubarão, a favela of around 7,000 located near some of Rio's wealthiest neighborhoods where criminals are effectively tied into a variety of governmental activities. Chapter 4 looks at Santa Ana, a favela of about 4,000 located near downtown Rio that experienced substantial state corruption and violence during the time I researched there. Chapter 5 examines Vigário Geral, a community of about 10,000 on the far northern edge of Rio, where twenty-one residents were massacred by police and residents were able to organize to demand better state services and lower levels of violence. In Chapter 6 I lay out comparative evidence of illegal networks in other parts of Brazil and Latin America and suggest how and why criminal networks vary across the hemisphere. In the concluding chapter I bring together my empirical observations with my general theoretical claims and set out an argument about the structure of state and society in Latin America today, as well as potential responses to the problems posed by criminal networks.

ONE

Setting the Scene: Continuities and Discontinuities in a "Divided City"

On 17 July 2003, *O Globo*, Rio de Janeiro's leading newspaper, reported that the wealthiest portion of the city's exclusive Zona Sul (South Zone) had the highest Human Development Index in the world as compared to full-scale nation-states. With a score of .988, this region of the city easily beat out Norway, the world leader, in terms of such factors as literacy, life span, and health care. *O Globo* ecstatically reported:

> This one is worth commemorating by singing "The Girl from Ipanema" and forgetting those problems typical of day-to-day life in the Zona Sul, like traffic jams, beggars, and informal car attendants. A still-incomplete study by the city government that will help with planning strategies for local development shows that if the region formed by Ipanema, Leblon, Lagoa, Jardim Botânico, Gávea, São Conrado, and Vidigal were an independent country, it would have the highest Human Development Index on the planet.[1]

Leaving aside the methodological problems of cherry-picking the wealthiest neighborhoods in the city (an area whose riches derive in part from the exploitation of poor labor in other parts of the city) and then comparing these neighborhoods to whole countries, this article engaged in the traditional upper-class Carioca (Rio residents) sport of aspiring to be European while literally "forgetting" and unsuccessfully trying to remove from the picture the large swaths of urban poverty that form part of the city's daily life.

For well over a century, Rio's civic leaders have worked to make and remake Rio into a city worthy of Europe while in many ways denying the intricate connections between wealthy and impoverished areas that give the city so much of its character. They have accomplished some of this through ambitious architectural projects at the beginning of the twentieth century that brought stunning Parisian building styles to this steamy tropical city.[2] In other epochs, government and religious leaders pursued these efforts through improving sanitation and public health, removing poor communities from prominent and visible places, and creating a police force focused on repressing freed slaves and other elements of the urban poor.[3]

Throughout the twentieth century, affluent and influential Cariocas have had an ambivalent relationship to the city's forms of popular housing. During carnival the whole city celebrates these areas, but for much of the rest of the year these communities have been seen as the opposite of the metropolis. Where the city was modern and urban, the favela was seen as rural and backward. Where the city was civil, the favela and other forms of popular housing were barbarian and had to be civilized.[4] As Alba Zaluar and Marcos Alvito aptly put it, "The utilization of the favela as an inverted construction of an urban civilized identity took various forms."[5] The favela, with its poverty and promise of violence, then, emerged as a negative constitutive myth of Rio as a civilized urban center and, hence, many state and civic leaders targeted it for removal.[6]

Ultimately, however, the problems of the favelas remained part of the city's problems. The favelas' intricate and important relationship to the city as a whole was only fully laid out with the 1977 publication of Janice Perlman's pathbreaking *Myth of Marginality*. Unfortunately, in the face of the violence that has emerged with the expansion of the drug trade into Rio, much of this notion of marginality has returned to current debates on favelas, as even activists and respected journalists argue that the city has become divided between violent and lawless favelas and suburbs and the democratic and orderly city of the downtown and the wealthy Zona Sul. Ultimately, the *O Globo* piece itself forms part of this history that divides the city and claims that with the removal of signs of poverty Rio could be a part of the developed world. In this chapter, I will set the scene for understanding Rio politics by analyzing how state policy, social choice, and economic and geographic structures led to the creation of favelas and their relationship to the wealthy parts of the city.

Inequality and Violence in Brazil and Rio de Janeiro

Politics in Rio today can only be understood in the historical context of inequality and violence in Brazil as a whole. By looking into the past to understand how conflicts were managed in colonial Brazil and how policing developed and operated in imperial and early republican Brazil, we can come to a more nuanced understanding of the nature of civic violence and the imperfect system of policing that exists in Rio today.

Finding a land largely bereft of immediate material wealth or even a ready local population of coercible labor, the Portuguese crown showed only a limited interest in the early process of colonization. Political power in Brazil was originally vested in a small number of Capitanias Donatarias in which the crown gave powerful soldiers and nobles near-plenipotentiary power over vast swaths of territory. The Portuguese took a very long time to set up any sort of official bureaucratic administration. This vested legal force in a very small number of colonists, who used that power to extract wealth from the land and from other settlers. This, combined with the African slave trade, led to the emergence of a system in which an immense amount of coercive violence came from the hands of a few private actors.

Over time, as Thomas Holloway has shown in his analysis of policing and gangs in nineteenth-century Rio, a discriminatory and unequal political and legal system emerged in Brazil. With much of the population held in slavery, private actors played a significant role in meting out punishment for lawbreaking in the pre- and postindependence period.[7]

The favelas and the violence that exists in Rio de Janeiro today are products of this complex history—in which the Brazilian state and powerful members of society have sought to exploit the labor of usually nonwhite poor people while, at the same time, devoting relatively few resources to their social well being or even, for that matter, their policing. This has resulted in the development of an extensive system of informal housing that includes favelas. This housing is abusively and, often, corruptly policed by undertrained and underpaid public servants who are usually drawn from the same social classes as those who live in those communities. Throughout its history, Brazilian politics has vacillated between periods of greater inclusion under decentralized and more or less democratic regimes and more exclusionary and formally centralized authoritarian forms of government. The current republican regime suffers from many of the same problems and tensions that have confronted its predecessors. The violence affecting Rio today is part of this history, and the ways that understandings, perceptions, and practices of this violence in both Rio and Brazil as a whole operate today have been shaped by the particular problems that have confronted Brazilian cities over the last generation. A brief analysis of major political shifts in Brazil will help situate this discussion.

With the abolition of slavery and monarchical government, Brazil embarked on a forty-year experiment with limited democracy in 1890, later known as the Old Republic. During this time the country experienced relatively free and fair elections, although with a limited franchise. In practice, most power lay in the hands of the elites who dominated particular regions. These elites negotiated among themselves who would run for the presidency, which typically alternated among the powerful states of Minas Gerais and São Paulo. The federal government had little power over the states, whose governors controlled their own military forces.

With the collapse of the Old Republic and the Revolution of 1930, Brazil took a more authoritarian, centralizing, and nominally inclusive path that culminated with the Estado Novo under the leadership of Getúlio Vargas.[8] During this period, state militaries were drastically weakened and reconstituted as more localized police forces, and the government worked to symbolically include, for the first time, the common people. It was during this period that samba, for example, became the national music, that police began to tolerate Afro-Brazilian cultural expressions, and that society as a whole began to officially celebrate carnival.[9] Despite these forms of cultural inclusion, politics remained dominated by a small group of elites, and mechanisms of popular dissent, such as labor unions, were formally incorporated into, and came under the control of, the state.

With the collapse of the Estado Novo at the end of the Second World War, Brazil established its Second Republic. This period represented the country's first experience with widely participatory democratic government. Politicians experimented with populism and large-scale development policies. Efforts to maintain popular support for the state and for political parties, however, resulted in tensions as workers began to make greater demands and business owners and conservative elements around the military reacted with growing fear and apprehension, especially in the years after the Cuban Revolution.

With the collapse of the Second Republic, Brazil once again adopted a centralized authoritarian political system under the military regime. During this period, the military pursued large-scale state-led development policies, in the process incurring substantial debt. The government also successfully repressed radical political dissent through the use of state force. The growing debt burden, oil crises in the 1970s, strengthening international human rights norms, and a more active local civil society led to the military stepping back and allowing the reestablishment of civilian government.

The New Republic that governs Brazil today is both inclusively democratic and relatively decentralized. The tensions that existed in earlier regimes have not disappeared but, instead, play out in new ways. In many aspects, Brazil's current president, Luiz Inácio Lula da Silva, is the heir to this tradition. On the one hand, he comes out of the antidictatorial social mobilization of the 1970s and 1980s that rejected excessive state power and abuse. On the other hand, he is also the heir to a development tradition going back to the Estado Novo, in which the state has played a substantial role in economic development and the inclusion of popular classes. Many of the challenges his government has confronted stem from these contradictions. Nowhere is this more visible than in recent federal public security policy. Government leadership has provided only lukewarm support to seriously needed criminal justice reform, and the traditional reluctance of the federal government to intervene in state level security issues has been tempered with occasional interventions during crises and the establishment of the Força Nacional de Segurança Pública (National Public Security Force), a small, heavily militarized, federal police force for deployment in emergency situations to supplement beleaguered state police. As a result, the current government has done very little to rein in the police and criminal violence that have had such a profound effect on the life of the poor elements of the population that the governing Partido dos Trabalhadores (Workers' Party, PT) claims to represent. To understand these issues in more depth, we now turn to the history of poverty and public security in Rio.

Favelas in the Old Republic and Estado Novo (1889–1945)

The first Rio squatter settlement called "favela" was a community on the Morro da Providência near the old War Ministry that, scholars generally agree, homeless federal soldiers settled after returning from the Canudos War—a conflict in which the Brazilian state put down a messianic popular uprising in the interior of Bahia—in 1897. The government had not paid the veterans, and their presence on the hill constituted a public demand for back pay and compensation promised by the state. The soldiers named their community "favela," after a plant that grows in the interior region of Bahia where they had fought.[10] This, of course, was not the first form of popular housing in Rio or the first squatter camp. Groups of runaway slaves had formed *quilombos* in other parts of the city in the early nineteenth century, and away from the city center squatting took place prior to the land occupation by the Canudos veterans.[11] The presence of former soldiers on a hill sitting over the War Ministry changed the meaning of informal land occupations in Rio by serving as a form of protest of the government's failure to live up to its obligation to those who had risked their lives for their country.

During this period, favelas existed almost completely without urban services. One set of reports from the early twentieth century noted that most houses on the Morro da Providência were built of wood with zinc roofs and, already negatively distinguishing favela residents from other city residents, that all the "vagabundos e criminosos [vagrants and criminals] who lived there were wholly without gas service."[12]

Almost from the beginning, the state proposed to move against favelas and other popular settlements in downtown Rio. Within three years of the establishment of the "favela" on the Morro da Providência, the police had surrounded and planned to remove the growing community. Over the next generation, city leaders would make similar unsuccessful efforts, often motivated by concerns over public hygiene, to remove this favela.[13] Between 1920 and 1922, the city leveled the nearby Morro do Castelo, a low-income housing district in downtown, as part of what Teresa Meade has referred to as the government's "renovation plan and civilizing goals." The city later hosted an international mercantile exhibition in the space to show off the city's industry.[14]

It is worth noting that at the turn of the last century, distinctions between different forms of popular housing were not as rigid as they are today. Places that we might consider favelas, often poor hillside settlements, could have been identified in other ways at the time. For example, the Morro do Castelo was an irregular neighborhood that was also the oldest settlement in the city of Rio—and which contained the ruins of Rio's first cathedral. During this period, many of these communities blended more easily with the wider environment of the city than they do today, especially in the Zona Sul.

Despite a growing recognition of favelas as an effervescent and valorized site of cultural creativity, the situation of the poor did not improve markedly during the Estado Novo (1930–1945).[15] During this period of state corporatism, the federal government extended limited citizenship and extremely attenuated worker rights to formal sector laborers.[16] For the most part, however, the Estado Novo government did little to politically incorporate the poor populations living in favelas. The government saw favelas as aberrations within the modern city, refused to list them on city maps, and slated them for removal.[17] Rio's government proposed eliminating the favela problem by strictly regulating the expansion of existing favelas and removing residents to *parques proletários*, a closed, state-administered form of popular housing with strict curfews. The Vargas administration built ties to *parque* residents by providing limited assistance and hosting social events. Eventually, authorities expelled residents from some *parques* where land values had increased to make way for higher-income housing.[18]

Favelas under the Second Republic (1945–1964)

During the years immediately following the Second World War, Brazil entered a phase of democratic government with the fall of the Estado Novo. From the 1930s onward, favelas grew significantly as a result of migration generated by industrialization in the major cities of the Southeast (Rio de Janeiro, São Paulo, and Belo Horizonte). With the growing population and the broadening of the democratic franchise, favelas first began to exercise a degree of political power and clientelist politicians sought votes by providing small favors to residents. This period, however, saw state and local governments alternately trying to extend services to favelas or to remove them.

Under the Second Republic, the state only rarely took an active and direct role in the administration of favelas. With the state often seeking to remove favelas and create alternative forms of popular housing, residents organized themselves. The first AMs were formed in 1945 to oppose potential removal efforts in several of the Zona Sul favelas.[19] As a result, local leadership began to play an important role in favelas' internal governance. During these years, favelas had little electricity and no internal plumbing. Residents had to go down to the city streets to find available spigots and carry heavy cans of water back up to their homes. Those who remember this era complain of long lines at available spigots and report fighting among residents as they waited. Some residents began to illegally cut into city power lines to bring electricity into their communities, and a few small-scale entrepreneurs strung power lines to other homes and resold the stolen energy. Groups of residents often organized themselves into *polícia mineira* (vigilante groups), which resolved disputes, controlled fights between residents, and stopped theft and other activity that violated neighborhood norms.[20]

Concerned that local organizing allowed favelas too much autonomy, the Catholic Church, under the Fundação Leão XIII and the Pastoral de Favelas, took the lead in administering these communities by regulating home building and providing assistance to residents. The unrealized long-term objective of these efforts was to remove the favelas and place residents in more regular housing. To this end, the church supported the construction of large-scale housing projects, provided education to favela children, and gave spiritual guidance to adults. In the late 1940s and 1950s, the church encouraged the AMs to help manage the communities and to more effectively channel charitable aid. On at least one occasion, the church intervened to stop city efforts to remove a group of favelas.[21]

This period of growth in community organizing coincided with Brazil's first experience with competitive electoral democracy in the context of wider popular suffrage.[22] From the early 1950s onward, politicians were quite active in Rio's favelas around elections, offering residents small prizes, such as soccer shirts, for their votes. Populist politicians put pressure on the state to provide more services to favelas. To this end, the state began to back the church's efforts to set up AMs in the early 1960s, when seventy-five new AMs were formed. The government would eventually supplant the church in favelas and work directly with AMs to deliver aid in exchange for political support.[23]

In the early 1960s, Carlos Lacerda, as governor of Rio, pursued a policy of removal as part of a "war on favelas" that he had declared when he had worked as a journalist fifteen years earlier.[24] In response, Rio's AMs organized themselves into the statewide Federação de Associações de Favelas do Estado de Guanabara (Federation of Favela Associations of the State of Guanabara, FAFEG) in 1963 to resist removal efforts and negotiate with the state.[25] In 1964, some months after the military dictatorship came to power, the Lacerda government began to remove the favelas, with the support of federal troops.[26]

Favelas during the Dictatorship (1964–1978)

In April 1965, a year after the military had taken power, Negrão de Lima, an opponent of removals and a former Rio mayor, defeated Flexa Ribeiro, Lacerda's chosen successor, on the strength of votes from poor areas of the city.[27] During the military dictatorship, the state government that controlled the city of Rio was nominally opposed to the authoritarian federal government. As a result, Negrão de Lima had weak political position and had great difficulty advancing policies that were in opposition to those of the military-controlled federal government.

Beginning in the late 1960s, with the hardening of the dictatorship, favela removal efforts began in earnest. In 1968, the federal government created the Coordenação de Habitação de Interesse Social da Área Metropolitana do Grande Rio (CHISAM, Coordination Agency for Habitation in the Social Interest of the Greater Rio Metropolitan Area), an organization that defined favelas as abnormal within the urban environment and considered the removal of favela housing as essential to the full integration of residents of these communities into the social and political life of the city. Three months after the founding of CHISAM there was already discussion of efforts to remove sixty-six favelas.[28] Legally, favelas were in an extremely precarious position since the state formally considered them illegal squatter settlements. During the period between 1968 and 1975 (a time that coincides with the most repressive years of the military dictatorship), the government forcibly removed approximately seventy favelas and 100,000 residents to other parts of the city.[29] Perlman offers a dramatic retelling of this story through vivid photos of the aftermath of the eviction of the Praia do Pinto favela at the edge of the wealthy Leblon neighborhood in 1969 when the favela "'accidentally' caught fire." Anthony Leeds and Elizabeth Leeds provide comprehensive analysis of the politics of removal efforts.[30] Despite these efforts, continued migration from the interior resulted in only a slight decrease in the percentage of favela residents in the city.[31]

With the onset of intensified removal efforts in 1968, the FAFEG declared itself publicly opposed to evictions.[32] AM leaders fought for the rights of residents to live in the homes they had built through both active protest and passive resistance but suffered the consequences of opposing an authoritarian state as government threats, abuse, and detentions led to the disappearance of many involved in these activities.[33] The severe damage that the dictatorship did to favela leadership caused the Federação de Associações de Favelas do Estado do Rio de Janeiro (Federation of Associations of Favelas of the State of Rio de Janeiro, FAFERJ), the successor to FAFEG after the integration of Rio city into Rio state in 1975, to adopt a basically passive attitude toward the government.

The state's efforts to eliminate favelas, and the state's use of AMs as local interlocutors, aid distributors, and land managers, caused residents to develop a system of limited internal governance.[34] After some feeble efforts in the mid-1960s to undertake housing stock improvements, the state provided few, if any, new services to favelas and did not recognize residents' rights. Remarkably, an informal system of jurisprudence evolved in favelas that paralleled, but differed from, the official jurisprudence of Brazil's courts. Since residents of favelas could not resolve property disputes through the court system, AMs began to register property ownership and validate contracts under their own "squatter" law. The leaders of the AMs worked to broker agreements between residents when disputes emerged, based on local norms and on popular (if inaccurate) understandings of the legal system.[35]

Under the military government, the state made very few efforts to improve conditions in favelas. Building on experiences from the 1950s and early 1960s, residents, usually through the AMs but also through other organizations, began to solve these problems on their own, engaging in *mutirão* (self-help) projects. Under the AMs' direction, residents built water reservoirs, laid pipes, and paved paths with funds from the residents, from private benefactors, and through state-level politicians in Antônio de Padua Chagas Freitas's political machine.

During the dictatorship, violence and crime played a significant, though not overwhelming, role in favela life. Rio de Janeiro's police often subjected favela residents to unreasonable searches, extortion, and arrest for vagrancy if they were not in possession of their work papers.[36] This harassment only increased during the military regime. *Bicheiros* (numbers runners) played a significant role in administering a drug trade dominated by small-scale marijuana sales and isolated from mainstream favela life.[37]

Favelas during Democratization (1978–1988)

Conditions improved in the late 1970s as the military regime allowed for more political competition. Elections once again sent politicians into favelas in search of votes, and residents began to draw on old-style political networks for assistance. As in the 1950s, most of these efforts were clientelist in nature, with politicians trying to set up an asymmetrical relationship of dependence with residents in order to ensure votes over the course of many elections.

In 1978, as Brazil began to open politically, Chagas Freitas was chosen governor of Rio. A member of the democratic opposition who maintained such good relations with the military government that his own national political party threatened to intercede in his state party operation, Chagas Freitas pursued intensely clientelistic policies to build his political base.[38]

In the late 1970s, AMs began to reorganize to make demands of the government. In the context of Rio's favelas, this democratic movement came to a climax with the 1982 gubernatorial election when Leonel Brizola built a winning populist coalition based on opposition to the dictatorship and on relationships with slum dwellers and their umbrella organization, the FAFERJ.[39] Recognizing the growing political power of the popular classes, Brizola shored up the support of favela residents by working to improve basic urban services. Unlike previous periods when individual politicians gave support for service improvements in exchange for votes, during the Brizola administration, government agencies delivered services directly to residents without the necessary intercession of a politician. This led to a series of programs that built comprehensive school–day care programs in many favelas, attempted to force police to respect favela residents' civil and human rights, and regularized water and electricity service to poor communities.[40]

On the negative side, Brizola worked hard to co-opt and demobilize the remaining leadership of the FAFERJ.[41] His strong and historical political presence (Brizola had been a national level politician prior to the 1964 coup and an eminent exile during the dictatorship), coupled with his expansive policies, resulted in a personalist populism that did little to build political institutions that could maintain his policies when his first government concluded in 1986. Instead of ending clientelism, through populism, Brizola took clientelism to its logical extreme by co-opting into his personalist government the very favela leaders who could have demanded the continuation of his policies after he left office.[42] To make matters worse, the effective delivery of services that favela leaders had so long sought undermined those same leaders. As the state regularized water and electricity services, the favela organizations that earlier had helped distribute those services weakened, as they could no longer charge residents for delivering those services. The decline in revenues from this regularization and other politicians' efforts to build their own reliable clientelist networks ultimately damaged the AMs, which grew even more dependent on the largesse of politicians to undertake local improvements.[43] This process disarticulated the favela movement and isolated individual favelas from one another as they began to compete for government aid. After Brizola's first administration ended in 1986, the political marginalization of AMs reduced the role of the state in favelas since politicians no longer had to work as hard to maintain the support of individual communities they had co-opted. As all this happened, large quantities of cocaine began to show up in Rio, and drug gangs vied with AMs for the leadership of many communities.[44]

Traffickers' power within favelas increased as a result of the expansion of the Andean drug trade into Brazil in the early 1980s. Traffickers started to employ many residents in their operations, provided needed assistance to the poor, and fortified their leadership role within favelas.[45] The consolidation of drug gangs has increased crime and violence in the city of Rio and provoked violent military and police responses that have resulted in the violation of favela residents' rights.[46]

The growing strength of drug traffickers did not simply stem from the ways in which they met the needs of residents or from the weakness of AMs. It also resulted from state corruption, a social policy dominated by personalist politics, organizational strategies learned by common criminals while incarcerated with political prisoners during the dictatorship, and the particular economic and political geography of Rio in an era of globalizing markets.

To fully understand the history of gang violence in Rio's favelas, we have to step backward for a moment to look again at the period of military rule in the late 1970s when the nuclei of the city's powerful gangs took shape. During the later years of the military government, penitentiary authorities housed common criminals together with political prisoners in the prison on Ilha Grande, a few hours outside of Rio. The jailed guerrillas, so the story goes, taught their cellmates organizational strategies that the criminals used as a basis to form powerful prison gangs. As they were released, former prisoners began setting up gang affiliates in the city. Drug trafficking and bank robbery, which had previously been highly diffuse and individualistic, became organized and subject to limited controls from inside prisons. The earliest and most important of these gangs was the Comando Vermelho (Red Command, CV).[47]

The popular press has sought to characterize these gangs as large-scale, hierarchical groups, but, in fact, organized drug trafficking at the local level has operated as part of a loose citywide network. Hierarchical criminal organizations have existed only within particular favelas where individual criminals have maintained limited top-down structures and have used their organizational skills to enforce order in favelas and provide social aid to residents.[48] Early on, some politicians realized the importance of these new traffickers as community leaders and began to work with them to obtain votes. In exchange, politicians supported the social projects of traffickers and provided assistance to the favelas.

In 1987, with the beginning of the administration of Wellington Moreira Franco as governor of Rio, the government adopted a much tougher line on drug trafficking.[49] The police raided favelas more frequently and violently than they had under the Brizola administration. Existing AMs, unable to stem the tide of police violence, lost support of residents and came under the sway of drug traffickers. During this period, traffickers often threatened and killed AM leaders who opposed them. With approximately 600 favelas in the city, in the last years of the 1980s, Rio's police recorded the murder of 240 community leaders.[50] The rapid ascension of trafficker power in favelas severely destabilized local politics. This shift disrupted existing patterns of political connections. In Santa Marta, in Rio's Zona Sul, traffickers murdered an AM leader associated with *bicheiros* (the owners of Rio's numbers game) who had become involved in drug trafficking.[51]

The increasing flow of money from dealing cocaine significantly contributed to this changing environment by giving drug dealers a huge infusion of resources that enabled them to buy light combat weapons, offer large bribes to police, and provide some minimal services to favela residents. Ultimately, the nature of the cocaine trade itself and the increasing resources needed to defend turf probably also contributed to the growth and consolidation of gangs. The marijuana trade had a relatively low overhead and moved small amounts of cash. As bribes grew more costly, narcotics prices went up, and the weapons needed to defend those narcotics grew more expensive. As a result, traffickers needed to organize themselves more efficiently and build stronger ties with other criminals who could give them material support.

Some scholars argue that the process of democratization in Rio's favelas led to the establishment of complex clientelist networks that incorporated both traffickers and politicians into the survival strategies of Rio's urban poor. These clientelist networks emerged from the failure of successive democratic governments to establish adequate formal political links to favelas and other types of poor communities. This reproduced historical systems of domination of Rio's underclass in which local leaders strove to obtain resources from the outside and delivered limited amounts of those resources to favela populations.[52] Although this approach provides important insights, this book differs from earlier accounts by looking more deeply at the operation of networks in specific Rio favelas. By closely and systematically examining the political life of multiple favelas, I will show that the criminal networks that operate in favelas engage in complex and varied clientelist operations but also go well beyond that in their activities. An ethnographic analysis of criminality within Rio's favelas shows that clientelism has evolved in complex, multilayered, and often dangerously contradictory ways as network member groups pursue different and, at times, uncoordinated goals. While general patterns remain the same, the structure of these networks varies from favela to favela, often tied directly to particular personalities in the community and the specific relationships those individuals maintain with one another. But, criminal networks go beyond this. In this volatile environment, some network actors play critical roles in mediating relationships both inside and outside the favela to create the political stability necessary to maintain at least tacit local support for drug trafficking.

Favelas under Brazil's New Republic (1988–Present)

Brazil's current democratic regime provides extensive formal rights to its citizens but assures few of the social guarantees necessary to take advantage of those rights. Rubem César Fernandes has characterized this system as one in which the historical formal ties, established during the mid-twentieth century between poor people and the state, have been broken.[53] Institutionally unmoored during a time of growing income inequality and declining formal sector job opportunities, the poor struggle to build ad hoc ties to state and social actors who can help meet their needs.

This leaves Rio's favelas today to pursue a mixture of double-barreled clientelism combined with a myriad of dynamic group activities designed to help favela residents accomplish individual goals with the assistance of the limited political capital and complex social networks that exist among favela residents. By doubled-barreled clientelism, I mean that both drug traffickers and politicians establish quantitatively and qualitatively different types of clientelist relations with favela residents. Both groups of patrons provide different goods and services at different times, in different ways, and with different effects. Further, traffickers interpose themselves on traditional clientelist relationships between politicians and residents in order to accrue significant amounts of the largesse distributed to favelas and then disburse that largesse to suit their interests. AMs help to mediate these types of clientelist relations by negotiating with residents, traffickers, and politicians and administering benefit distribution.[54] The social networks operating in Rio's favelas, however, do not stop at clientelism. AM leaders negotiate a myriad of other relationships among traffickers, residents, and outsiders, helping to effectively enforce order in favelas and overcome potentially destabilizing internal disputes.

The Drug Trade in Rio de Janeiro

Partially as a result of certain basic structural and geographic factors, Rio today is a hub for the retail and wholesale Latin American drug trade. As the home of the second-largest port in Brazil (the fourth-largest in South America) and an important tourist hub, Rio is a major site of drug transshipment and, over the years, has also become a large-scale consumer market.[55] Rio's favelas, which are sometimes built on very steep hillsides, provide ideal places to hide drugs and arms. The young, poor, nonwhite men who dominate trafficking in the favelas are the public face of the city's drug trade. Different parts of the metropolis confront different criminal problems based on particular local characteristics, with the wealthy Zona Sul providing the most valuable retail markets, and areas on the northern edge of the city, with the proximity to major highways and port facilities, playing a role in wholesale drug storage and transportation.

Despite these facilitating factors, drug trafficking has reached a saturation point in Rio. Over the past ten years, homicide rates have declined from a record 73 per 100,000 in 1994 to 43 per 100,000 in 2003, although rapidly growing rates of "disappearances" may suggest that murder levels have more or less held constant at around 75 per 100,000 per year.[56] In recent years, homicide rates in other major Brazilian cities, such as Belo Horizonte, Porto Alegre, and Vitória, have increased dramatically as those cities have begun to experience significantly higher rates of drug crimes and murders. During this same period, rates of cargo robberies in Rio more than tripled, from around a thousand to over three thousand per year. Favela residents reported that drug traffickers, because of the amount of police pressure on retail drug sales, were involved in providing protected storage areas for cargoes prior to fencing. This suggests that at least some of the possible improvements in overall crime levels in Rio have resulted from the maturation of the drug market and a concomitant decline in competition over marginally less valuable urban turf.

Rio's criminals organize through loose, though sophisticated, institutional frameworks that make arrest and detection difficult but also help to co-opt state and social actors who could undermine their activities. The drug trade in favelas is controlled by a *dono* (owner), who may be imprisoned and/or may control multiple favelas. The *dono* will usually appoint a *gerente geral* (general manager) to run day-to-day operations. Depending on local economic and political dynamics, gangs can include submanagerial positions such as *chefe de segurança* (security chief), accountant, and separate *gerentes de cocaína* and *maconha* (managers of cocaine and marijuana sales). At progressively lower levels, drug gangs will generally include *vapores* (dealers), *soldados* (soldiers), *aviões* (literally airplanes, i.e., carriers who ferry drugs to clients outside the favela), and, at the lowest level, *olheiros* (lookouts).[57] Children become involved in the drug trade as young as ten or eleven, although most street-level dealers appear to be in their later teens. Males make up the bulk of gangs, but women and girls are increasingly playing roles.

Most favela trafficking operations are based around the *boca de fumo* (mouth of smoke). *Bocas* have a double meaning in Rio's drug trade. Most often this refers to a specific point of sale that may change frequently. A *boca* can also mean something more fixed, like a headquarters. When a resident needs to communicate with traffickers, the person will often say that he or she is "going up to the *boca*" where a group of senior traffickers direct operations.

Above the level of the favela, Rio's drug trade is loosely organized into four *facções* (factions), the Comando Vermelho (Red Command, CV), the Comando Vermelho Jovem (Young Red Command, CVJ), the Amigos dos Amigos (Friends of Friends, ADA), and the Terceiro Comando (Third Command, TC). The largest and oldest is the CV. The TC was formed later in opposition to the CV. The CVJ is a dissident offshoot of the CV that gained prominence in the mid- and late 1990s. The CV uses some leftist rhetoric in public statements, although it does not appear to have a wider political platform.

The gangs that control individual favelas have only loose ties with their *facção*, which has virtually no control over illegal activities on the street. Alliances of *facção* members are limited to personal ties or the confluence of mutual interests, and members may switch between *facções*. Under some circumstances, such as when a favela faces coordinated attack by another *facção*, it may receive assistance from its allies. Some groups in the CV, however, do not trust each other, and residents of these favelas cannot travel to favelas controlled by rival CV gangs. The real power of the *facções* lies in prisons, where they play a major role in protecting members and resolving disputes.[58] *Donos* who violate certain rules, such as disclosing information about the *facção* to the press, may have to provide some sort of accounting to *facção* leadership.[59]

Little is known about the shadowy upper levels of Rio narcotics dealing. *Donos* buy their drugs from *matutos* (literally, "people from the woods"). *Matutos* are not associated with any particular *facção*, although they may have previously been part of one. According to the norms of Rio's drug trade, faction members cannot attack them. The famous trafficker Fernandinho Beira Mar (Little Freddy Seashore) was painted in numerous news reports and in an important congressional inquiry as the most important drug trafficker in Rio. Those familiar with Rio's drug trade, however, argue he was only a *matuto*.[60] *Matutos* buy their drugs from shadowy *atacadistas* (wholesalers), who are believed to come from some of the most powerful segments of Rio society. Some believe that *atacadistas* include wealthy *bicheiros* (the owners of Rio's numbers game), although evidence suggests that some are associated with people linked to the federal military.[61] *Atacadistas* bring drugs in from abroad and have significant financial resources and international contacts. There is evidence that powerful *atacadistas* have built linkages with members of the Brazilian Congress.[62] Around a hundred *matutos* and *atacadistas* operate in Rio.[63]

Politics within Rio's Favelas

Rio's favelas experience a complex political and legal pluralism in which different organizations enforce order over different aspects of life. No longer are AMs the primary leaders of communities. Rather, drug traffickers, AMs, religious groups, and NGOs all participate in the management of favelas. Relationships among these organizations, needless to say, are often in a state of flux, and conflicts can lead to violence. In this context, traffickers have the upper hand, but, since they ultimately depend on the tolerance of favela residents themselves for protection against police and outside traffickers, drug dealers must often work peacefully with other favela leaders to resolve differences.[64] With community support, traffickers take it upon themselves to enforce these norms, with punishments ranging from beatings to ritualized murder.[65] Retribution, however, is often uneven and dependent on the potential victim's social position in the favela.[66]

In general, local political participation has decreased strikingly over the past thirty years.[67] AMs still formally administer most favelas. Residents theoretically choose their leaders through regular election, but, since traffickers have so much interest in the leadership of the AM and the (formally unremunerated) job of AM president exposes its holder to so much danger, AM leaders often run unopposed.

The official duties of the AMs are to improve conditions in favelas by organizing residents and to maintain links with the state and other outside organizations. This involves brokering contacts with politicians to obtain benefits, working with bureaucrats charged with locally implementing state projects, administering garbage removal, delivering mail, and bringing residents together in mutual self-help programs. AMs are still expected to resolve disputes among residents where possible, maintain an inventory of the ownership of local land, and make requests of state agencies for infrastructural repairs. It is extremely risky for community leaders to protest police abuse since the police often retaliate against those who denounce their illegal activities. Since AMs depend on the government for aid, their leaders must also avoid publicly criticizing the behavior of state agencies and politicians.

As the state has withdrawn some forms of basic support from communities and as contacts among politicians and favelas have become tenuous, nongovernmental and religious groups have stepped in to fill the gap. NGOs generally provide relatively limited programs, such as child care or human rights education. Few NGOs are able to provide large-scale assistance or work in more than a handful of favelas. The most prominent NGO in Rio is Viva Rio, which, through an extensive network of contacts in the international nonprofit community, the state, and among the wealthy, provides important services to many poor areas.

Protestant religious denominations, especially Pentecostals and Neo-Pentecostals, have grown rapidly since the return to democracy.[68] The practice of Protestant Christianity in Rio's favelas is both a political and a social statement. Those who have entered these churches in earnest adopt different forms of dress and public comportment.[69] Churches, often composed mostly of women, strongly encourage congregants to spend their free time with other members of their faith, and members of some of these churches rarely partake in the street life characteristic of favelas. These groups provide one of the few ways for gang members to leave criminal life. Members of certain denominations take active political roles in favelas.

Residents maintain multifaceted relations with drug traffickers. The protection and aid provided by traffickers and their explicit threats of violence lead nearly all residents to at least tolerate criminals' presence.[70] Residents must constantly remain aware of changing politics in the favela in order to be on good terms with traffickers.[71] On the other hand, especially for the young and the poor, traffickers emerge as folk heroes because of their efforts to provide aid to residents and enforce order.[72]

Donos build on and exploit their image as folk heroes and local patrons because they depend on residents for their continued freedom and livelihood. With its isolated space and confusing street patterns that make assault difficult, the favela is invaluable to their business.[73] In cases where traffickers have killed or expelled too many residents, those remaining may turn against them and help police or other traffickers force them out.[74] As a result, traffickers seek to establish patronage relations with favela residents that arise from the tradition of Brazil's urban clientelism, in which powerful social and political actors were expected to provide aid and services to poor clients and employees. Moreover, traffickers also exist in the context of a history in which bandits, such as the famous Lampião (who was linked to some powerful landowners), supposedly righted injustice in the name of the poor.

Policing and the State in Rio's Favelas

Despite prevailing popular opinion, trafficking has not developed in the absence of the state.[75] Evidence of government activity is in the form of expended shells from gun battles between traffickers and police and weapons in the hands of traffickers sold by corrupt officers and soldiers, not to mention the fact that projects funded by state agencies and clientelist politicians literally fill favelas. A 2002 wiretap reveals traffickers' discussing payoffs of between R$500 and R$1,000 to police to loan traffickers official trucks to move drugs and otherwise not interfere with dealing.[76] All three of the communities analyzed in this study benefited from significant government investment, including schools, water improvement projects, funding for housing, and, all too often, intense, but corrupt, policing. If the absence of the state accounted for trafficker power then one would expect to see that communities with less state investment would have a greater presence of traffickers than would communities with more state investment. This, however, is not the case. Some favelas, especially those in the Zona Sul, receive considerably more state outlays than outlying favelas, yet all suffer from relatively high levels of violence. The activities of corrupt police, disinterested bureaucrats, and personalist politicians all empower criminals. Although numerous state actors, including police, do work to improve residents' lives, self-interested actors take advantage of their positions at the expense of the polity.

Crime in Rio can only be understood in the context of the police forces operating in the city. As in France, Brazil uses a bifurcated policing system in which the uniformed Polícia Militar (Military Police, PM) carries out the ostensible duties, while plainclothed Polícia Civil (Civil Police, PC) perform investigations. The contemporary functions of the police developed during the military dictatorship. From 1934 to the late 1960s, the PM had a formally auxiliary relationship with the military but were generally limited to specific paramilitary operations, such as guarding government installations and maintaining antiriot troops.[77] The military regime, however, gave the PM a direct day-to-day role in public order and expanded its national security function. The dictatorship attached elements of the PM to "anti-terrorism" units and created more informal death squads focused on repressing the very limited armed opposition—and dissent in general. Generally, "anti-terrorist" units would develop informal relationships with sympathetic police. During off-duty hours, these informal groups undertook repressive actions. Later, after the military began to rein in its repressive units, the informal death squads continued to operate.[78]

After the dictatorship, the PM made an uneasy transition back to civilian control. Today, they remain quartered in barracks. While individual soldiers often do not cut military figures on the street, bases are maintained with a military degree of cleanliness and officers often have the straight posture characteristic of career soldiers. The PM is known to have some significant problems with corruption. Indeed, among favela residents, there is almost constant talk of PM extortion.

The PC, however, is believed to be much more deeply corrupt. A fundamentally civilian police force, all PC wear plainclothes, and the officer corps, the *delegados*, has legal rather than military training. *Delegacias* (precincts) are typical offices and usually contain overcrowded holding cells where those arrested wait indefinitely for trial. There is significant evidence of pervasive corruption within the PC, with important *delegados* leading major corruption operations.[79]

Since the early days of the return to democracy, policing practices have been heavily tied to the policymaking of gubernatorial administrations. Leonel Brizola (1982–1986 and 1990–1994) tried to rein in police behavior in poor communities. Governors Wellington Moreira Franco (1986–1990) and Marcelo Alencar (1994–1998) adopted more confrontational approaches. The recent administrations of Anthony Garotinho (1998–2002) and his wife, Rosinha Garotinho (2002–2006), have adopted very different crime control strategies at different times. Garotinho came to power in 1998 in alliance with the Rio Partido dos Trabalhadores (Workers' Party, PT) on the basis of a progressive public security policy designed by a team of social science researchers led by Luiz Eduardo Soares. For two years, the gubernatorial administration sought to implement this platform, while at the same time mollifying hard-line elements in the police forces by delivering critical commands into their hands. Eventually this unstable state of affairs collapsed, and Garotinho forced Soares, who had been serving as a high-ranking adviser on public security, out. A period then followed in which conservative elements in the state public security establishment controlled policy and sidelined reform efforts. In 2002, Garotinho stepped down to run for president, passing control of the government to Benedita da Silva, his PT vice governor, who reimplemented the reform platform. In late 2002, Garotinho's wife, Rosinha, defeated da Silva in the gubernatorial election. Since that time, the state government has pursued generally more conservative policing policies on the ground, while continuing with administrative reform efforts that have led to the computerization of PC precincts and have standardized criminal justice recordkeeping in the state. This has led to improved crime statistics over the last five years.

The Operation of the State in Rio's Favelas

This history highlights some of the characteristics of weak states. Many of problems of the favelas emerge from the mis- and malfeasance of state actors. Upper-level politicians, police, and bureaucrats usually do not have effective control over lower-level state representatives. Police engage in brutal operations that result in violations of residents' rights.[80] Many bureaucrats, police, and politicians take bribes and steal from funds targeted for social aid. These actions strengthen drug traffickers, who, as a result of bribes to police and politicians, operate freely in favelas and provide aid to residents.

The Brazilian state, however, is not all that weak, and to understand it we need to appreciate the ways that formal and informal links to favelas help in policy implementation. Despite all of the problems facing favelas, some elements of the state do attempt to assist citizens. In general, the state provides some aid that helps residents deal with infrastructural matters. Following traditions of allowing favela leaders to administer many aspects of local life, the state pays money and delivers many services to the "elected" leaders of AMs. This, of course, reinforces existing local patterns of authority and dominance. With AM leaders closely linked to traffickers, this system invariably provides aid to criminals and supports their political role in favelas.

Thus, with a huge amount of wasted and misallocated resources, the state does not effectively meet the needs of most favelas, guarantee the rights of residents, or prevent crime. In fact, since many favelas are still technically squatter settlements, the state does not fully recognize the extent of their problems or extend full rights to residents. Though the state provides some aid to favelas and is legally obligated to protect residents' rights, the favela remains a place in which the protection of citizens' interests falls into the hands of private actors.[81] Rights are only partially assured through the mediation of powerful local leaders linked to criminals. The result is that individuals with intimate ties to the AM leadership, and hence traffickers, effectively have more support in guaranteeing their constitutional rights and obtaining government services than more law-abiding residents.[82] The state has chosen to pursue political strategies that empower traffickers with policy choices that put state resources into the hands of leaders allied with criminals.

The interaction between civil society and the state in Brazil's favelas raises serious questions about how state and society can work together to create a viable democratic order. For the past hundred years, the lives of those in Rio's favelas and the city's politics have been deeply interlinked. Today those connections continue through complex networks that tie together police, politicians, civic leaders, favela residents, and criminals. Clientelist politicians have given the poor small benefits without working to implement policies that will improve their conditions over the long term. At the same time, clientelist politicians have weakened local movements of favela associations that threatened their efforts to build up reliable political networks in the city's slums. Some corrupt politicians work with drug traffickers to secure votes in favelas in exchange for political favors. The police, for their part, allow traffickers to operate freely in favelas. This has led to localized violence, which has raised the costs of public activism and pushed AMs further into the arms of drug traffickers in a desperate search for needed funds that have not been provided by the state.

TWO

Network Approach to Criminal Politics

The challenge of this book is explaining the resilience and extensiveness of criminal activity under a consolidating democratic system, despite an international consensus to control drug trafficking and a willingness on the part of governments to use high levels of force to bring crime under control. Essential to understanding the persistence of violence in Brazil is an examination of the necessary links that criminals sustain with actors in state and society—actors who have reciprocal interests in maintaining connections to criminals in order to accomplish personal and political goals. This occurs in an environment where state power has dramatically changed as a result of transnational institutional and market pressures. Through networks, criminals establish long-term relationships with individuals in both state and society who can provide needed help in avoiding arrest and detection, expanding illegal market share, and building the trust and legitimacy necessary to perpetuate and bring to fruition complex illegal activities. Increasing criminal connections between state and society have deleterious effects for democratic governance and basic rights. Government repression and efforts to build local institutional capacity may have little efficacy in controlling this type of illegal activity because of the ability of criminal networks to co-opt potential opponents. In this chapter, I discuss the nature, composition, and operation of illegal networks, examine the effects they have on democratic governance, and look at alternative types of organizations that may address the problems they create.

Defining Illegal Networks

Following Walter Powell, Margaret Keck, Kathryn Sikkink, Laurel Smith Doerr, and Phil Williams, I argue that "networks are voluntary, reciprocal, and horizontal [though not exclusively equal] patterns of communication and exchange" that can be contrasted with both markets (short-term, contract-based horizontal exchanges) and hierarchies (long-term vertical systems of control).[1] As institutions, networks are based on flexible links among component parts that work to achieve mutual interests.[2] Groups work together collaboratively to accomplish what they would not be able to accomplish in either closed formal organizations or in diffuse market relations. In other words, when groups need to maintain trust and cultivate enduring stable contacts but where it is impossible or inconvenient to form strict hierarchical structures, networks will provide an effective alternative form of organization.[3]

Criminal networks perpetuate illegal exchanges by flexibly and variably incorporating criminals, state actors, and members of civil society to assist in unlawful enterprises.[4] Though many network members have full knowledge of their connection to criminals, some will have only a vague awareness of these connections, and others may know nothing of these links. Although particular network nodes are often based in geographically constrained localities, they necessarily spread beyond a specific place. Illegal networks do not have clear boundaries and will often merge seamlessly into completely legal enterprises, in the process crossing national/international and state/nonstate frontiers.

This model of networks builds on but differs significantly from existing network approaches. Williams argues that transnational criminal organizations are based on instrumental material and information exchanges.[5] Criminals work with state officials and business owners to gain access to specific resources unavailable to them as a result of their illegal status. Civic and state actors work with criminals to gain access to resources and to accomplish objectives that may be unattainable without the skilled use of violence. Crossing boundaries between state and society allows criminals to acquire the materials and services they need to continue operating.

My understanding of illegal networks incorporates and goes beyond these claims. Following writing on civic society and transnational advocacy, I argue that networks play an essential role in building trust and diffusing norms.[6] Like advocacy networks, illegal networks mobilize resources and create and spread the norms and ideas necessary to sustain criminal activities.[7] Through network activity, criminals position themselves and their allies as defenders of group norms against state organizations' claims to legitimacy and use networks' capacity to build social capital and political power.

The illegal networks model also disaggregates state and civil society as a set of actors involved in these networks. More so than either Keck and Sikkink or Williams, I examine the different modes in which state and social actors work with criminals. Illegal networks, in fact, are lodged within a world that includes competing and complementary policy and advocacy networks that operate inside the state and across political and social boundaries. Illegal networks use contacts into policy networks to accomplish their objectives, not just by undermining state functioning but also by altering how the state and the political regime operate. They are embedded in political systems, undermining human rights and public order by deploying the state and social forces that are supposed to uphold that order against it. Criminals behave differently from actors in both state and civil society as a result of their regular use of violence, their position as often very powerful but low-status social actors, and their operation outside many legal and social norms. As a result, they must delicately mediate interactions with state officials to gain the space necessary to carry out certain types of activities. If their actions have significant political implications, we must move beyond a model of the polity focused on the give-and-take between state and civil society that dominates discussions in political science. Networks provide a flexible model to conceptualize criminals as political actors different from both state and social actors, but also integrally connected to them. Finally, by helping to unpack state institutions, networks provide perspective in understanding the ways that state actors, criminals, and civic leaders work together to manipulate other actors and networks.

Actors in Illegal Networks

One of the key elements of network organization is the ability of networks to loosely and contingently bring together actors with reciprocal interests, needs, and skills sets to help accomplish those actors' individual and collective goals. Although the traditional literature on state-society relations almost wholly excludes criminals from politics, relegating violent actors to the realm of protest and revolution, a number of scholars in recent years have suggested a role for criminals in our understandings of politics.[8] A network approach, which carefully examines the diverse operatives working in the criminal underworld, in the state, and in society, provides a framework for understanding why and how these radically different and technically antagonistic actors work together.

Amid the global "retreat of the state," Susan Strange argues that criminal organizations have stepped in to fill states' regulatory and governance roles through marketized and informal systems of control.[9] Carolyn Nordstrom, William Reno, and Mark Duffield suggest that war in Africa today does not represent anarchy (as Robert Kaplan argues in his famous essay)— but instead a networked system of social control where ongoing conflict depends on access to illegal markets and international institutions that can only be achieved through the organized collusion of state, civic, and criminal actors.[10] In the domestic sphere of more-ordered political entities such as Colombia, Bolivia, Brazil, or Anton Blok's Sicily, high levels of crime, far from revealing a failure of state institutions, reflect a degree of state power and the specific ways in which that power, often combined with social forces, is deployed in the polity.[11] Because of the dynamics of how state power has changed in the neoliberal era and, as Julia Paley has argued, how these changes have caused individuals to internalize certain ideas about their participation in the political, social, and economic systems they live in, criminals, state, and civic actors depend on each other to achieve their political, personal, and market objectives.[12] Thus, globalization, the retreat of the state, and seeming anarchy in poor areas of Rio, rural Colombia, or West Africa reflect not the breakdown of state power but, rather, the redeployment of state power and social forces through new forms of political networks that necessarily involve criminals, state officials, and social groups. The illegal nature of many of these activities necessitates that member groups work together with actors from other sectors of the polity to gain access to the resources and skills necessary to achieve political aims in this unstable environment.[13]

The conceptual domains of state, society, and crime are not homogeneous and must be thoroughly unpacked in order to understand how alliances across these sectors of the polity can affect social and political outcomes. Each of these domains contains within itself multiple types of actors who may engage in dramatically different activities. As we look more closely at the edges of these different fields, we will also find that the borders of state, society, and criminal activity are gray and amorphous. These sectors overlap, with some groups sitting at the intersection of two or more. Further, actors operating in one field can, with varying degrees of difficulty, move between different fields. Thus, a leader of a civic organization may be named to public office or, under other circumstances, could become a criminal. Criminals, of course, confront more serious challenges when trying to move into civil society or into the state, but this is not impossible under all circumstances. Further, criminals' status is defined almost completely by their relationship to the law and state and social institutions. Changes in the structure of these institutions, in the relationship between criminals and these institutions, or in the law itself can change criminals' social and political position, moving them from one domain to another. Despite this ambiguity, a model that looks at actors working together across domains provides insights into how actors in these different segments of the polity can make use of the specific skills and resources available to them to help accomplish collaborative objectives. Nevertheless, we must keep in mind the contingency and flexibility of the place of actors within these domains and the structure of the domains themselves.

The State

Most social scientists approach the state from a Weberian perspective, seeing it as an institution with sovereign power and a monopoly on the use of legitimate violence in a given territory, interacting domestically with subject populations and internationally with other sovereign governments. States, however, are much more complex entities than these basic definitions reflect. They are composed of numerous types of actors, ranging from high-ranking elected officials and general officers in the military to beat cops and customs inspectors.[14] States, in fact, may be viewed as a series of processes and effects rather than as sets of juridical institutions. The many politicians and bureaucrats who compose modern states do not always act in harmony and, in fact, are often at odds with one another. What holds them together, however, is that they work within the juridical state, have internalized this affiliation, and, as a result of that affiliation, will have access to particular resources and contacts that come from their stations to pursue personal and political objectives.[15] For the purposes of this book, state officials include police, politicians and elected officials, and bureaucrats.

Actors who work within states have access to particular types of resources and contacts unique to state actors. Even in some of the weakest states, the privileges of international sovereignty provide public officials with access to certain types of claims and resources that other members of the polity do not have. For example, government representatives may sign agreements with the IMF, the World Bank, and other international organizations. In West Africa, governments in danger of falling to guerrilla armies have made arrangements with mercenary organizations to fend off enemies and build ties to international NGOs for humanitarian aid.[16] State actors in these environments can charge extortionate fees for passports or can sell documents legalizing shipping licenses or weapons sales.[17]

Of course, in the better-established polities of Latin America and Asia, officials not only make claims to resources in the international community but also have access to much more extensive internal state assets and social networks—providing them with monies to spend to achieve political goals, the ability to dictate the terms of state contracts, influence over information broadcast through government-owned media services, or direct control of legitimate coercive violence.[18] More broadly, in functioning states, actors often operate within political networks, which bring them into contact with other state actors who have access to resources or the means of violence that can be used to help achieve their objectives.[19]

Unlike state actors who are skilled at gaining access to and using public resources and official violence, criminals are specialists at operating in illegal markets and are adept at using clandestine force. In a world where structural adjustment has significantly decreased funds for state officials' salaries and where overall state resources are scarcer than they used to be, some state actors may have an interest in exploiting criminals' access to illegal markets. Police and politicians may want bribes to supplement their income, and local officials, pursuing reelection, may need illegal funds to complete projects for which tax dollars are not available. With global democratic norms making the use of overt state violence politically costly under conditions where states are drained of the money needed to maintain basic order, state leaders may establish relationships with criminals to attack political opponents or simply to enforce their decisions.[20] Finally, with fewer available forms of social assistance and where contacts between state and society have been broken, criminals occasionally help citizens seek social assistance and solve collective problems.[21] For politicians seeking public office, contacts with these criminals can help build ties to potential votes.[22]

These dynamics reward state actors who work with criminals by allowing them, if they are not caught, to reinforce their own political networks and position within the state. Politicians who are able to work with criminals who can provide them with access to votes may be more likely to get elected. Police who make money from criminals and can deliver better pay-offs to corrupt superiors may be more likely to obtain promotions to powerful positions in the security hierarchy.[23] Thus, criminal contacts help some state actors advance at the expense of others, creating powerful constituencies in state institutions tolerant of growing illegal activity and more susceptible to criminal influence.

These contacts with criminals, however, are dangerous for public servants, who must manage them with considerable skill and delicacy. As representatives of the state, government officials must retain at least a public posture of legality. To have notorious links with criminals could directly undermine state legitimacy and would almost certainly result in these officials losing their jobs or going to prison. Even in countries with a limited rule of law, such as Brazil, actual public evidence of corruption or other serious malfeasance can lead to prosecution and incarceration of public officials.[24] To this end, state actors must keep their contacts with criminal and corrupt activities quiet—or face the possibility of losing position or going to jail. Further, criminals are generally dangerous people, and politicians whose relations with them sour could run the risk of physical violence. As a result, state actors who need ongoing ties with criminals will tend to work with criminals through safe proxies.

Civil Society

Although there is a great deal of debate about what exactly civil society is, for the purposes of this book, civil society means collective nonstate institutions and groups that mediate relations between other actors in the polity, such as isolated individuals and businesses, and the state.[25] These institutions generally eschew violence in order to effectively build consensus, represent the interests of constituents, and attempt to influence (or resist) state policy. Some see civil society as having a fundamental normative component as an essential bulwark between a possible tyrannical state and atomized individuals.[26] The role of civil society, however, is considerably more ambiguous, and under certain circumstances civic institutions can advance the agendas of groups inside and outside the state that have little interest in either protecting human rights or consolidating democracy.

Civic leaders are specialized in negotiating with other actors in state and society and in building broad consensus under difficult circumstances. When states want to implement unpopular policies, these actors can help to create agreement among the population and can also improve state policy proposals by helping to communicate public concerns to state officials.[27] By having good contact with civic leaders, then, state officials can maintain open lines of communication to make policy and ensure public compliance with programs. Civic actors also mediate complex disputes among members of society. Thus, under certain circumstances, church leaders may be brought in to negotiate settlements to ethnic conflicts or violent strikes.[28] Further, in the wake of smaller government budgets, many look to civil society to provide social services to the population in some places.[29]

Under these circumstances, some civic groups may find it tempting to work with criminals. With their access to the illegal marketplace, lawbreakers can provide monies to civic actors to undertake projects. In an environment of increasingly less-effective and corrupt state security services, illegal actors may provide better security for civil society projects than the state. Alternatively, in an environment where the state fails to adequately enforce the law, civic actors may need to establish basic relationships with criminals to avoid harassment. Further, given that certain underserved populations may depend on delinquents for security and social services, civic groups may need to build ties to criminal groups in order to effectively work with these populations. On the other hand, in an environment where criminals provide security and regulatory services to some populations, civic leaders may also mediate the sometimes-contentious relationships between criminals and the citizens they attempt to control.

Despite declining levels of state support for effective policing and the growing role of security firms and illegal actors in providing public protection, democratic norms today require politicians to campaign for votes. Criminals can provide important access for politicians to groups of poor people not adequately served by the state. Since politicians are unlikely to want to have regular or open ties with delinquents, they build contacts with them through civic actors. This work makes social leaders useful to politicians in channeling funds to powerful criminals and providing votes to politicians.

Although contacts with criminals entail some risks for civic leaders, those risks are both less avoidable for them and, in some ways, less compromising than they are for state actors of comparable status. Even if they are caught, civic actors will probably not immediately lose their jobs. Moreover, it is less likely that the press or other groups will pursue a story of contacts between criminals and social leaders than the story of contacts between criminals and state officials of commensurate prominence and prestige. Nevertheless, the potential of criminal violence against civic leaders exists, and there is a risk that the public exposure of civic leaders' contacts with criminals could undermine the ability of civic leaders to negotiate with state actors. As a result, any civic actor will tread carefully in building relationships with illegal actors.

Criminals

Specialized in operating outside the law, taking advantage of illegal markets, and using publicly illegitimate violence, criminals play increasingly important political roles in a world where the expansion of global markets has dramatically reconfigured the ability of states to provide services to their citizenry. Criminals' status is not necessarily static, as it is defined by the law and can be altered with changes in the law. In this environment, some criminals resolve disputes, provide some forms of security and social services to underserved populations, and act as clandestine intermediaries between political and social actors and black markets.[30] Embedded in social norms and networks, criminals may also take active roles in enforcing communal behaviors in some places and supporting popular organizations. Connections to state and civic actors help in achieving these goals by effectively connecting criminals with actors who have a higher degree of social stature and who can transmit norms, negotiate conflicts, and gain access to some resources. For the purposes of this book, this category includes a wide variety of operatives, ranging from large-scale international criminals and leaders of some forms of paramilitary groups to street-level drug gangs and human-trafficking organizations.

Despite the roles that illegal actors play in the polity, criminals are dependent on contacts with politicians and others in society to remain active. As "outlaws," they find themselves confronted by threats of violence from diverse sources within the state and the criminal community. This situation is worse for territorial criminals, including some urban drug dealers, who depend on access to particular spaces and the support of the population that lives in those spaces in order to do business.[31] To prevent arrest and limit the damage of attacks from competitors, many criminals maintain links to the population that lives in the area in which they operate, since members of that population could work with state actors or other criminals to displace them.

Contacts with civic actors can play an essential role in providing safety for criminal operations. Their normal advocacy work brings them into contact with politicians, and, as a result, they can broker agreements between criminals and the state. The collaboration of civic leaders, who often have long experience building consensus and working with the population, can help to smooth over difficult relations between criminals and individuals living in areas where they are active, preventing conflicts from emerging by keeping communications open. Civic actors, with their ability to open bank accounts and control property, can manage criminals' resources, organize events, and provide services to the population. Indeed, networks allow criminals and civic actors to converse over extended periods of time, learn from one another, diffuse their ideas, and collectively build norms. Conversely, criminals linked into networks learn from their civic contacts about the views of state and social leaders, allowing them to react quickly to challenges and maintain good relations with network partners.[32] The variable strength and density of network ties helps member groups build and transfer legitimacy, facilitate learning and the diffusion of social norms, and reinforce criminals' roles as political actors.[33] More concretely, civic groups can also negotiate with government bureaucrats about the implementation of regulations favorable to criminals. They can file papers with government offices and conduct other basic legal activities that criminals would have great difficulty doing on their own—but which are important to territorial efforts to provide services to a population and secure more general operations.

Criminals also depend on state actors. Contacts with police can help buy protection for illegal activities. Under other circumstances, criminals' links to politicians give criminals access to resources to help provide services to populations. Through assistance to politicians, illegal actors can also gain access to the state policymaking machinery to prevent repressive actions or minimize the effect of legal proceedings against them. Without contacts with the state, long-term organized criminal activities would be difficult or impossible to undertake.[34] To understand how these relationships work, we need to look at the details of network organization.

The Structure of Criminal Networks

Despite the interests that criminals and state and civic actors may have in working with each other, their relationships are fraught with danger (see Figure 1). Although state and civic actors may want the resources that criminals can provide, these same actors usually do not want these relationships to become public, because if that were to occur they would risk losing their positions or could even go to jail. On the other side, while criminals need ties to state and civic actors to succeed at certain forms of activities, they run risks whenever they build relationships and, as a consequence, provide information about themselves to others. To overcome these challenges, criminals and their partners operate in networks composed of complex combinations of nodes and links, which enable them to work together with a degree of safety by providing a flexible framework to build and maintain their connections.

Illegal networks are characterized by a combination of both "strong" and "weak" ties between member organizations. In some cases, criminals or other member groups will need strong, tight links with other network members, based on long-term mutual trust and reciprocity that involve extensive information-sharing and activity-planning. In cases where groups worry about the embarrassment that may come through connections to criminals or where it is difficult to build trust, such as in relations between police and criminals, more distant, weak, ties will better meet network members' needs. These flexible and variable connections allow legal and illegal actors to mediate their relations thorough proxies, to choose exactly what types of links they will use to set up connections with partners, and to weave together different types of ties to mediate information among members and carry out criminal activities, while avoiding arrest or detection. This allows for criminal groups to protect themselves from outsiders whose help they need—but whom they may not fully trust—and allows groups interacting with criminals to do so, while at the same time avoiding direct public contact.

Territorial criminals can use strong, intimate, ties with local residents and some civic leaders to maintain an intense inward-based trust in specific places, build their leadership roles, and exclude state actors from significant local functions, all the while drawing in government aid and using connections with state officials to

FIGURE I. State-Society-Criminal Exchanges

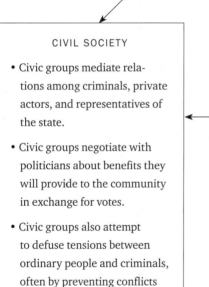

THE STATE

- Politicians provide aid and protection to criminals. They control police operations against them and intervene to limit judicial actions.

- Government bureaucrats provide some support for criminals in terms of helping them to provide basic services.

- Police sell protection. This protection can come either through persistent relationships or through arrests that lead to ransom payments for the release of traffickers.

CIVIL SOCIETY

- Civic groups mediate relations among criminals, private actors, and representatives of the state.

- Civic groups negotiate with politicians about benefits they will provide to the community in exchange for votes.

- Civic groups also attempt to defuse tensions between ordinary people and criminals, often by preventing conflicts from coming to a head.

CRIMINALS

- Criminals provide resources and some protection to residents.

- Criminals sell votes in areas they control to politicians.

- Criminals pay off police and supplement police income.

minimize police actions against them. In different situations, criminals can use contacts, such as lawyers, to maintain loose and weak ties with local business leaders and politicians who may be able to provide important resources—but who may not want to have direct contact with criminals. Through this complex set of ties, criminal networks draw in resources to reinforce local illegal activity, provide politicians with access to votes, and, at the same time, ensure that government officials have neither direct contact with criminals that could endanger criminals' political or legal position nor allow a political presence in a particular community that could undermine criminal leadership.

Through networks, actors engaged in illegal activities can transfer legitimacy and trust—not with the security afforded by the state judiciary apparatus, but sufficiently to ensure continued business operations.[35] By participating in these organizations, network actors gain introductions to counterparties that they have some knowledge of. An introduction to a third party through a trusted network partner can help a criminal in deciding who to do business with. Further, in a network based on multiple overlapping linkages in a world where trust and reputation determine your business, an introduction increases the chances that both parties will act in a reasonable way, since to cross each other could also damage relations with the party that made the introduction. Second, networks operate based on protocols that facilitate group interaction. Members of networks share behaviors, such as dress, slang, and communication style, that simplify their transactions and create a sense of trust. Those outside of networks are less likely to know these protocols and, as a result, are less likely to be trusted.[36] Further, networks provide a system of peer surveillance, whereby member groups can inform one another if one group has abrogated an agreement or violated collective norms.[37]

The nonhierarchical structure of networks further restricts information flow, allows norm building, and prevents network deactivation under violent conditions. Since no actor has a command role that would result in the centralization of information, the arrest or murder of a single member will do little to destroy the organization. Further, since no discernible hierarchy exists, the apprehension of a single group in the network will not lead anywhere in particular. State agents cannot arrest a network member and ask who gives them orders since, effectively, no one does. Rather, actors with close ties to the arrested will simply disappear for a while and cut ties to groups at risk of exposure. Despite the loss of one member, the rest of the network will remain active and wait for a new actor to enter and take up the activities of the group that left. As one journalist writing about the cocaine trade puts it, "That fluidity is another key factor of the rapid-reaction narcotics business: push it down in one place and it simply pops up somewhere else."[38]

Not only is it difficult to shut down a network without deactivating many of its members simultaneously, but the flexibility of criminal networks allows them to quickly change shape and membership to respond to changing outside pressures.[39] As government and social actors try to undermine networks, network members will often adapt and respond in innovative ways. Over time, with the ability to co-opt potential opponents, networks can undermine even innovative efforts to control their activities. These flexible contacts also allow the network to change over time, bringing in new groups as necessary and excluding groups that become unnecessary, thereby optimizing network operations and promoting security.[40]

Although criminal networks maintain variable node densities according to the needs of particular members, they tend to concentrate connections through a few trusted actors who can serve as interfaces between different political realms. These people face unique risks and pose particular challenge to criminals because they have direct information about criminal operations but must maintain connections with noncriminals who might collude with police. This flexibility and secrecy allows network members to quickly co-opt legitimate state and civic actors into the network and undermines efforts to reduce crime. Criminals need not directly contact politicians or police whom they wish to work with. Rather, through proxies, often in civil society, they can approach government representatives who may not even be aware of their links to criminals.

Since illegal networks have the ability to co-opt state actors and civic leaders, the pluralist and social movement mechanisms that many argue guarantee rights in democracies fail to function properly.[41] For example, state leaders allied to criminals may simply ignore popular calls for reforms or may alternatively develop hollow "get tough on crime" policies to mollify public sentiment, while allowing illegal networks free rein. On the other hand, the leaders of social movements may be threatened or co-opted by criminals and their allies into not pressing for reforms. As a result, violence seems to spin out of control and the population calls for more potent state reactions to crime. Giving police more freedom and resources to control crime, however, may only create the groundwork for more violence.

Corruption of the state is progressive and insidious.[42] As governments devote more resources to repressing these groups, either through police actions or by building local institutional capacity, criminals have more opportunities to co-opt members of civil society and the state. For example, better armaments may provide police with more incentives to become corrupt, since it will be easier for them to stage operations that may result in the arrest of traffickers or to threaten operations against traffickers. Those willing to provide traffickers with intelligence may find their information is in significantly higher demand if police, with better funding, carry out more antinarcotics operations. As funding to repress the drug trade increases, corruption will penetrate more deeply into the state and trafficking will become more pervasive. Those police not on the take will face criminals who have intelligence about their activities from other police. Police who would normally not take bribes may start to take bribes out of a sense of hopelessness, because it is less risky than actually trying to enforce the law when other police actively work with criminals, or because pervasive corruption renders corrupt activity one of the few ways of moving up the career ladder. This progressively undermines the rule of law, leads to higher levels of human rights abuse, and can pose profound challenges to democracy.

Political Effects of Criminal Networks

Expansive transnational organized crime creates new forms of authoritarianism.[43] On the domestic level, the presence of illegal networks can have the effect of radically altering governance and warping democratic systems. Although formal democracy may exist, rights will only be effectively guaranteed to classes that have adequate funds to buy security and gain access to the courts and other state administrative systems.[44] Those left on the outside will enjoy few of the advantages of the democratic system and will, in fact, be subject to transient forms of authoritarian rule in their day-to-day lives, depending on the structure of police activities in a particular neighborhood and the actions of criminals. As civil society becomes closely linked to criminals, the potential for opposition to criminal activities is reduced and the situation can spin out of control. In different places and historical contexts, this leads to different outcomes. In any case, it forces us to reconsider the structure of the state at the local level.

Understanding the practical experience of the rule of law in Latin America is essential to understanding the challenges facing the region today.[45] Guillermo O'Donnell argues that Latin America can be divided into "blue zones," where a rule of law operates; "green zones," where that rule is more constrained; and "brown zones," where the state is virtually absent. In each country, there are different mixtures of these three types of areas, with a country like Brazil having large swaths of brown in the countryside and in some parts of major cities and a country like Argentina having significantly larger green areas and more limited brown areas.[46]

This spatial model provides important insights into the variances of the rule of law across Latin America, but it provides only a limited understanding of what really lies in "brown" and "green" zones—or the relationships between those zones and places where the rule of law operates. The network model outlined in this chapter turns this limitation on its head. While recognizing the importance of O'Donnell's insight about the existence of differences in the rule of law over different parts of territory, this approach allows us to systematically unpack the political structures that support the existence of "brown" and "green zones." Through networks, we can not only learn about how political systems operate in these areas, but we also can understand how these places of democratic deficit differ from one another and relate to broader political structures. We are able to do this because rather than premising the lack of rule of law on the failure of institutions or the rise of parallel states, the network approach suggests that the rule of law fails as a result of the specific types of relationships that emerge in the broader political system and how those relationships foster and link to alternative political structures operating in "brown" zones. Thus, in this formulation, the limitations of the rule of law reflect not the weaknesses of institutions but the way in which the strengths of institutions are deployed in the interests of powerful criminal or authoritarian actors.

A considerable amount of evidence suggests that the persistence of authoritarian practices in Latin America and the emergence of new forms of violence under democratic regimes is linked to the ways that violent and repressive actors tie themselves in to other actors in the political system.[47] This chapter argues that how this linking occurs, the ways that particular links operate, and to which state actors these different groups are connected will shape the character of institutions and places that lie outside the normal rule of law. In the context of Latin America today, three major issues stand out that affect the types of political problems seen in the region.

One of the driving characteristics of the shape of illegal networks is the structural contours of criminal opportunities in that area. For example, the production of cocaine requires the planting and harvesting of coca in large fields and secure installations to process the coca into cocaine hydrochloride. Undertaking this difficult process requires access to an undisturbed countryside, which the state repressive apparatus has difficulty penetrating. Thus, in Colombia and Peru criminal organizations devote considerable time to gaining control over whole mountain valleys and buying the support of powerful military leaders who can prevent large-scale crop eradication efforts. On the other hand, drug transshipment requires access to quality port and airport facilities in close proximity to relatively secure, short-term storage facilities. Thus, Kingston, Jamaica, and Rio de Janeiro, with their large tourism and export trades located near nodes of urban poverty, provide ideal locations to store drugs in underserved communities as they wait for shipment to consumer markets in Europe and North America. Finally, large-scale money laundering tends to take place in countries with very strong bank secrecy laws. These conditions tend to arise in places with relatively small populations, which require only limited government services. Thus, the Cayman Islands, the Channel Islands, and Hong Kong play major roles in illegal financial transactions.

These different conditions create very different criminal opportunity structures. In Colombia and Peru, large-scale guerrilla armies defend and offer protection to some coca growers, while other coca growers receive protection from powerful drug traffickers who have the resources to buy off whole military or police units. In Kingston and Rio, on the other hand, violence is implicated not in guerrilla warfare and pay-offs to military commanders but, rather, becomes embedded in petty police corruption and traditional clientelist dealings between politicians and the poor communities that store the drugs. Finally, in money laundering sites, criminal activity and connections will tend to reach very high up into the state and business community but will have little impact on the ground, since bloodshed on the streets interferes with the efficient processing of funds.

The nature, history, and the types of civic institutions that exist in a particular place can also have a profound effect on the types of political and criminal violence that occur there. In some locations, for example, political clientelist organizations might have been the primary link between the population and the state. Under conditions where relatively low-level criminals need to build links with the state, they may do this through traditional clientelist interlocutors. On the other hand, in places where politics are elite-dominated, long-term criminal activities will need to find ways to operate through the elite groups that dominate society. Finally, in some places, religious organizations may play powerful political roles, and criminals must find ways of incorporating the leadership of those groups into their activities. Regardless, the particular historical shape of social relationships and organizations in a specific place will affect the ways that criminals establish spaces for themselves to operate.

Finally, the institutional characteristics of the state itself also shape the contours of criminal activities. At the most basic level, weak states create certain types of opportunities for criminal activities that differ from anarchic environments or territories controlled by strong states.[48] The type and degree of centralized control that high-level state officials maintain over lower-level state actors can affect how criminal networks are built in particular places. The depth of state penetration into certain communities and the extent to which social welfare services are provided to populations create different types of possibilities for criminal activities and also engender the conditions under which criminals negotiate with state officials. The structure of the state in a particular place affects how criminals establish links to the state and the shape of the criminal network. Figure 2 graphically illustrates these effects.

Although these variables result in a myriad of different effective forms of rule, in countries as complex and diverse as Brazil—that can appear, following O'Donnell, as a three-color patchwork mapped across national territory—they also suggest a much more complex story. First, pockets of state-based order and areas subject to high levels of social violence are contingent, due to both historical conditions and changing structures of state and social institutions and to the specific economic dynamics affecting a particular region. Second, the existence of pockets of violence and poor law enforcement stem as much from state absence as they do from state involvement and the particular links that violent actors build into state institutions. Third, the pockets of violence that exist, then, also can differ dramatically from one another. Instead of "brown" and "green" zones that represent discrete forms of nondemocratic practice in formally democratic polities, we have a myriad of different forms of violent practices in these areas that depend on the specific social, governmental, structural, and historical conditions that exist inside them. The nature of micro-level democratic breakdown differs considerably from São Paulo to Rio—and, to an even greater extent, from Medellín to Kingston. These differences, however, can only be understood in the context of how these variables change over space and time. As types of criminal opportunities and social and institutional circumstances change, different types of criminal organizations develop. Consequently, different types of nonstate violence, abuse, and authority emerge.

The types of network relations that exist in particular "brown" and "green" areas, then, structure the specific forms of politics that operate in them. "Brown" zones are not places where there is simply an absence of a rule of law, but, rather, are places where there is a presence of a particular kind of order that varies across "brown" zones, depending on the particular relationships that sustain that space. Favelas in Rio do not just lack state order; they embody a different form of order that depends on actions by criminal, state, and civic actors. To take this a step further, the important variable is not institutional strength in a particular space but the types of relationships that exist in that space and the relationships among the individuals who occupy that space. As a result, the interactions of individuals who occupy a space give shape to the seeming disorder that exists there. Understanding the dynamics of networks and how they affect political order can also help us to understand how we can work to reestablish basic rights and the rule of law.

FIGURE 2. Factors Affecting the Structure of Illegal Networks

CONDITIONS	EFFECTS
Structural Constraints	• Economic conditions lead to illegal opportunities that shape the types of criminal organizations that develop. • Geographic constraints affect the political pressures and economic opportunities that exist in particular places.
Social and Historical Constraints	• Criminal organizations will build ties to the social groups operating in particular places, depending on their specific needs. • Some forms of civic organizing will be more susceptible to criminal ties than others. • A history of conflict, long-term exclusion, or tolerance of criminality will aid criminals in building ties to civic groups. • Basic norms that exist among social groups will affect how criminals and civic actors network together.
Institutional Constraints	• Organizational coherence of the state, particular institutions in the state, and the degree of state centralization will affect how state and criminal actors network together. • Tolerance of corruption in the state apparatus will affect the degree of corruption. • Resources available for internal state policing and structure of internal and external accountability will affect the possibilities of state-criminal ties.

Counternetworks: Resistance to Criminal Activity

The persistence of localized authoritarian enclaves characterized by state impunity and criminality bring into question basic assumptions about the project of democratic consolidation in Latin America. Neoliberal reforms and a difficult transition from authoritarian rule have limited poor peoples' access to the state and have exacerbated conditions of violence.[49] Criminals pose serious challenges to democratic rule and when organized in networks undermine many conventional efforts by state and social actors to control violence by easily co-opting or threatening potential opponents. How does a democratizing state guarantee order in crime-ridden neighborhoods, when even draconian force seems to lead to more criminal activity?

Any group focused on controlling crime in the context of networked illegal activity must have broader support and protection not just from drug dealers but also from the corrupt police allied with them. Given these particular challenges, one of the only available solutions to these problems is tightly linked and densely organized networks composed of both state and social actors. By working together, these groups and individuals can tap in to broader social and political networks to pressure more powerful state officials to control the corruption criminal activity depends on, provide aid to the population that relies on illegal actors for services, and implement effective crime control policies. This notion of densely linked, civic-state organizing to promote better governance is a popular idea advocated by scholars working in the social capital/civic society school. This section will examine the possibilities and pitfalls of civic networking as an alternative strategy to control violence.

State engagement plays an important role in any effort to control ongoing social violence. Under the prevailing conditions in Latin America, many argue that political elites must reform judicial institutions to treat citizens more equally and hold police accountable under civilian laws.[50] Further, to end ongoing abuse of poor and minority populations, these same leaders must also reform the police by "inculcating" them with democratic values and ending corruption.[51] This will help not only in limiting police violence but also in decreasing criminal violence, as police, responding to reform efforts, break ties with criminals and begin enforcing the law. Ending state corruption, however, is only part of the battle. Government efforts to politically incorporate the poor also help in extending the rule of law by reducing the dependence of the population on criminals for employment, informal security, and welfare services. Hernando de Soto argues that by offering basic welfare guarantees and by recognizing irregular urban land tenure, states can decrease the dependence of squatters on criminals for loans and protection.[52]

There is little reason, however, to believe that governments will implement these suggestions. Why, for example, would officials initiate reforms if they are tied to criminals and if the principal beneficiaries of those changes have little presence or representation within the state? Further, even if the government actually does initiate reforms, how do those policies get implemented on the ground if criminals are able to draw government agents into illegal networks?[53]

The literature on civil society and social movements provides some answers. Writers on social movements argue that mobilization and protest is one avenue for political change in exclusionary democracies.[54] By taking to the streets, populations can put pressure on the government to alter policies and behaviors.[55] Movement activism does not stop at pressing for policy change but also acts to reform authoritarian and repressive practices in society.[56] In the times between marches and public clashes, more formal civic institutions act as bridges between citizens and the state. Representative groups work with state officials to help implement policies and to hold government officials accountable through political networks, the press, and, occasionally, public demonstrations.[57] These ongoing contacts build public accountability and ensure effective governance.

But how can these societal efforts to create reform work in extremely violent communities? Under dictatorships, civic actors often become the focus of government repression. Today, corrupt officials or criminals target social leaders working to control violence.[58] Contemporary writings on social networks suggest that dense civic-state organizing can provide channels for communication, collective action, and representation in conditions where traditional forms of political activism are ineffectual. By bringing together functionally and spatially diffuse actors, localized networks facilitate the delicate political tasks required to bring peace to areas suffering from both state and criminal violence. For example, significant evidence shows that transnational networks that bring together NGOs, IGOs (international governmental organizations), and governments have had success in protecting human rights under authoritarian regimes that made domestic political opposition difficult. By deflecting attention from particular actors exposed to violence and using alternative channels of communication and representation, network connections helped to achieve political change under difficult circumstances.[59] At the local level, the involvement of networks raises the costs of violent actors silencing individual groups. Further, the activity of civic groups in particular neighborhoods helps make state leaders aware of community problems so that they can either change existing policies or discipline negligent officials. Civic networks facilitate efforts to build up norms of social and political behavior that contrast with those propagated by traffickers and their allies.[60] The interaction of local level activists, more powerful NGOs, and state officials helps transmit local-level knowledge to more powerful state and social actors under conditions where normal bureaucratic lines of communication do not function properly. Finally, networks allow groups with different and often contradictory strategies to work together to achieve similar objectives. Thus, a group engaged in open protest can operate in conjunction with a group that puts more weight on negotiating accommodations with the government.[61] Through informal networks, different local organizations can interact with outside NGOs, residents, and the state to bring in external assistance, develop innovative solutions to problems, change state policy, and extend the rule of law.

As we will see in this book, the distinct challenges posed by criminal groups that are strongly connected to some civic leaders and government agents in Rio's favelas create an environment in which civic networks provide an effective way to extend democratic governance and protect citizens' rights over the medium term. Only by building connections between residents and the outside can groups with resources to help reduce violence effectively penetrate neighborhoods dominated by criminal organizations. The specific flexible structures of networks allow groups concerned with controlling conflict to work together to build the confidence of fearful and isolated populations necessary to undertake significant political reforms and decrease their reliance on traffickers.

There are, however, some serious structural, institutional, and historical barriers that interfere with the long-term success of civic networks in controlling violence. Economic influences keep crime and violence vibrant. There is a huge market for drugs and weapons but a lot less interest in supporting the types of social programs or even the types of effective policing that will control these activities. Further, working to control social violence, particularly in the very poor places that suffer the most from this violence, has only limited rewards for state and social actors. Skilled NGO activists, police, and bureaucrats who may begin work in particularly dangerous places often come from middle-class backgrounds and have only a limited interest in working in these locations. As they succeed at bringing violence in particular places under control, they are likely to move on to better jobs in other areas, leaving behind their work and those they worked with. As violence declines, less highly skilled professionals will be attracted to work in these communities, and efforts to control violence will consequently suffer. Successful criminals, on the other hand, usually remain, since their growing wealth is tied to continuing illegal activities. Even if they are arrested or killed, there are always others who are interested in taking their place. To make matters worse, given the many risks involved in resisting criminal activity, individuals living in these areas are unlikely to become involved in trying to repress violent activity unless it has reached a crisis level or there are specific external incentives that induce them to act. Thus, civic networking may take off after a series of murders, but, as that crisis passes, there will be many incentives, including ongoing threats from criminals, for individuals active in violence control efforts to give up after a short time. Criminals, on the other hand, rarely face reciprocal dangers as a result of their efforts to intimidate potential civic opponents. Occasionally, a heightened police or media focus on preventing crime in a neighborhood and, specifically, on protecting activists can place some restraint on the ability of criminals to threaten those seeking to reduce violence. This type of attention, however, is usually short-lived. As a result of all this, even with coordinated, well-organized activism, it is usually only a matter of time before activists are threatened into inaction, co-opted by criminals, or murdered.

A second, related problem is that civic and state actors seeking to work in a place suffering from high levels of violence will often need some engagement with the criminals who dominate the area in order to gain access and undertake operations. These contacts increase the risk of co-optation and, over the long term, pose serious challenges to any networked effort to control violence.

THREE

Tubarão

In the early morning hours of 15 May 2000, a PM murdered five residents of the adjacent favelas of Tubarão and Ceuzinho. The angry populace, not accepting the police story that the men were drug traffickers, descended the hill into the streets of the wealthy neighborhood below, where they rioted. Televisions broadcast images of the tumult across the country, and within a month the government began to implement an innovative public security program based on contacts among police, NGOs, and local leaders that significantly decreased levels of violence in the two favelas. Although these reforms achieved some success, within three years they had unraveled and violence had returned to the previous high levels. Caught between the sea and the sky, the Morro do Tubarão stands out as an example of the contradictions of wealth and poverty that define Brazil.

This chapter is the story of Tubarão and its close neighbor, Ceuzinho, two favelas that are home to 15,000 to 17,000 residents, located on an extremely steep hill above one of Rio's wealthiest neighborhoods. For many years prior to the 2000 massacre, Tubarão suffered from such significant violence that a doctor who tended to the community reported that residents had "substantial problems with anxiety." According to a local plumber, many of the bodies were simply carelessly thrown on the main streets of the favela. Another gang war in 1997 resulted in a shooting on one of Rio's most glamorous beaches on a hot and crowded Saturday afternoon. Throughout all of this, bullets rained down from the favela into apartments in the affluent neighborhoods nearby. A banker with whom I attended college recalled that he spent his first night in a posh Rio hotel watching the traces of bullets fly over the hill. During the nine months that I worked in these favelas in 1998 and 1999, ten murders occurred; another ten followed during the first six months of 2000. In 1996, a war between rival gangs in Tubarão and Ceuzinho left over one hundred dead. Because of its location close to wealthy neighborhoods, Tubarão and its neighbor have strong connections with state officials and have long received much more substantial assistance, from both the government and wealthy private citizens, than most other favelas. Given all of these efforts and concerns, how can violence in these favelas remain so high? The answer lies in the political connections traffickers maintain with civic leaders, police, and politicians.

The Historical Geography of Tubarão

Tubarão, located in the wealthy Zona Sul (South Zone), shares a very steep hillside with its neighbor and sometime rival, Ceuzinho. Until the 1980s, most of Tubarão's populace came from Rio, but today 75 percent of residents come from northeastern Brazil. Many of these new migrants, in Brazil's complex system of racial categorization, are not considered Afro-Brazilian by residents whose ancestors lived in the favela. Despite the high percentage of northeasterners in Tubarão, local leaders are either Cariocas (Rio natives) or childhood migrants. The leadership of the local AM lives on the southern side of the hill. Residents on the northern side say they feel ignored.[1] The neighboring community of Ceuzinho is populated almost exclusively by Cariocas of Afro-Brazilian descent. The racial and regional differences that characterize these communities contribute to a sibling rivalry that has occasionally led to violence.

Today, Tubarão has a lively social life with weekly *forros* (a popular northeastern dance) and *baile funks* (parties featuring a version of hip-hop common in Rio that has similarities with Miami bass). Tubarão and Ceuzinho have even set aside some of their rivalries to form a samba school that competes in Rio's famous Carnival parades, although residents bicker about which community's composers and lyricists will have their work chosen to represent the school.

The terrain of Tubarão is extremely precipitous. Some streets rise at very steep inclines. These high grades have, over the years, resulted in numerous mud and trash slides that have destroyed homes and killed residents.

Most homes that I visited during my research were overcrowded, with extended families making use of small spaces. The owner of one three-story structure had turned the building into a honeycomb of small rooms that were rented by single men and young couples. The owner also operated a bar on the first floor. My notes of a visit to one small two-bedroom apartment highlights the crowding: "I go up to Elizete's apartment. Nine people live in there: her mother, her father in law, her brother, Elizete, Wilson (her husband), another person I don't know, and her three children. She says there aren't that many people living in their apartment compared to others. In another similar apartment they have fifteen people living there. She says its cramped and that if I came on the weekend then I would see everyone sitting in the apartment."[2]

The favela is oriented along a main path that runs up the hill. Many businesses, the AM, and two crèches (day care centers) are located on the path. On summer days, the pungent smells of sewage flowing through partially covered gutters and garbage thrown down a ramp that runs perpendicular to the street mix with the salty sea breezes blown in from the nearby beach. While police posts stand at either end of the path, traffickers maintain a sales point in the middle, near the AM. About a third of the way into the favela, the path widens into a *quadra* (plaza) where traffickers and the AM hold parties. Standing in this space, one can feel as if in an arena, with the hill rising precipitously and dwellings towering above the head. PMs patrolling this plaza aim their rifles up into the homes above as they walk through.

Endowed with spectacular views of Rio's crescent beaches, the community has long been locked in conflict with the affluent neighborhoods below. Although many favela residents provide essential services to the city's elite, the media focuses almost exclusively on the favelas' petty thieves and drug traffickers who, respectively, relieve tourists of their valuables and provide the wealthy with narcotics. Politicians and rich neighbors have given assistance to Tubarão over the years, and the government has tried to provide effective policing. But at other times, the state has tried to remove the favela altogether in order to clear valuable land for construction, and wealthy neighbors have built walls to contain the community and to prevent muggers from escaping into it. Tubarão's large drug sales have created intense conflict among rival gangs for control of the favela. To make matters worse, state agents have tried to impose order, but often the police, bought off by one gang or another, are complicit in the violence.

The high levels of intervention by the state and private citizens peaked during the mid-1980s, when Governor Leonel Brizola built a large school nearby and improved many residents' homes.[3] During a conversation on a hot, rainy December evening, one resident said:

> Brizola was a primary factor in changing the community. After the *caixa d'agua* [water tower] fell in the middle of the community and knocked over all the houses he came in and put in the road and rebuilt many of the homes. Up until then most of the houses . . . were made of wood. Brizola rebuilt them and made them out of bricks. Those houses which remain built out of wood were people who disagreed with Brizola. They chose not to have their homes improved. Everyone supports Brizola.[4]

During this period, the state government also regularized water and electrical service to the favela, taking distribution away from local organizations and setting up accounts for residents with public utilities. The Brizola government and later state administrations also built a day care center, a citizenship rights center, and numerous apartment buildings.[5] In addition, the favela has received significant assistance from NGOs and religious organizations attracted to the community because of its location in the Zona Sul.[6] This connection is reflected in one story recounted during a long conversation by a religious activist whose family has worked in the community since the 1980s and who runs a crèche:

> One night, there was a heavy rain storm and a rock fell moving over many houses. Most homes at the time were made of plywood and *pica-pau* [daub and wattle]. That night we could hear lots of screaming up in the hill. The next day [her family] went up to see what we could do and when they got to the AM they could see that the AM was full of people left homeless. After the people were housed again we held [religious] services on a rock in the community once a week. Soon many people were coming. Not just those who we had helped and we realized we had a mission in the community.

As a result of their close proximity to the favela, the activist family heard the cries of residents from their home and went into the community to offer help. Through their personal wealth and connections to other wealthy donors, including the author Paulo Coelho, they brought resources to the favela and opened the crèche and school.

Although this was not the case with the program described in the above story, most outside assistance has flowed directly through the local AM, which, for example, controls access to spaces in the government apartment buildings and receives state funds to maintain the water system and another crèche. Sitting one day at a public school high on the hill, one very active older Ceuzinho resident reflected that despite the AM's control over collective resources, the regularization of water and electrical service in the 1980s weakened the AM since it could no longer threaten to cut off water or electrical service to ensure that residents paid their AM dues.[7] These shifts transformed the political and social resources available to local groups and contributed to the conditions under which AM leaders would later develop strong ties with traffickers.

Structure of the Illegal Network in Tubarão

Tubarão is the site of a powerful illegal network that brings together politicians, traffickers, local leaders, and police in efforts to enrich each other by disrupting formal governance and perpetuating criminality. These groups work together to ensure the social order necessary to promote criminal activities. The members of this network discourage the creation of other alternative political coalitions by providing resources to residents and by threatening or co-opting outsiders who might want to become politically involved. Local civic leaders and traffickers work to resolve disputes and promote an intensely inward-looking community identification among residents that makes it difficult to build the civic institutions and political relationships necessary to control violence.

The AM: Resolving Conflicts and Mediating Relations

The two principal internal organizations in Tubarão, the AM and the drug gang, have been closely aligned since the early 1980s.[8] The traffickers provide the AM with a monthly subsidy and the backing to implement difficult decisions when resolving conflicts among residents or dealing with internal dissent. In exchange, the AM helps the traffickers organize parties, minimize conflicts, legitimize their power, and maintain open channels with politicians, some police, local businesses, and the state bureaucracy.

The AM was formed in the mid-twentieth century out of a *polícia mineira* (vigilante group) that had successfully controlled crime in the community. In the early 1960s, support from a wealthy storeowner helped build the headquarters of the AM, a small school, and a few apartments for residents. Civic leaders later used contacts with politicians to improve local conditions.[9] Government aid largely halted during the dictatorship, but with the return of democracy in the 1980s, Governor Leonel Brizola developed close relations with AM leaders and, as described earlier, invested heavily in the community.

The current president of the AM, Bernardo, came to power in the early 1980s after helping a drug gang gain control of the favela.[10] Before this, an unstable, paranoid, drug-abusing trafficker ran Tubarão. He threatened residents and obliged many to leave their homes. Eventually, he forced the leadership of the AM, including Bernardo, who was then vice president, to leave the favela. As a result, Bernardo brokered a deal with members of the CV, at the time an up-and-coming prison gang, in which he agreed to help them take over Tubarão if they would let him run the AM. The traffickers agreed, and he prepared the community for their entry. The CV succeeded in forcing the old trafficker out and installed Bernardo as president.

Bernardo is a large, heavyset, combative, and compelling figure in local politics. As the nexus of relations between outsiders, traffickers, and residents, he mediates some of the most difficult issues facing the community. Since the 1980s, he has maintained close relations with powerful traffickers, and one NGO worker familiar with the community described it as having the largest arsenal in the Zona Sul. Over the years, Bernardo has skillfully negotiated the dangerous shoals of favela politics, remaining in power despite changes in trafficker leadership. Describing Bernardo's relationship with the jailed trafficker who retained tight control of the favela, Jorge, a former president of Ceuzinho who at one point had been publicly beaten by traffickers and who later was driven out of the favela for working on a police reform project, said: "[Bernardo] is tied to one group of traffickers and . . . he knows that their life is short so he is planning to leave the community when this one leaves. He used to run the community for Flavio but then Alberto [the current head trafficker] had him killed and [then] he worked with Alberto. . . . He is his *compadre* [the godfather of the trafficker's child]."[11] Indeed, Bernardo had such a close relationship with Alberto that he took calls from him nearly every day, invariably referring to the trafficker as *meu compadre* and discussing both weighty issues such as a transfer of power in the Ceuzinho AM and mundane things like progress in organizing local festivities. Asked how Bernardo remained in power, despite frequent violent changes of criminal leadership and his standing alliances with traffickers who eventually went to jail or were killed, Jorge responded, "Bernardo has a lot of *jogo* [short for *jogo de cintura* or political skill] and changes between one [trafficker] and the other."[12] In the early 1990s, as the number of evangelical Christians expanded dramatically in Rio's favelas, Bernardo too converted to evangelical Christianity. He would often hold prayer meetings in the AM and, although he privately drank wine, publicly avoided consuming alcohol.

Bernardo's long tenure gave Tubarão a political stability rare in favelas, successfully resolving conflicts between residents and helping improve the favela's basic infrastructure. Asked about Bernardo's success as president, Elizete, a sometime drug dealer, former prisoner, and resident of Ceuzinho, responded this way: "Bernardo is the only one . . . who has everyone's confidence."[13] Jorge, the former Ceuzinho leader, added: "One of the reasons why things work so well in Tubarão is that he [Bernardo] has the power of the traffickers to collect residents' dues."[14] His long experience allowed Bernardo to hone skills in dealing with residents, traffickers, bureaucrats, politicians, and the press. These skills enabled the AM to make substantial improvements in the favela and informally adjudicate residents' disputes. His skills in community management were on display one hot January night when he advised Ceuzinho leaders on how to improve local water service. In this conversation, he offered suggestions on which politicians to call and when to call them, on the bureaucrats they should contact, and on how to deal with the press in efforts to promote a positive state response.[15] Through a combination of public works, investment, and threats, the AM has sustained conditions for drug trafficking.

Today, the AM maintains contacts with businesses and politicians to help criminals build local support and to provide services to residents. When the traffickers wanted help in putting together Christmas and children's parties, Bernardo ordered AM officers to go to the neighborhood below to ask local businesses for money.[16] On one occasion when a bar owner did not provide the requested assistance, Bernardo told residents to drink at the bar and not pay. For his failure to help, the bar owner lost a great deal of money.[17] These efforts provided services to the favela but limited residents' ability to develop independent institutions to make demands of the government.

The AM also eases relations between traffickers and residents. One day, an angry, nervous, powerfully built man came to the dark AM headquarters to tell Bernard that a trafficker from Ceuzinho had threatened to kill him and begged Bernardo to intervene. Bernardo advised him to "give a *papo* [chat] to Jacaré [a trafficker's nickname]. He will automatically pass it on to Alberto who should be able to take care of it." Angry and afraid, the threatened man responded, "If you can't take care of it I'll kill the guy to set things right even if I have to leave the hill." Bernardo calmly responded, "There is nothing I can do about it during the day but . . . you should give Jacaré a *papo*." Later that day, Bernardo made some inquiries and complained to a group of AM activists about how residents expected him to resolve problems, but later did not show gratitude: "Yesterday a guy came [to the AM] who had arranged some problems for himself with the *vagabundo* [criminal] in Ceuzinho by getting himself involved with his [the *vagabundo*'s] girlfriend. The guy got punched in the eye and was told the night guys would come to kill him." Bernardo continued by saying that he "resolved the problem and the next day he was wearing a Ruy Ceasar shirt [a political candidate whom Bernardo was not supporting]."[18] Bernardo attempted to use his resolution of this problem to affect politics in Ceuzinho. During a delicate transition during which Bernardo tried to take over the AM there, my notes reflect the following statement Bernardo made to Alexandre, then Ceuzinho's AM president:

[The guy who had been threatened] doesn't have the minimum conditions to run for president. One of the traffickers is chasing him around with a knife. [I had a] guy in here the other day who had gotten himself in trouble with the traffickers because he had gotten together with a girlfriend of theirs and was being threatened and he wanted me to do something about it. The guy can't be the president of Ceuzinho. My *compadre* won't allow it. They have to find someone who can stay on there and not create problems. It would be great if you could stay.[19]

The AM tries to reduce conflict among residents and minimize the chances that these conflicts could involve traffickers. One day, two residents asked Bernardo to take forceful action against a former resident who had stolen their car radios. Bernardo counseled them to move cautiously, saying he could not do anything, "because if I call my *compadre* they will kill the guy. The guy doesn't have any money that he could use to reimburse you." Bernardo continued: "[I don't] want the guy's death on my hands" and suggested that they contact a PM named Guilherme to have the man arrested. The victims showed little enthusiasm for this. Concerned about drawing the traffickers into his conflict and compromising their political position, Bernardo said that he and other leaders in the AM had "to minimize the problems so as not to arouse the ire of my *compadre*."[20] Eventually the conflict was resolved peacefully when traffickers forced the man to pay for the radios. In all of his mediations of trafficker-resident relations Bernardo tried to prevent serious problems before they occurred to minimize the possibility of violence in the favela that could draw traffickers into conflict with residents.

Under some circumstances, Bernardo will communicate information to help traffickers act quickly to allay residents' concerns. On one occasion, Bernardo told Alberto by phone that "the robbers below don't even respect São Bento [a nearby street] anymore. They rob on the Rua dos Gafanhotos [another nearby street]. Something has to be done about them." Bernardo concluded that "the merchants in the area are ready to work with us to solve the problem."[21] In this case, Bernardo conveyed information to Alberto that he could use to provide more effective protection to the businesses operating around the community.

A climate of fear regarding Bernardo pervades the favela and minimizes criticism among Tubarão residents. On three occasions, residents refused my request for interviews.[22] This had only happened to me on one occasion in the two other communities that I studied. Zinha, an older and well-respected woman, rejected an interview request by loudly stating, "I won't talk about the AM because it has been sold out [*esta vendido*]. Nothing in the community should be sold to anyone. The community shouldn't have an owner but now it does. Bernardo makes it pretty [*bonito*] for him. Talking about the community could get you in jail. It is very dangerous. . . . There is lots of stuff that you can't talk about and I will only talk about things if I can talk about all of it."[23] Zinha made this statement in front of an

AM representative who had introduced us, almost as if she were challenging him to respond. Though Zinha did not want to be interviewed because of dangers associated with speaking her mind, she clearly did not restrain herself from speaking anyway. She believed that the affiliation between Bernardo and the community's *dono* (literally, owner, a common way Cariocas refer to the head trafficker in a favela) made her feel uncomfortable discussing how the community worked. Ceuzinho leaders had more intense criticism. Asked about Bernardo's long run as president, Denise noted that "no one would accuse Bernardo of being a criminal," but "no one in Ceuzinho has their *rabo preso* [literally, tail imprisoned]. Bernardo does."[24] Describing Bernardo, Jorge said, "Bernardo's family has lots of problems. There are lots of crazy people. He doesn't have it but sometimes it shows up in him. He is religious and has an obligation to be good but sometimes evil descends in him and you can see it."[25] This fear among residents cannot help but limit the work of outside NGOs, internal political dissent, and efforts to reduce violence.

The AMs' efforts keep residents calm and stem possible collective responses to traffickers. Political mobilization against traffickers is unlikely because residents are too afraid of Bernardo to challenge him and because he actively works to resolve conflicts and provide services. In one case, a group of residents formed an alternate ticket for AM elections, but Bernardo instead offered them places on his directorate. After they accepted the positions, however, he promptly began ignoring them.

The AM, thus, has a complex role in the favela. On one level, it provides basic services and mediates relations between the community and outsiders, much as it did before the 1980s. On another level, the AM acts as a public face for the traffickers, mediating relations among traffickers, residents, and outsiders. The AM is a clientelist organization, operating in a complex new context that dramatically changes the basis of patron-client relations. The residents of the community are clients of both the traffickers and of the politicians. These different patrons expect different types of loyalty. Given the levels of violence that traffickers bring into the community, the AM also has to make efforts to ensure that residents do not repudiate traffickers as their patrons. On the other hand, although the AM must work with politicians to bring in assistance, it also needs to prevent politicians from becoming more important to residents than the traffickers. To further muddle matters, politicians usually will not work directly with traffickers but, instead, will work through AM leaders, with the understanding that traffickers will guarantee the agreements they make with AM leaders. Although the AM mediates relations with traffickers, politicians, and residents, it also carries out agreements between traffickers and politicians and undertakes planning social events for traffickers. At the same time, the AM works to strengthen its position vis-à-vis traffickers and politicians. The violence that affects the community creates a complicated environment that, in the words of one AM officer, necessitates that those who run the AM have "*jogo de cintura*" (political skill).

The Traffickers: Efforts to Maintain Order and Guarantee Security

Alberto, the *dono* of Tubarão and Ceuzinho, was in prison in 1998 and 1999. Nevertheless, he retained control over the favela as a result of his pseudofamilial relationship with Bernardo, his *compadre*. Alberto chose who would lead the traffickers and they then paid a tithe to support him. During this period, there was some dissension that led to gunfights among traffickers, but the faction that supported Alberto won.

To preserve some degree of harmony and prevent residents from driving them out, despite the violence they bring to the favela, criminals involve themselves in many aspects of local life.[26] For example, traffickers throw parties, including a children's party, run with the AM's help, that provided toys to the favela's many needy children.[27] For adults, the gang organizes *baile funks*.[28] The traffickers actually own the sound system and employ the DJs that work at these festivities.[29] In addition to throwing parties, traffickers work with the AM to provide jobs to residents. Although the number of people employed is small, the funding provides the AM with increased capacity to help residents and pay for basic services. In explaining employment conditions to one worker on the DJ team, Bernardo said that he "can't pay much," but if the young man took the job, he "will never be without money."[30] Finally, as Marcos Alvito observed in Acarí, traffickers maintain close relationships with their extended families, which often involve multiple long-term girlfriends, in order to garner protection from the police.[31]

The AM plays a critical role in these efforts by providing administrative leadership to organize events and connect different actors who may not want to work publicly with traffickers. One spring day, Bernardo complained of being tired of all the toil facing him. An accountant who worked in the AM responded by saying, "Alberto wants to have a *forro* in the community." Bernardo then began talking about what bands they could hire, shifted to talking about hiring clowns for a children's party the traffickers also wanted him to run, and with some exasperation said that "he [Alberto] wants it all again for the Christmas party." The conversation moved on to raising additional money for the parties through local businesses. My field notes read:

Bernardo sends the accountant off with some letters to turn in to different businesses to ask for presents for the Christmas party. He gives Ricardo some other cards. There is a letter with a place for 6 signatures which Bernardo signs. Bernardo sends Julio to one business and instructs him to talk only to the manager. Letters requesting funds are going to Zona Sul, Paes Mendonça and a large bingo parlor [major businesses in the area].

In addition to planning and raising money for parties, the AM also sends *ofícios* [official memo's] to police to prevent actions during parties. My notes of one interaction in the AM demonstrate this: "Bernardo gets a call from his *compadre*. First he says that there have not been any arrests of late. The police haven't done much. He says that someone must not have given *mole* [gone soft]. He talks then about all of the *ofícios* which he has turned in to approve the parties which they will be having." Elizete and her husband, Wilson, a drug dealer, noted the importance of these *ofícios*: "There are no problems with violence during the [samba] rehearsals because the police have *ofícios* sent to them about the event."[32] A similar process of gaining official sanction for parties through civic actors will be seen in the chapter on Santa Ana.

Traffickers also reinforce their position by working to advance the perception that they support local norms. For example, many residents believe that traffickers do not tolerate theft in the favela or other crimes against residents they have not approved.[33] Elizete notes: "The traffickers there [in Tubarão] killed someone for rape . . . the other night. You can't rape or rob in the community or you will be killed. Robbery is rare in the community." Elizete went on to say that if she "were robbed she would denounce it to the traffickers and they would take care of it."[34] During the period of this research, traffickers frequently disciplined residents. Rumors also spread that traffickers had beaten and killed someone accused of sexual assault. As described earlier, the traffickers caught an ex-resident who had stolen car radios and forced him to pay back those he had robbed.[35] In general, traffickers do not steal from residents and avoid assaulting residents, except when enforcing order, because doing so would undermine their own support in the favela and perhaps cause residents to try to force them out of the favela.

Trafficker decisions, however, are political choices designed to improve support among certain groups of residents critical to their safety. Pedrinho, an ex-trafficker who had converted to evangelical Christianity, said that "the basis of the law [of the hill] is your respect in the community." He went on to say that "respect is based on whether you drink, smoke [marijuana], sniff [cocaine] in public or go after women who aren't your own. . . . Those who do not do these things earn the respect of other residents. Those who engage in these activities lose respect." It is notable that men and women who hold positions of respect in favelas are rarely seen drinking at the many bars that dot community streets. He said: "It would appear as if this was not a big deal but it is. . . . If you get yourself in trouble but are respected no one will do anything to you. If you get yourself in trouble but are not respected people might beat you up."[36] This practice helps to reinforce local norms but also reflects the fact that traffickers will avoid taking actions against particularly well-connected residents, since this could weaken their position in the favela. On one occasion, I was robbed while I rented a room in the favela. I discussed the robbery with several neighbors but did not take the issue formally to either the traffickers or the AM. Several weeks later, while discussing my decision not to renew my lease on the room, my landlady, a resident married to a jailed trafficker, reported that a boy had been taken away by traffickers for stealing. Another resident who was present at the conversation, a former business associate of a powerful trafficker, said that the real thief was the nephew of a powerful trafficker and he was unlikely to ever be punished for committing a small robbery. The boy who was punished had been involved in a different set of robberies in another part of the favela.[37] Pedrinho's observations about the role of respect are confirmed by one event in January 1999 when, after a Ceuzinho AM meeting, I ran across traffickers brutally beating a man accused of rape in front of a crowd. During the assault, the adolescents attacking the man threw an entire metal market stand on top of him. Someone standing near me wanted to intervene to stop the beating, but a woman prevented him, saying, "There is nothing to do." Later a distraught Jorge, the former Ceuzinho president and a member of Alcoholics Anonymous who also witnessed the beating, said, "The guy is a drunk who loses himself but isn't a rapist." Jorge went on to note that "he will probably get himself killed."[38] Clearly, one of the factors in this attack was the man's alcoholism. The unpredictability of trafficker actions is also reflected in one conversation with Elizete about a woman who had been beaten by her husband. The following notes, taken as an angry beaten woman desperately wandered one street of the favela, reflect the complexities of gaining the traffickers' help: "First, Elizete says maybe she is going to get the police and then she says that the police aren't going to do anything because it is a problem between husbands and wives. She goes down the hill and Elizete says that she will go get os meninos ["the boys," slang for traffickers] because they are responsible for what happens in the community. She says they probably won't do anything either."[39] This statement reflects the ambivalence of traffickers toward certain types of violence in the favela. Although traffickers are responsible for what "happens" on the hill, they also are not likely to act in a domestic dispute. This story goes back to local politics and the question of respect. Traffickers will not intervene in disputes, robbery, or violence if they believe that such an intervention might weaken their position among segments of residents critical to their safety.[40] Thus, traffickers might beat a drunk but are less likely to punish a man who attacks his wife.

These conversations also reflect a gendered element to trafficker order. In both Pedrinho's and Elizete's statements, gender plays a role in the interpretation of both community norms and the possibility of trafficker action. For Pedrinho, one of the bases of one's respect in the community is staying away from other men's women. At the same time, Elizete notes that traffickers are probably unwilling to intervene in a local case of domestic abuse. Further, the most severe and repeatedly discussed punishments appear to be reserved for rapists. These bits of information suggest that traffickers respect and attempt to police the boundaries of a private sphere in which some women are tied to certain men. These relationships, in view of these norms, appear not to be subject to outside interference. Traffickers will avoid crossing this line in dealing with domestic disputes and they will police the line by punishing those men who improperly interfere with this domestic sphere.

Even those closely associated with traffickers feel ambivalence about their power. While the gang might maintain a certain order in the favela, there is little recourse if traffickers themselves create difficulties. One day, Elizete noted that certain powerful traffickers, still in their adolescence or early twenties, regularly flew kites from the roof of her apartment building, breaking water pipes and damaging the roof. She said, however, that since they are dealers she could do nothing to get them off the roof.[41]

Because of its connections to the traffickers, the AM can also claim a role in keeping order. For example, several people had broken into a crèche building owned by the Spiritists, had caused some damage, and had stolen paint. One of the group's leaders, a woman from outside the community, spoke to Bernardo. After hearing her story, Bernardo said he would figure out who had done it and declared that those responsible would have to make repairs and pay for what they had stolen.[42] I am not aware of whether or not the crèche was repaid, but its leader was well aware of Bernardo's connection with the traffickers and seemed confident in his assurances.

Traffickers also maintain political control of Tubarão and Ceuzinho through the leadership of the Tubarão AM. During the period of this research, there was only one drug trafficking operation for the sibling hills. Although the traffickers have a close relationship with Tubarão's leadership, their relationship had been tense with Ceuzinho leaders. In late 1998, the then-president of Ceuzinho's AM, Alexandre, wanted to leave office because of threats made against him and his family.[43] Bernardo and Alberto did not approve of any of the candidates to replace him. As a result, Bernardo tried to mediate a transfer of power that would leave him in control of Ceuzinho. At one meeting, he noted that he helped to create a peaceful transfer of power in another nearby favela where many knew that traffickers had forced the AM president out so that they could install a friend. Ultimately, a group of old leaders formed a coalition that the traffickers accepted.[44] Although Bernardo's efforts did not leave him in control of Ceuzinho, he did force Ceuzinho leaders to form a slate of candidates acceptable to the traffickers.

The interests of the AM and the traffickers are not completely congruent, but they usually work toward similar goals because the traffickers' firepower backs up the AM, enabling its leaders to enforce difficult decisions. The traffickers' subsidy helps the AM to employ residents and pursue their own projects. Although the AM occasionally receives outside support for larger capital investments such as a community radio station, the monthly expenses of the AM appear to be under R$2,000. Excluding any personal remuneration for Bernardo, traffickers probably provide the AM with no more than this amount.[45]

The AM and the traffickers maintain a delicate balance. The traffickers' leadership depends on the AM to mediate relations with both the state and the residents. At the same time, the traffickers frequently undertake activities that endanger residents. Thus, the traffickers depend on the AM to maintain support in the favela but regularly do things that complicate the lives of AM leaders by putting residents at risk. It is unlikely that traffickers could have a better ally than Bernardo since he knows how to get what he wants from both residents and state actors. This close relationship allows Bernardo a considerable degree of political independence but, at the same time, constrains him.

State Actors' Contributions to the Network

Public officials also play an important role in Tubarão's illegal network. Police and politicians have access to state power, can provide money and building materials to the community, and can aid criminals. Corrupt politicians provide financial support that reinforces trafficker legitimacy, and both politicians and police facilitate crimes by interceding with judges or by not enforcing the law.

The Police: Selling Protection and Undermining Legitimacy
Until the 2000 reforms, law enforcement officers in Tubarão were extremely corrupt and violent. Police, maintaining posts within one hundred meters of a *boca*

de fumo, rarely bothered traffickers. Groups of armed adolescents, some of whom appeared to be as young as twelve, openly dealt drugs at the entrance of the favela and in the street below. The occasional violence the police directed against dealers had little effect on trafficking because they used that violence haphazardly to extort money from traffickers.

Prior to the 2000 reforms, residents had only negative things to say about the police, who, according to one resident, did not adequately secure the community. Jorge, the former Ceuzinho AM president, angrily noted, "The state does not guarantee security the way that it is supposed to. The police work down here and up in the hill. Down here they are well dressed and behaved. Up there they have big weapons and shoot people. They take bribes." Evaldo (another resident) says that " things are different because down here everyone is watching them all the time and will complain about them. In the hill it doesn't work that way. People have to make demands of the state."[46] Elizete observed that police had a limited presence in the favela. Looking out on the hill one day, she pointed to a peak just ahead of us, commenting, "The police don't go up there. The police have a presence in the community but it is only on the lowest street. They rarely get higher into the hill. There are many gunfights in the community."[47] Indeed, although it was common to see police in the lowest parts of the favela, they rarely patrolled higher up. Bernardo complained one day of having to go to a meeting where awards would be given to police by noting that the police were *safado* (scummy, lying).[48] On another occasion, Bernardo said that the colonel in charge of the PM battalion responsible for Tubarão wanted to have lunch. Bernardo asked rhetorically, "How can I have lunch with the Colonel when his *pragas* [plagues] are here making life difficult." Hearing this, someone else in the AM complained that the police had shot up all of the lights on her street.[49] Some police behaved inappropriately in the community. One night, an angry PM officer walked around claiming that he would kill a resident in earshot of this researcher and a number of residents. Others complained of police harassment. One resident noted, "Now you can't go into the *mato* [forest] above the community because the police bother everyone even if they know you are a resident. Two police sit by [a nearby school] at a bar and bother people they know are residents."[50] The police stopped and searched me on many occasions. Once they asked that I wear an identity card to indicate I was a researcher. I thought this was ridiculous, but Bernardo was not surprised and offered to make up a card for me.

Some police violence is a result of overzealous law enforcement efforts and the errors that arise from fear, but some police violence results from corruption. The police in Tubarão take bribes and use the means of violence available to them to enforce deals with traffickers. I myself witnessed a minor case of police corruption, fortunately with no violent consequences other than an intimidating show of arms.

At about 3:00 P.M. one day in August 1998, three police appeared in the AM with their guns drawn. I was sitting in the back of the office with the owner of a pirate cable system, Carlton, and the AM's extremely quiet receptionist, Roberto. The police came in waving weapons and addressed Carlton and me, saying that they were "not joking" and asking us if we knew about the *combi* (a van used to take residents up and down the hill). Confused at this hostile opening gambit, Carlton and I directed them to Roberto since neither of us worked for the AM. Roberto, who was an employee of the AM rather than an officer, said he could only take messages. When he told the police he did not know what was going on, the officer became angry and repeated that they were "not joking" and that the president should call the Batalhão (Battalion Headquarters). Later, Roberto related the story to Ricardo, the AM vice president. Ricardo had no idea what the officer had been talking about but found out that the police had assessed the *combi* an illegal "fine." The owner of the *combi* had said he was working with the AM and never paid the police off. Angry, the police went to the AM to obtain their payment.[51]

One resident, closely tied with traffickers, told the story of how a police officer who showed up for work one day in a bad mood shook down a group of minor traffickers. He walked around the favela angrily looking for some low-level drug dealers to bother. Not finding any, he went to the nearby beach where he located the dealers and, finding narcotics, forced them to come up with some money to ransom their own freedom. The traffickers went off and got the money by borrowing or stealing.[52]

Another story highlights the mixture of cooperation and conflict between traffickers and police. One trafficker's girlfriend said that all the police did was take money from traffickers and harass residents. Her mother, Carolina, a socially active evangelical Christian, said that one day she found the police assaulting a low-level dealer in an empty house. The police told her to go away, but she refused because she believed the police might kill the man. After the police left, she convinced him to file a complaint and denounced the beating herself. Shortly afterwards, however, a terrifying encounter occurred when a police soldier came to her house. She recalled that "he came in with a weapon without asking and sat down and talked to my daughter," who had recently suffered a miscarriage. When Carolina arrived, the police told her that "it was unfortunate that your daughter had lost the child." On another occasion, two police came to her house. The experience is recounted in my field notes as follows: "One was in her house pointing his gun at her. She was scared. He [the police soldier] said that they had arranged for the Terceiro Co-mando [Third Command, TC, a rival drug gang reputed to have close connections to the police] to invade the community so that people in the community would learn to appreciate the police." After this, she was so afraid that she let the matter go. When internal affairs officers came to take a statement from the beating victim, Carolina reported that he refused to discuss the issue with the officers out of fear.[53] Higher-level traffickers had worked out a deal with the police, and the victim dropped the complaint.[54] On another occasion, residents confirmed the presence of this type of high-level collusion when they pointed out that the chief of state security had cashiered the former head of the local Batalhão after the government found that he had taken bribes.[55]

An interesting example of police corruption took place in October 1998 before the beginning of the children's party sponsored by the traffickers. By 3:00 P.M. on the day of the party, all of the entertainers, including clowns and a DJ, had set up, but the festivities had yet to begin, despite a 1:00 P.M. start time. Just before the DJs went on, two police appeared at one end of the plaza and began communicating with a group of traffickers who sat in a box above the crowd.[56] One of the traffickers started running back and forth between the group communicating with the police and somewhere else on the hill. A series of hand signals ended with the traffickers giving the police a "thumbs-up" sign and the police nodding. The music then started to play, and the party went off without further complications.[57] It is likely the police were going to receive some sort of payment for this. Certainly, in the context of residents' broader accusations of corruption, this exchange makes clear that there is a businesslike relationship between the two groups, and the existence of such an open relationship indicates some corruption.

This evidence shows that police corruption is rampant but disorganized. Each new set of police transferred into the favela must establish its own relationship with the dealers.[58] A resident noted that when a new group of police came into the community, things become quite tense as the police got the lay of the land and made contact with traffickers. Sitting under an overhang, just outside a public school looking out over the hill on a sunny late afternoon, Elizete noted that police commanders had changed the *turma* (group) of police because they did not harass traffickers enough: "They only left Osmar and Diodoro's [two police sergeants assigned to the community] *turmas* in Tubarão because they *pertubar* [perturb, create difficulties] a lot. All the rest changed. The [new] police came in from the Baixada [the poor suburbs around Rio] and don't know the hill yet. . . . they sit in the post and don't do very much. When it is time for them to go through the community they go in groups of eight . . . They don't go in at night."[59] Senior commanders had moved out a significant number of police in the favela because they had worked out payment arrangements with traffickers and no longer actually interfered with criminal activities, leaving only those police who engaged in substantial violence. Elizete expected that things would calm down again after the police and the traffickers made new arrangements. Until then, however, there would be more conflict. In the weeks after this conversation, traffickers and police engaged in a series of gun battles.

Police are a critical component in the network, in that they both provide protection to traffickers by not enforcing the law and they build criminal legitimacy within the community by actively working with traffickers. The combination of police violence and corruption delegitimizes the police in the eyes of many residents, who regularly repeat stories about their conduct and links to criminals. Although they take bribes and provide necessary services, they also engage in frequent conflicts with traffickers, resulting in arrests and deaths. Different police units have different relationships with traffickers. Over time, groups of police assigned to the community may be reassigned, and traffickers then have to establish relationships with each new group of police.

Politicians and State Officials: Resources and Respectability
The connection between politicians and the favela is consistent with the way politicians have historically treated favelas in Rio. Most politicians come from the upper classes and only have contact with favelas in the period prior to elections. Since politicians have limited funds to secure support, they try to distribute a minimal amount of largesse to each community in exchange for votes.

The behavior of politicians during the 1998 elections suggests that politicians today use two approaches in dealing with the favela. Some politicians work with the AM only to get votes. These politicians know that Bernardo is well-connected to traffickers and provide the AM with resources in order to gain access to the favela. To increase his bargaining power, Bernardo makes apparent his associations with traffickers when negotiating with politicians, who like the reassurance of this connection but do not want to deal directly with criminals.[60] Most politicians support the network in this passive way by doing business with Bernardo, much in the manner machine politics traditionally takes place in big cities, but with the knowledge that Bernardo's connection to the traffickers guarantees community access. Other politicians negotiate with traffickers through different connections and provide benefits directly to traffickers.

During the 1998 elections, Bernardo engineered relationships with a number of competing politicians to obtain resources for the community. Bernardo negotiated direct monopoly access to the favela with one candidate who had worked with traffickers in another favela during the 1990 campaign. That candidate then employed five residents to promote his campaign and provided resources to the AM. The residents Bernardo chose to work on the campaign all had close relations to the traffickers and included the expectant mother of Alberto's son, the wife of the AM vice president, and a jailed trafficker's girlfriend. In discussions with his campaign manager, Bernardo asked for money to improve a stairway and the plaza the traffickers used for parties. In addition, he said that the candidate would have to provide three "clean" cellular phones for use by him, the imprisoned trafficker, and the trafficker's girlfriend.[61] In these negotiations, Bernardo clearly wanted to indicate to the campaign manager that he had an association with Alberto and that he could guarantee him access to the community. The politician's manager accepted the requests, willingly believing that he had established a relationship with the traffickers, and employed a number of residents associated with Bernardo and the traffickers to campaign for him.

To the chagrin of this politician, Bernardo also developed more limited relationships with other politicians, in which he agreed to provide workers to campaign in the wealthy neighborhoods nearby. This did not violate the letter of the initial agreement since the other politicians did not campaign in the favela, but it led to significant tension when representatives of the first candidate found signs for one of their competitors in the AM.

To further complicate matters, the traffickers brokered another deal with a separate group of politicians. A few days before the elections, Bernardo told those working for the first politician to take down his signs and put up the signs of the politicians the traffickers negotiated the new deal with. Bernardo was very angry and said that he wanted to get himself out of "these problems." He went on to say that he took "a subsidy from them [the traffickers] so when they decide to support a candidate I have to also. This was our [the favela's] chance to be respected again. We had a candidate from the same party as the mayor and had he been elected people would have paid attention to us. Now we are forced to support a candidate who they [the traffickers] had closed [the agreement with] without consulting me."[62] On election day, Bernardo's anger grew when he realized that one local neo-Pentecostal congregation had backed a third candidate. In the end, none of the politicians won, but their contributions helped the AM improve the stairway and plaza and gave the traffickers access to an improved space to sustain their efforts to gain residents' support.

Bernardo's connection with traffickers gave him leverage with the first politician, even though the traffickers had no connection to the negotiations. The politician worked with the AM because he thought the AM acted on behalf of the traffickers and could help him get votes. Nevertheless, this story also makes clear that the politician had little intention of directly seeking out the traffickers. The candidate worked through the AM because dealing with the AM did not entail the same risks as dealing with criminals. In the end, the traffickers provided no such guarantee and made a separate deal with other politicians. The failure of the traffickers and the AM to work together created confusion in the favela and opened a space for the neo-Pentecostals to support a different candidate. This lack of coordination split residents and decreased their political clout.

The AM acts as an intermediary between traffickers and politicians and continues to play this role between elections. One young ambitious political appointee appeared regularly in the favela to attend state-supported events, and, on one occasion, he posed with Bernardo for photos in a major Rio newspaper.[63]

The AM will also use contacts with government officials and politicians to deal with some of the more egregious problems caused by traffickers. One AM project is a crèche, which was set up in the mid-1990s with assistance from the mayor's wife. The area where the crèche was built had been filled with tables where traffickers dealt drugs. One night the police came through and destroyed the tables. Bernardo used the opportunity to ask the city for money to build a crèche in the space. The crèche provides day care to about forty children and employs five women closely associated with the AM. They have a VCR and a TV and provide the children with two meals a day. Parents pay R$20 per month for the service and children between the ages of two and four can attend.[64] The crèche receives aid from outside sources and offers a televised adult education course.[65] Despite having their activities displaced by the new crèche, traffickers did not interfere with efforts to bring in outside aid because this would have upset the residents whom they depended on for protection. In some sense, this was a dream project for the AM. By starting the crèche, they developed a revenue stream to serve residents and provide employment. By making use of the space to deliver a service to residents, they forced traffickers from a very public area without creating tensions.

Traffickers allow city officials to come into the favela to do work that will benefit residents. At no time during my study did traffickers interfere with any projects the state developed in the community, since doing so would have undermined their support among residents. Nevertheless, since residents associate Bernardo with the traffickers, his public connections to state officials reinforced his power in the community and perceptions that traffickers and state officials work together. Public association with politicians confers legitimacy on Bernardo as a local leader. His successful efforts to gain improvements from the state strengthened the illegal network's position in the favela. As another leader boldly stated, "We are the government here."[66]

Why the Criminal Network Emerged

Several factors enabled this criminal network to emerge. The first was timing. The 1980s was a period when cocaine trafficking grew dramatically in the city. Residents reported that the shift from marijuana to cocaine put more money into the hands of criminals and intensified competition for drug sales points. Bernardo took advantage of this dramatically increased competition to broker an alliance to bring in traffickers, whom he felt could benefit him and other residents.

The illegal network also developed from traffickers' ability to use the resources they had earned through cocaine dealing to provide services to residents, such as sponsoring social events and providing medical care for residents. In exchange for a subsidy, the AM helped deliver these services and undertook the administration of large-scale projects, such as infrastructure improvements and parties funded by traffickers.

Finally, the criminal network emerged as a result of state officials' complicity in local illegal activities. The expansion of the illegal network occurred in the context of the transition to democracy and the first gubernatorial administration of Leonel Brizola. Since his strong connection to favela residents was one of his primary electoral bases, he pumped a huge amount of resources into the favelas. Tubarão was a main beneficiary. Despite the alliance between traffickers and AM leaders, politicians continued to work with the community and, in fact, invested a staggering amount of resources (by Rio standards) in the favela, despite the growing power of traffickers. Politicians and other officials filtered these resources into projects that had, in Rio's clientelist tradition, a connection to the AM. Since the Tubarão AM worked with traffickers, these funds reinforced the illegal network.

How the Network Affects Political Order in Tubarão

Why is the criminal network in Tubarão so successful? If any favela in Rio could have been expected to have low levels of violence, Tubarão would have been a good candidate. The location facilitated residents' efforts to make demands of the state and build contacts with outsiders who could draw attention to the community. Wealthy neighbors and hotel owners pressured the government to decrease local crime and violence, but little came of this other than more repressive policing. Despite all of these factors, neither residents nor the government took any significant action to control violence because of the existence of a well-linked criminal network, involving the AM, traffickers, and state officials.

The political order in Tubarão does not reflect simply a failure of the rule of law and state governance but, rather, reflects a particular type of political order based on state, civic, and criminal relations, which has both strong similarities to and differences from other poor communities in the city. The internal politics of Tubarão are created by the way the particular environment that the community exists in interacts with local state and social structures. The result is a community where politics is driven by strong retail consumer demand for narcotics, ongoing intense political concerns with violence in the area, the easy access of outside activists to the favela, and a narrow civic base dominated by a clientelist AM.

The location of the favela puts it inside of some of the most valuable retail drug turf in Brazil, with easy access to both a wealthy local clientele and many tourists. This creates intense competition over the site of drug sales and has led to several wars between drug gangs. The value of the drug market creates some serious pressures on the part of police for bribes. These conflicts and the other hazards associated with the drug trade also bring immense pressure from wealthy neighbors for intermittent police crackdowns and broader reforms. From a longer-term perspective, the favela has always been well positioned to receive many benefits from the state, in terms of both clientelist support from politicians and large-scale government projects, which serve residents and showcase government policies for powerful social figures who live nearby and visiting dignitaries.

These particular conditions can only be negotiated with a great deal of political skill. As a result, the head of the AM, Bernardo, plays a very significant role in the community. He, among the three community leaders I examine in this book, is the only one with a fully intact body and effective public-speaking skills. He regularly talks to reporters and, as a result of the community's prominence, appears in local papers. Over the course of the decade in which he has been AM president, he has survived many different traffickers as a result of his political skills. Although someone else could probably take over for him, no one would have comparable abilities in dealing with residents, the press, and state officials.

Bernardo is the dominating figure in Tubarão political life and has a close but loose relationship with traffickers. He has a considerable degree of operational flexibility to bargain with state officials and has the strategic freedom to develop plans for the community and for himself. This allowed him to negotiate in the traffickers' name without gaining their formal approval. It also allows him to calm residents and defuse potential problems before they reach traffickers or result in violence.

With all of the state services coming into the favela, it is essential that elements of the illegal network control distribution of those services. With his top-notch political skills, Bernardo was able to do this. The AM, for example, had power over access to public housing and could help residents gain access. The AM also controlled which residents received certain jobs that the government channeled through the AM, such as plumber, fumigator, or sanitation worker. Traffickers might have wanted someone more beholden to them, but having a powerful but partially independent AM president was a worthwhile sacrifice in exchange for a stronger network.

The role of Bernardo and the AM shows how civic actors can aid and abet illegal activities. The normal function of civil society to mediate relations between state and civic actors to ensure effective policy adoption and implementation is altered in this case, as the AM takes on the role not just of linking residents to state officials, but also of mediating relations between traffickers and residents and traffickers and a variety of state actors. Without the skillful mediation provided by Bernardo, it would have been very hard for the illegal network to function or for the traffickers to remain active, since he helped to defuse conflicts within the community before they erupted in ways that could damage the traffickers—and because he provided a safe conduit between certain public officials and traffickers. Bernardo's efforts to control the community were assisted by the fact that most state resources that came to the community flowed through the AM. This enabled him to provide jobs to his and the traffickers' allies and, during one four-year period, to take over a powerful state institution responsible for defending citizen rights in Tubarão and other nearby favelas. In this position, Bernardo was able to denounce one police occupation, resulting in a partial withdrawal of police from the favela. The AM also tried to weaken and co-opt other potential civic actors in the community. Their threats against the Spiritist crèche forced that group into the traffickers' arms, and their studied exclusion of the Catholic chapel and clinic helped to marginalize those organizations.[67]

The evidence here, then, shows that the AM performed some of the classic functions of civil society in providing mediation and in affecting state policy, but, unlike some in the civil society school argue, it used this position to weaken the rule of law in the community and to promote criminality. In addition, the AM also undermined other civic groups, leading to a relatively sparse civil society compromised to the interests of the drug gang. Rather than serving as a bulwark against tyranny, the AM operated as a conduit to redirect state and social power away from enforcing the law toward building micro-authoritarian power in the favela.

One of the negative political implications of this structure is that the semipublic nature of the relationship between Bernardo and the traffickers limits the ability of residents to demand reductions in police violence through their official representatives. On one occasion, Bernardo told a resident, who had publicly complained of police abuse during a pre-electoral candidate forum, to go directly to the leadership of the Batalhão. He added, however, that he could only offer her limited assistance with these matters since the police did not trust in him. After the meeting, Bernardo told others in the AM office that "it was good the woman [who criticized the police] was there because they [the police] don't listen to me."[68] Outside awareness of Bernardo's relationships undermined the AM's efforts to control violence.

This case also shows an apparently divided and uncoordinated state institution. Different police are engaged in very different types of activities. Some behave unprofessionally by making casual death threats in the street, while others extort money. At the same time, some police actually worked to stop crime, either within the law or by brutally pursuing traffickers in contravention of basic human rights guarantees. To make matters worse, police have virtually no role in actually dealing with basic law enforcement issues, such as protecting homes against theft or investigating other major crimes. What order the police do establish is both geographically and temporally contingent, based on the spaces they occupy and the particular shift of officers on duty at that time. As a result, most residents see police as corrupt threats to their lives.

The problem with the management of state violence reflects several structural and institutional factors. First, it indicates a lack of resources to adequately pay and train police in Rio, leading not just to poor discipline and corruption but also to bad police practice. Further, the existing public security institutions appear not to have the ability to enforce internal discipline or ensure that the police in their command adequately serve the population. One could argue that police leadership actually encourages corruption among the ranks, but there is little evidence for this in Tubarão, since it seems that each different *turma* under the command of a particular sergeant approaches its job and the possibility of corruption differently. This does not mean that high-ranking police officers are not corrupt, but it does suggest that at this time they are not directly involved in quotidian corruption within the ranks in this particular place. This evidence also suggests that the system of military courts in which police disciplinary proceedings are adjudicated in Rio is ineffective at controlling either corruption or police violence.

Other state activities are no better. Bureaucrats and politicians invest in the community, usually by channeling money through the AM, while at the same time making public statements about the need to control crime. Unlike the AM, which has a relatively fixed presence, state actors regularly rotate through the community and rarely develop strong ties to residents. The result is that, other than police brutality, the state is perceived to have little effect on local lives (to say nothing of a possible positive impact). What money does come in goes through the AM, which then ends up getting most of the credit for the benefits those resources bring.

This evidence suggests that political relationships between elected officials and the favela are dominated by old clientelist models, which were created in the 1950s. These efforts focused on building up AMs as almost corporatist structures to represent the community as a whole but were co-opted by politicians to serve as conduits to give resources to favela residents in exchange for votes. The result was the emergence, which Robert Gay has amply documented, of influential AM leaders serving as effective interlocutors between the favela and the state.[69] Today, this operates in the context of powerful criminal elements who are allied with the AM leadership. The infusion of resources into the community through the AM, including government centers, improved roads, and a day care center, only increases the power of AM leaders. The AM uses those resources to provide assistance to those who have good relations with traffickers. Further, the traffickers do not act as simple patrons in their relationships with residents, since they depend on residents to remain active. The violence their activities brings to the favela creates resentment that the AM has to overcome in order to avoid efforts to push traffickers out of the favela. In the end, the strength of the AM, which results from outside funding and the elimination of competing civic groups, makes it possible for the traffickers to buy its leadership. The AM also provides a conduit for both traffickers and politicians to deliver services. At the same time, though, politicians, again through the AM, also act as patrons to the drug traffickers. Thus, the more state and political investment, the more powerful the illegal network.

The connections that state actors have to criminals and allied civic leaders seem to have a greater effect on their actual decisions than do either their ties to superiors in the state or their commitment to the abstract principles of the rule of law, democratic governance, and civil rights. The state clearly is a powerful institution, with many more resources than any other group operating in the favela. Its representatives build roads, housing, and schools and pay for teachers and a regular police presence. The traffickers cannot compare in terms of resource expenditure and, indeed, are partially dependent on state agents' favors. The problem is that state power is deployed in the community for particular rather than public benefit.

Police use state power to extort money from traffickers. State institutions channel funds through the AM, propping up its leadership and providing jobs to their allies rather than providing direct benefits to most residents. Trafficking, then, is strengthened by the specific way the state is present in the favela.

This particular configuration of localized power relations, ironically, tends to strengthen the state in the wider political system. Despite neoliberal cutbacks in government spending and global democratic norms that supposedly restrict human rights abuse, the seeming emergence of a powerful "parallel state" in the community and anarchic gun battles at night above Rio's ritziest neighborhoods provide the justification for increasing state repression and expenditures of resources around the community. Looked at from the inside, the state is very much present in this community. The perceived weakness that comes from conflicts that emerge out of the state/civic/criminal alliance seen here only strengthens the hand of the state to spend limited resources on crime control and violate basic civic guarantees in poor neighborhoods.

Criminal organization in the community plays an important role in holding all of these groups together. With access to limited illegal funds and the use of force, the traffickers concentrate the power of the AM and give it leverage to negotiate with politicians to provide services to residents. Criminals also provide some semblance of order in the community by preventing certain types of crimes. These efforts, however, are politically contingent and depend on the particular political interests of the traffickers, who will tend not to punish those who are well connected in the favela, since to do so might upset important residents, thereby weakening the traffickers' political position. They will, however, attack those who command little respect in the community. Further, through their powerful positions in the favela, criminals play a role in granting outsiders access and have some control over how residents vote.

As operators in illegal markets and purveyors of private violence, criminals have a significant role in community life in an environment of dwindling state expenditures on welfare guarantees, erratic police and bureaucratic behavior, and growing resident fear. Both state and civic actors gain from their connection to criminals, and criminals depend on their connection to these other actors. Without these links, it is hard to imagine that the gang would be as powerful as it is, since it would be subject to regular pressure from police and local civic groups. The traffickers, however, are able to use their access to violence and funds to gain control of civic and state power. Through this, they play a role in local political outcomes. They prevent state agents from becoming too powerful and also reduce the chances that any significant internal opposition to their activities will develop. Understanding politics in Tubarão, and, indeed, in any other community in Rio, is contingent on understanding the role that criminals play in the community and the connections that they maintain to other state and social actors.

In the end, a very specific kind of political order emerges in Tubarão, which is based on the ways that clientelism has evolved in Rio and the roles that the drug trade, politicians, and civic leaders play in this particular community. This environment necessitates a very powerful civic component to the network to mediate the uniquely complex relationships among the community, the state, and its powerful neighbors. Criminals maintain order, but they do so in the context of these existing relationships. They depend on the AM to reduce the burden on them of maintaining an order that could make them unpopular among some segments of the neighborhood population by redirecting residents' concerns to other possible mediators. Although the criminals claim to enforce a certain order, they do so within a specific political calculus and are aided in this effort by the AM, which helps resolve conflicts before they reach the criminals. The state plays a large role in the community, but most of its resources are co-opted into the network, either through bribes to police or through the ability of the AM to gain control of resources coming into the community and then using them in the interests of Bernardo, the traffickers, and their allies. The political order that exists in Tubarão reflects a divided and poorly organized state that is only able to intermittently enforce a limited rule of law operating in the context of a single powerful civic organization allied with criminals. The perceived localized disorder, however, strengthens the hand of more powerful state actors to develop programs and devote resources to repressing certain types of criminals and, more generally, the poor in an otherwise hostile fiscal environment. What funding the state does put into the community is either bought off by traffickers or funneled through their allies in the AM.

Efforts to Control Violence in Tubarão

For years, Tubarão suffered from high levels of violence, yet residents failed to take constructive steps to bring this situation under control. Then, in September 2000, Rio's PM, in conjunction with leaders in the neighboring favela of Ceuzinho and outside civic activists, initiated a community policing program that significantly decreased violence and, for a time, cut official homicides to zero. Government actors began this program in response to riots sparked by the murder of five residents at the hands of a purportedly corrupt police officer. Unfortunately, murder rates began to climb again about three years after the program was implemented. To understand this partially successful effort to control violence, we must answer several key questions. First, why did this intervention succeed? Second, what factors motivated intervention? Third, what challenges did this reform encounter that led to a return of higher levels of violence?

Why Did the Intervention Succeed?

Conditions in Tubarão and Ceuzinho began to change on 15 May 2000, when elements of the PM went into Ceuzinho and murdered five residents. Police claimed that they had killed traffickers, but residents disagreed and rioted in the streets below, breaking windows with rocks and cooking gas canisters. Many believed that traffickers regularly bribed the police accused in the murders. In the aftermath of the riots, with extensive news coverage on everyone's minds, the state government promised to improve local policing and began to meet with angry residents.[70] PM major João Antunes worked with Viva Rio, an important NGO, to develop a community policing program. Viva Rio leaders knew about Operation Cease Fire, a policing program that had successfully controlled violence in the Dorchester section of Boston, Massachusetts, and arranged for Antunes and other police to travel there.[71]

Upon his return, Major Antunes began the collaborative process of implementing a policing program based on the Boston experiment that involved building the confidence of residents to denounce police abuse and establishing an effective law enforcement presence to prevent serious crimes. Initially, Antunes tried to work with Bernardo but encountered resistance. He then made contact with Jorge, the president of Ceuzinho's AM. Long an important local figure, Jorge had many contacts with outside political and civic leaders and had little sympathy for the drug traffickers who, years earlier, had briefly driven him out of the favela. Jorge readily gave the police access and helped them build local contacts. Eventually the traffickers threatened Jorge's life but, with Bernardo's intervention, allowed him to leave the favela unharmed. By this point, however, Viva Rio and the police had already successfully initiated the program and had established independent ties to many residents.

On 22 September 2000, the PM began a social occupation of Tubarão and Ceuzinho. A team of 100 police cast off from other battalions, often for disciplinary reasons, took control of key points in the favela and adopted a nonconfrontational crime control strategy based on monitoring access to the hill and slowly suffocating trafficking. PM officials worked with Viva Rio to set up a police training program focused on increasing professionalism and improving service to residents.[72] Antunes told arriving police that they should see their primary responsibility as serving the needs of residents and quickly removed police who did not follow orders.

In conjunction with the change in policing, Viva Rio and the state government began a series of social programs designed to build local confidence in police and reduce dependence on traffickers. The state government invested in high school completion courses that provided classes and a stipend for 300 at-risk teenagers. Former members of the Ceuzinho AM and other respected residents took a lead in these programs to help build up the confidence of residents. Viva Rio provided legal assistance, helped set up a volleyball program, started a second high school equivalency class, organized local religious groups to address neighborhood problems, and helped build local capacity.[73] Viva Rio and the Fundação Roberto Marinho, a foundation associated with the Globo television network, worked with UNESCO to open a sports program to serve 1,500 children from the hill and surrounding neighborhoods.[74] Finally, Viva Rio organized a community forum to give local leaders a space to meet with each other, police, and NGO workers.

The efforts of police, local leaders, and outside groups had a significant effect on Tubarão. Residents and police reported a decline in shoot-outs. One resident noted that "things have gotten a lot better in the community. There are no more shoot-outs. There is no violence."[75] Although residents remained wary, relations with the police thawed. Residents reserved special complements for Antunes, whom they thought was a good man in a bad institution. As one NGO worker put it, "Many people say that they don't like the police but say that Major Antunes is okay."[76] One resident, deeply linked to trafficking and who had once served time in prison, sought out Major Antunes for help when she had no work. She said that although she could not trust most of the police she felt she could trust him.[77] Finally Carolina, the evangelical Christian, said that although she did not trust the police she did think the major was a little better than the others.[78] Growing confidence in the police hierarchy allowed residents to denounce police behavior to officers. As a result of residents' assistance, in the first year, Major Antunes removed 40 of the 100 police assigned to him for disciplinary reasons.[79] A resident close to Viva Rio stated,

> The work of Viva Rio and the new policing program has changed people's vision of the police. Now they [the police] have a way to talk to the community. The police walk in the community, residents have access to the police; they talk to them. [When there were problems with other police] . . . the Major went to

the Batalhão to fix things. He gave his cell phone number to leaders. Residents didn't trust the new program at first but after they [the 40 police accused of extortion] were removed it gave a new viability to their work.[80]

Many contributed to this success. Major Antunes and a few other highly placed members of Rio's PM played a central role in the reforms. His commitment to this program and his ability to negotiate the complex relationships among the state, the favela, and NGOs allowed this program to move forward. Through his contacts with NGOs, Antunes developed clear ideas about strategies for effective police reform. By maintaining these contacts, he enlisted the help of Viva Rio in advancing the project and obtaining outside funding to achieve the social goals of the program. Through his position in the PM, Antunes secured the resources to set up and maintain the project. Antunes and other high-level police also maintained extensive contacts with the press to promote international awareness of the project and obtain additional support.

The work of Viva Rio also played an important role. Viva Rio helped Antunes develop his program by putting him in touch with Operation Cease Fire. Later, Viva Rio monitored violence, trained police, and offered advice to both residents and state representatives. The participation of a civic organization showed residents that the project had support beyond the state, thereby giving it a degree of legitimacy. Further, Viva Rio brought funds to the social and educational sides of the plan and also served as a liaison between residents and the government. Through this connection, Viva Rio helped to meet local needs, gave small stipends to at-risk teens in equivalency courses, and generally decreased local dependence on traffickers. Finally, Viva Rio helped build local capacity to pressure police and traffickers to control violence by building a community leadership council to discuss problems, establishing a network of religious organizations to develop new programs to help residents, and setting up a training program to professionalize the police. As one resident put it, "The community is growing and learning. The [leadership] council is proof that the community is uniting and making demands of the government."[81]

Local leaders advanced this process. As mentioned earlier, Jorge, Ceuzinho's president, brought the police in and set up social programs after Bernardo had refused to help. Jorge walked around with Antunes and other outsiders and introduced them to residents. This allowed outsiders to build a strong network of contacts that proved invaluable in implementing the program. Having community leadership was essential to this project since the target audience was underserved at-risk teenagers, a group close to drug traffickers who had reason to distrust outside authorities.

Various factors, however, posed challenges. As a result of his ties to the police, traffickers forced Jorge out, and, in 2001, Bernardo took over the Ceuzinho AM. Bernardo tried to limit the role of the police by demanding the removal of several police posts in the favela. Some police took bribes—and not only allowed drug dealing but also provided traffickers with information about police operations, preventing on one occasion the arrest of an important trafficker. Viva Rio, moreover, had some internal divisions that led to poor decisions and the hiring of outsiders to work in the community when residents could easily have done the job. Over time, this decreased support for the reforms. Alexandre, by then a former Ceuzinho AM president who was involved in the program said, "[A foundation] gave them [Viva Rio] a lot of money [to start the UNESCO sports program] and they used it to hire outsiders." He went on, "They pay them R$2,000 or R$3,000 a month and they run things. Residents were only given jobs as janitors."[82] To make matters worse, these custodial positions were awarded to friends of Bernardo's, who had been appointed to the board of the program.

Despite these problems, the contacts that had already been established within the favela helped maintain the program. Community leaders gave legitimacy to the police presence by publicly speaking out in favor of it, even after Bernardo took over the Ceuzinho AM. The vice president of the Ceuzinho AM said at a leadership council meeting, "The police are in the hill everyday. If the police go down the hill the community will pay. They [the residents] need someone to go to directly [like the major] to make sure they are satisfied. If they get rid of these police other police will go up and invade the community."[83] Though Bernardo immediately admonished him, other Ceuzinho residents at the meeting expressed support. Statements such as this reinforced community backing for positive police actions. Viva Rio helped to resolve some of its own problems in the community by hiring Eduardo, an activist from a nearby favela, to act as their intermediary and by employing Cédric, a local Baptist pastor, to work on a number of their projects. As a result of their own strong local contacts and long-standing relations with community leaders, Eduardo and Cédric helped immeasurably in dealing with difficulties within Tubarão. When Bernardo resisted the program, they could speak with him and point out that by not cooperating with the program he hurt their work as residents of favelas—a politically untenable position for Bernardo to take, as a result of his position as a local leader who portrayed himself as committed to defending local interests. By establishing a strong network of contacts in the favelas, efforts to maintain the new policing program succeeded. Residents who previously may not have had the courage to speak out were now connected to others who shared their concerns. Without support from such diverse participants as government agents and outside civic actors to local leaders, activists, and residents, the intervention would not have succeeded.

The Role of State-Level Politics in Motivating Intervention

The efforts of the government and Viva Rio were part of a broader public security policy undertaken by the administrations of Governors Anthony Garotinho and Benedita da Silva between 1998 and 2002 that were based on a public security platform written by Luiz Eduardo Soares, a sociologist and Viva Rio collaborator.[84] Government policies during this period focused on building links among favelas, civil society, and the state to decrease the power of traffickers and control violence. Antunes had been Soares's aide while he served in the state government. Soares himself was also aware of Viva Rio's activities in Vigário in the mid-1990s. Any decrease in the growth of violence in Rio during the Garotinho and da Silva administrations can be partially attributable to a broad set of policing policies that involved increasing transparency, administrative reform, and strengthening ties between poor communities and the state. What these data imply is that although macro-level administrative reforms are important in controlling violence, the coordination of those reforms at the local level through the networking of state agents, local civic actors, and NGOs is essential in implementation. The data also indicate that the process of reform is often initiated, and consistently supported, through the activities of the residents themselves. With the extremely limited formal ties that exist between the poor population and the state in Brazil, networks provide one of the only conduits for these populations to communicate with government officials.[85]

Although the orientation of political leaders played an important role in the timing of reforms, the Garotinho administration had been in office for almost two years before this program was implemented. Reformist government attention turned to this favela only as a result of the media's focus on the murders of May 2000. As we will see in Santa Ana and Vigário, the killing of innocent residents by police is a singular factor that motivates public organizing and demonstrations. In the case of Tubarão, the murders led to riots in the streets below the community, closed transit near a tourist area, and heavy media coverage. Coming in the wake of the televised "Bus 174" killing in June 2000, the Garotinho administration was under pressure to respond to this type of unrest.

The decision by the government to take action on residents' demands was helped by support from Viva Rio, an organization that has learned from its experiences addressing violence in Vigário since 1993, where its activists, who had been quite young at the time, took a role in local reforms. The understandings they had developed in Vigário and other places contributed to their efforts to build and coordinate the program in Tubarão. All of this, of course, was helped by the fact that Luiz Eduardo Soares, who had been involved with Viva Rio, played a major part in creating the public security policy and in influencing the thinking of some members of the PM.

Finally, in explaining the reform's timing, it is essential to remember the participation of Jorge, the Ceuzinho AM president. He had only returned to power a year before the murders. In the past, he had made efforts to promote reform and had been forced from the community by the traffickers. He still had a bad relationship with the traffickers and was happy to work with police to control violence. Others leaders would have been less likely to take these risks. Eventually, of course, he was forced out. Bernardo's efforts to make sure traffickers did not kill Jorge maintained the viability of the reforms, since Jorge's murder might have scared away government leaders, residents, and civic activists.

Limitations of Reform Efforts

Despite these accomplishments, the efforts of the post-2000 period did not resolve all of the problems lurking in Tubarão. Even during the height of the reform efforts, traffickers remained active, secretly carried out killings, and kept many residents in a state of fear. In the small world of Tubarão, the AM leadership remained quite powerful and other factions of Rio's police engaged in highly violent actions against traffickers.

Over time, murders increased, and, indeed, within three years significant violence had returned to Tubarão. In the end, the long-term failure of the reform efforts stemmed from a variety of sources. On one level, the criminal network lingered. On another level, police commanders, which changed with some frequency, each adopted substantially different strategies to deal with crime in the community, which ranged from slowly suffocating trafficking in order to avoid the types of violent conflagrations that would endanger serious social reform efforts to aggressive anticrime tactics that eventually resulted in the abuse and killing of residents not involved in criminal activities. Finally, police never fully stopped trafficking in the favela and left large segments of the illegal network in place.

Simple fatigue also contributed to this failure. In the broad structural and institutional environment that exists in Rio, it is much harder to build and maintain efforts to control crime than it is to engage in criminal activities. Police and social reform efforts required a significant commitment of resources on the part of the state and a huge personal commitment on the part of those leading projects. There was never a promise for long-term funding for the various social programs associated with this project. Viva Rio had to search for support from donors and eventually would settle on the project with the United Nations, which ultimately was poorly managed and partially co-opted by people associated with trafficking. Viva Rio leaders and activists, coming principally from the middle class, had little personal long-term commitment to the community and, within a few years, would move on to other, often more prestigious, jobs, leaving residents with their problems. This, of course, is understandable. Viva Rio is an important organization and has many commitments around the city. The organization had done good work in Rio and its efforts were needed to resolve other pressing problems. However, there was never a plan as to how local organizing would be maintained once Viva Rio's efforts were scaled back and subsumed into the UNESCO project. Long-term involvement in these programs was extremely difficult for favela residents, who endured regular pressure from criminals to minimize their contacts with police. Without significant outside support, it is hard to imagine how residents of the favela would have the energy and courage to devote themselves to supporting the program after Viva Rio and the state lost interest.

Finally, the policing program was intertwined with the vision of Major Antunes, who eventually left the leadership of the program. By 2002, he received his promotion to lieutenant colonel and left to serve as the chief of staff to Soares, who by then had been appointed national secretary for public security in Brasilia. The officers who followed him did not possess his political skill in dealing with residents and the police hierarchy. This led to a slow unraveling of the program. Police units from other jurisdictions began to poach on the favela and conduct independent operations there. Violence returned.

As this brief summary makes clear, all the principal players in the reforms had left the community by 2003. Without committed, skilled actors, it was difficult to keep up the quality of the program. Unfortunately, few incentives exist to keep government officials, residents, and outsiders working to reduce violence in a particular community. Violence continued in Tubarão because of the resilience of the illegal network. The structural and institutional environment in Rio leads to drug dealing and corruption. Violence continued apace, and within three years of the beginning of the program nearly all the original contingent of police had been transferred out of the favela.[86] In other words, even under these unique circumstances, traffickers networked well enough to remain active and undermine police operations. The money associated with the drug trade, the institutional incentives that lead to corruption, and the adapted forms of clientelism that characterize relationships with politicians result in ongoing crime in the absence of some countervailing force.

Conclusion

Sitting on a hillside towering over the glittering neighborhoods of Rio's Zona Sul, Tubarão's residents live the inequality that defines Brazilian life in a very intense and personal way. Every day the community's denizens awake to look down at the wealth of the city sitting below and see around them squalor and the violence of the community that they live in. No one has a greater awareness of these inequalities than the leaders of Tubarão and Ceuzinho, one of whom observed that policing in the neighboring wealthy areas operated very differently from policing within the favelas, in large part because civic institutions existed in those parts of the city that could control police violence.

Undoubtedly, the formal democratic institutions of Brazil's New Republic have failed the residents of these hills, who, despite the efforts of some of their leaders, police, and civic activists, suffer from high levels of trafficker and police violence. Clearly simply having the vote and formal juridical rights does little to guarantee residents' safety.

Evidence presented in this chapter indicates that despite the fact that the political regime systematically discriminates against favelas in terms of local services and policing, residents are in fact quite well connected to politicians, who come to the favela to get votes and, in turn, provide services. State officials do make efforts, usually through contacts with the AM, to provide some limited assistance to residents. The problem is that despite the existence of democratic institutions and formal rights and, in fact, a large amount of public pressure from the wealthier classes to control violence in this favela, contacts between the community and the state are dominated by an illegal network that brings together AM leaders, criminals, police, and politicians. The result is that while clientelist contacts provide resources to the community, those resources actually end up in the hands of groups connected to criminals. The configuration of state-society relations allows government and political resources to reinforce illegal activities in this community. Evidence in this chapter reveals that even under excellent circumstances, in a community closely watched by the best connected among Rio's wealthy classes, an illegal network operates that can use state resources to engage in criminal activities.

Understanding politics in Brazil depends much more on understanding the networks that link state officials, civic leaders, and criminals together than it depends on understanding either the structure of political institutions or the opposition between those institutions and violent and nonviolent social actors. Evidence from Tubarão shows the importance of moving beyond traditional notions of state-society relations that have for many years defined the study of politics in Latin America. Preponderant state power can effectively change social conditions only when it works constructively with social actors. At the same time—and this may fly in the face of common assumptions about politics in the developing world—this chapter makes clear the extremely ambivalent role of civil society in supporting democracy. Civic groups clearly play an important role in mediating state-society relations, but the story of Tubarão and Ceuzinho shows that civic leaders can mediate those relations in such a way as to undermine basic rights and the rule of law. Further, criminals, people who are part of neither state nor civil society but who possess attributes of both, play a critical role in politics at the local level. Only by understanding the specific role of criminal organizations in the political process can we understand politics in Brazil today. With considerable effort and commitment, the relationship between state, civic, and criminal domains may be restructured or reformed in order to better protect residents' rights. Such efforts, it is sad to say, do not appear to be sustainable over the long term, due to basic structural and institutional factors. A close analysis of two other favelas, in the coming chapters, will deepen these theoretical arguments.

FOUR

Santa Ana

At 2:00 P.M. on Friday, 4 August 1997, I climbed the gentle slope of Santa Ana Hill to visit a crèche run by the Catholic Church, which serves approximately forty children between the ages of two and four. To get there, one has to walk up a roughly paved path lined with small bars and stores from a city-maintained road that runs into the heart of the favela. All along the walk, smells of sewage and garbage running down the rocky slope in iridescent streams assault the climber. Just before arriving at the crèche, the path comes out into an open sunny area next to a large rock that overlooks the favela and, beyond, downtown Rio and the shimmering Guanabara Bay. Here young children fly kites during the day and traffickers and other adolescents flirt and gossip at night.

That day, I arrived in the crèche, a two-story, five-room building used for both day care and other church activities, to visit with Camilla, a short, voluble, and rotund middle-aged resident who serves as the cook and supervisor. Around 3:00 P.M., I sat in the window of one of the activities rooms, talking with the room coordinator about her life and the favela and watching a couple dozen toddlers, when a series of fireworks went off in a rapid sequence that ended with a loud boom from a higher caliber explosive. This, as all favela residents know, is one of the signals traffickers use to indicate that police have entered the hill.[1] The coordinator and I looked at each other warily, knowing this could mean trouble, and I briefly thought that I should probably wait awhile before going down the hill. Then, with stunning rapidity, several bursts of gunfire broke out behind the building. The coordinator ran across the room screaming to get the children down closer to the ground, and I crouched and crawled to the relative safety of an interior wall where the children had congregated. For a few minutes, while the gunfire blazed behind us, I sat on the floor surrounded by scared children, one of whom, in the midst of the firefight, told me that she thought the police were "bad." When the gunfire abated, I sat for a time with the children, talked about meaningless things, and drank their imaginary coffee and tea.

Later that afternoon, I walked down the hill. My contacts at the AM told me that police had carried out two of their wounded who were taken to the hospital and, as I later found out, died. Residents had worried about the police retaliating over the weekend, but nothing particular happened. The next week, my contacts reported that the gunfight had actually involved two factions of the police who disagreed about how a corruption scheme should work. One group of police led another group into a wooded area of the hill and opened fire.[2]

Even by Carioca standards, Santa Ana is exceptionally violent. Killings here do not occur simply as a result of drug dealers' operations. Rather, Santa Ana is the site of a powerful trafficking organization linked to civic leaders, politicians, and police. The traffickers, with the help of their lawyer, bribe the police and, through their contacts in the AM and the crèche, work with politicians and provide services to residents. Local leaders and state actors collude with traffickers in propagating drug dealing by helping align residents with traffickers, assisting traffickers in delivering services to residents, building internal norms and trust among residents, and aligning government and civic actors with criminals.

Geography

Located near downtown Rio, Santa Ana sits on a hillside that overlooks a declining middle-class neighborhood. A large private school operates nearby and contributes to the local drug trade with, as one resident put it, "kids coming up from the . . . school taking drugs."[3] Around the hill, one can see, not too far away, a number of older favelas, which one resident referred to as the "cradles of samba." This small favela, with a population of 4,000, sits on the northern face of an outcropping of a hill that contains several other favelas, with a total population of 50,000. On the ridge above the favela sits a larger community containing a small police post, a public elementary school, and some businesses. With its easy access to downtown Rio and wealthy neighborhoods, this location attracts a brisk drug business. At the same time, since the favela rises directly out of a fairly bleak district, it has only attracted passing government attention. This leads to a heavy police presence with little official oversight and a favela political life dominated by a criminal network built out of an alliance of traffickers, police, and local civic leaders.

The community is oriented along a single main street that is the center of Santa Ana's social and economic life. Arrayed along this stretch of pavement are the AM's office, some bars, a hardware store, and, further up (after the street has narrowed to a sidewalk), the drug traffickers' *boca de fumo* (point of sale). The front of the AM has a panoramic view of the street below. Up the main boulevard is the local traffickers' *boca*, which is frequented by addicts buying drugs, residents asking for assistance, and police seeking bribes. Residents and outsiders, including students from the nearby school, often take drugs openly on the street. The road feels like a canyon, with three-story brick homes rising on one side and an imposing wall dividing the favela from the middle-class homes that border it on a somewhat shabby tree-lined lane. The only exits from the street are steep stairways that lead onto the hill and the path that runs up to the *boca*.

Caught in the all-too-common crossfire between the police and drug traffickers, Santa Ana is a dangerous place. The favela is full of signs of violence, ranging from damaged walls and satellite dishes, to scars on the bodies of young men, and the tired faces of residents who have difficulty sleeping. The failure of the state to effectively govern Santa Ana has resulted in the growth of violence. In the early 1990s, average murder rates in Rio de Janeiro were around sixty per hundred thousand residents.[4] During one three-month stretch here in 1997, there were twenty-eight gunfights, twenty-seven murders, and fourteen occasions when residents denounced police abuse.[5] Despite this violence, traffickers have maintained local support by providing social assistance through a network that includes civic leaders, members of a church group, and politicians. The only force outside of the control of traffickers is a small social club supported by an NGO dedicated to promoting human rights, which is, nevertheless, tolerated by traffickers and their allies for the services they provide to at-risk children.

Conflict in Santa Ana

These numbers alone, however, do not do justice to the extremely tense experience of life in the favela. Stories of police violence ranged from the slow stabbing death of one minor dealer in an effort to force information from him to regular beatings of residents. One trip I made to the favela on a gloomy Sunday afternoon after a two-year absence reflects these tensions. My field notes from that day read:

> Coming up to the hill someone is sitting in a chair right in the middle of
> the street that leads into the hill. Someone else [a young man] is nervously
> staring around the corner. I think they are traffickers but I'm not sure. As
> I walk up to the entrance I notice the guy has a gun in his hand. My heart
> pounds so hard it hurts and I walk a little too far past him to make it seem
> that I am casually walking into the hill. I'm not sure if I want to go up into
> the hill. I decide to make a wide turn in . . . [to] walk past them. I expect

them to ask me what I am doing there and I turn around to look back at about the time I think they would be asking me where I am going. The guy is looking at me but they don't ask anything. There are about four guys standing with him staring down the street and anxiously waiting for whatever may come into the hill.[6]

This was not the only time that I had encounters like this at the entrance of the favela. Whenever I heard anything that sounded like gunfire I would duck, often drawing laughter from residents, who usually would shake their heads and tell me that gunfire sounded nothing like the car backfire or fireworks that had provoked me. No other favela I worked in produced these types of internal reactions on a regular basis.

Of course, those who lived in the favela experienced the violence in a much deeper and more emotionally disturbing way. Maria, an elderly resident and wife of a former police officer, reported that the high levels violence prevented her from sleeping: "It used to be that people helped each other. Now there are only *malandros*. . . . There used to be fewer residents, less craziness."[7] The AM treasurer also had trouble sleeping, and, when he appeared particularly haggard one day, he said that a man had come to his home late the previous night and had told him that they "both were going to die"[8] Bête, the director of the children's club, noted that many young residents play with the word *morrer* (to die). She said that the children have a saying, *"porque medo se o futuro é a morte"* (why be afraid if the future is death).[9] Camilla wanted to return to her native city of Natal in the impoverished and parched Northeast, saying that she "would rather deal with the dryness of the north than the violence of Rio."[10] With gunfights occurring nearly every night, local nerves often frayed. Manoel, the AM vice president, put it best when he said that with all the tension he needed to get out for a while to *"esfriar a cabeça"* (cool his head).[11]

The banality of this violence is brought home in one brief interaction with Bête when I arrived in the favela on a Monday morning. She motioned me up the hill to the club headquarters and we sat down to talk. She started the conversation by saying that she had to attend the funeral of a baby who had died on Thursday as a result of "an enlarged skull." I noted that I had heard that someone had died that morning from what I was told were similar causes, and I asked her if this was the same person. She said that the person who had died that morning was an adult man who had had a severe headache. I then asked her how the weekend had gone for her, and she whispered, happily, "It was good since no one died." Confused at this response, I asked how this could be the case if residents had died on Thursday and Monday. She replied, with some awkwardness and a knowing laugh, that she "didn't count them because they died of natural causes."[12]

Unlike Tubarão and Vigário, where there was a substantial history of intergang violence, most of the violence that affects Santa Ana results from ongoing conflicts between traffickers and different elements of Rio's PM. Overzealous efforts to control crime result in some violence and in the past residents reported conflict with traffickers from other favelas, but much of the conflict in Santa Ana when I studied there and in the year before I arrived was due to corrupt and ineffective policing.

Law enforcement agents and drug dealers contribute to high levels of violence in Santa Ana in different ways. Due to a lack of oversight or effective engagement between government officials and residents, police abuse residents and use violence to extort money from traffickers.[13] Trafficker violence results from efforts to maintain local order, suspicion that residents or others may be informing on them, and conflicts with police and other traffickers.

A typical example of violence in Santa Ana was the accidental shooting death of Josias's wife. The police conducted a raid around 11:30 one night and took positions on the path in front of Josias's house. The police shot the streetlights out before they began to fire on a position held by traffickers higher on the hill. Josias was awakened by the gunfire and dove to the floor. He tried to wake his wife but she did not respond. By the time he was able to turn on a light, she was dead, lying in a pool of her own blood.[14] That night the police would not let anyone up the hill or into the house to help Josias with the body. It was only in the morning that they called for an ambulance to take his wife to the hospital.[15]

Josias took no action against the police after his wife's murder, and he asked that no autopsy be performed on the body. Further, he did not press the state for damages, expressing fear that pushing the case could result in harm coming to him.[16] Others reported that police threatened residents who denounced them.[17]

The ongoing violence affecting Santa Ana creates a general climate of distrust between residents and the police. One group of residents noted of the police "that the blue shirts [regular duty police] are bad and the black shirts [elite police from the Batalhão de Operações Especiais, Special Operations Battalion, BOPE] are worse. They *abordar* [aggressively stop and search]. . . . they used to beat people up in the street. Now they knock doors down."[18] After an intervention during which the BOPE briefly stopped and questioned me, Nilo said he saw no difference between police units, noting that "they [the BOPE] are specialized in killing from the waist up while the others are specialized in killing from the waist down."[19] Josias advised whomever would listen to make sure the police did not plant drugs on them.[20] One resident, who later became romantically involved with Josias, explained violence this way: "The community is very calm during the day. [You can go anywhere you] want to. There is no trouble. . . . At night it is a different matter. It is very dangerous and you shouldn't come to the community. Even in the day you shouldn't go above the bar [about 50 yards from where we sat]. The community is very nice. Everything is calm up until his [Josias's] house [just above the AM]."[21]

Police abuse and violence toward residents exacerbates already high levels of distrust. According to those who live in the community, police mistreatment ranges from unwarranted searches to sexual assault, beatings, and torture, in which police alternately asphyxiated and drowned victims in an effort to obtain information about traffickers' whereabouts.[22] Referring to the murder of one minor, but well-liked, dealer, Joselino lamented, "The police captured him thinking he was someone else more important. They tortured him in the street to get information from him about where their drugs and weapons were. He didn't say anything. They started stabbing him to get information. He didn't tell them anything and he died. Everyone could hear him being stabbed in the street but couldn't do anything because the police would hurt them."[23] A second report of this killing also sheds light on police violence. Camilla states,

> The police had caught him in [an adjoining favela] around where he
> lived and shot him in the hand and foot. He escaped but the police, with
> flashlights, followed the trail of blood. He escaped to Celso's house. There
> he cleaned and bandaged his hands and feet. Afterwards Celso began to
> clean his house. The police arrived there as he was cleaning. . . . They asked
> him why he was cleaning . . . in the middle of the night. They had beaten
> him several times already and he had his wife, a *gringa*, their child, and an
> older woman there so he gave up [the victim]. The police pulled him out
> of the house and killed him.[24]

These types of actions that involve gratuitous torture and a slow painful death increase the animosity between residents and the police. Joselino noted that while he has problems with the traffickers, 90 percent of the community would rather have the traffickers maintaining order than the police. This of course is only exacerbated by traffickers' family commitments. As one resident noted, "Those who die always leave pregnant women."[25] Traffickers have grown up in the favela and have many long-standing personal and familial relationships.[26] Police, who never come from the favela, beat, harass, and extort money from both *trabalhadores* (workers, a term used to positively identify residents who work in legal informal or formal sector jobs) and dealers. In this context, residents have little doubt about whom to ally themselves with.

The following story offers an interesting example of police use of physical coercion to extract information from residents. Santa Ana, as is the case with Vigário Geral and Tubarão, is the beneficiary of a city program that provides regular garbage services to favelas. A man who lived high above the woods at the upper reaches of the favela administered the program. Santa Ana's *garís* (street cleaners) had to cross the woods to draw their pay. One morning, the police, who in the months before Pope John Paul II's October 1997 visit had hidden themselves in the trees, stopped two *garís* and harassed them for intelligence about the traffickers. Not receiving answers, the police beat them, causing one mentally disabled *garí* to lose his intestinal continence. The complex relationships among residents, the police, and the drug traffickers left the *garís* in a difficult position. If the *garís* had given the police information, they would have risked retribution from the traffickers. For not talking, the police assaulted them.[27]

A final story, however, makes clear much of police motivation in these activities and casts in relief the problem of violence in Santa Ana. On 19 July 1998, a group of military police entered the community to arrest traffickers dealing on the main street. The criminals fled and the police opened fire. A bullet struck and killed Nelsinho, a middle-aged day laborer and father who had been standing in the street drinking a *guarana* (a soft drink common in Brazil). Angry residents quickly surrounded the police and threatened to riot. The police fired bullets into the air but failed to disperse the crowd. Fearing that more violence would break out, Joselino helped get the body into the ambulance and out of the community. The police withdrew with the ambulance. Bête then convinced residents to protest peacefully and block the street below rather than riot. A major newspaper carried a report about the protest. At the behest of Joselino, traffickers moved their point of sale to a safer place, further inside the favela, and violence decreased for a period, as both police and traffickers avoided confrontations.[28]

The gunfights that led to Nelsinho's murder were not uncommon. The traffickers dealt near the favela's entrance to gain easier access to buyers. This location, however, prevented traffickers from quickly escaping when police appeared, since they either had to quickly climb a steep stairway or run straight up the main street. Both choices exposed them to gunfire. The police conducted many raids since they could apprehend traffickers and their narcotics and then ransom the freedom of the traffickers and sell the drugs to other gangs.

These incidents show that a significant chunk of Santa Ana's violence stems from police efforts to obtain bribes and the conflicts that result from this practice. Law enforcement strategies directly contribute to violence in the favela. By allowing traffickers free run of the hill, the police permit traffickers to deal drugs and take strong defensive positions that complicate police operations. When the police do intervene, then, it provokes violent trafficker responses. Police allow this because they are not interested in controlling crime but, rather, in apprehending traffickers and drugs to hold for ransom. Allies of traffickers, such as the AM, make a point of playing up their concerns about police, in part to reinforce their political position.

Traffickers do engage in violence, but residents hold them less accountable than police since they make some efforts to help residents. The comments of Ângela, an outside church activist, capture many residents' feelings. "The people," she said, "hate the police but they don't hate the traffickers. The police knock down people's doors and steal from them. They don't respect the residents. Traffickers do not treat residents badly. Even if no one is home they won't steal from residents. Traffickers fight each other but do not bother people." Camilla added, "The traffickers are not as bad. They are children most of whom haven't left the favela. They don't know the Zona Sul. . . . They don't [even] speak Portuguese well. They can't be involved in the international arms trade the way the police are because they don't have any way of leaving Brazil."[29] Traffickers, as a result of their dependence on residents for protection from the police, are careful not to take actions against respected residents. This, combined with the way they use local ties to build support, contributes to further antipathy for the police.

Persistent Violence in Santa Ana and the Illegal Network

Violence in Santa Ana, as in many other parts of Rio, is driven by an illegal network composed of the local drug traffickers, community leaders, residents, politicians, and police. The sale of narcotics enriches traffickers, and, through the network, other members gain access to some of this wealth. Network actors provide different services to each other and, as a result, create conditions in which criminality is economically and politically sustainable. Further, local groups work together on projects that reinforce their own positions and help cement certain understandings of community norms.

Traffickers, the AM, the Church, and NGOs in Santa Ana

Four organizations operate in Santa Ana. The AM manages local infrastructure and maintains links among residents, outsiders, and traffickers. The local drug gang provides some basic services to residents and brings considerable resources to the community. The traffickers and the AM are closely tied together by family bonds and work with two outside groups (police and politicians) to help accomplish their goals and legitimize their activities. The Catholic parish located below the favela supports a center in the community that contains a crèche for working mothers and public space for religious classes and tutoring. Camilla, the leader of the crèche, maintains positive relations with the AM and the traffickers. Although a small public elementary school operates in a nearby favela, it has no direct role in Santa Ana politics. Finally, an outside NGO supports a social club that provides young people with education about human rights and leads activities to help keep them away from crime. Three local women, led by Bête, run the center, but it has very complicated relations with the other favela groups.

History of Organizing in Santa Ana

The illegal network in Santa Ana emerged in the late 1980s when Doca, the son of Josias, and Arturo, a former resident of Santa Ana and a trafficker whose gang controls a group of favelas, including Santa Ana, displaced the bank robbers who had dominated local criminal activities. Joselino recounted that "they robbed banks all around Rio but never robbed any bank that members of the community worked in. A former resident was the manager of a bank branch. No one ever bothered him and his bank was never robbed."[30] Doca and Arturo were involved in minor criminal activities and served time in jail where they developed connections with the TC and the CV, powerful drug gangs. Arturo was released first and began to consolidate a number of favelas under his power in conjunction with the CV. When Doca was released, he took over trafficking in Santa Ana.[31] The AM closely aligned itself with the traffickers in the mid-1990s when Josias became president. To understand the favela today, however, we need to start our story during an earlier era.

Residents founded the AM in the early 1960s to mediate relations with the government. Initially, the AM focused on ensuring better water distribution. Indeed, one of the AM's first acts was to raise money to build a *caixa d'agua* high in the hill. Over time, water service grew from a small number of spigots, ones provided by Carlos Lacerda's gubernatorial administration, to full-scale internal plumbing. The AM also came to administer electric service by maintaining power lines and paying the favelas' electrical bills. During the 1960s and 1970s, the AM grew wealthy by skimming money off the top.[32] Joselino said that when he was young "the AM was very corrupt. It ran the water and the light. The people who ran it all stole from the money." He went on to say that his family would not allow his father to participate in the AM because "he would have been associated with thieves."[33] Activism in the AM increased in the 1960s and 1970s as a result of fears that the state would try to evict residents.[34]

Local collective organizing was vigorous through the early 1980s, as residents fended off these limited removal efforts, and during the three years of heavy political activity that occurred during the transition from authoritarian rule, as politicians returned to search for votes.[35] As in Tubarão, the favela benefited from the first administration of Leonel Brizola, when the government built a sewage system, paved roads, and regularized the distribution of electricity and water.[36] Today, many residents remain loyal to Brizola, but Nilo complained to me that "Brizola was treated badly by the poor" in the 1994 election when they provided him with little support in his run for Brazil's presidency.[37] The regularization of state services weakened the AM and meeting attendance dropped.

Growing violence also damaged local political institutions. Joselino reported:

> In the past, people followed the orders of community leaders and they
> could control who built where and ensure that things were paid to the AM.
> Now everyone is afraid to tell those who are associated with traffickers that
> they are doing the wrong thing. This started in the seventies when the light
> in the community was run by a resident. He disconnected rigorously the
> lights of those who hadn't paid their bills. One day he was very high in the
> hill and a guy pointed a gun at him and told him to get down from a ladder
> which he was using to disconnect the lights in someone's house. The guy
> who had pointed the gun at him was one of the leaders of the traffickers
> . . . at the time. After that no one could really organize the community.[38]

With the growing violence and the increasing independence of the traffickers, local political institutions ceased functioning as effective regulators. When criminals challenged leaders and those leaders had no collective response, the AM lost respect. This contributed to AM inactivity that only ended when the AM allied itself with criminals.

As basic infrastructural improvements made in the 1980s deteriorated and residents felt they again needed to make demands of the state, the AM reawakened. The group that came to power in the re-formed AM included Josias, as well as most of the current officers and a handful of other local activists, such as Bête, who has since left the AM leadership.

Santa Ana, however, was a different place in the 1990s than it had been in the 1980s. The massive influx of cocaine into Rio after 1983 allowed Doca's group of drug traffickers to displace the bank robbers who had dominated local criminal activity. Over time, Josias would emerge as the leader of the AM, in large part because, as Doca's father, he could best mediate relations between residents and traffickers.[39]

Local Network Activities

Between 1997 and 1999, the AM and the traffickers supported a variety of activities to help increase resident support for traffickers. A party held in July 1997 illustrates how close relations between traffickers and civic leaders reinforce trafficker legitimacy.

In the months leading up to the night of Saturday, 6 July, there had been regular shoot-outs between police and traffickers that had forced traffickers to abandon their usual point of sale. Residents became concerned about their safety because many shells had pierced the walls of their homes during firefights. Worried about resident discontent, Arturo decided to throw a party for the community.

Saying that he was concerned about local violence, Arturo asked Camilla if she would put together some sort of party because, Camilla reported, he knew that people would follow her lead.[40] Concerned about helping residents and flattered at being asked, Camilla agreed. She already worked with a group associated with traffickers to put on events to dispel the community's violent image. The original idea had been to organize events and send out press releases, but this had failed since the drug traffickers did not want to attract too much outside attention.[41]

Camilla began to discuss possible activities with colleagues at the crèche, and a nun, unaware of the funding source, suggested a *festa junina* (June party), a folkloric event held in the winter to celebrate saints' feast days. The centerpiece of many of these parties is a *dança de quadrilha* in which competing dancing groups enact a farcical rural wedding. Camilla liked the idea and took a budget to Doca, but Doca told her to cut costs. She revised the budget downward to R$1,380 to cover party expenses and funds to dress the *quadrilha*.[42] She insisted that no traffickers participate in the *quadrilha* and that no one bring weapons to the party.[43] Camilla then found a group of teenagers to dance, hired a choreographer, found a seamstress to make the costumes, and let the dancers practice in the crèche.[44] The funding source for the party became an open secret in the favela. Residents would talk salaciously among themselves about the traffickers' support and would comment on elaborate costumes the dancers would wear. Camilla decided to hold the party on the main street, which she divided into booths that she offered to community groups and the dancers' families to sell food.[45] The social club refused to participate because of the traffickers' involvement. With some tension in her voice, Bête said that "the perversity of traffickers is that they do this for the community while they hurt the community." She added that if the club attended they would be showing support for the traffickers and said that "people do not understand that accepting money is how people are brought into trafficking. . . . Camilla should know better."[46] Others accepted the booths.

Residents, however, were apprehensive about violence. To help reduce fears, Josias sought authorization from the PM battalion, the PC precinct, and the *região administrativa* (the lowest level of city offices) to close the favela's main street. Josias and Eusébio, the AM treasurer, reported with some surprise that when they went to turn in the forms to the police, the bureaucrats who attended them "were very nice."[47] Discussing a *festa* held the following year, Camilla recalled that "the police didn't come in because they filed a paper [with the police] asking for a truce that night."[48] Just before the party, a letter arrived from prison to inform the traffickers that another gang planned to invade Santa Ana. Some residents worried that, with neither an armed trafficker nor a police presence, other traffickers would invade during the event.[49]

Despite these tensions, preparations continued and excitement grew. The day before the party, Josias worried about clearing the street of cars and of the illegal activities that might go on in the AM building where the dancing groups would dress.[50] Because the street had to be cleared of cars to make room for the party, Josias spent most of the morning of 6 July on the AM loudspeaker telling residents to move their vehicles. Frustrated by the failure of his requests, Josias and other AM leaders jokingly asked a trafficker to help.[51] The man teasingly responded that he would shoot those who did not cooperate. Although Josias protested, the trafficker assumed responsibility for the matter. By the afternoon, all residents had moved their cars without any overt use of violence.[52] A couple of weeks later, Camilla furtively told me at another performance of the dance group that "the cars were moved because Josias's son ordered it. People follow his orders."[53]

On the night of the party, a DJ contracted by the traffickers played *funk* under a clear starry sky. Asked about concerns regarding bloodshed, one mother said that she would not have let her daughter attend if she thought violence would break out. The traffickers had invited *quadrilhas* from other communities allied with them to dance at the party. The competition was to start at ten and end around two.[54] The dancing, however, did not begin until midnight when a group made up of younger adolescents opened with a short skit about a rural wedding. After the skit ended, the group danced frenetically for about forty-five minutes. From the opening notes, the performance captivated the revelers. Different groups went on dancing until five in the morning. At the end of the night, party organizers awarded prizes to the dance groups and to Josias and Doca for their support. That night, no one fired any shots and many said that the party was the nicest thing to happen in a long time.[55]

Just below the surface, however, tensions lingered. Some worried the police might raid the party, and a few thought another gang might attack. At one point, a car drove up filled with some men in it looking for a fight, but they went away. After I talked to a high school student whom I had met earlier, a group of teenagers ran up to him and nervously asked about me. Josias had to tell one trafficker to take his weapon back to the *boca*. On the whole, however, residents seemed much calmer than on other nights.

The party highlights many aspects of politics in Santa Ana. The traffickers and the AM play an important role in distributing goods to residents. The traffickers hired the DJs and paid to costume the *quadrilha*. The relative serenity of that night shows why the residents support traffickers. The drug dealers realize their business creates difficulties for residents, but residents blame most problems on the police. Traffickers, in contrast, provide services (albeit from a material point of view relatively insignificant services) to make their lives more pleasant. In exchange, residents offer the traffickers their silence and support.

The efforts to move the cars before the party also shed light on local politics. Having no place to park, residents leave their cars on the main street. The AM made extensive, though unsuccessful, efforts to get residents to move their vehicles. The AM's power seems to be based wholly on the ability of Josias to convince residents to follow his lead or to convince other factions in the community to support him.[56] In this case he used his connection to traffickers to gain the outcome he needed. Under threat from traffickers, residents moved their cars.

Despite his garrulous personality and his almost continuous joking with close friends, Josias, a compact man with always perfectly combed brilliantined hair who got around on crutches as a result of losing one of his legs to a garbage truck he worked on, was often anxious about traffickers doing things that would compromise the integrity of the AM. When festivities were scheduled to take place in the AM headquarters or when the AM had to file papers with the police to close the street for public events, Josias went out of his way to request that traffickers not bring weapons or drugs into the AM or the street. He often had to tread the difficult line between police, traffickers, and residents in resolving conflicts and providing services. He complained that "running the AM is very tough" and said that "if you screw up you die."[57] Josias also believed that he did not get enough support from residents and said, "I would have as much support as my son if I had a gun."[58] He added that he would lend his name to his son but "not to the traffickers."[59] During the period that I worked in the favela, he often threatened to retire, something which did not happen until mid-2003.

Although Josias provided support to his son, he expressed considerable ambivalence about his son's career. One resident who said that Josias was a good leader noted that he was "perturbed because his son is involved in that life."[60] One day Josias described his disappointment at his son, saying that "Doca could have had a job but he let all that go and spent his youth in jail. He had all sorts of diplomas. He had one for photo developing. He had gone to a private school that I paid for. He could have had a different life but he let it all go for trafficking." Josias went on to say that his "life and my brother's was much better [than Doca's]. . . . all we thought about was partying and dancing. My wife never knew how much I betrayed her. I had a car at one point but . . . don't now. I lost a lot of things." Josias noted sadly that "children give shame to their parents. They do what they do."[61] He went on to say that "one day I will have to go see my son in jail."[62]

Camilla's contribution to the *festa junina* also reveals much about Santa Ana's politics. As the leader of the church crèche, Camilla commands a certain amount of prestige because she provides an important service and has the confidence of parish leaders. Her access to the church center provided the *quadrilha* with a place to practice. Camilla voiced no concerns about the apparent contradictions between her religious convictions and her work with traffickers. She lives in a particularly poor part of the community and had children involved with crime. Camilla seemed to believe that both her day care work and her efforts to promote the party were compatible because both helped improve residents' lives.

The *festa junina* reflects not only the relative power of the traffickers but also their dependence on others to achieve their goals. Josias put it particularly forcefully, if not completely accurately, saying, "Trafficking is shit. . . . we don't need help from them here." Traffickers, he argued, need his help.[63] This claim is partially born out by several events. To guarantee that the police did not intervene during the party, Josias had to obtain police permission to close the street. Traffickers could never have gone to police precincts to request that the police close the street or not intervene in the favela. Traffickers also enlisted the support of respected residents who could get people to come to the party. The traffickers, further, legitimized their position through their network of relationships with other local leaders. Had only the traffickers organized the party, they would have had more difficulty in attracting the participation of middle-aged and older adults and children and they would not have made the links to bureaucrats needed to run the party safely.

But the impact of trafficking on the community does not end with parties. Gang leaders also provide financial assistance. Almost daily, a line of residents forms in front of the *boca* to ask for help. Residents requesting assistance for medical expenses or funerals are generally considered deserving by traffickers and other residents. By helping the needy, traffickers bolster their position on the hill.[64] Given the extremely limited assistance that the Brazilian government offers the poor, their financial assistance to residents helps legitimize the traffickers' presence and reinforces their network of contacts, which encourages residents to reciprocate by helping traffickers in times of danger.[65]

Traffickers, however, must take care in choosing whom to assist, since their position in a favela is always a little precarious. Not only do traffickers engage in activities that anger residents, they are also younger and not considered as wise or respectable as other local leaders. Doca is barely into his thirties and most dealers are considerably younger. Although giving aid to residents will in general increase the support for the traffickers, traffickers must be sure to offer support to residents in politically astute ways consistent with the views of other respected residents in order to maintain and build legitimacy in the community.[66]

Traffickers also maintain public order on the hill by punishing residents who break rules.[67] Police do not become involved when interpersonal conflicts break out.[68] While many commented about traffickers' efforts to ensure order, one conversation with Joselino sheds light on the role of traffickers in controlling crime:

> All assaults around the hill have to be approved by the trafficker. You can't assault in the community. If someone from the outside does they will be killed. If a resident of the community were to assault in the community they would be expelled. The street leading up to the community is also protected. Addicts, however, rob there to get the money to come up the hill and buy drugs. They could get themselves killed doing this. Very powerful traffickers prevent robberies in the streets around the community such as the Rua X [a major street that runs by Santa Ana]. . . . Traffickers are very concerned with not *sujando a area* [dirtying the area]. Thieves operating in the area ask permission of the traffickers. Once, a thief planning on doing some robberies in the neighborhood asked permission of the traffickers to come into the hill if he were to get into trouble. The traffickers refused him. . . . If he had come into the hill he would have been killed. Once, a number of computers were robbed at the [nearby] school without their permission. The traffickers forced the robbers to send the computers back. Traffickers beat or kill those who steal. Outsiders are treated worse.[69]

Joselino's comments suggest that traffickers attempt to manage crime in and around the community within certain broad guidelines. For traffickers in Santa Ana, there appear to be two distinct zones they are concerned with. The first zone is within the favela itself, where they categorically do not allow theft but where, under some circumstances, traffickers may provide a haven for thieves. The second zone is the immediate surroundings of the favela, where crimes could draw police attention to the hill but where they will not directly inconvenience residents. In these cases, traffickers may okay criminal activities but only under particular circumstances.

The central concern of traffickers in controlling crime is to avoid "dirtying the area" in such a way that they would interfere with trafficking by drawing the police in to resolve a crime at the behest of residents or businesspeople from the surrounding neighborhood. Traffickers try to ensure that residents do not go to the police to resolve crime problems. Ignácio, a former police officer, and Maria, his wife, reported that "in the past, the police were called by . . . residents. Now the police can't be called because the traffickers think that the residents are telling the police about them and they don't want the police in the community. The traffickers themselves break up fights between residents."[70] Joselino echoes these claims: "If the police work in the community the traffickers might run into them and there would be a gunfight. . . . If this happens the people who called the police . . . might have to leave. In general the police won't involve themselves in resolving problems in the community. They tell the people to go to the traffickers."[71] Joselino's comment not only suggests the very high stakes of residents contacting police but also indicates that police are reluctant to involve themselves in local disputes. By keeping control of crime, traffickers provide a service to residents, reduce their dependence on the state, and reinforce social norms supported by residents.

Residents can, under some circumstances, make demands of traffickers. Joselino suggests that "traffickers are respectful of residents. Residents are not forced to be addicted to drugs. Traffickers don't addict young children to drugs. If parents ask traffickers not to sell to their children they will not sell to their children. The first couple of times a kid comes to the *boca* the traffickers will not sell to him." Ricardo, a friend of Joselino's who worked in his store, added, "People have nothing to complain about." Joselino continued, "If the traffickers do things which people don't like they can go and talk to the *boca*." Traffickers, he continued, set up a *boca* near his store, and he had "talked to the *dono* about not setting up the *boca* there because it was dangerous for the community because it could create a shootout on the main street." The *dono* agreed and moved the *boca,* although later traffickers set it up there again.[72]

Joselino argued that the ability of residents to make demands of traffickers was based on their respect in the favela: "Many in the community are complicit because they have fear" but "as long as traffickers respect you, you have no problem. To maintain respect it is necessary that you don't become involved in drugs." Asked if he had an advantage in dealing with the traffickers because he had lived in the community his whole life, he replied: "If a resident has lived in the community five years he has just as much ability to deal with the traffickers as long as they have respect."[73] Here, as in the case of Tubarão, the relationship between residents and traffickers is linked to the respect residents have in the favela and is based on adherence to local norms. Traffickers are unlikely to punish those who are well connected in the favela.

The AM helps mediate relations between residents and traffickers by resolving their differences and maintaining an open dialogue. The power differential between these two groups can make disagreements tricky, and residents' insecurities about their prestige in the favela can make them reluctant to raise their concerns publicly, causing resentment to fester until unhappiness reaches a boiling point.[74] Josias, a man who has immense prestige in the favela, helps mediate these relations so that crises do not emerge.

For example, traffickers in Rio often insist that nearby shops close the day after a gang member dies. Businesses, however, resist for fear of losing revenues. On 12 August 1997, traffickers ordered businesses closed until 6:00 P.M. after police killed one young dealer. Most owners did not readily agree, and Josias hobbled up and down the street negotiating with each owner over the terms of their closing. He compromised with one obstinate merchant and let her leave the shutters to her store half open. Just before closing the AM offices and leaving for home, Josias declared that his son "is a citizen."[75]

The issue of business closings creates tensions. From the perspective of merchants, the demand of the traffickers specifically disadvantages them. From the perspective of the traffickers, however, the forced period of mourning recognizes their legitimacy in the face of police violence. Josias obtains compliance with his decisions by calmly talking to residents and convincing them to go along with traffickers' demands.

Over the long term, Josias's leadership reduces tensions and maintains residents' support for traffickers. In return, the AM receives the backing of the traffickers and support in conflicts with residents. This was illustrated in the efforts of traffickers to remove cars from the street prior to the *festa junina*. On the surface, traffickers do not interfere in the political decision making of the AM, but the close relationship between Josias and Doca both facilitates and conceals the connection between the AM and the traffickers, since most conflicts between the groups are worked out in private. Despite high levels of violence, Josias's mediation helps create support for traffickers. As a result, residents have little desire to undermine Doca and other gang leaders.

The Role of the Police and Politicians in Santa Ana

State actors help maintain conditions for ongoing criminal activity. Police seem to have a much more hostile relationship with residents of Santa Ana than they do with the residents of either of the other two communities in this study. Despite high levels of violence, a close examination of the relationship between traffickers and state actors illustrates the enduring ties that maintain criminal activity in the favela.

Relations between police and traffickers are both violent and disorganized. Residents report that while one shift of police takes direct payments from the traffickers, other shifts maintain more distant relations. Most police do not directly take bribes from the gang. Rather, they arrest traffickers, confiscate contraband, and then ransom the jailed traffickers' freedom and sell the drugs and weapons to other gangs. For example, after one lucky arrest, police ransomed Arturo for around R$50,000.[76] Similarly, a group of traffickers apprehended by the police bought their freedom for R$30,000, although police retained a cache of weapons they had seized during the same raid.[77] Finally, on a third occasion, police released three low-level traffickers for a total payment of R$1,000.[78]

A good example of these relations occurred one afternoon in August 1997, when a group of off-duty police entered the favela by car and quickly ran up the hill to catch some traffickers at the *boca*. One of the police screamed to a dealer, "You again. We saw you two weeks before and you owe us."[79] The police then rounded up a few more people, and residents seemed sure that they would face assault by the police. Josias and a public health worker took down their cars' license plate numbers and sent someone to tell the traffickers' lawyer what had happened. After the police left, a resident explained to me that the lawyer's job was to negotiate a fee with the police. The next day, one resident told me the police had released them that night in exchange for a payment. The police who had screamed, "It's you again," had captured the same trafficker the previous week and freed him on the condition that he would pay his own ransom, but he had not made good on the promise.[80]

The arrest and ransom were typical of police-trafficker relations. As Josias put it, the "police bother [my] son every day. . . . Why should he give anything. He fills the bellies of other people."[81] The regular arrest of traffickers did nothing to control violence in the community because the police quickly released them after contact with their lawyer. Over the course of 1998 and 1999, however, these relationships unraveled. In 1998, one group of police, over a period of months, went through and killed many of Santa Ana's low- and mid-level traffickers. In 1999, the traffickers murdered their lawyer and his girlfriend on a nearby hill because they believed that he had skimmed ransoms for himself.[82]

Even the draconian efforts of police in 1998 did little to eliminate criminality because the police still used an inefficient crime control strategy. The PM spent most of its time outside the hill and only came in during operations. Since the police never occupied the hill, as eventually happened in Vigário Geral and Tubarão, nothing stopped the traffickers from dealing drugs openly. During this period, a group of police continued to demand ransoms. Police killed Nelsinho during one of these raids. All of this may have occurred as a result of efforts to systematically and brutally slay traffickers to extort higher payments. Nevertheless, the traffickers replaced their comrades with new ones from other favelas.[83]

Dealers also maintained indirect contacts with politicians through the AM and their lawyer. Joselino noted that these relations are a necessary part of campaigns: "Politicians can only get access to a community if they make deals with traffickers. The work between the traffickers and the politicians is limited to the election."[84] In 1998, for example, candidates for federal and state legislatures made contact with Santa Ana through the traffickers' lawyer and agreed to provide resources to build a recreational quadra in exchange for exclusive access to the favela during the campaign.

In the months before the election, a banner flew over the main street proclaiming that Josias and the traffickers' lawyer supported the candidates. Building materials arrived, and residents in Doca's employ carried the supplies up to the plaza and helped in construction. The candidates even provided extra materials for Josias and Doca to build a bar on the dance floor. The candidate for federal legislature won and then, again with the support of the Santa Ana AM, won reelection in 2002. According to one resident, in exchange for the quadra, the community delivered 2,400 votes.[85] As of 2002, Doca's girlfriend controlled access to the space, which is used for parties, political activities for politicians associated with traffickers, and some NGO events. Despite these uses, one young evangelical complained of the quadra, saying, "They [the traffickers] have bailes all the time now and they are very loud. You can hear the beats up here. The houses around the quadra have all been devalued. . . . [No one] who lives there could sell one of those houses now.

Traffickers patrol around the dance with large weapons. You can't get the dances changed because they run them. Eventually the dance will end because the police don't like them."[86]

Through these links to politicians, the traffickers worked with the AM to deliver services that helped reinforce their legitimacy among residents by establishing relations with a federal deputy and then built a space that traffickers could use to support community activities. These contacts, however, undermined residents' support for politicians. Joselino makes this clear: "They [politicians] are all liars. Naldo [a politician] agreed to pay for the materials for the *quadra* if the traffickers paid for the *mão de obra* [labor]. Teixeira [another politician] came in with him and knew what was going on." He noted that if someone is willing to work with criminals when they run for office there is no reason to believe that they won't work with bigger criminals when they are elected. He added sarcastically, "The guy who was elected will work with the Medellín cartel."[87]

Mechanisms of Network Creation

The Santa Ana network contains components from the criminal underworld, the state, and civil society. The participation of actors from different sectors of the polity provides specific resources and skills that facilitate crime. The AM ensures positive relations between traffickers and residents and mediates relations between traffickers and politicians. State actors provide resources to the community and protection against law enforcement. In exchange, traffickers provide protection to politicians during campaigns, aid to residents, and support to the AM.

A crucial factor in the Santa Ana network is the close relationship between Josias and Doca, which facilitates contacts between traffickers, the AM, and residents. Josias has much more flexibility in leading the AM than others would. Concerned with residents' complaints about the noise and violence associated with the traffickers' *baile funks*, Josias convinced traffickers to cut down on their *bailes* and organized an alternative party on Saturday nights, which appealed to more people and decreased resident discontent. The relationship between Josias and Doca facilitated maintaining a positive environment at parties. When traffickers showed up armed at public events Josias told them to take their weapons back to the *boca*. It is extremely unlikely that other residents could have successfully made similar requests. Residents felt that Josias's presence in the AM prevented the traffickers from fully taking over.

The leadership of AMs closely affiliated with drug traffickers often believe their alliance with traffickers benefits the community by reducing conflicts and ensuring that residents' interests are represented. This relationship, however, is a double-edged sword. Although AM leaders use their connections to traffickers to help residents, these ties prevent them from dealing directly with the violence that has such a large impact on local life. Not only do some state officials ignore AM leaders when they raise questions about violence, but an alliance with traffickers prevents AM leaders from working actively to control crime.

Although police corruption does not appear to be formally organized, the mediated structure of network ties facilitates ongoing crime. Through bribes, often negotiated by a lawyer, traffickers make certain that police have an interest in the narcotics trade. Since police earn money when they catch a dealer, they use an intervention strategy that ensures that there will always be trafficking activity. Thus, their efforts focus on arresting individual traffickers and letting them go for a fee rather than destroying the gang as a whole.

The illegal network in Santa Ana provides a number of public goods. The gang and the AM, in collaboration with politicians, make basic improvements, as seen with the construction of the *quadra*. Traffickers also back many social events such as the *festa junina* and the *baile funks*. The importance of these events is illustrated by Doca's thirtieth birthday festivities. The week before this party, residents discussed the massive preparations and talked of how they had heard that Doca had ordered four cows slaughtered, had the beef shipped to Rio, and had purchased over fifty cases of beer. Traffickers refuted these exaggerations, but this account shows that traffickers will throw excessive parties to build their own local stature and residents will readily ascribe mythic proportions to traffickers' festivities. This storytelling helps to reinforce residents' own sense of their importance and establishes a legend of a powerful trafficker who can protect them.

Through contacts with civic leaders, traffickers build local support for their activities. Josias's particular relationship to Doca allows him to maintain a measure of independence that can be used to build consensus in the favela. Traffickers work to respond to residents' demands. Joselino, for example, asked traffickers to move their *boca* from near his store to protect the many children who played there, and traffickers, for a time, complied. Gang members also punish residents who commit crimes within the context of local norms, thereby protecting residents and creating conditions under which residents feel safe and included, even while they are formally excluded by society at large.

The evidence presented here suggests remarkable similarities between Santa Ana and Tubarão. In both favelas, traffickers worked with local leaders to make their presence felt and to prevent their political role within the favelas from becoming public knowledge, since to do that could bring even more state attention and undermine trafficking. Police and politicians could lose their jobs if the media reported their contacts with traffickers. If the leaders of the Catholic Church parish had known of the connection between the traffickers and the *festa junina,* the local pastor probably would not have allowed the group to practice in the crèche. In both favelas, the AMs made residents aware that they and the traffickers supported political candidates by using the names of AM leaders and the trafficker's lawyers as public proxies. Similarly, the AM and other civic leaders served as the public face of the community in managing social events sponsored by traffickers. Residents who filmed the *festa junina,* for example, did not film part of an awards ceremony when organizers recognized traffickers for supporting the event.[88] As a result, traffickers simultaneously hosted an event that benefited residents but erased their public presence from the festivities. Neither the Santa Ana nor the Tubarão networks would function properly if it were more public.

As in Tubarão, the Santa Ana network is characterized by limited connections. Each member group has contact with few other member groups, and volatile relationships are mediated through third parties. Thus, politicians maintain contacts with the traffickers' lawyer and the AM but not with the traffickers. The AM maintains more connections than other groups and acts as a hub bringing together traffickers, residents, and many outsiders. Criminals and their allies minimize the presence of outsiders in the favela in order to create a secure area to conduct criminal activity, reinforce local ties, and prevent residents from building the types of links to the outside that could actually change government policy or cause residents to put trust in outsiders.

The strategic use of strong and weak ties reinforces network resistance. Groups within Santa Ana and Tubarão maintain strong ties with one another. Residents and leaders readily share detailed information with each other about the activities of criminals but do not share the same information with outsiders. When respected leaders such as Josias and Camilla work with traffickers they confer on traffickers some of the trust and respect they have in the community. Outsiders do contribute to the community, but their assistance only comes to the favela through specific residents, usually associated with traffickers, who then receive credit for bringing that aid to the favela. The result is a series of very strong local ties inside the community, combined with much more limited and distant links to outsiders.

From a policy perspective, the horizontal quality of the network enables members to co-opt state and civic actors who would ordinarily work to control crime and violence. Instead of an ongoing police presence designed to prevent drug dealing and build positive relations with residents, police focused their efforts on extremely dangerous and unpredictable raids that resulted in few arrests and high levels of extortion. On the other side, traffickers build connections into and co-opt civic organizations.

Controlling Violence in Santa Ana

The activities of the criminal network in Santa Ana not only increase levels of violence but also prevent the organization of alternative network links that could help residents diminish bloodshed. Of the organizations that operate in Santa Ana, only the local social club does not maintain connections to traffickers. This position gives social club leaders flexibility in protesting police actions and building ties to outsiders, but its lack of connections to traffickers marginalizes the group within Santa Ana. Intense inward-directed network ties limit the ability of residents to put pressure on outsiders that could decrease conflict. Nevertheless, some efforts on the part of the AM, social club leaders, and other residents do show how connections to outsiders can have a positive affect on the favela.

A Rio-based human rights NGO set up the social club and funds eight similar clubs around the city that also provide after-school activities for young people, who participate in discussion groups and retreats that address issues such as violence, sexuality, and health. Due to funding constraints, however, only about thirty local children participate, and many Santa Ana residents resent the money that the club receives.[89] This detachment, along with the distance from trafficking, has helped the club organize protests against the police and serve the needs of at-risk adolescents and children.[90] This same distance, however, has prevented club leaders from establishing a broader local network focused on controlling violence in the favela.[91] One story provides an example of this.

In 1997 I won a *cesta basica*, a bag containing sixty pounds of staple foods, in a raffle operated by one of the *garís*. Since I had no cupboard space or containers for the rice, farinha de mandioca, fubá, sugar, and coffee, I decided to donate the bag to the social club. The next day, my contacts in the AM and their friends expressed their disappointment at my decision. They said I had given my food to "the beast," a term commonly used to refer to a devil in Brazil, and accused the club leaders, all residents of the hill, of getting easy money and using it for themselves.[92] Manoel, the AM vice president, said the club does not do "anything for the community. . . . Poverty is a source of money for people. The residents . . . are revolted by this."[93] Joselino, a resident whom I would have otherwise thought would be sympathetic to the club, also had misgivings, saying that "they just do that to get money.

They have a project but they don't do anything. People come from the outside and film people in the community and make them look good to show that they are doing something with the money. People in the community stupidly smile in the camera to get themselves filmed."[94] Bête, the club leader, of course had deep concerns about this but argued that it was the nature of favelas: "There is jealousy in the communities about public work. People do not like people who are democratic. People think that everyone is dishonest and they don't trust you when you say that you are going to be honest. . . . People ask . . . for things because they think that the club has money." But she said she could not give to them, "because there won't be anything left in the club."[95] It is worth noting that the crèche, which also receives similar outside support but has better contacts with traffickers and engages in no political activism, does not suffer the same types of criticisms.

The feelings of suspicion directed toward the club would have also been directed at any other group trying to set up local operations that did not have connections to the AM or the traffickers. Residents fear external actors and suspect even long-time residents who receive money from outsiders. At one point early in my contact with community leadership, Josias said that people claiming to represent a foreign NGO came to Santa Ana and took pictures, promising to come back and help, but never returned. On another occasion, a man came to the AM saying he wanted to hire women to distribute pamphlets. Manoel was very circumspect, asked for the man's phone number, and then never returned his call. He said the man might be seeking prostitutes and the AM had to protect residents. Finally, many outsiders enter the favela to buy drugs. Because of these experiences, external groups wanting to work in the favela would have to spend considerable time and energy to build trust. Traffickers contribute to this by encouraging suspicion, constraining the ability of residents to build relationships with outsiders, and preventing residents from communicating with the police. Further, groups that develop connections to traffickers have an advantage operating in the community. The crèche works closely with traffickers and comes in for less criticism than does the social club, which explicitly eschews these contacts.

Because of this distrust of outsiders, no local group checks police violence. The AM and church organizations work with drug traffickers and would only get themselves in trouble if they denounced police violence too forcefully. Bête has organized protests but cannot act alone because of the suspicions of other residents, and long-standing mistrust of outsiders prevents other groups from setting up operations on the hill.

Successful Efforts to Reduce Violence

Despite the failure to build an alternative network to control violence, some efforts to work with the press and build links with the outside have led to lower levels of conflict in Santa Ana for brief periods. Residents report that violence has decreased when they have succeeded in drawing outside attention to the community. This can clearly be seen in the media reports in three cases: those that followed the death of Josias's wife, the effect of a visit by Pope John Paul II to Rio, and in the murder of Nelsinho.[96]

These incidents reveal several details about violence in Santa Ana. They confirm earlier observations that public protest and press attention could contribute to a decrease in violence. These stories add an additional dynamic in showing how resident discontent and public attention constrain both police and trafficker behavior. Criminals made efforts to reduce the potential fallout that their conflicts had on residents. Finally, these stories make clear the role that trained local leadership can play in changing these situations. Bête is one of the few politically active members of the community. Her efforts played an important role in refocusing residents' energies away from attacking the police and toward public protest after the murder of Nelsinho.

It is also clear that certain linkages between the community and the outside had a role in decreasing violence. A stray bullet killed Josias's wife at about the same time that a stray bullet killed two women who lived near the community. This coincidence helped to attract press attention that resulted in a slight dip in local violence. The presence of Pope John Paul II in an area near the favela in late 1997 caused the state to take actions to control violence. At least one resident reported that she was happy with the military occupation because it led to a decline in bloodshed. Finally, the protest of Nelsinho's shooting brought residents out into the city's streets to block traffic, attracting attention and briefly decreasing violence.

These events alone did not stimulate the formation of an alternative to the illegal network because the organs of power in the favela are too deeply tied to drug traffickers. Only the leaders of the social club seem to have the desire to create some change, but they are isolated politically. For real change to occur, there has to be greater investment in educating and training local leaders, and more outside groups need to initiate programs in the favela. The services that traffickers provide to residents, the deep familial and social web of connections between traffickers and residents, and traffickers' efforts to build community norms prevent residents from looking at alternatives to control local violence. Bête led residents in their protest, but without broader network support she could not maintain media attention or mount the long-term projects that would reduce residents' dependence on traffickers. There is no indication that leaders concerned with organization building would receive broad support from residents or could create the types of links with the outside that would provide them with protection from police retribution.

Building Strategies to Control Violence in Santa Ana

The crèche and the AM try to reduce violence, but the illegal network renders them powerless to demand changes in state policy. Despite his anger at state law enforcement, Josias was reduced to making occasional phone calls to newspapers to complain about individual police. Because of his ties to the traffickers, he also had a vested interest in the status quo. Camilla tried to work with a group in a nearby favela to stage events to attract notice, but the traffickers stopped them in order not to attract outside attention.[97] Further, Josias's and Camilla's illegal connections, as occurred with Bernardo in Tubarão, prevented them from working publicly with outsiders to improve life in Santa Ana. The social club, without contacts with traffickers, is free to build contacts to outsiders but the club alone was hardly able to accomplish what groups in Vigário or Tubarão were able to do through their larger networks. Unfortunately, the government and outside NGOs do not take the initiative in setting up these types of relationships. With so much violence in Rio, the attention of these organizations focuses on places with more prominence and stronger networking skills.

Nelsinho's murder shows that police violence against residents not involved in trafficking can provoke crises that can lead to mobilization. His murder so angered residents that they overcame their individual fear to collectively criticize police violence. Further, crises of this type could provide the opportunity to create sustained and successful efforts to change policing policy and control trafficking. Unfortunately, another tragedy on the level of Vigário or Tubarão might be necessary to spark an outside response. Like Scott's Southeast Asian peasants, Santa Ana's residents are unlikely to take public risks to promote political change when there is not a direct threat to their lives.[98]

This evidence suggests five factors that could contribute to the creation of a political movement to control violence. One is the training of high-quality local leaders who can jointly solve local problems and work with outsiders. Santa Ana has some good leaders, but, because it has few links to the outside and local leaders work with the illegal network, they cannot build the types of institutions that could control violence. The training of a new generation of leaders will play an important role in future political mobilization.

A second factor that prevents political mobilization is the trafficker/AM connection. If this tie weakened, significant difficulties could be created for the criminals. When that shift takes place, it may be possible for other local leaders to organize to change the community's political situation.

A third factor is the possibility of a crisis. Gunfights at night kill traffickers and create stress but do not cause residents to protest. On the other hand, the killing of a working resident in the middle of the day caused a riot. The difference lies in how endangered residents feel. If they think they face direct personal threats, they may act. If they feel the peril focuses mainly on criminals, they will probably not act. Leaders and outsiders concerned with forming a network to reduce violence need to monitor the community so that they can encourage action when residents are in a mood conducive to taking action.

Fourth, Santa Ana is a fairly small community and needs to build connections with outside groups. It is likely that a political movement that emerged there would have to connect with organizations in surrounding favelas and outside NGOs. These links would provide significant benefits to residents by helping to reduce the level of organization needed in Santa Ana.

The last factor that could promote a political mobilization is the ability of groups to meet residents' basic needs. Traffickers will not stop such groups from helping the community since their activities help build resident support for the status quo. Thus, while members of the criminal network are uncomfortable with the social club, they do nothing to stop its activities because the club's efforts to help adolescents get jobs and receive better health care are good for residents. Groups from the outside will need to focus on providing services rather than political leadership until they are well established.

Ultimately, improving conditions in Santa Ana will require police assistance. The connections that drug traffickers maintain to community and political leaders, however, undermine hopes of reform. Instead of pressing the government to control violence, local leaders work with traffickers to build ties with politicians to bring aid into the community to help traffickers. Even if government officials obliged police to change policy, top-down reform efforts would not succeed without pressure and ongoing monitoring from below. Lacking serious efforts at police reform, it is difficult to imagine any serious change in levels of violence.

With considerable effort a political movement against violence could emerge in Santa Ana. To do this, groups that want to operate in the favela will have to build close ties to residents. Outside groups will need to find a way to build social capital within the community that will help residents link themselves to other groups in the city by overcoming residents' distrust of outsiders and the intense inward-looking trust that ties residents tightly to drug traffickers. This is a complex task that involves not simply building social capital but also overcoming the challenges posed by the intense inward-based social capital that criminals have hijacked—to redirect the use of that inward capital toward positive ends and to build a weaker, linking, social capital to tie groups to the outside.

Comparing Santa Ana to Other Favelas

Located near downtown Rio, in a decaying working- and middle-class area, Santa Ana has access to a less valuable and, hence, less competitive retail market than Tubarão. As a result of this and of Santa Ana's location in a complex of favelas all run by the same gang, violence generally stems from police-trafficker fighting rather than from criminal conflict. Whereas trafficking wars are characterized by many-days-long battles that can shut down whole neighborhoods, police-trafficker conflicts are more regular but less severe, creating fewer headlines and constant but, on a day-to-day basis, lower casualties. The decaying neighborhood surrounding Santa Ana contains no prominent tourist hotels, and those who live nearby rarely have the same resources and political contacts as those of neighbors in the well-off Zona Sul. Finally, Santa Ana is a much smaller and more closely knit community than Tubarão.

These basic structural and geographic conditions contribute to political outcomes. In a small, tight-knit community, traffickers are under pressure to maintain positive relationships with specific residents in a way that is not necessary in larger favelas. As a result, Arturo appointed Doca, a native son, to manage the community. In contrast with Tubarão, where trafficker leadership comes from another favela, many residents have known Doca personally for their whole lives. The location of the favela in a decaying neighborhood with weak neighbors and little press interest has resulted in less government attention, giving local police a freer hand to engage in dangerous shoot-outs. The political weakness of the favela's neighbors also leads to fewer efforts at civic intervention than in favelas in wealthier parts of the city.

Socially, Santa Ana is a more pluralistic place than Tubarão. The favela contains three prominent and relatively powerful local organizations: the AM, the church crèche, and the social club. As in Tubarão, the AM is the central local organization mediating relations among traffickers, residents, and politicians. The Santa

Ana AM, however, is notably less dominant than Tubarão's. Although its leadership does not trust the social club, they make no effort to displace the organization or to co-opt it. This does not mean that these groups are actively interested in working with the social club or that they do not feel threatened. They do not, however, appear to have an interest in eliminating it. The crèche, run by Camilla, is also independent, although it works with traffickers when their interests converge.

One of the major reasons for this pluralism is the position of the AM. As a place with much less state investment in schools, services, and roads than Tubarão but, nevertheless, with a basic infrastructure, the favela has had little reason to develop a strong AM. Residents neither had to protest for basic improvements nor were so many resources sent to the community that a strong AM was needed to distribute services. Indeed, for much of the 1980s, the organization closed its doors. The result was an AM primarily focused on serving as a liaison with politicians and local state officials.

With a relatively acquiescent surrounding neighborhood and almost no press interest, a powerful outwardly oriented AM was unnecessary. This and the small close-knit nature of the favela led to Josias's leadership. He was a tough and respected local who had very close ties with traffickers but also, as a result of his paternal relationship to Doca, a considerable degree of independence. These qualities gave Josias the stature in the community to easily negotiate the complex relations between residents and traffickers. Josias was the right person to negotiate internal relations, but he had some difficulties dealing with outsiders. He did not have a commanding public presence or an ability to speak to the press and government officials. Not only did he not represent the favela well in public forums, he displayed some naïveté when dealing with the press, bureaucracy, and politicians. Nevertheless, in a place where the media and much of the state had little interest, there was no reason to have an AM leader who could reach out. The only exception to this was when politicians came searching for votes. In this case, the AM worked with the traffickers' lawyer to make contacts and negotiate deals.

The favela's pluralism also lay in its relationship to the Catholic Church. Santa Ana had been the site in the 1970s and 1980s of a strong Comunidade Ecelsiastico de Base (Ecclesiastical Base Community, CEB), the central teaching unit of Catholic liberation theology, which educated many residents, including Bête and Camilla. A strong cadre of trained local leaders coupled with a historically weak AM led to conditions where multiple groups could operate locally.

Traffickers faced little long-term threat from any of the groups working in the favela. Traffickers could tap into other organizations' prestige by working with them on occasion, as was the case with Camilla. By not challenging those who did not work with them, as with the social club, they did not risk their local stature by threatening long-time residents who were doing positive things for the favela's children. This resulted in a flexible social environment, which led to general resident tolerance of the traffickers along with some possibility of internal civic mobilization.

The institutional state also affected local political organizing. In terms of clientelism, Santa Ana appeared to have received very little help from politicians between 1986, when the first Leonel Brizola administration ended, and 1998, when a powerful conservative state deputy campaigning for federal congress came to the community and made a deal with the traffickers and the AM to build the *quadra*. This effort led to the creation of a public space completely under the control of the traffickers, reinforcing their position in the community, by helping build their local prestige and giving them control over the only large public space that could be used for dances and sports activities.

The most prominent state presence is haphazard and corrupt law enforcement. Like police in Tubarão, the type of police-trafficker relationships that operate here depend on the group of police that is on duty at a particular time. Some police take money directly from traffickers and leave them alone, while others conduct raids and then ransom traffickers' freedom. Unlike Tubarão, Santa Ana suffers more interventions by different police units, with the violent BOPE occasionally showing up and, at one point while I worked there, armed members of the famously corrupt PC walking up to the *boca* for an extended talk with the traffickers while the entire community watched.

This evidence suggests that, as in Tubarão, most police corruption is relatively haphazard and managed by particular sergeants rather than higher officers in the PM. Police appear to believe they have a freer hand here than in Tubarão, since they actually conduct many raids in broad daylight and engage in nightly, as opposed to weekly, gunfights. It is also clear that the different police units not assigned to the Batalhão with responsibility for the area have more flexibility in operating in Santa Ana. Police were certainly not a positive presence in Tubarão, but I never saw any notoriously violent police units deployed there, and when I saw PC in Tubarão, they would typically sit at PM posts, rather than march, in full public view, up to the *boca* for a chat. This does not mean that the Polícia Civil were not taking money from traffickers in Tubarão, but it does indicate that they were much more careful about how they made contact with criminals.

By this I do not mean that corruption is not systematic in Rio's police. Certainly the presence of two PC at the *boca* could reflect larger demands by high-ranking *delegados* (police officers) in that organization. Further, even if the mode of collecting bribes in the PM is guided by sergeants, this does not mean that those police do not have to systematically provide pay-offs to their superiors.

Facing more limited outside pressures and in an intensely personal political environment, the illegal network in Santa Ana is not as tightly organized as Tubarão's. Santa Ana's network has only a limited concern with altering public opinion, government policy, or working with the press. Without an immediate threat of outside trafficker takeover, it is also less important that one group dominate all social organizations. Rather, the members of the criminal network tried to ensure that residents did not become so alienated from the local traffickers that they would turn against them. In this environment, it makes sense for traffickers to allow multiple groups to operate and to have open relationships with them so that their leaders can more effectively provide services to residents. The traffickers' most pressing concern is maintaining local morale amid grinding police violence. To this end, traffickers provided services through the AM and tolerated the social club. All of this leads to a community where residents closely identify with the gang and harbor high degrees of anger toward the state.

Conclusion

The rate of violence in Santa Ana easily exceeded that of Rio de Janeiro as a whole. In Tubarão, a community much larger than Santa Ana, only half as many murders occurred in a similar period. Why was there so much violence in this place at this time? Why did residents do so little about it? What could be done to improve conditions in the community? An analysis of Santa Ana raises a number of important issues.

The democratic system that has evolved in Brazil has not effectively included the poor and, in the context of a proliferation of drugs and arms trafficking around the world, has led to the increasing levels of violence being directed at Santa Ana's residents. Bête put it best when she said, "Democracy has done little for the residents of the favela other than provide them with the right to talk. Prior [to that] individuals were not allowed to talk, but the politics have not changed. The poor do not have what they need, and politicians tend to provide things to the poor via clientelism. The poor have little more ability to interact with politicians than was available to them under the dictatorship."[99] As Rubem César Fernandes has argued, Brazil's postauthoritarian regime was built specifically on breaking the formal ties that bound the poor to the state, enabled the poor to make demands, and provided a minimal standard of living to the urban working classes. The result has been the emergence of a highly exclusionary political system in which the poor depend on informal actors and clientelist politicians to help meet basic needs and in which public security forces continue to devote huge amounts of energy, as they have historically, to repressing poor nonwhite Brazilians. Citizens who live in Santa Ana and other favelas do not have the resources to effectively make demands of the politicians on their own—nor do they have the resources to vote with their feet and move to safer parts of the city. As a result, they are stuck in the middle, depending on civic leaders and criminals for connections into the state and for access to what basic services exist.

Violence remains at high levels in Santa Ana because of an active network that brings police, traffickers, policymakers, and civic leaders together in perverse and undemocratic ways. At its core, the illegal network that operates in Santa Ana links actors from different sectors of state and society to perpetuate illegal activity. As both Tubarão and Santa Ana have shown, this is not an unusual outcome and, in fact, characterizes the political life of favelas throughout Rio. These complex criminal networks not only provide basic services and some feeling of security for the poor, but they also act as the primary link between the urban poor and the state. Ultimately, criminality and violence depend on state involvement, and the particular structure of the state in Rio, characterized by corruption and repressive policing, depends on the ongoing violence produced by the involvement of police, criminals, and civic leaders.

In the context of Santa Ana, and more broadly of Rio's favelas, both the state and civil society are ambivalent actors. Ample evidence from this chapter suggests that a greater state presence does not necessarily control violence. Tubarão and Santa Ana suffered regular police interventions, received substantial money from politicians, and enjoyed the use of a government-funded school in a nearby favela. Not only did these contacts with the state not reduce violence and criminality, for the most part these contacts actually *contributed* to violence and the abuse of favela residents, by providing civic actors linked to criminals with access to state resources. Civic actors in the favela actively contributed to the maintenance of the criminal network. Both the AM and the crèche in Santa Ana used the material and social resources available to them to help criminals. Clearly, simply having more civic institutions did not help control crime in the favela. In fact, the resources the Catholic Church put into the crèche actually strengthened the criminal organization through contacts criminals maintained with Camilla. Civil society, then, can do as much damage to democratic life as it can contribute to building it. The question about civil society, then, is not how to create more civic institutions—but how to create the correct civic institutions and help those institutions build the types of relationships with other state and social actors that help to control violent crime and promote democracy.

In this world, connections between civic, state, and criminal actors are more important in determining political outcomes than are hierarchical relationships between state actors, as many institutionalists would predict, or the conflict between elements of society and the state, as writers on social movements and state society relations would argue. Rather, cooperation between state and nonstate actors and the way they ally themselves against other coalitions of state and nonstate actors is the essential factor in understanding politics in Santa Ana. Further, the activities of criminals and their use of civic actors such as AM leaders or their lawyer to build contacts with the government suggests that the existing two-sided model of state and society is insufficient to describe politics under the circumstances that exist in Santa Ana. Here, criminals operate as an independent force apart from, but engaged with, state and society. The criminals that operate in Santa Ana share certain attributes in common with state actors, such as access to weapons and the ability to use violence to achieve goals on a regular basis. At the same time, the criminals share other attributes with social actors, such as their relative isolation from seats of power and the illegality of their use of force. On some level, finally, the criminals in Santa Ana differ from both civic and state actors in their strategies to make money and in their need for mediation from lawyers or other allies to make contacts with many public and civic actors. The next chapter will examine these problems in the context of Vigário Geral and will provide data on how favela residents can work together to control violence.

FIVE

Vigário Geral

On the night of 16 July 2003, a group of drug traffickers from the favela of Parada de Lucas invaded Vigário Geral, killed traffickers, and threatened the lives of other residents. Nearly ten years earlier, in the predawn hours of 30 August 1993, a group of police from the 9th Batalhão de Polícia Militar (Military Plice Batallion, BPM) invaded Vigário and killed twenty-one residents in alleged retaliation for traffickers killing a group of police the night before.[1] In response, residents organized themselves and began to work with outside groups to control police and trafficker violence. These efforts had many repercussions in Rio and throughout Brazil. As a result of internal organizing, murder in the community dropped almost to zero during a period in the mid- to late 1990s. However, for a variety of reasons, violence began to creep upward in late 1999 and in the new decade. By 2003, despite continued NGO attention, regular violence had returned to the favela. The 16 July attack closed the door on an era in Vigário's history and, perhaps, on popular mobilization in Rio.

With approximately 10,000 inhabitants, Vigário sits on the outskirts of the city and, until the 1993 massacre, rarely drew significant governmental attention. As a result, the community developed a strong internal political structure based around a powerful AM that delivered water service and laid out a regular street plan. With the growth of drug trafficking in the 1980s, the AM and other independent political organizations weakened, as newly empowered traffickers started delivering resources to residents. In 1986, an extended war began between traffickers from Vigário and Parada de Lucas, after a soccer game that resulted in the shooting death of a Vigário trafficker. During this period, residents note that police took bribes from traffickers and would stand on one of the bridges leading into the favela and watch traffickers deal drugs. Only with the breakdown in relations between police and drug traffickers after the 1993 massacre did favela residents organize effectively to counter both criminal and police violence and draw the attention necessary to push through longer-term policy reform. In this chapter, I will examine how an illegal network operated in the favela in the period prior to 1993, how a movement network emerged after the massacre that helped control violence, and why violence has increased since the end of 1999.

Historical Geography of Vigário Geral

The Parque Proletário de Vigário Geral is located on the far northern edge of Rio de Janeiro in a low-lying area bordering on a mangrove swamp, on the frontier with the impoverished suburb of Duque de Caxias. Vigário's residents live on a wedge of land that is bordered on the west by the favela of Parada de Lucas, on the south and east by the heavily polluted São João de Meriti River, and on the north by train tracks leading from downtown Rio into the impoverished suburbs of the Baixada Fluminense. The favela is unusual in that it has well-laid-out streets that, in many places, are large enough for trucks to pass through. Until 2000, when the city built a highway exit ramp into the favela, cars could only drive into Vigário on a road that runs through Parada de Lucas. Pedestrians could enter by crossing one of the two bridges built over the railroad tracks or by making a quick dash across the tracks themselves.

A single main road bisects the community, with areas to the west and south (toward Parada de Lucas and the surrounding neighborhood) sitting on higher ground and, as a result, less prone to river flooding. These areas contain the oldest and least impoverished neighborhoods. Those parts of the community closest to the train tracks were originally constructed as housing for railroad workers. Here residents have built their homes of brick and cement and occasionally covered them with comparatively expensive tiles. As one moves to the north and east, toward the river, the neighborhoods become progressively poorer and more prone to flooding. Here many residents built their homes of wood and some, as of the late 1990s, sat on stilts over the pungent black waters of the Meriti.

Vigário's location on the city's border influenced the history of local politics. This distance allowed the community to escape the dictatorship's policy of favela removal.[2] Nevertheless, in the 1960s and 1970s, the government resettled residents to Vigário who had been evicted from downtown favelas to make room for new skyscrapers.

With few basic services provided by the state, aside from a handful of water spigots installed by politicians, residents had to fend for themselves by building their own electrical systems, internal plumbing, and sewage networks and laying out wide streets.[3] Residents formed an AM in the early 1960s at the behest of the Fundação Leão XIII. The AM's initial concern was establishing more regular water service to the favela and making basic infrastructural improvements. After a takeover of the local electric commission in the 1970s, the AM started distributing electricity.[4] Haphazard and corrupt law enforcement led to some difficulties for residents, from whom the police would occasionally demand bribes.

Vigário's residents came originally from the city of Rio and from the nearby state of Minas Gerais. In those early years, much of the favela was built on a *mangue* (mangrove swamp) at the edge of the river, and much of the land on which the favela now sits was created by residents carrying in buckets of earth. One younger resident recalled that "the community had been built on the *mangue* and residents had walked on wooden bridges. The Rio Meriti passed by the community and was very nice. It was full of fish and alligators. When kids would fall in the *mangue* their parents would have to [take] them out before the alligators ate them."[5] Over time, the growing population slowly filled in the swamp on orders from AM leaders, who required residents to bring in one bucket of earth for deposit in public areas for each bucket brought in to fill private lots. Years later, that same resident said, "The streets were filled with a fine sand, like the beach."[6] In the 1980s, migrants arrived from northeastern Brazil and the interior of the state of Rio. Today, virtually all of the favela is on dry, if low-lying, ground.

Crime and Violence in Vigário

Until 1993, Vigário was the site of a strong illegal network that brought together police, local political leaders, and drug traffickers. This network facilitated localized violence and criminality but also maintained a certain type of order. Understanding the activities and history of this network will help in understanding the operation of illegal networks in favelas in general and will also help show the factors that led to the emergence of the later antiviolence network.

History of the Illegal Network

Prior to the late 1970s, the principal political actor in Vigário Geral was a powerful AM that focused on maintaining the local infrastructure. Violence increased significantly in Vigário in the 1980s as cocaine flowed into the community. One well-connected resident noted that in 1978 the police became more actively complicit with criminals. In 1979, conditions in the favela worsened as traffickers started a war with Parada de Lucas. Although the war ended in 1983, trafficker power in Vigário grew over the course of the next decade.[7]

Vigário's traffickers again came into conflict with Parada in 1986 when a dealer from Parada killed a Vigário gang member during a soccer game.[8] This conflict, which only ended with the 1993 massacre, was a seminal moment in the life of the favela, and nearly every resident has a version of that day's events. As the story goes, traffickers from the two favelas were enjoying a precarious peace and had arranged a soccer game to take place in Parada, which residents of both favelas attended. The most poetic account of the game came from Wesley, a teenager active in an NGO who was a young child at the time:

> The problems between the two communities started long ago, before
> the streets were filled in, when the houses were still made of wood. There
> was a soccer game between the two communities. Then the bandits used
> small weapons like .38 revolvers and pistols [which they carried in the
> waistbands of their shorts during the game]. Now they have rifles and
> grenade launchers. The game was tied at 1 to 1, and Parada had a penalty
> kick. The goalie defended the penalty kick, and the guy who kicked the
> penalty shot him while he still had the ball in his arms.[9]

Other residents reported that during the ensuing firefight Parada traffickers fired on Vigário residents. Trapped inside the enemy favela, some fled into the *mangue* and into the heavily polluted river; others escaped out into the high-speed traffic of Avenida Brasil, a major six-lane highway that runs to downtown Rio. The attack only ended when riflemen from a nearby naval base on the other side of the *mangue* fired over the heads of the Parada traffickers.[10] Three Vigário residents died.[11]

This traumatic conflict sundered two communities that historically had had a symbiotic, if contentious, relationship. Romantic affairs abruptly ended, families were divided, and Vigário's residents, who depended on the road though Parada for vehicle access, found themselves partially cut off from the outside world. The two favelas shared a large, full-service, public school that the state government had built in the early 1980s after an extensive political fight by the leadership of the Vigário AM. Now Vigário residents could no longer attend the school since it was located slightly closer to Parada. The corridor between the favelas, where the school sits, was rebaptized "Vietnam," and the walls of homes in this area became covered in blossoms of bullet holes. Charles, a young activist and longtime local activist, recalled, "When there were gunfights, [residents] would wait outside the community until the gunfight ended to let the drug traffickers kill each other. Sometimes they would shoot for hours and no one would be killed. They would shoot all their money into the air for no reason. The police never made an effort to calm things down for the residents."[12] This war lasted for seven years.

The conflict was hard on residents, as traffickers, constantly fearing for their lives, developed deep suspicions of those around them. Charles noted, "Bandits, especially those at war, have a very limited vision. Most are illiterate. They believe that anyone who comes into their community is spying on them."[13] Evanildo, a resident from a poor part of the favela, recalled a murder during this period that took place just outside his home of a man whom traffickers suspected of treachery. He remembered, "The [traffickers] said to someone that he was going to die. Then they screamed, grabbing him, [and] put the pistol to his head and shot him. Then some guy said, 'He's not dead, shoot him again,' [and] bang." He reported that afterwards he "was not well the rest of the day." In a second case of extreme trafficker violence, Evanildo reported that another resident was friends with a man from outside the favela who worked for the police as a common clerk. His job, however, did not pay him much money, and he began a small business selling flip-flops in Vigário. Seeing that his friend was also short of cash, he "took his friend . . . to the factory [where he purchased his supply] and said he could sell flip-flops, but not in Vigário because it was his territory." Eventually, the Vigarío resident decided he wanted the whole business for himself and arranged for the murder of his partner by spreading rumors that his partner was an x-9 (informant) for the police. Soon afterward, on one of his trips to the favela, the traffickers had the man killed. Eventually, however, the truth came out, and the traffickers forced the resident to leave the favela.[14]

To avoid arrest or murder under these circumstances, Vigário's traffickers needed the support of residents to help them hide in this community with a geography that made retreat difficult and escape nearly impossible. To build support, traffickers did not just rely on fear of retribution. They also worked closely with local civic leaders to deliver services. Criminals provided assistance to residents, such as improving water quality, giving presents to children during certain seasons, providing for home improvements, and offering financial assistance during times of need.[15] Roger, the owner of a hardware store and a former president of the AM, explained one day, sitting in the kitchen of his home, that "[the traffickers] maintained the water, built homes, had parties, and maintained security." He reported that "they spent R$2,000–5,000 per week at [his store]." He continued: "They built the *quadra* in the back of the community to show movies and have concerts. They improved the community a lot during this period but also caused problems. They didn't allow crime in the community. Someone who stole was killed."[16] Charles reported that the traffickers provided similar services, when he noted that Flavio Negão, the main trafficker in the years before the massacre, "tried to help the community a lot." He reported that they built a soccer field and stage in the favela, "asphalted the streets," and "bought medicines" for residents. He went on to say that "Flavio Negão was supposed to have been very religious and a worker, though he was very cruel with other people involved in trafficking." Charles concluded by saying that Flavio Negão was "just with the people."[17] Sitting on the roof of the partially completed headquarters of the Grupo Cultural Afro-Reggae (Afro-Reggae Cultural Group, GCAR), Wesley recalled, "You could go out and come home at night whenever you wanted to. You could walk around in the streets . . . whenever you wanted to. Traffickers helped residents with money, they had *combis* [vans] to take residents to the hospital. . . . Drug traffickers only provided assistance when they wanted to, not necessarily when it was needed. Traffickers had to provide benefits to the community in order to maintain the support of the residents."[18] One older community member lamented that water service had been much better during the time the traffickers funded the system.[19] By providing assistance, traffickers maintained public support, despite the violence that their activities visited on the favela.

These efforts created attachments between residents and traffickers that led many residents to complain about their absence after the police occupation began in 1996.[20] All residents, however, did not uniformly support the gang. The traffickers could be brutal and often threatened residents who became uncomfortable with their presence.[21] Charles noted, however, that "if you weren't involved with them they wouldn't bother you."[22] It seemed that poorer residents, those who benefited the most from traffickers' services, were most likely to report favorable impressions of the dealers. Charles said, "The traffickers didn't have a lot of control in the community. . . . [Their] power was based in the poorest parts of the community . . . [where] [t]hey would intervene in conflicts in homes. Traffickers' power is not as extensive as most imagine. They didn't control everyone. They didn't control the AM though they gave advice."[23] In a local restaurant, Jorginho, an outsider who led an NGO, reported, "In the past, traffickers used to be involved in making decisions. [R]esidents didn't go first to the traffickers. If they couldn't work things out on their own they would talk to the traffickers. If issues became problems, traffickers would become involved. . . . The traffickers resolved fights among residents."[24] The support criminals provided enhanced their legitimacy among residents and facilitated their efforts to hide from police attacks.

During this period, the drug gang maintained complex relations with the AM, which was dominated by Seu Tarcísio, a leader who rotated in and out of office as term limits allowed and who died in 1996. ("Seu" is an honorific that is a corruption of "senhor" (mister). People in favelas generally use it sparingly for respected very old men. In Vigário it is used in reference to all politically important men, especially AM presidents and past presidents from later middle age on.) Residents disagree about the penetration of the traffickers into the AM. Over lunch in her spacious home, Seu Tarcísio's widow, Paula, said, "The traffickers tried many times to take over the AM . . . but Seu Tarcísio refused their offers. They would come over and sit unarmed and talk with [him] about the AM. He would tell them 'no,' but every few months they would pressure him again. . . . [t]hings could have been worse had they been political because they would have been able to organize themselves. They were illiterate, which helped Seu Tarcísio maintain organization in the community."[25] Seu Almeida, the AM president in 1997 and 1998, told a different story, saying, "During the time of Flavio Negão, the traffickers [had] a lot of power . . . and things were very violent. They used to collect money by force. They would come to your house and put a gun in your face and force you to pay your [AM] dues. This was during the time of Seu Tarcísio's directorate. Flavio Negão's brother . . . was . . . first secretary and paid all the bills."[26] During a long interview in the poorly lit living room of his home, Miguel, a former community plumber employed by the AM and paid by the traffickers, told a different story:

> The traffickers never officially controlled the AM though they gave
> advice. Seu Tarcísio had always been an effective leader . . . and had
> maintained good relations with the traffickers. Eventually, however, Flavio
> Negão decided to get rid of Seu Tarcísio. He expelled him from the AM, went
> through all his documents, and took things. He convinced them to let him
> organize the elections. This had to be done twice because the traffickers
> didn't like the results of the . . . elections. [For the second elections] they
> agreed on two candidates, Seu Gérson and Seu Almeida. It was agreed that
> Seu Gérson would lose. Seu Almeida was chosen by the traffickers to win.
> Seu Gérson later left the community because members of his family had
> been killed. Seu Almeida had always believed himself to have the skills to
> be a good president. He had connection in politics and politicians knew
> him. The trafficker liked that.[27]

Miguel said that he "told [Almeida] he was crazy to be president," and that, despite their friendship, he "would not be part of the directorate." He concluded, "During the early years of Seu Almeida's term, Vigário was under the control of Flavio Negão . . . [who] had about forty people working for him."[28] Through these intermittent and tenuous connections, the traffickers worked with the AM and paid the AM's bills.[29]

These descriptions show that connections between traffickers and the AM varied over time. The evidence suggests that traffickers had a persistent interest in the AM and that there was some interest on the part of the traffickers, especially when Almeida took office, of using the AM as a conduit to politicians. The traffickers used the AM to provide some day-to-day services to the community and to employ residents who worked for them.

During this time, traffickers had contentious relations with law enforcement. There had always been some bribe taking by police, but corruption intensified dramatically in the 1980s. Defending her husband, Paula stated, "When the police became corrupt as a result of the trafficking, Seu Tarcísio fought to have the police removed from the community."[30] Prior to the massacre, the traffickers paid the police a regular bribe so that they could openly deal drugs in the favela. Residents said police would stand on the bridge leading to the favela and would watch drug deals but do nothing.[31] During this period, Vigário was located in the jurisdiction of the 9th BPM, a unit known at the time to be one of the most corrupt and violent in the city. Some evidence suggests that when the massacre occurred a large-scale corruption network operated within this entity, which both executed criminals and extorted money from traffickers. In one version of the story of the Vigário massacre, the traffickers' decision to stop paying the police led directly to the killings of residents. Paula remembered, "The traffickers had worked out with the police a system [to pay] them . . . money to let them operate. In 1993 the traffickers decided to stop paying the police. They let three payments go by and on the fourth they . . . attacked [the police]. They killed the police and went and hid in other favelas. The night the police came the traffickers were in other places, so they killed the workers who were there."[32] After the killings, police and traffickers, the core of the illegal network, no longer trusted each other and could not work together. The now public nature of their relationship and ongoing media scrutiny undermined any efforts to rebuild the network.

The police also harassed residents. Sitting in their living room on a hot January afternoon, Daniel, a former community activist, and his mother noted that the police "used to cross the *pasarela* [bridge] shooting. Once Seu Tarcísio was caught out there [using a telephone at the entrance of the favela] and he had to go and hide in a friend's house for the night." Police violence, however, did not stop with raids. Recalling the fear she had while raising her son, Daniel's mother, Joana, notes, "The police used to treat residents very badly. Many were beaten and killed. Once they stopped Daniel and put him in the back of a police car and didn't let him out for several hours. Eventually his uncle heard him screaming and they let him go."[33] Similarly Clarinha, an activist whose entire family was killed, said, "Before the massacre [the police] would just break into homes when people weren't home. They said they were suspect homes."[34] Charles, who also suffered police harassment as an adolescent, echoed these experiences, saying, "The police would come in and beat people up. They especially like to get young poorly dressed men and beat them up."[35] This abuse damaged relations between residents and police and elicited some sympathy for the traffickers who lived in the community and suffered some of this same abuse but who provided residents some services.

Dynamics of Violence in Vigário

Research on Vigário was conducted during a period when criminals were extremely weak, making it difficult to directly observe interactions between them and other groups. Nonetheless, the community does provide some insights into criminal network activities. To keep resident support, traffickers maintained contacts with the AM, providing them with links into the legal marketplace and the state bureaucracy. Although traffickers paid for water services, the plumber they hired to maintain the system worked for the AM. If Roger's estimates are correct, they spent between US$100,000 and US$250,000 on supplies each year to improve homes and build infrastructure. The *combi* service traffickers offered residents also ran through the AM. Nonetheless, attempts by some AM leaders to resist traffickers created tensions. Although traffickers could remove recalcitrant AM leaders, finding a competent, well-connected resident to take over was not easy. As a result, traffickers did not move decisively to replace leaders, since this might have weakened their position. There is also, typically, very clear evidence of collusion between police and traffickers. Despite these similarities, Vigário differed considerably from Santa Ana and Tubarão.

Located on the far edge of the city, Vigário was long forgotten by the government and had to fight for the provision of even basic services. The community is partially isolated from the rest of the city, since it had vehicular access only through Parada de Lucas. In an environment of intense gang conflict, residents and dealers had little means of receiving shipments or even, in the event of a medical emergency, of going to the hospital. The favela's flat topography, coupled with well-laid-out roads, made the area very difficult to defend. Finally, the proximity of the favela to major highways and the airport created conditions for running a substantial drug wholesaling business. These factors led to intense competition for the favela with other traffickers and to a very brutal and militarily effective criminal gang.

The isolation of the favela and the particular way that the city settled the area—first with railroad employees and later with residents displaced from other favelas

—led to the emergence of a robust AM. What services did come to the favela had to be fought for by a politically savvy AM in a community that occasionally suffered raids during the dictatorship. As drug traffickers gained power in the 1980s, it is clear that the AM had some ability to operate independently, although eventually the AM and traffickers developed a strong relationship. Unlike some other favelas, however, the AM was not directly controlled by the traffickers, and, after the massacre, it rapidly distanced itself from criminals.

Owing to its distance from potential funders, there were few active civic groups in the favela. The Catholic Church had a very limited presence. There were also various growing Protestant congregations, which, until the massacre, took virtually no public role in the community. These churches did provide some very limited social assistance, but the only real sources of help were the underfunded AM and the much more powerful traffickers.

The state's presence in the community also differed from that of Tubarão and Santa Ana. After considerable protest, the Brizola government built a full-service public school, which also provided day care on the frontier between Vigário and Parada. After the two favelas went to war in 1986, Vigário residents could not attend the school. Electricity had been regularized, but, unlike the other two favelas, water service was provided directly by traffickers.

The only regular state presence came in the form of the systematically corrupt 9th BPM. The involvement of a large number of police in the massacre was possible only with the collusion of high-ranking officers. There was evidence at the trial of the police accused in the massacre that the unit's duty logs had been altered in an attempt to provide alibis to the police involved in the killings. Further, the 9th BPM's leadership also tolerated a tremendous amount of violence on the part of its company in undertaking law enforcement activities. Corruption in the pre-1993 period was based on a level of violence not seen in either Santa Ana or Tubarão. Police violence went a long way toward facilitating trafficking and only drove residents further into the arms of criminals.

The reasons for this coordinated violence and corruption are many and varied. Clearly, the distance from downtown and from places where powerful citizens lived gave police a freer hand to allow long-term gang warfare and corruption. Further, perhaps in an effort to show efforts at fighting crime, the PM hierarchy tolerated more abusive police practices here. Unlike in other police units, there appears to have been a degree of internal discipline in the 9th BPM that enabled more serious and pervasive corruption. This internal discipline likely had to do with the history of this particular unit and its relationship with other neighboring units.

This evidence provides robust confirmation of the role of network activities in aiding crime. As in Santa Ana and Tubarão, criminals maintained connections with civic and state actors to sustain their activities. The failure of the connection between traffickers and the police ultimately undermined the network and opened the space for the emergence of organizations that significantly limited crime and violence in the favela.

Controlling Violence in Vigário

In the early morning of 30 August 1993, a group of thirty Rio de Janeiro military police invaded Vigário Geral and killed twenty-one residents in alleged retaliation for the murder of several police officers the night before.[36] As the story told by residents goes, the traffickers gunned down the police who had gone to a small plaza near the community to collect a bribe. Knowing the police would retaliate, the traffickers went into hiding outside the community after warning residents to stay off the streets. The brutality the following night went beyond what anyone could have imagined. At one small bar, police killed several men celebrating Brazil's victory over Bolivia that day in a qualifying game for the 1994 World Cup. Across the street, a policeman tossed a grenade into a home, murdering an entire family while they prayed for the shooting to end. Since the traffickers did not return fire, the police were able to attack residents with impunity.[37]

The next day, angry residents went to the traffickers, who had returned from hiding, seized their weapons in rage, and, as one resident reported, threw them on the ground. As the day went on, the press arrived to report on the massacre, and by evening the story had been broadcast throughout Brazil and around the world. The attention of civil society, politicians, and human rights activists put traffickers and police on the defensive. In the days following the massacre, using the civic resources available in Brazil's fledgling democracy, residents organized the Movimento Comunitário de Vigário Geral (Community Movement of Vigário Geral, Mocovide). Angry young adults, upset with the killings, led the movement, which quickly grew to involve civic leaders, survivors of massacre victims, and AM leaders from Vigário and the neighboring favela of Parada de Lucas.

Mocovide's first success was to compel Vigário's and Parada's traffickers to make peace. In a dramatic gesture of solidarity, Robertinho, the head trafficker from Parada, came to Vigário for the victims' funeral and sealed the peace by hugging his bitter enemy, Flavio Negão, the leader of Vigário's gang. Mocovide then held events designed to bring together residents to deepen the peace. These events included a dance, a soccer game, and a party for older residents of the two communities.

In the weeks after the massacre, Mocovide's leaders began to build alliances with organizations from other parts of the city. At the time of the killings, Rio teemed with concern about burgeoning social violence as a result of the murder of eight street children outside the Candelária church at the hands of police, a spate of kidnappings, and a series of *arrastões* (mass muggings) on city beaches. As a result, several groups, which had vivid memories of recent protests to end authoritarian government, had already organized, and Vigário's new activists had an easy time tapping into this. Over coffee in a Cambridge, Massachusetts, Au Bon Pain, Caio Ferraz, a central Casa da Paz (House of Peace, CdP) organizer who had fled Brazil after threats on his life by police, said, "The massacre of August 1993 came at a time when other massacres had occurred in Brazil. One-hundred and eleven were killed in Carandíru, twenty-one in Vigário, eleven in Acarí, eight in Candelária. . . . The movement that started then in Vigário resonated with a crisis which was occurring in the country. In the middle of a democracy the poor were being killed by the police. No democracy exists for the poor."[38] Another activist suggested that the confluence of events gave Vigário residents the position to make claims of the state: "The killings in Vigário came in one large group [of] many of the massacres in other parts of the city. . . . It was hard to say that the police weren't to blame. This let us point the finger in the face of the governor and say that he had to do something about Vigário."[39] Shortly after the massacre, two Mocovide leaders went to a meeting on violence at the city hall, where they met Mateus, a biology teacher, who later became active in the movement. Following Mateus's advice, residents staged a march on the one-month anniversary of the killings, from the Candelária Church in downtown Rio to Vigário, nearly forty kilometers away, to symbolically link the two events.[40]

These alliances helped Mocovide attract media attention and bring in assistance. Cash from a progressive evangelical group whose leaders worked with Viva Rio, a new NGO, helped Mocovide purchase the house where police had killed eight residents during the massacre. With help from Manoel Ribeiro, a progressive architect, they transformed the dwelling into the headquarters of the new NGO, the CdP. With additional outside help, the CdP began professionalization courses for adolescents and advocacy programs focused on reducing violence.

Many in the favela believed that this outside assistance had more to do with middle-class interests than with those of residents. This is particularly apparent in one local activist's statement:

After the massacre, a number of parachutists came into the community. Manoel Ribeiro was the first. He had seen the *arrastões* (mass muggings) and had begun to do research on the *funkeiros* (generally poor youth who regularly attend *baile funks* and were accused of organizing *arrastões* on Rio's nicest beaches). When he saw the crisis in Vigário, he became involved in the community and began to attract more interest. Rubém César came afterwards. . . . He used the crisis in Vigário to bring a lot of attention to Viva Rio. Later came Zuenir Ventura, who spent ten months living in Vigário drinking cachaça to understand the community [for] writing his book. They were all part of a Zona Sul bourgeoisie who had nothing better to do than scratch their crotch. Caio Fábio also participated in this. They envisioned the Casa da Paz as an organization which would fight for human rights. [T]he Casa da Paz was a great victory for Viva Rio. There was a tape cutting at which all of the important people were present but which had little to do with the community.[41]

These statements clearly reflect a strain of anger at what many residents saw as the opportunism of outsiders engaging in social work that also provided benefits to themselves and their organizations. At the same time, however, these interventions and the contacts they would leave in the community brought considerable benefits to residents.

In the year after the massacre, a number of other organizations came into Vigário with the CdP's help. These groups included the Médicos Sem Fronteiras (Doctors without Borders, MSF); the Grupo Cultural Afro-Reggae (Afro-Reggae Cultural Group, GCAR); the Fundação Municipal Lar Escola Francisco de Paula (Francisco de Paula Home School Foundation, FUNLAR), a government program to assist the disabled; a Swiss-supported crèche; a workers cooperative; and the Centro de Valorização do Ser (Center for Personal Development, CVS), an environmental and social welfare group that worked in the poorest parts of the community. These organizations focused on delivering different services to residents and offering advocacy assistance to help improve the favela.

In the three years after the massacre, despite the peace between traffickers and ongoing NGO activity, high levels of violence continued as police retaliated against traffickers. One resident noted, "In the years between the massacre and the police occupation, the amount of drug trafficking increased and the traffickers became stronger as a result of the money and weapons that came into the community. The police raids that would make the traffickers hide were ineffective at controlling trafficking."[42] During these years, regular shoot-outs occurred between traffickers and law enforcement. At one point, police dropped grenades from a hovering helicopter onto a home suspected of harboring criminals, leaving the owner deeply traumatized. The police had no permanent presence in the favela and only entered the community to conduct operations. When police were not present, traffickers walked the streets, armed, and sold drugs from a central building located within a block of the AM, the CdP, and one of the bridges that linked the favela to the outside. These interventions resulted in intense conflicts between different heavily armed groups controlling the streets of Vigário at different times of the day.[43] During this period, stories abounded of police and trafficker violence, ranging from unjustified searches of homes and illegal detentions to beatings and killings.[44]

Still, ongoing activism and media attention resulted in significant changes in the favela. Wesley, the young GCAR activist, made this particularly clear:

> In the years since the massacre, the community has attracted international attention. First that attention was directed at the violence. People who worked outside the community had trouble getting jobs because they were suspect for living in the community. In the past year, things have improved considerably. Attention has focused on a decrease in violence in the community. It has focused on the Casa da Paz and Afro-Reggae. The positive news has made residents proud and gotten attention for the community, which allows residents to receive the approval of co-workers.[45]

A newspaper reporter with whom I conversed in the streets of the favela agreed: "The massacre brought the community to the world's attention and enabled lots of money and attention to come to the community. . . . the community has improved because of that attention."[46] These connections to the outside reached their peak in September 1996 when one resident exhibited a sculpture of a family made of 11,000 bullet casings that favela children had collected and exchanged at the CdP for candy.[47] Local and international media came to Vigário to report on its unveiling. Working together with Charles, the sculptor, the CdP attracted more attention than if the organization had worked independently. Charles might have been able to build the sculpture on his own, but the CdP turned the job of gathering the casings into a highly meaningful collective experience and gave Charles access to their media contacts to help promote his art. In addition, Charles's art gave the CdP the visual resources and the cause to call up their contacts in the media to draw attention to the community. Although the CdP had regular access to the media, the ordinary routine was to wait for a shoot-out to call the press. This resulted in overwhelmingly negative coverage. The public exposure of this creative and interesting sculpture in the CdP attracted a new kind of positive attention that helped force the hand of the state to change local policing policy. Sitting in the entryway to the CdP late one afternoon, Dé, an activist from another favela, noted, "The sculptures were responsible for the government occupying the community, because a week after they were unveiled and . . . received much attention in the national and international press, the governor signed the order for the police to occupy the community. The occupation has been directly responsible for the decline of the violence. . . . All of the [main] traffickers have now left because of the police."[48]

A clear consensus of residents reported that the police occupation led to a precipitous drop in violence. Daniel and Joana noted: "Things have gotten better with the police in the community. The police post has repressed trafficker activity. The police stationed at the post are responsible for the community. If traffickers are active or someone dies in the community, local police have to answer for it. They still, however, beat residents but not in the way they used to. People are more aware of their rights now."[49] Cynthia, the AM secretary, said, "People speak more freely now because there is less violence. Violence has been declining since the police came in. People are very relaxed."[50] On a hectic day when an important foreign dignitary and many reporters had visited the community, Charles said to me, "Things have been at peace in the community for the last year. . . . violence has dropped to zero. . . . Residents have demanded of the police that they not contribute to the violence in the community."[51] One young activist from the GCAR gave some insights into why the police occupation succeeded: "The police operations did no good because the traffickers always hid. The police occupation has been effective in reducing crime because they placed soldiers in the community [who] take over each corner, preventing the traffickers . . . from acting. There is no space to deal drugs [and] only a few small traffickers are left."[52] Roger agreed: "The occupation of the police saved the community. The presence of the police has suppressed the trafficking. The people are still afraid . . . but . . . they will become accustomed to [the police]. The traffickers created terror and now the police are eliminating that. The change will take time. The future in Rio is the police in every community. The trafficking will go away forever if the police stay long enough for the people to have confidence in them."[53] One resident, a former employee of the traffickers, offered a slightly less optimistic analysis, saying, "The Casa da Paz and Afro-Reggae have done some good . . . in giving kids things to do, but they haven't been successful in the elimination of violence. Violence only ended when the police came in last year . . . [although] [t]here is still violence. It is 30 percent lower than what it was. Traffickers still deal. There are still shoot-outs. The president [of the AM] still has to watch his position."[54] Perhaps the most emphatic statement about security in the favelas was offered by an outsider who worked as an AM accountant: "The community has a bad history, but, thanks to God, they are going through a calm season."[55]

These comments show that although many residents continued to distrust the police most recognized that the occupation had a positive effect on their lives. Residents' comments highlight the strategic failure of policing tactics prior to the intervention, noting that the process of intermittently intervening and withdrawing from the community, a strategy used in nearly all favelas in Rio, allowed the traffickers to consolidate their power and encouraged higher levels of violence. The regular presence of police at major intersections in the favela forced important criminals to go into hiding in other parts of the city, ended regular shoot-outs, and suffocated drug dealing, thereby reducing the interest of outside traffickers in attacking the community. Residents, as a result of their mobilization and the activities of NGOs, had a greater sense of their rights and used that knowledge to control police violence. The ongoing vigilance of the NGOs kept the police in check, and continued to do so through mid-1999, by pressuring state leaders to reform government policy directed toward the favela.

Unfortunately, serious political problems eventually developed in the antiviolence network. In early 1995, Caio Ferraz, the president of the CdP, upset the police with public denunciations of their corruption. Fearing for his life in the face of death threats, he went into exile in the United States and the board appointed Balduíno as executive director to take over the day-to-day management of the CdP. Caio's complaints were politically unpopular in the favela in that they highlighted tensions with the state and attracted violent police pressure against the leaders of other local groups. Political decisions by successive CdP leaders would cause the group to collapse and transform the Vigário network. Most complaints about the CdP were linked to local political competition and poor decision making among the leadership of the organization. Many former Mocovide activists felt that Ferraz had used the CdP to promote himself. Roberto, a GCAR leader, made this very clear:

Caio had no *jeito* [style] to deal with the problems that he was confronting. . . . Caio and Mateus decided to do the external work for Mocovide while others did the internal work. Caio took that external work and his experience with sociology [Ferraz has a bachelor's degree] to . . . draw attention to himself. The CdP was envisioned by many people. . . . Caio excluded every-one except Afro-Reggae from . . . decision making. . . . With everyone excluded, Caio isolated himself. Caio used to use words that alienated other people. . . . He had no charisma. . . . In order to keep power, he forced other people out of the Casa and only kept the quietest people. . . . The people who worked in the house thought that he was the owner and they couldn't get rid of him. Caio was corrupted.[56]

Others echoed Roberto's feelings.[57] Some complaints, however, focused on the missteps in how Ferraz and others dealt with the police occupation. Charles noted that Ferraz, at the time in exile in Boston, took a long time to support the police occupation:

> When the police began the occupation, Caio was against it. He wanted Balduíno to help [denounce] the police intervention. The problem was that people actually liked the intervention. When they occupied the community, the PMs were told not to create any problems because of the international repercussions. . . . [They were told:] "For God's sakes, don't create any more scandals." When they went into the community, they didn't create many problems and began to control the trafficking. Sure there were some new incidents, but they generally involved drunks and they were doing good work. The community was incredibly happy . . . because violence had pretty much subsided. Caio was radically against [this but] . . . Balduíno wouldn't follow him because the people didn't want it. [Caio's opposition] *não tinha razão* [made no sense], the people . . . supported the intervention. . . . Caio had the audacity to defy everyone and protest from the United States. It was crazy. After about a month, Caio realized he was wrong and stopped protesting.[58]

Deep, long-standing, personal animosity was at play in some of these very pointed criticisms of Ferraz, who, as a result of his exile, could not defend himself. Nevertheless, Roberto's and Charles's statements reflect the fact that poor management of relations with residents, activists, and CdP employees, a lack of political savvy to deal with delicate political issues, problems with successive executive directors, and the distance of Ferraz from Rio contributed to political difficulties for the CdP and Ferraz.

After Ferraz left for the United States, the CdP experienced financial troubles, with one resident reporting the institution running a R$15,000 deficit.[59] This led to the dismissal of Balduíno, a dramatist with a common touch, and his replacement with Jorginho, a middle-class activist who managed an international Protestant faith-based NGO in a well-known Zona Sul favela. Whereas Balduíno allowed the CdP's finances to fall apart and focused on managing the political relations in Vigário, Jorginho worked well with funders and kept the massacre trials in the news. As a result, he alienated residents and CdP workers, who believed he was too aloof and who wanted to forget the killings. One resident said, "The Casa is more interested in working with people from the outside. They treat people from the outside well but treat people from here badly."[60] Another said, "Jorginho doesn't get around the community. He only walks on the main street [far from the neediest areas]."[61] Relations between Jorginho and Marcelinho VP, an important Zona Sul trafficker, made matters worse, creating tensions between the CdP, other NGOs, and local traffickers.[62] Evanildo said that Jorginho "brought people in from the outside to do work that he could have hired in the community. . . . He brought people in from Santa Marta and Borel who no one knew in the community. They were all from places which were run by other gangs. Santa Marta is CV they say, but not the same CV as Vigário. No one really likes Jorginho because he was from Santa Marta."[63] Rúbia, a restaurant owner, added that "he is the number two guy in Santa Marta after the *chefe* [boss]. He is not accepted [here]."[64] While Rúbia's assertion about the degree of Jorginho's power in Santa Marta is open to argument, her perception of him as the second most powerful person in Santa Marta is telling. Charles put the question of Jorginho's ties to traffickers most eloquently when he said, "Another problem with Jorginho was his very close links to Marcelinho VP, the bandit leader of Santa Marta, and one of the most important traffickers in Rio. His relationship with Marcelinho made his relationship with the other NGOs very complicated. He is friends with Marcelinho and has helped him hide from the police. He publicly defends bandits. Given this, his image is very compromised. It was very dangerous to have someone like Jorginho in the community. It was bad for Vigário."[65] Charles noted that other NGO leaders complained that Jorginho's presence hurt their work.[66]

These tensions came to a head on 20 January 1998, when residents, traffickers' allies, and CdP workers gathered in the CdP for a conference call with Ferraz. A shouting match ensued in which Seu Rafael, the Parada de Lucas AM president, hyperbolically accused Jorginho of being a "sambista" as a result of his ties to the samba school in Santa Marta and, hence, to traffickers there. In Jorginho's case, his association with samba was a particular indictment because of the degree of respect he possessed as a result of his publicly Protestant religiosity, which in the tradition of many Rio Protestants excludes participation in Carnival. By the end of the phone call, Ferraz and Jorginho had agreed to step down. Over the next several weeks, a major newspaper published a story on the conflict, as different groups wrangled over the CdP's leadership. The CdP failed to reorganize and significantly decreased its operations.[67] Public pressure on issues of violence decreased drastically. In November of 1998, with little comment, the Supremo Tribunal de Justiça, Brazil's highest court, acquitted eleven of the police accused in the massacre and other courts released two other police who had been convicted earlier.[68] Press coverage of the CdP's infighting undermined the ability of its leaders to raise funds and pursue projects.[69] By mid-2000, Onda Azul, a growing NGO that recycles plastic bottles to make furniture, had taken over the CdP building.[70]

Dissatisfaction with the CdP stemmed from popular dissatisfaction with Ferraz that led to an alliance of Mocovide activists and massacre survivors. Mismanagement of funds under Balduíno worsened the situation. With this deficit, the CdP could not pay its employees. Local unhappiness with Jorginho and his contacts with Marcelinho VP built an alliance between disgruntled residents, unpaid workers, NGO leaders, and traffickers that helped push Ferraz and Jorginho out.

Fortunately for Vigário, the activities of other network groups began to fill the void left by the CdP. The AM, for example, started to provide some of the services that the CdP had offered by opening a number of classes for residents. An NGO formed in 1998, the Movimento de Gestão Comunitário (Movement for Community Management, MOGEC), along with the AM, provided a space from which the FUNLAR could operate. At the same time, the GCAR and the MSF continued consciousness-raising efforts and served as a check on police violence. In 2000, leaders of the GCAR used links with Viva Rio to contact state officials to demand better policing to avert a conflict between Vigário and Parada. The government intervened and, for a time, prevented conflict. The network, thus, provided a back-up system to make up for the loss of the CdP.

Community Organization: Countering Violence in Vigário

As we have seen, after the massacre, important local leaders, the survivors of victims, and many young residents who had no previous political experience all came together to change the favela. Leaders of Mocovide realized they would need outside help to get resources for the community and to bring those responsible for the massacre to justice. After the CdP was organized, the MSF and the GCAR came to Vigário to develop programs. Later, as the traffickers weakened, the AM emerged as an independent organization. These four groups formed the core of the new Vigário network.

The AM

Seu Almeida, the AM president between 1996 and 1998, was elected with the support of traffickers, but, as traffickers weakened, he staked out a new position for the organization, developed closer relations with NGOs, and used those connections to bring in new government projects. The following statement by Miguel illustrates the difficulty of the transition from trafficker to resident leadership of the AM:

> The job of president of the AM is very difficult. The police think they are working with the traffickers and the traffickers think they are working with the police. The president has to be able to convince both groups that he is working with them. Almeida's life was threatened several times. Most of [these threats were] done jokingly by Ulises [the gang leader after Flavio Negão], though you have to take those things seriously. The other time he was threatened by Flavio Negão's brother after Flavio Negão had been killed [because he] believed that Almeida had been involved in his [brother's] death.[71]

Almeida's effectiveness at bringing resources into Vigário was belied by his physical presence and demeanor. A short, heavyset, nearsighted man who was missing several fingers, Almeida had difficulty speaking. As a result of these traits and his former connections with traffickers, he inspired little confidence in residents. Mateus, an outside activist, discussed this newfound independence: "The AM could not have existed the way it is today under the traffickers. The president of the AM couldn't do much of anything. They had the support of the traffickers. . . . presidents of [the] AM had to defend what traffickers did but since it is impossible to defend traffickers eventually presidents of [the] AM took *pau* [stick]. Things were messed up in Vigário once."[72] One former AM president noted that this shift resulted in considerable improvements in the community: "Things have improved 100 percent since the massacre because of the activities of the AM and the CdP." He went on in some detail: "The international attention led to a reduction of violence in the community. More money hasn't come into the community, but it has led to an ideological reorientation that has made residents more aware of their rights and more willing to fight for them. The Associação and the Casa are now willing to make demands of the state to improve the community and reduce violence. . . . No longer are residents simply viewed as bandits. . . . Now organizations complain about violence and people are made aware of their rights."[73] The specific activities of groups in the favela, and the ways they can voice residents' concerns to the powerful, has increased public respect for residents. In 1998, residents voted to replace Almeida with his vice president, Lorivaldo, a large gregarious man who led Vigário's soccer team to the favela soccer championship final game in Maracanã stadium. Most saw him as having fewer connections with the traffickers and a more active and commanding presence. Lorivaldo kept Almeida on as his vice president. In this capacity, Almeida continued to bring resources into the favela.

NGO connections helped the AM deliver services to residents. On one occasion, the GCAR brought Tony Lloyd, then British foreign secretary, into the favela to see their project and participate in a show. During the visit, Lloyd met with Almeida and asked him what he wanted to communicate to Rio's mayor, whom Lloyd would meet with later that day. Through this contact, Almeida put pressure on the city government to deliver services to the community.[74] On another occasion, Almeida went to a GCAR show sponsored by a federal job assistance program and met with a variety of government officials. Later, this group opened a computer training program in the AM.[75] Regular community forums held in late 1997 contributed to the AM's capacity to place demands on state officials who attended the meetings. Finally, the media attention the NGOs brought to the favela reinforced the AM's efforts by keeping the favela in the press.

In addition to working with the state, the AM also helped the NGOs that were operating in the favela. A community forum, sponsored by the MSF, was held in the AM on a monthly basis in 1997 that brought together residents, NGO leaders, and city representatives to discuss community problems.[76] The AM also provided space for other activities, including an MSF community management class and a televised primary and high school completion course offered by Viva Rio. The AM used the trash collectors it paid to provide security for a concert that the GCAR held.

The elimination of traffickers had created some hardships for residents in terms of a decline in water service, fewer social activities, and higher rates of petty theft. The AM's efforts helped reduce nostalgia for traffickers by delivering some of the same services that traffickers had provided. The AM also supplemented the efforts of other groups by providing necessary local information to help them develop projects. When state officials would come to Vigário, for example, they frequently relied on the AM to help in implementing programs. This was most visible in the AM's extensive efforts to assist in an urbanization and water improvement project. The AM also resolved disputes between residents and monitored local property ownership. The strengthening of the AM and the growing connections between it and other organizations played a critical role in minimizing the social activities of traffickers during this period.

Despite all of these successes many difficulties remained. The AM constantly found itself short of money. Cynthia noted in a conversation with one older resident that "when Seu Tarcísio, Seu Roger, and Seu Luís were here there was always a box with a little money. They used to work hard on Friday and Saturday transferring property. Now no one transfers property in the *associação*. . . . No one pays attention to the *associação* anymore."[77] Further, the ongoing trafficker presence created significant tensions that boiled over into AM dispute resolution. In one particular case, Cynthia worried that Almeida might "end up with a bullet in his head if he keeps working on" a particular dispute.[78] Other residents complained that the AM was too weak to even maintain the favela's infrastructure against the predations of residents. One local homeowner said that in the past the "president was sovereign and had the force to knock down things which were improperly built. Now everything is a mess. Everyone could be a president now but couldn't be as powerful as Seu Tarcísio was."[79] Almeida complained that he had little support from residents, saying, "They won't participate in the AM but expect the AM to do things for them." Daniel, on the other hand, complained that the AM did not make enough demands and that residents needed to push them: "The AM has to know how to demand things but it doesn't. The leaders whine and don't do anything. They need force behind them. Any demand that comes out of the community must be signed by the AM. They need the AM's support, but they also need to push the AM. The AM is very willing to say that things will get done in the future, but they aren't willing to do what is necessary to get things done. The AM needs to *bater de frente* [hit things head-on]. They need the people to push them."[80] Despite these observed weaknesses, these statements about the AM reflect a clear desire to strengthen the institution. Indeed, the inability of the AM to stop the expansion of homes into the streets may have reflected a democratization of local power.

The CdP

From the time of the massacre until 1998, the CdP took a leading role in local organizing in two principal areas: controlling police violence in Vigário and in Rio more generally and reducing residents' dependence on traffickers. To this end, the CdP maintained links to the media, lawyers, and international NGOs that kept Vigário in the spotlight and pressured state officials. Unfortunately, in 1998, conflicts both within the CdP and with other favela groups caused the CdP to collapse and contributed to an upturn in violence.[81]

To bring the police accused in the massacre to justice, the leadership of the CdP stayed in touch with the lawyer for the relatives of the victims and pressured the prosecutors in the trial. During a visit of the lead prosecutor to the favela, the CdP's leadership called the press and other activists to the community.[82] During the trial of a police soldier accused in the massacre, CdP activists held a candlelight vigil outside of the courthouse.[83] On another occasion, the CdP took coffins to the court to represent the victims of the massacre.[84] These efforts kept the media's focus on Vigário. The CdP also maintained contacts with Amnesty International and the international press to promote global awareness of police violence. These activities brought to light the experiences of the powerless and made compelling demands for change.

The CdP facilitated the delivery of direct assistance to residents and ran a variety of professionalization and educational programs to provide residents with the skills to reduce dependence on traffickers. Jorginho recalled:

> The state provides no direct assistance to the community. Some aid
> to families and food goes through the Casa. In the past, a large amount of
> social aid flowed through the traffickers. Since the police have come in, the
> *boca* has been shut down and . . . the traffickers haven't been able to . . . fund
> social assistance. [This] loss . . . has been tough on the community. The main
> street in Vigário used to be five times as busy as it is now with people coming
> to the *boca* and buying drugs. The state has come in with a police presence
> and no social presence. As a result, they have suppressed the drug trade but
> not the reason why people demand it in the community. The Casa is trying
> to convince the state to increase social assistance.[85]

Among the services the CdP used to break this dependence were computer classes, televised school completion courses, and a reading room to provide children a place to study. During a major flood that inundated a third of the favela in 1998, the CdP made requests for donations through the media and arranged for food for needy residents.[86]

The CdP played a critical role in promoting NGO activities in the favela, and resources generously flowed into the organization from 1993 until 1998.[87] Both the MSF and the GCAR came into the favela through the CdP, which in the year after its founding acted as an incubator for new projects. Later, as differences emerged, the MSF and the GCAR established independent operations.[88] The CdP also attempted to bring together different local factions, including young activists, massacre survivors, and outside workers. Through 1998, the CdP helped mediate relations between traffickers and outsiders, ensuring that traffickers knew what was being planned in the community so they would not create problems.[89] This contact contributed, in part, to the CdP's collapse.

Over time, conflicts developed between the CdP and other organizations as a result of poor decision making by CdP leaders and the CdP's efforts to memorialize the massacre. A conversation between Almeida and Jorginho shows the tensions between local organizations. Almeida began by saying that he "could have killed Caio Ferraz and his father," adding that if he "were a more vengeful man I could have put Caio in the *vala* [sewer, a place bodies might be dumped] instead of the

United States." He went on: "Everybody wanted to *acertar contas* [settle accounts] with Caio and his father. When the Casa started, it was very strange for the traffickers. Flavio Negão didn't know what to make of the Casa since all of the money for it came in from the outside. The Associação used to be nice but Flavio Negão tore it down. Caio chose to have conflicts with the Associação. Many things which he did, in terms of denouncing the police, were not helpful to the community and contradicted the interests of the Associação." Jorginho, who was trying to repair relations with the AM, responded: "After Balduíno [his predecessor] took over, the Casa became even more distant from the rest of the community. It was so far away, the Associação wanted to have nothing to do with it." Almeida agreed, saying that the AM "was about a billion kilometers away from the Casa. As far as I wanted to know, it might as well have been in Niteroi [a city across Guanabara Bay]."[90] This conversation reflects the feelings at the heart of difficulties between the CdP and other groups. Almeida was angry that the CdP had distanced itself from the AM and, during a time when it was bringing in resources, that it showed little interest in working with others, seemingly hoarding largesse. Almeida also expressed near homicidal rage that the CdP had gone off on its own in denouncing police corruption, an act that resulted in Caio Ferraz fleeing the country, and which Almeida felt had put him and others in danger.

This concern with Caio Ferraz and others denouncing police reflects a tension identified by Sérgio, a filmmaker who considered making a documentary about Vigário. Sérgio reported that Almeida had said that he "wants to move on with life in the community and not continue to look back at the massacre" and denied remembering the massacre. Sérgio believed the CdP had "a negative image because it is the museum of death. The GCAR is the museum of life. Kids [there] don't talk about death, they talk about going to Europe [where the GCAR band would tour during the 1998 World Cup in France]."[91] Indeed, even within the CdP, there was some debate about the extent to which memories of the massacre should drive the CdP's image. At one point, for example, CdP activists building a web page argued about whether the links to other pages should be represented by coffins or something more uplifting. Sérgio's interpretation of the CdP's political challenges are born out by the comments of one woman, a massacre survivor, who expressed concern about testifying at the trial: "[The] community is tired. [I] don't want to go to the Valão [the big sewer] to become crab food."[92] Here, the survivor reflects the exhaustion of dealing with violence and the real fear that activism could result in her murder. The CdP was caught in these difficult emotions, which caused Almeida and the survivor to want to forget the past and made her reluctant to denounce corruption.

The failure of the CdP shows that specific political choices of NGO leaders and the social context into which those organizations are inserted can have profound affects on their long-term durability. Conflicts within networks can result in the expulsion of one network group that other members deem to be at odds with their interests. The relationship between Jorginho and Marcelinho VP posed particular problems for the entire network. The failure of the CdP resulted in decreasing pressure on the government to control violence. Networks also do not operate in a vacuum. Elements of opposing networks, such as Seu Rafael, the trafficker's ally in Parada's AM, can mobilize and build ties to other actors to destroy a group that threatens their interests. Weakness in network members can give opponent organizations the opportunity to mobilize and limit the capacity of the network. In this case, criminals worked with other groups to destroy an organization that had done much to control violence.

Perhaps the best epitaph for the CdP is heard in conversations I had with Caio Ferraz and Charles. When I met Ferraz in August 1997 he told me that he was "the biggest *malandro* from Vigário Geral. While all of the other guys who were involved in crime are either dead or in jail," he "is in the United States studying at one of the world's best universities."[93] After Ferraz had been forced from the CdP, Charles, with his usual eloquence, said that eventually the "*malandro* takes one too many steps and trips himself. *Ele dá mole a um otário.* [He gives in easily to a dupe.] Eventually the people of Vigário got rid of Caio. What Caio doesn't understand is that what was happening in the Casa is not a *golpe* [coup] by a small group but rather a movement which came out of every *beco* [dead-end street] and *viela* [alley] in the community."

The GCAR

Shortly after the CdP was founded, Mocovide activists invited the GCAR, an organization that promotes Afro-Brazilian culture, to set up a program in Vigário. Prior to this, the GCAR's primary activities involved publishing a newsletter and throwing parties where they played music from the African diaspora. The GCAR provides adolescents with dance, music, and capoeira (an Afro-Brazilian martial art) classes, as well as work opportunities and counseling. Wesley said: "[The GCAR] started four years ago after the massacre. It originally focused on getting kids out of trafficking but that has diminished because there is no significant trafficking in Vigário right now. Afro-Reggae brings people in with culture and then offers them information and community to keep them out of other things. Afro-Reggae envelops the kids when they come into the program and gives them lots of things to do . . . jobs, activities. It tries to get people to go to school. [We] give lots of information to kids about why trafficking is bad so that they will not become involved."[94] The GCAR earned the respect of residents with their daring efforts to reach at-risk teens. As Roberto put it, "When there was a *boca* we would go to the *buraco* [hole] to get people."[95] Although little is required to enter the program other than a desire to participate, members are eventually asked to attend school and break off illegal activities. The GCAR has attracted extensive international NGO support and has helped to raise awareness about violence and cultural activities in the favela.[96]

The GCAR is formally based outside of the favela, but the organization's long-term contact with the community, its investment in a headquarters building, and its integration of locals into leadership positions have helped it to be seen by residents as a community group. A GCAR leader noted:

> Afro-Reggae is a particularly good community organization because it is the only one which directly draws residents to run the organization. Wesley and others come from the community. They are trained to be leaders. Other groups bring people in from the outside to make money from the community being needy. The community isn't really needy. The people who participate in the Fundação Afro-Reggae are not needy and are not necessarily more needy than people who are from the *asfalto* [asphalted streets, parts of the city that are not favelas]. They go out into the community to recruit people to the Fundação Afro-Reggae.[97]

Cynthia and Kleber, a relative of Caio Ferraz's, conversed about this one day in the AM headquarters: "The CdP is run by Caio [Kleber adds "and his wife"] from the U.S. The Fundação Afro-Reggae is better organized. They are more democratic and include people from the community."[98] This commitment to recruiting leadership within the favela stood the GCAR in good stead with local leaders, who maintained support for the group even in difficult times.

The GCAR, the most visible group in Vigário since 1998, projected a new, more positive image for the favela. Members have traveled around the city and the world performing. The main band, which released an album in 2001, has appeared in Europe and the United States, where it gave a show at Carnegie Hall as part of a tour sponsored by Caetano Veloso, one of GCAR's *padrinhos* (godfather). GCAR would grow to include several bands, a health-awareness acting troupe, and a capoeira group. By maintaining attention on the favela long after the massacre, the GCAR built a basis for long-term organizing and reinvented local activism. The GCAR also has an agreement with another NGO to finance lawyers to assist residents in making complaints against the police. As violence increased after 1998, the GCAR provided a structure to help residents bring complaints against abusive police.[99]

The GCAR receives funding from many sources. Both Breda Rio, a bus company, and MW Barroso, a silk screener, have provided funds locally.[100] The GCAR also receives support from international sources, including the European Union, the French and Italian governments, the British Council (a UK quasi-nongovernmental organization), IBISS (a Dutch NGO), Cirque de Soleil (a Canadian dance theater troupe), and the Ford Foundation.[101] The GCAR established these contacts through their connections with the CdP and the MSF but also developed these contacts through links to other outside groups. Finally, they were sponsored by a number of prominent Brazilian artists, including Caetano Veloso and Regina Casé. The GCAR's success in obtaining funding and working with outside groups has helped other local organizations build contacts and raise money.

Despite this overall positive impression, the GCAR was occasionally criticized. Sérgio, the filmmaker, said that once he tried to converse with Roberto at an GCAR event but that Roberto ran off to talk to a funder, saying that he "had to talk to his *patrão*" (the colloquial term for boss but also patron). With some irritation, Sérgio went on: "The people at the Casa want something from you but [at least] they are good about talking to you."[102] A few residents whispered that the GCAR was more concerned with bringing money in than with helping residents. Most, however, seemed proud of the achievements that the sons and daughters of the favela had made through their participation in the GCAR. Because of the GCAR's efforts, the media began to paint Vigário in a more positive light. Correspondents appeared at the GCAR, at first to write human interest stories and later on to report on the many artistic and social events promoted by this group.

The MSF/MOGEC

The MSF is a Belgian NGO that provides medical services in conflict areas around the world. The MSF also came to Vigário after the massacre and, like the GCAR, operated out of the CdP until it established its own headquarters. In 1998, the MSF formally pulled out of Vigário. Before it left, the MSF worked with residents to set up MOGEC to carry on their work. Jaime, an AIDs activist who went on to serve in the municipal and federal governments, headed the MSF operation. He was named to the board of MOGEC in an advisory capacity and continued to have contact with the community.[103]

The MSF provided basic medical care and health education to residents through a post in the favela staffed by nurses and part-time doctors. In addition, the group provided health education classes for pregnant women and new mothers and more general classes about health and human rights. The MSF also offered community management classes to residents of Vigário and other favelas to prepare local leaders to start their own NGOs focused on community improvement and health care.[104]

The MSF helped the community obtain public funds and effective government response to resident demands. Its reaction to a flood in 1998 provides a good example of this. The day after the worst flooding, Jaime took city health officials to the most beleaguered areas of the favela. The officials quickly declared the community a disaster area, and the city moved to bring assistance to residents. Jaime's understanding of public health and his skill in dealing with bureaucrats helped in this.[105]

The MSF had a broad vision of relations among the local groups and helped to solidify the various organizations operating in the favela into a network. In 1997, Jaime organized monthly forums to bring together activists, residents, and city officials to exchange ideas to promote local collective action to redress grievances. Jaime made this clear in a speech at a meeting of a community management class the MSF offered: "People should demand changes if they don't like what is going on. Lots of things are better than they used to be, and for those improvements to be reflected people need to participate." He went on to say that he was "profoundly happy about the changes in the community."[106]

Efforts to repair a sewer pipe show the effectiveness of the forum and the broader MSF efforts. A company contracted by the city had opened a sewer pipe but had failed to close the sewer after it went bankrupt. The stagnant water in the open pipe emitted noxious odors. Numerous petitions by Almeida to the city had failed to resolve the impasse, and residents brought the issue up at several forum meetings. This gave residents the opportunity to hear city officials' arguments and to talk among themselves and with NGO leaders about what they could do to solve the problem. During one meeting and in informal conversations afterward, many expressed anger and determination to change this situation. Daniel's comments make this clear: "[We are] missing a scream of war but in peace. Vigário has no leadership. [The] hole will kill people. There was leadership before the Casa. In the past [the community] *mostrou a cara* [showed its face]; now we are prisoners in ourselves. People have to carry water [to solve this problem]."[107] Later in a private conversation, Daniel told me that "the people have to organize and take the street because they have no judicial recourse. The poor can't use the judicial system to demand change."[108] These comments, and those of others, reflected a sophisticated understanding of the political strategies available to the poor to obtain redress from the state. Some activists suggested holding a rally and circulating a petition to pressure city officials. Most leaders concurred. Residents and activists attended the protest the following Saturday. The GCAR sent a group of drummers to draw attention.[109] After these activities, the city took care of the sewer.

The community forum itself ended in 1998 when the MSF pulled out of Vigário, but the board of MOGEC was composed of a number of residents, AM leaders, and NGO activists. It continued to provide the basis for ties among the different groups in the favela and a place for ongoing conversations about the community. In the wake of the collapse of the CdP, the MOGEC went on to become one of the most important service providers in the favela. MOGEC eventually took over many of the government contracts that had gone to the CdP and was, after the return of trafficker power and the takeover of the AM by allies of the traffickers, the main interlocutor, along with the GCAR, between state agencies and the community.

Other Actors

A number of more minor groups operated around Vigário during this period. These included a worker's cooperative focused on getting jobs for residents and a crèche supported by funds from Switzerland.[110] In 1997 and 1998, the most politically active of these was the CVS, a group formed by disaffected Mocovide activists to work on the poorest segments of the favela and on environmental problems. Larger NGOs helped smaller groups obtain support from the outside and also helped in organizing new groups. The GCAR, for example, provided space for the CVS to hold meetings. By mid-1999, the CVS had started a few projects and had begun to build a headquarters.[111]

Some residents and activists worked independently to help others. For example, during the 1998 flood, activists aided residents whose homes were inundated. During the flood, Rúbia, the restaurant owner, asked outsiders to donate food, which, with the help of friends, she delivered to residents.[112]

The State

The Brazilian state is neither a coherent nor an efficient entity, but government officials have helped groups active in the favela control violence. Some state representatives actively engaged network members and pushed other state actors, such as police, to limit conflict. Over time, officials supported programs to improve local living conditions.

Following resident demands, high-level state officials implemented new policing and public works policies. In 1996, Marcelo Alencar, then governor of Rio, ordered the police to occupy the favela and addressed infrastructural problems. After a series of petitions and public mobilizations driven by forum meetings and undertaken by local NGOs, the city fixed the sewer.[113] During election seasons, politicians provided resources to make local improvements.

Career bureaucrats also play a role in these networks in helping implement large government projects. City engineers spent time in the favela listening to leaders and ensuring that contractors correctly completed the project. The head of a water project, for example, regularly spoke with AM leaders to ensure that the project met community needs.[114]

The Brazilian state is an extremely heterogeneous institution that contains many who operate within the law, others who break the law, and some who do both. State actors concerned about controlling crime and those who work with criminals are often political competitors. Groups in the state concerned with controlling violence build alliances to help control other state actors with whom they disagree.

Difficulties Created by the Breakdown of the Trafficker Network

The growing importance of NGOs and the weakening of the traffickers created new challenges that groups operating in the community had to find ways to deal with. Events during the 1998 national elections showed some of the challenges facing the favela in the wake of the failure of the trafficker network. With the AM seemingly uninterested in working with political candidates, Rúbia took it upon herself to bring a candidate for state deputy to the favela. This candidate hired a few residents to campaign for him and funded repairs to a soccer field that traffickers had originally built. His campaign posters carried the name of the gubernatorial candidate from his party. The traffickers, however, supported a left-leaning gubernatorial candidate and asked Rúbia to take the signs down. She refused. A more powerful trafficker then arrived from another favela and had local gang members kidnap her boyfriend and hold him at gun point. Eventually, Rúbia compromised and removed the name of the gubernatorial candidate from the posters.[115]

Without a connection to the AM, the local traffickers did not possess the political capital or skills to directly go out and establish ties to a politician who would deliver services to the community. The AM, which was quite well connected politically, likely chose not to bring in a candidate, specifically to avoid this type of conflict. Without an ally in the AM, the traffickers lost control of the clientelist process. This created difficulties, since the larger gang that the traffickers were affiliated with, the CV, supported a specific gubernatorial candidate. Without having a direct hand in determining the stipulations of the agreement between Rúbia and the candidate, the traffickers had little control over what signs went up in the community.[116] Finally, without a link to the AM, the traffickers seemed to have no skilled political mediator to deal with Rúbia. As a result, the traffickers had to resort to violence to achieve an acceptable outcome. In political terms, they embarrassed themselves. Although they succeeded in removing the name of the candidate from the signs, the traffickers alienated residents and, despite a partial monopoly on local violence, did not even achieve their initial objective of removing the signs.

The weakness of the traffickers also led many homeowners to complain of increasing theft, saying they could no longer leave their doors unlocked. One man standing in the street, as NGO workers asked residents to evacuate their homes during the flood in 1998, said, "Most people aren't going to leave because they are afraid of getting robbed. There didn't used to be robbery in the community but things have gotten *mole* [soft, easy] now. Inferninho [a poor neighborhood near the river] is where most of the robbery is going on."[117] Another resident, speaking with Cynthia, expressed a longing for the order that traffickers had created in the past: "Things have been a mess here since Flavio Negão was killed. [There is] lots of *bagunça* [mess, confusion]. . . . People need more order."[118] To make matters worse, the decline in drug trafficking decreased the number of addicts who, after purchasing drugs, would stop at local bars to purchase drinks or snacks. This led to economic stagnation in the favela. As a result, a resident complained that despite additional medical services provided by the MSF, residents were not as well off as with traffickers in power, because they did not have the money to buy the drugs they were prescribed. NGOs, hence, tried to stave off nostalgia for the trafficking organization.

Success of the Network

Associative network connections, that bring groups together, helped change conditions in Vigário by facilitating communication and learning between groups, enabling groups to specialize within a network, transferring legitimacy between members, helping members support and compensate for each other, and, finally, creating a level of economic and political efficiency they could not have achieved on their own. At the heart of network success are loose and malleable ties that, as Mark Granovetter has suggested, allow groups to engage in different types of activities.[119]

Meetings of network members, whether formally through the community forum, or more casually in the streets, helped to keep activists aware of local problems, share ideas, and make decisions. A good example of this was the effort to close the sewer pipe. The AM, acting independently, had petitioned the city to fix the pipe, but only when local leaders met together to discuss the problem, debated possible solutions, and, finally, choose a collective course of action did the city respond. The network helped local groups build ties to like-minded organizations outside the community and allowed members to use contacts with the media to maintain pressure on the state and attract outside funding. Charles's creation of the sculpture made of bullet casings in conjunction with the CdP and community children, for example, produced a symbolic work that drew national and international press attention. By working together, network members also learned from each other. We can see this in the MSF's efforts to train activists in community management and the creation of MOGEC. Residents said that they learned about fund-raising techniques from NGO activists.

The Vigário network also succeeded as a result of the ability of members to specialize in what they did best. Thus, the GCAR focused on cultural education and work, the CdP pursued police accountability and professionalization courses, the MSF concentrated on health care, and the AM worked on bettering community infrastructure. By contributing with their strengths, these networked actors solved problems more effectively than a single group could have and avoided some of the intense political pressure that would have come to bear on any single group that tried to address all these questions.

This contrasts with other favelas discussed in this study that have fewer organizations and fail to meet residents' needs. In those cases, criminals provide assistance or take control of the groups delivering services. Thus, as we saw in Santa Ana, while the AM maintains the local infrastructure, traffickers provide medical care and entertainment. This is not to say that the traffickers do a good job at providing services, but that they provide better services than would otherwise be available. By offering a single service efficiently, groups in Vigário chipped away at the services that traffickers provided. Ultimately, by working together, network members provided much more extensive and effective services than traffickers could.

Specialization creates a resilient source of opposition to violent practices. If a single group succeeded in providing the services the CdP, GCAR, MSF, and AM provided, its concentrated power may have made traffickers very uncomfortable. This type of situation leads to traffickers either lashing out against the leadership of their opposition or trying to co-opt them.[120] But it takes greater work to co-opt five separate groups than to co-opt one large one. By working independently, each group engaged in fairly innocuous activities that only chipped away at a bit of trafficker power while helping residents. Even so, the traffickers contributed to efforts to close the CdP. Collectively, however, the network undermined trafficker power and changed state policy. The same logic applies to the relationship between the community and violent police. Each of the organizations active in Vigário attracted attention to police violence in different ways and put different types of pressure on the government. Since each group focused on their own efforts, the police did not single out any one as responsible for creating trouble.

The exception that proves the rule was Caio Ferraz's exile from Brazil. When Ferraz left, the GCAR itself had yet to come into its own and traffickers still had some control over the AM.[121] As president, Ferraz took the lead in denouncing police abuses. This resulted in death threats and his exile. A more active network may have been able to deflect attention away from Ferraz and may have limited his own need to aggressively denounce police as other leaders took up part of this burden.

Finally, specialization allowed groups to simultaneously adopt different political strategies. The GCAR worked through outside NGOs and engaged in artistic efforts to raise awareness and improve Vigário's image. The MSF used connections to the international NGO community to raise local concerns and worked with health officials to better conditions. The CdP led protests and helped to bring the police accused of the massacre to justice. By specializing in different activities, groups in Vigário could engage in contradictory strategies, while working together to improve the favela. Thus, a group like the CdP could take the lead in putting people in the streets protesting violence, while leaders of the MSF could take the case directly to the same state officials that the CdP protested.

The network also helped transfer legitimacy among member groups and build trust with residents. For example, the MSF and the GCAR originally set up their operations in the CdP and had come into the favela at the invitation of local activists. Without an anchor, these groups would have had trouble setting up operations since residents and traffickers would not have trusted them and thus would not have had access to residents. Conversely, residents and activists in Vigário gained credibility with the government, the NGOs, and the media as a result of their attachment to other outsiders. The MSF and GCAR built links between residents, bureaucrats, and foreign officials who control much of the aid that flows into Rio's favelas. Almeida, for example, met with the British foreign minister, Tony Lloyd, who offered to carry a message to Rio's mayor after a GCAR event.[122] Further, residents' claims about police abuse in the favela became more credible because of their repetition in Amnesty International and Human Rights Watch reports. Contacts with outsiders who had credibility with government officials and the media gave legitimacy to local claims. At the same time, outsiders working in Vigário increased their credibility with government officials. As Charles put it, "Rubém César [Fernandes] is a guy from Ipanema who made a name for his organization [Viva Rio] through the [Vigário massacre]. Manoel Ribeiro is a mediocre architect who has been able to make a name for himself through his relationship with Vigário and will make a lot of money."[123] One can certainly disagree with the tone of this statement (both Rubem César Fernandes and Manoel Ribeiro contributed in important ways to efforts to control violence), but it is clear that outsiders benefited from links to Vigário.

The participation of multiple groups in the favela allowed political activism to continue when one member group was destroyed. When Caio Ferraz went into exile, other member groups continued to operate. Since the network had no leader, the removal of one actor did little to endanger the entire organization. When the CdP closed, it did hurt the network. Nevertheless, although other groups engaged in different activities, those groups remained active and worked to help the community. Since a network continued to operate in Vigário, new groups could come in and develop new projects, as occurred when Onda Azul set up operations in the favela.

Having multiple groups active in the favela created a system of peer monitoring that forced organizations to operate in ways consistent with the interests of residents and other network members. For example, when it became clear that many were dissatisfied with the CdP, NGOs and activists removed the CdP's leadership. Groups that formed later used organizational models that had broad local support. As we can see in the case of the CdP, the observation of the activities of groups also ensured that groups did not become involved in illegal activities.

Finally, the network created economic efficiencies. MW Barroso's links to the favela provide an example of this. After the network formed, Barroso, which had long provided money to the AM, continued to work with the AM but also helped the CdP and the GCAR. Similarly, the MSF introduced GCAR leaders to European Union representatives, who then provided them with funding, and Viva Rio helped put the leaders of Mocovide in touch with an evangelical NGO leader who helped purchase CdP headquarters.

The End of the Counternetwork and the Reemergence of Violence

Despite the collapse of the CdP, network members continued to control violence until well into the new decade.[124] Nevertheless, as time went by, traffickers played a larger role in the community and violence made a slow and steady comeback. Residents date the real return in violence to the building of a highway connection directly into the community, which decreased the need for cooperation between Vigário's and Parada's traffickers. Increasingly, Vigário's gang began to host *baile funks* (which police had prohibited between 1996 and 1998) and, with the death of the important traffickers involved in the 1993 massacre, developed new ties to the police. Traffickers forced Lorivaldo, then AM president, from power and replaced him with one of their relatives.

In July 2003, the situation deteriorated when traffickers from Parada invaded, massacred a number of Vigário traffickers, and threatened to kill residents. One local NGO leader said that he had attempted to get in touch with reporters and state officials to initiate a quick response, but they had shown little interest in doing anything. Traffickers from Vigário regrouped and drove the Parada traffickers out. A day later, the police briefly sent in an occupation force, but the damage had been done. A new war had begun, and residents had started to look to criminals again for protection. In the month immediately after this attack, there were no new initiatives from the state government, which, under the administration of Rosinha Garotinho—the wife of Anthony Garotinho, a former presidential candidate, and, at the time, state secretary for public security—seemed to have little interest in directly addressing violence in the favela.

On 29 August 2003, local leaders held a small memorial service to commemorate the tenth anniversary of the massacre. For all that had happened in the previous month, the event was remarkably subdued. A full-scale war erupted in Vigário in October 2004 when Parada traffickers invaded Vigário, forcing hundreds of residents into the streets of nearby neighborhoods. The NGOs that still operate in Vigário, principally MOGEC and the GCAR, have been unable to force the state to restrict this violence. Despite ten years of organizing, Vigário had returned to some of its earlier obscurity and conflict.

The Failure of the Vigário Counternetwork

Efforts to counter violence in both Vigário Geral and Tubarão resulted in dramatic drops in violence for periods of two to three years. In both communities, collaborations among local leaders, outside activists, and state officials (including police) achieved significant results. Nevertheless, despite continued activism in Vigário, these coalitions unraveled and violence returned.

Civic networking as a solution to entrenched social violence has clear limits when confronting the structural and institutional factors that favor violence. Rio is one of Latin America's largest ports, and it plays a role in the growing global drug trade. A significant retail drug trade exists in the city that infuses money into the criminal marketplace. High levels of inequality, low levels of government social spending, and limited opportunities for upward social mobility force many poor people to look for work in the informal sector. Some of these informal workers are drawn into the lucrative narcotics economy. Amid all of this, the state is unable to adequately pay police. This encourages corruption and inadequate law enforcement. Many politicians see favelas simply as sources of cheap votes they can obtain through small social projects and pay-offs to traffickers. There is little inclination on the part of political leaders to adopt serious long-term plans to deal with the institutional and structural factors that favor social violence.

This environment makes local-level reform attempts a dubious proposition. It is to the credit of Vigário's residents and the state officials and activists involved in these projects that they were able to take the massacre and, unlike so many similar tragedies in Rio, turn it into the beginning of a broad-based localized movement to demand better policing. While people remained active and the massacre itself stayed at the forefront of public thought about Vigário, these groups suppressed the abuses of traffickers and police. As the massacre and the events that led it to it receded from memory, however, things began to unravel. Successful activists moved on to other jobs, leadership changed, the press lost interest, and state leaders felt less pressure to closely monitor local policing. This allowed traffickers, who had never really gone away, to begin to reassert themselves in what proved to be a divided community prone to internal conflict. They threatened local leaders and established constraints on the activities of NGOs operating in the favela. Residents, and local leaders, cowed by a lack of outside support and resurgent trafficker audacity, could not continue to mount pressure to control violence. The vast majority of local activists will eventually tire and stop protesting when subject to constant threats. In Vigário, as in Tubarão, this appears to have been the case. In one form or another, criminals, who had much to gain from remaining in the community and controlling the narcotics trade there, stayed on through the entire period of NGO activism. After state and social interest in the favela began to wane and some of the most successful activists moved out of the favela, the traffickers who remained reasserted themselves.

Ultimately, civic mobilization does not occur in a vacuum. Traffickers and other violent actors can strategize against groups concerned with controlling violence and work to undermine groups that oppose them. To understand how to control violence, the data in this chapter show that we need to understand not just how groups organize but how they deal with opponent groups that might want to increase violence.

Local organizing can control conflict over the medium term. Studying successful reforms is worthwhile because we can build on their successes. Nonetheless, given the structural and institutional conditions that favor violence, these mobilizations are like pushing a boulder up an endless hill. Eventually, the groups that do the work tire and the boulder rolls back down. For focused mobilization to have any chance to succeed, the state must work to correct institutional flaws that lead to violence, deal with broader structural issues that contribute to crime, and work to support and broaden local efforts to control violence to encompass a larger number of neighborhoods and individuals.

Conclusion

This chapter provides further support for the arguments made in the chapters on Tubarão and Santa Ana. Evidence from before the massacre shows that traffickers depended on networks of civic leaders and politicians to provide services to residents and engage in criminal activity. The data from Vigário suggest that criminals actively worked to penetrate the AM and to maintain positive relations with some residents.

In terms of controlling violence, the Vigário case shows that the organization of a network focused on promoting human rights provided the political capital to force the state to implement a more effective policing program, while ensuring that police did not violate residents' rights and, through NGOs, developing programs to reduce residents' dependence on traffickers. The anger created by the 1993 massacre and specific conditions in Rio at the time triggered the emergence of this network. Vigário's experience suggests a few factors that are critical in creating viable opposition to illegal networks. First, as we saw in Tubarão and Ceuzinho, there has to be some group active within the community that is not tightly affiliated with criminals and that can serve as a bridge to the outside. A number of external organizations then either have to set up operations in the favela or other groups have to emerge within the community to pressure the state and provide assistance to residents. Second, community groups need to have the capacity to build links with outside institutions. Third, organizations active in the favela need to focus on solving limited problems so as to attract little attention while working on bigger issues.

Unlike Tubarão, where reform was a top-down effort initiated by state actors and Viva Rio, Vigário's reforms were part of a bottom-up process led by residents who built ties to better-off social activists and political entrepreneurs, who, in turn, helped build links to state officials and international actors. In Tubarão, outsiders interested in addressing Tubarão's problems spent considerable time overcoming the residents' resistance. In Vigário, on the other hand, the principal problem was not gaining residents' acceptance but, rather, was maintaining outside interest and overcoming the challenges created by the intense infighting among constituencies involved in those projects.

At the same time, Vigário and Tubarão reflect enormous similarities. In both communities, activities that controlled violence involved police reform, NGO intervention, and internal mobilization. Resident monitoring helped control police violence and corruption in both places. In Vigário and Tubarão, when police reform was combined with the establishment of internal monitoring mechanisms and programs to help residents ease their dependence on traffickers, violence decreased precipitously.

In the end, both projects slowly unraveled for similar reasons. Each favela suffered a degree of political fatigue. It takes a lot of energy and sacrifice to maintain a program to control police and trafficker violence. In both places, those involved gradually lost interest in undertaking the arduous activities necessary to keep these programs going. Further, in each case, leaders willing to take public stands against either police or criminals were forced out. Finally, both programs were victims of their own success. As violence dropped, the press lost interest, pressure decreased on the state, and successful outside program leaders moved on to better jobs. Despite these early successes, illegal networks returned and violence again increased in each case.

One could argue that conflict decreased in Vigário not because of the network but because of the immense media attention attracted to the favela as a result of the massacre. Undoubtedly, media attention had an effect, just as the heavy coverage of the riots outside Tubarão led to that police reform program. Media attention alone, however, was not enough to decrease bloodshed. Violence is all too common in Rio's favelas, where many multiple murders have occurred over the last ten years. All of this violence, however, does not necessarily lead to the type of press attention that helps control conflict, since most journalists' only access to dangerous favelas comes through the police, and press reports tend to reflect their perspective.[125] NGOs in Vigário played a critical institutional role in getting word out about violence. The effect of the network in reducing conflict can best be seen in the timing of violence reduction in Vigário. The massacre and massive press attention to the favela occurred in 1993. The favela, however, did not experience a dramatic decrease in violence until late 1996 when the police occupied the community. In the intervening three years, groups operating in Vigário maintained press attention on the favela, and, only after years of work, did the government make the changes in policing policy that led to a decrease in violence. Only by consistently pressuring the government over time did groups in the favela improve local conditions. The next chapter will examine how networks operate in other parts of Brazil and Latin America.

SIX

Comparative Analysis of Criminal Networks in Brazil and Latin America

The foregoing chapters have outlined a model of criminal networks and provided evidence of their structure and operation in Rio de Janeiro's favelas. Criminals operate through functionally organized networks that bring them together with actors in state and civil society. These interactions give traffickers access to existing political networks and social capital that enable them to buy protection, build the support necessary to maintain ongoing criminal activities, and co-opt some of their potential opposition, thereby undermining state and social efforts to control violence.

Through an examination of data from four Brazilian cities and from other Latin American countries, this chapter will look at how criminal networks operate beyond Rio. This evidence will show that networks, in different localized forms, play an essential role in enabling criminal activity throughout the region.

Drug Trafficking in Rio de Janeiro

The structure of trafficking in Rio emerges out of the particular political and social circumstances that exist in the city. The combination of having Brazil's second-largest port and airport facilities, along with mass poverty located in areas with difficult outside access, results in an ideal environment for drug transshipment. High-level traffickers buy their way into political power and operate in the city through mediators, who connect them to both the powerful in state government and to the poor usually nonwhite men who take most of the risks in holding and protecting their drugs. Lower-level drug traffickers reproduce these arrangements within and between particular favelas to protect themselves from arrest and attack.

Crime in Other Parts of Brazil

The past several years have seen a stabilization of Rio's overall homicide rates while the rates of homicides in other major cities of southeastern and southern Brazil have exploded. A good deal of this change has resulted from the saturation of the consumer markets for cocaine in Rio and São Paulo and the efforts of criminal entrepreneurs to develop new markets in other municipalities. The specific nature of criminal activities and the particular local social and political issues in different places have affected the growth of criminal networks in Vitória, Belo Horizonte, Porto Alegre, and São Paulo.

Vitória: High-Level Criminal Networking

Vitória, the capital of the state of Espírito Santo (just north of Rio de Janeiro), has one of the highest per capita murder rates in Brazil. A seemingly sleepy, wealthy, and peaceful city, in the late 1990s, Vitória experienced a massive increase in homicides, jumping from around 55 per 100,000 inhabitants in the early 1990s to more than 100 per 100,000 later in the decade. In 1999, Vitória led Brazil in homicide rates per inhabitant, with 107 homicides per 100,000 residents. At the heart of violence in this state is the Scuderie Detetive Le Cocq (The Shield of Detective Le Cocq, SDLC), a remnant of the police execution teams formed in the 1950s and 1960s in Rio. The SDLC was initially organized to avenge the murder of the eponymous detective and death squad leader. Under the dictatorship, the group, which was structured as a "charitable" entity, grew into a statewide and then interstate network of death squads. In the 1970s, the Espírito Santo SDLC, which had a particularly tight relationship with the military-appointed governor of that state, began to traffic in illegal arms and drugs. The group, which was seen as a threat to central power by Brazil's ruling generals, came under intense political pressure, and some members were even prosecuted during the dictatorship.[1] The Espírito Santo SDLC, however, survived and during the 1990s counted among its number hundreds of "members of the political establishment," including state and federal police, business owners, politicians, prosecutors, and judges.[2] Although this group had a long involvement in local business dealings and "cleansing" operations against the city's poor, over the course of the 1990s it greatly expanded the scope of its activities and political power, as the organization involved itself more directly in large-scale drug trafficking and racketeering.[3] The driving force behind this shift was the displacement of powerful *bicheiros* (illegal lottery bankers) from Rio, who developed operations in this town to take advantage of lucrative public works projects and Brazil's third-largest port. At its height, the president of the Espírito Santo Legislative Assembly directed a large-scale corruption scheme that involved the awarding of state contracts to a *bicheiro* and his allies who, in exchange, provided heavy pay-offs.[4] A report by Global Justice lists the murders of nine prominent opponents, including a priest and various trade unionists. The same report also lists extensive threats against police and prosecutors investigating the SDLC.[5] All told, police actively took part in killings and received bribes, not only to look the other way on the issue of state contracts, but also to allow an expansion of drug trafficking through Vitória's port.

Things became so bad here that the government of Fernando Henrique Cardoso and then the government of Luiz Inácio Lula da Silva, at the behest of a federal senator representing the state, decided to intervene and took over the public security apparatus.[6] A federal police *delegado* (investigative police officer) with a reputation for honesty took charge of a corruption investigation and large-scale police reforms. The *delegado* worked jointly with public prosecutors, other federal police, and the justice ministry to investigate organized crime in the state and to force elected representatives, including the president of the Legislative Assembly, out of office. This seems to have had some effect in controlling rampant crime.[7] Federal prosecutors eventually succeeded in having the SDLC's nonprofit status revoked.

Vitória conforms to the expectations of criminal networking and politics laid out in this book. A network of actors from the criminal underworld, the business community, the political world, and the bureaucracy came together through the Scuderie to undertake the wholesale looting of the state treasury and the murder of their opponents. Connections to criminals provided the necessary expertise in illegal activities. Political links gave criminals access to the government budget and the port. Business leaders undertook illegal state contracts and provided kickbacks to bribe police and elected officials. Judges stopped possible investigations. Finally, police and criminals supplied the muscle to keep the complex operation in place. Through diffuse organizing and operations in different segments of society, this group engaged in large-scale criminal operations over the course of more than a decade.

The complex structure of the network made crime control quite difficult. Few important actors from the state tried to attack the network. Those who did took substantial personal and professional risks. In one particularly disturbing case, a witness for an investigation of the Scuderie was assassinated while in federal police custody.[8]

The location and political conditions in Espírito Santo determined the structure of criminal activity there. With a population of only 1 million in the metropolitan area and few favelas central to the city, Vitória did not develop into a major site of narcotics consumption or provide effective places to hide and protect drugs. A sleepy state, wedged in Brazil's industrial heartland, the town provided an ideal place for extensive corruption. Criminals were well located to build contacts and develop operations in the area but faced little competition from locals. Further, as a small state in the hands of a small political elite, Espírito Santo provided criminals with ample opportunities to build links to legitimate actors and gain access to government resources. In the end, an illegal network developed around criminals from other states working with local leaders to extract government resources for private exploitation and used criminals and police to maintain their hold on those illegal activities.

The role of the SDLC in Espírito Santo politics raises questions about the broader activities of death squads in Brazil. In recent years, death squads have not had such a prominent political impact in other states, but their activities provide insights into how violence is privatized in different places and, in particular, the different forms of networks that can emerge to cross the state/society and legal/illegal frontiers. Martha Huggins has suggested that death squads were a critical form of liminal actors initially sanctioned by the state to engage in extralegal political repression that began, especially in the later years of the dictatorship, to cross the line into clearly illegal activities, such as drug trafficking and arms smuggling. As the state encouraged, permitted, and enabled public security officers to work outside the law, other state representatives became increasingly implicated in these activities. Police operating in death squads had superiors who knew what they did, and they had friends in other segments of the public security apparatus who occasionally needed their help. The result was a further weakening of state control over these units and, as the dictatorship gave way to civilian government, a failure to reestablish centralized legal control over the state's sprawling violence machinery. Today death squads, such as the SDLC, are involved in a host of illegal activities and play important roles in different types of criminal networks in Brazil.[9]

Belo Horizonte: A Secondary Consumer Market and Effective Public Response

Belo Horizonte, a major metropolitan area and the capital of Minas Gerais (a historically and economically important state that borders Rio and São Paulo), has recently developed a strong consumer narcotics market. Over the course of the 1990s, violent crime rates doubled—from around 100 per 100,000 to around 200 per 100,000 inhabitants.[10] Murder rates, which were once very low, reached 35 per

100,000 in the late 1990s. The six Belo Horizonte favelas that had a prominent role in the retail drug trade accounted for a significant percentage of the skyrocketing homicide levels.[11] These communities had two important things in common: a close proximity to the wealthy regions of the city and, as in Rio, locations on hillsides that made police intervention difficult.[12] Many believe that the presence of "crack" cocaine has contributed to the city's growing violence.[13]

Although corruption here is not as bad as in Espírito Santo or Rio, there is significant evidence of police malfeasance, ranging from petty graft to actual police-managed drug dealing operations. In 2003, a group of civil police forced prostitutes working around the central business district to sell narcotics.[14] In at least one case, police worked closely with a drug trafficker who ran a favela. In other cases, significant amounts of low-level corruption occurred, in which traffickers bribed police. The most serious corruption is concentrated in the civil police.[15] There is some evidence of police impunity, especially among the civil police, who have been involved in killings of suspects and others who have in some way offended members of this force.[16]

Criminal networks do not appear to extend broadly in the state, but they do appear to have had a significant effect on social life in the most violent favelas. In these places, gangs have not fully developed, although in a few areas they have taken over official civic groups. As in Rio de Janeiro, some criminals also provided social assistance to residents.[17] Nevertheless, as of June 2003, the drug trade had not fully consolidated, even in these violent favelas. In a number of cases, multiple small gangs operated in each favela and competed for control of territory, principally for affective reasons. These gangs were not uniformly involved in the drug trade, although some members associated with particular traffickers who operated in the community, dealt drugs for them, and helped protect and expand turf. Other gang members would occasionally deal drugs or fight under contract to defend territory against encroaching outside gangs and dealers.[18]

Belo Horizonte offers significant evidence of the success of networking in controlling crime. A group of academics based at the Universidade Federal de Minas Gerais (UFMG) have long worked to build ties to police. This started during the democratization process when one senior PM officer sought advice from a UFMG professor on how to adapt policing techniques to the newly emerging democratic system. This resulted in a collaboration that led to a series of classes. Eventually all senior police were required to take these classes. These contacts led a mayor of Belo Horizonte to ask UFMG social scientists to conduct an extensive crime-mapping project in the city.[19] Using close contacts with the police, the academics helped build a system of uniform crime reporting and data entry that led to the production of an annual series of local crime maps, resulting in the best crime data set in Brazil. The program at UFMG has received funding from the Ford Foundation, and UFMG faculty have traveled in Latin America, the United States, and Europe to discuss their work.[20]

In collaboration with UFMG, the PM set up a community policing program in the city that used the data from the crime-mapping survey as a basis for new crime prevention efforts.[21] The program was based around community policing councils formed in each of the twenty-five companies of the PM and distributed around the city.[22] These councils provided a space for public debate about security issues and allowed neighborhood residents to participate in establishing local public safety priorities. Early feedback was positive. Overall crime rates in the city, which had increased nearly fivefold between 1995 and 2000, leveled off after the implementation of this project. Violent crime rates in eleven of the twenty-five council districts dropped in 2001, and in ten of the remaining sixteen districts crime rose at lower rates than in the previous year. In the remaining districts, significant increases in crime rates continued, although at less spectacular rates than in the previous two years.[23] Poor communities suffering from high levels of armed violence benefited from this program the least. One major reason for this was that the government expected local civic groups to subsidize improvements in policing. Less well-off communities, of course, could not make these types of contributions. In some poor areas, residents derisively labeled this program *"polícia chapéu na mão"* (police with hat in hand).[24]

In response to the limitations of this broader community policing initiative, a more intense and targeted community-oriented program called Fica Vivo! was implemented in particularly violent favelas.[25] This program, developed in a collaboration among city and state officials and UFMG faculty, explicitly uses local networking and social capital building strategies to construct links among state service actors, police, and community residents to address crime. In the places where it was implemented, it resulted in a 47 percent decrease in homicides in 2003.[26] These efforts suggest that, as in Vigário Geral, Ceuzinho, and Tubarão, effective contacts between favela residents, community leaders, police, state actors, and civil society, represented here by university faculty, can help control violence over the medium term.

Porto Alegre: Corruption and Trafficking in the South

Porto Alegre, the capital of Rio Grande do Sul in the far south of Brazil, faces many of the same problems as Belo Horizonte, but without the type of effective civil society–state collaboration that has helped ameliorate problems there. As with other second-tier state capitals in Brazil, Porto Alegre has experienced a rapid expansion of the illegal drug trade over the past several years. Homicide rates in the city have increased from around 40 per 100,000 residents in the mid-1990s to around 60 per 100,000 at the turn of the century.[27] The mortality associated with this, as in other parts of Brazil, is concentrated in poor areas of the city, which are also generally underserved by the state.[28] Criminals operating within the impoverished communities, as in Belo Horizonte, cannot keep police at bay but do provide some services to community residents to build local support, and they also work to prevent other crimes in the favelas they operate in. Police reported that traffickers provided loans, money, and basic security to poor communities. Criminals also used resources to buy off investigative police when they were arrested. As in Belo Horizonte, criminal gangs are smaller than in Rio and hire contract killers to carry out murders.[29] Current and former governments have rigorously pursued corruption, and in 2002 prosecutors brought some police up on corruption charges.[30]

During the period between 1998 and 2002, the administration of PT governor Olívio Dutra attempted limited community-oriented reforms. Working in one of the most violent outlying areas of the city, reformers within the police, actors in civil society, and academics undertook building a community council in one neighborhood to work with police to address pressing local problems. In order to help with this program, the government provided significant amounts of state aid to the population. The plan reportedly decreased violence dramatically in the community. Luiz Eduardo Soares, a sociology professor and former national secretary for public security, who had worked in developing the community policing program in Rio and who had collaborated on a number of Viva Rio's projects in the 1990s, played a major role in this program. One senior police officer in charge of reform efforts noted that his interest in changing the police came out of contacts that he had with Soares while studying for a postgraduate degree at a local university.[31] The reforms discussed here collapsed after the transition from the PT to the more centrist government of Germano Rigotto, who had campaigned on a zero-tolerance policy.[32]

Despite a reputation for professionalism, the Brigada Militar, Rio Grande do Sul's PM, is a deeply divided institution that experiences what seem to be moderate levels of petty corruption but that today has an almost paramilitary attitude toward crime control. The Rigotto administration defunded community-oriented reforms and put in place a conservative hierarchy, heavily criticized by reformers in the state during the time in which I visited, within the police that has pursued an extremely hard-line, anticrime policy, contributing to violence in the city, while doing little to reduce crime. One senior police officer interviewed stated that he thought it was good that police kill possible criminals in armed confrontations and that he believed that "racial miscegenation" led to much of the violence that Brazil experiences today.[33]

São Paulo: The Big City

Unlike the other cities discussed in this section, high levels of homicide are nothing new to São Paulo. Like Rio, international trafficking penetrated the city over fifteen years ago, causing a spike in violence in the 1980s and 1990s. This city of 20 million people does not have the dramatic hillside geography of Rio, and, as a result, drug dealing is diffused across the metropolitan area. Traffickers do not have the same degree of geographical control of parts of the city as in Rio. There is some indication that crime in São Paulo is much more diverse than in other areas of the country because of the city's large legal marketplace. The overall levels of wealth enable extensive bank robberies, burglaries, kidnappings, and other crimes.

In general, illegal organization is considerably more diffuse in this environment. For the most part, criminals in São Paulo organize themselves into specialized crews dealing with particular crimes. Since territory is not a primary concern, criminals put little effort into organizing defensive capabilities. Rather, as in Belo Horizonte and Porto Alegre, traffickers often contract out murders to third parties.

The most prominent gang in the state is Primeiro Comando do Capital (First Command of the Capital, PCC). The PCC is a prison gang with the ability to strike outside the prison system. São Paulo criminals affiliate to guarantee their safety when arrested.[34] Members outside prison pay a regular fee to maintain their connection. The gang staged a series of prison uprisings in 2000 and 2001 in response to the terrible conditions of detention common in Brazil. Later PCC affiliates set off bombs in the city to pressure government officials and draw attention to the gang's concerns. The government responded by transferring powerful members to a super maximum security prison in the state's interior. These efforts, however, seem to have had only a limited effect. In May 2006, in response to fears that more members would be transferred to the super maximum prison and as a result of information sold by a sound technician working for a Brazilian congressional committee on arms trafficking, the PCC staged prison rebellions and carried out attacks on police and civilians throughout the city resulting in the murder of forty-two police and a number of civilians. Police retaliated by killing over one hundred people they accused of being bandits. The confrontation only concluded when the state government apparently negotiated with high-level gang members to provide some limited improvements in prison conditions in exchange for an end to the attacks.[35]

Like law enforcement agencies in other parts of Brazil, São Paulo's police are also known for corruption and violence. Police death squads have acted with impunity throughout the metropolitan area.[36] Efforts to put down prison rebellions have led to mass killings. The most famous case occurred in 1993 when an uprising at the Carandiru prison in metropolitan São Paulo led to a police operation that resulted in the deaths of 111 prisoners at the hands of state public security forces.

Of all the cases I examined, I found the least evidence of criminal networking in São Paulo. The diffuse nature of criminality limits emergence of powerful criminal networks. In the end, however, criminals clearly operate through low-level networks that bring them together with other criminals and some actors in the state. There is also fairly extensive evidence of serious political corruption throughout the metropolitan area.[37]

The Operation of Criminal Networks in Latin America

The evidence presented thus far suggests the existence of functional criminal networks in Brazilian cities that bring together civic, state, and criminal actors to engage in illegal activities. The persistence of these networks provides ongoing political challenges to order in numerous urban areas. This section will look at the similarities and differences between criminal networks in Brazil and other parts of Latin America.

Colombia

In terms of criminal activities, Colombia has become almost a caricature for the rest of Latin America. Brazilian newspaper writers anxiously wring their hands about the "Colombianization" of Rio.[38] The U.S. government pumps billions of dollars into Colombia in the hope of stopping cocaine exports. As a result of its position as a drug-producing country and as the center of illegal entrepreneurial activity, Colombia brings in a huge amount of money every year through the drug economy. Estimates vary broadly, but the cocaine trade probably accounts for three to five billion dollars in earnings for the economy, or approximately 10 percent of the gross domestic product.[39] Between 1980 and 1995, the country experienced 300,000 murders.[40] The cocaine trade has empowered criminals and guerrillas, undermined state institutions, and provoked a generalized crisis of political legitimacy.[41]

On some levels, Colombia radically differs from Brazil and other countries in Latin America. As the center of the international narcotics trade and a major producer of cocaine, Colombia and its Andean neighbors face challenges that the rest of the region does not. On the other hand, like Brazil, Colombian criminals have organized through networks that bring them together with state and civic actors, much in the same way that occurs in Brazil.

The current situation in Colombia is immensely complex. Guerrillas, trafficking cartels, and paramilitary organizations operate as loose coalitions with similar interests rather than as coherent hierarchical organizations. The Fuerzas Armadas Revolucionarias de Colombia (Revolutionary Armed Forces of Colombia, FARC), a guerrilla group, for example, contains some sixty independent units that contend with each other over both ideology and strategy.[42] Drug cartels operate as violent business interest groups, using bombs and bribes to influence policy and sell insurance to members. Although traffickers from the same city have aggregated their interests through cartels, there seems to have been little coordination between traffickers from different cities.[43] Finally, paramilitaries in Colombia also operate independently. The Autodefesas Unidas de Colombia (United Self-Defense Forces of Colombia, AUC), the country's largest paramilitary organization, contains at least eleven independent member groups.

All of the different organizations engaged in violent activities in Colombia also participate in drug trafficking and extortion. Guerrillas have survived the decline of the Soviet Union and the collapse of guerrilla movements in other parts of Latin America, as a result of their ability to tap into illegal sources of revenue by taxing drug production and shipment through parts of the countryside and by extorting protection fees from mineral extraction corporations. These activities, Daniel Pécaut notes, require "[a] certain degree of cooperation between guerrillas and drug traffickers," and "the implicit complicity of other local forces, including the military, the police and politicians."[44] Drug traffickers and guerrillas, in other words, have become parasitically integrated into the political and economic activities of the country. These groups do not work to stop business activity, but rather, through connections into state and civil society, profit by extorting money from businesses.

Drug traffickers depend on connections into civil society and the state to maintain ongoing illegal activities. The Medellín and Cali cartels' operations during the 1980s and 1990s provide ample evidence of this. Through the simultaneous use of bribery and threats, *plata o plomo* (silver or lead), as Colombians called this practice, traffickers in the Medellín cartel succeeded in corrupting huge segments of the local judiciary and police forces.[45] Traffickers also connected themselves to political parties and politicians by funding many electoral campaigns, and Pablo Escobar was even voted an alternative representative to the national Congress.[46] Escobar, Carlos Lehder, and other traffickers put significant resources into building local political support for themselves by establishing civic and political groups that constructed homes for the poor, built local infrastructure, and beautified cities.[47] Significant evidence also suggests that former president Ernesto Samper Pizano's election campaign received heavy funding from the Cali cartel.[48] Though there is some debate about his culpability in receiving the bribe, this concern led to Colombia's decertification as an "ally in the war on drugs" by the U.S. Congress in 1997.[49] The cartels also developed the *apuntada* system, in which proxy contacts were used to allow legitimate businesspeople to buy into cocaine shipments. This helped traffickers gain access to whole new sources of financing for their operations and fortify connections into legal society, which built public support for their activities.[50] These contacts in the licit economy also created other commercial opportunities for traffickers, enabling them to invest in legal business ventures that hid illegally acquired funds.[51] The Colombian government facilitated the repatriation of illegal funds by allowing the central bank to exchange drug traffickers' dollars for local currency in order to increase foreign exchange revenues. Traffickers from Medellín and Cali also provided substantial financial support to local soccer teams.[52]

Paramilitaries operate in collusion with both criminals and government forces and have had the support of some members of civil society who express concern about kidnapping and extortion.[53] Created by landowners and drug traffickers to stave off kidnapping attempts by left-wing guerrillas, paramilitary organizations have grown into political organizations in their own right that have built strong ties to elements of the Colombian military and right-wing politicians.[54] AUC leader Carlos Castaño had a prior career as a trafficker in the Cali cartel, and many active members had previously worked as criminals or had served in the military.[55] Like criminals and guerrillas, the paramilitaries exist as a result of the ways that they can bridge different elements of Colombian society. They raise money by providing illegal protection to powerful families, make alliances with the military to gain the weapons they need to fight, and work with other criminals to make money by dealing drugs.[56]

As with Brazil, network connections that bring together actors from different segments of society to accomplish long-term strategic objectives drive criminal activity in Colombia. As one observer discussing connections among traffickers, guerrillas, and paramilitaries has noted,

The equation that links illegal narcotics to insurgency and the paramilitaries in Colombia—and elsewhere—turns on a combination of need, organizational infrastructure development, ability, and the availability of sophisticated communications and weaponry. For example, the drug industry possesses cash and lines of transportation and communication. Insurgent and paramilitary organizations have followers, organization, and discipline. Traffickers need these to help protect their assets and project their power within and among nationstates. Insurgents and paramilitaries are in constant need of logistical and communications support—and money.[57]

As observed above, traffickers, paramilitaries, and guerrillas work to varying degrees with legitimate elected officials, bureaucrats, and civic actors, who can provide them with other services and resources they might need to undertake their activities.

While illegal actors work with one another and with other political and civic actors, these relationships vary across time and space. The FARC voted in 1982 to work with drug traffickers to help support their own guerrilla activities, but their alliances with different criminals are intermittent and violent.[58] For example, in cocaine-producing regions, traffickers often find themselves acting in coalition with criminals to protect and deliver the cocaine crop. However, when traffickers cannot come to an agreement with the guerrillas, they may employ paramilitaries to protect their supply and put pressure on the guerrillas. On the other hand, in agricultural areas where traffickers invest resources in farming and ranching, they often find themselves threatened by guerrillas imposing revolutionary taxes and extorting money through kidnappings. Traffickers, guerrillas, and the military also maintain difficult relations as a result of the drug trade, with traffickers and guerrillas bribing military units for protection of drug production operations. At times, however, these relationships break down as a result of the failure of traffickers or guerrillas to meet the bribe demands of military units.[59]

Illegal networks in Colombia and Brazil also differ in certain critical ways. Unlike Brazil, Colombia is one of the centers of the world drug trade, and drug trafficking there reaches much higher levels and has had a much more intense effect on state and society. The huge amounts of wealth acquired by traffickers have enabled them to buy substantial stakes in the legitimate economy and to gain a deeper control of politicians and political parties than occurs in Brazil.[60] Further, since Colombia is a major drug production site, many illegal activities take place in the countryside and require specific types of political arrangements that are not required in Brazil. Thus, the need to control territory to grow coca results in traffickers and state agents making deals that sustain guerrilla groups whose avowed goal is the destruction of the state. Under these conditions, armed organizations end up controlling a substantial portion of the national territory. This results in rural violence having major impacts on urban areas. Finally, the resources and structure of illegal activities lead to the emergence of multiple and differentiated types of illegal actors, who themselves work together to accomplish different goals. Since most criminal activities in Brazil are located near port facilities as a result of the drug transshipment activities that occur there, most of the disruption of state governance occurs in large coastal cities. The conditions that exist in Brazil do not facilitate the emergence of either guerrillas or large-scale paramilitary groups, since the countryside, which experiences intense conflicts over land, plays such a small role in the Brazilian narcotics trade. In Colombia, rural and urban violence are often deeply interconnected, whereas in Brazil they are not.[61]

The evidence presented here suggests that criminal activities in Colombia depend on illegal networks that have developed differently as a result of the specific place that Colombia has in the international drug trade. This would seem to indicate that Brazil itself is not in danger of "Colombianization," since Brazil experiences the problem of the drug trade in a very different way. Brazil may, to be sure, become more violent and develop greater problems of corruption than already exist, but this will likely result from the strengthening of existing Brazilian criminal networks, which themselves have different structures and effects than Colombian criminal networks.

Jamaica

Jamaica displays a similar pattern to those exhibited in both Brazil and Colombia but also differs from those cases as a result of the particular history of the island and its location in the international drug trade. Of all the other cases examined in this chapter, the politics in the capitol, Kingston, share the most in common with those in Rio. Here criminals and their civic interlocutors have maintained direct contacts with high-level political actors that, over time, have resulted in a radical transformation of traditional clientelist political practices.[62]

Like Colombia and Brazil, violence has long played an important role in Jamaican politics. In the 1940s and 1950s, just prior to independence, the Jamaica Labour Party (JLP) and the People's National Party (PNP) competed to dominate the unions in particular workplaces, in order to gain control of votes. This process involved hiring thugs who could effectively drive off supporters of the other party and resulted in a deadlock that contributed to the emergence of a two-party system. Since independence in 1962, there have been regular shifts in power between the JLP and the PNP that have led to intense political competition characterized by leaders in both parties hiring local toughs to establish their control over poor districts in urban areas on the island.

Over the course of the late 1960s and 1970s, these clashes worsened, and political leaders increasingly delivered firearms into the hands of supporters, who would then use those weapons to defend their turf and break up the opponent's political rallies.[63] Politicians also used local gunmen as brokers in clientelist relations with poor city residents. Once in power, those politicians bulldozed shanty areas in Kingston to make way for housing projects that they filled with loyal supporters. The government would give resources to gunmen to distribute to the communities. Increasingly threatened by violence, politicians developed even closer relations with these gunmen, some of whom acted as personal bodyguards, in the 1970s. Escalating violence culminated in the 1980 election, which resulted in over 800 murders on this small island and, for the first time, the murder of a political candidate.[64] After this, politicians started to distance themselves from violent supporters—and even turned the names of some over to police when they felt they could no longer control them. Although elections remained violent as a result of the continuation of some of these practices, in the 1980s, violence increasingly became linked to the drug trade. Today, criminals retain some connections to politicians and state actors but also operate separately and maintain a very high level of violence in Kingston.[65]

During the 1970s, Jamaica's major illegal export was marijuana. Many of the gunmen who associated with politicians and served as their clientelist interlocutors were involved in small-time drug dealing and exporting during this period. As politicians started to distance themselves from the gunmen in the 1980s, their gangs looked for alternative ways to support themselves and defend their neighborhoods. The solution to this problem came through the expanding international cocaine trade. Colombian traffickers began to use Jamaica as a major transshipment hub. Local gang leaders in the Kingston area were well positioned to take advantage of this new trade, as a result of the high-quality port facilities associated with the island's agricultural and mineral export trade, as well as the quickly growing tourist trade. With limited territorial control over certain parts of Kingston, as well as intermittent alliances with politicians and state security forces, local political-criminal leaders increasingly could import, protect, and reexport cocaine to the United States. Over time, these gangs would use their connection to expatriates to gain control of lucrative distribution networks on the East Coast of the United States and in the United Kingdom. This helped drug dealers raise large amounts of money, which they used to maintain some basic social services in the slum areas they controlled and which helped them to import weapons bought in Florida gun shops.[66] This resulted in an expansion and generalization of violence within Jamaica's major cities during the 1980s and 1990s.[67]

Another element of the structure of illegal networks in Jamaica is the relationships among public security forces, political parties, and criminals. Both Jamaica's military and police are quite violent institutions. Police actions account for approximately one-third of all homicides in Jamaica.[68] A deeper understanding of conflict here can be achieved through a more thorough analysis of the problems of corruption in local security forces. Unfortunately, this is beyond the scope of this book.

Jamaican gang leaders work to maintain relations with different social and political leaders. Historically, the heads of criminal gangs, "dons" as they are known in Jamaica, operate as direct interlocutors with politicians. Important political leaders, in fact, have attended the funerals of deceased gang allies.[69] Actual civic actors only involve themselves in this political patronage process at a lower level. Politicians directly deliver funds for local projects and maintenance in housing projects for dons to redistribute to local contractors, who may or may not have direct connections with illegal activities.[70] As politicians reduced their support for traffickers in the last twenty years, drug dons began to use cocaine profits to deliver services to the communities they operated in—to maintain local order, to support neighborhood soccer teams, and to plan social events.[71] Gangs would also provide services for the elderly and, in at least one case, work with local business owners to maintain a neighborhood school and provide educational supplies to children.[72]

Connections among criminals, state officials, and politicians play a large role in maintaining ongoing criminal activity. Links to politicians have provided criminals with resources and protection. In exchange, politicians have received monopoly access to certain slum communities and an effective way to distribute largesse. Police corruption and association with different political parties has affected the ability of the government to effectively deal with growing crime problems over the last few decades. As connections with politicians have weakened, criminals have embedded themselves in the international drug trade. This has enabled traffickers to raise money abroad to provide services to the residents of their communities and guarantee protection.

The particular political history of Jamaica and its place in the international drug trade, however, has created a very different environment for criminal networks than exists in other countries. Relatively low-level drug traffickers, for example, seem to have much more prestigious political connections than low-level traffickers do in Brazil. A former head of government in Brazil would not attend the funeral of a known trafficker. Further, historical alliances within Jamaica's two-party system help to define conflicts among gangs active on the island. Finally, the alliances of politicians with the police and the military also affect the structure of relationships between police and criminals.

Mexico

From the early twentieth century until the summer of 2000, the Partido Revolucionario Institucional (Institutional Revolutionary Party, PRI) dominated Mexican economic, social, and political life through a series of hierarchical clientelist networks known as *camarillas*. Every six years, with the election of a new president, tens of thousands of jobs turned over in the Mexican state, within state governments, in state-owned enterprises, and in party institutions. Individuals allied to those who gained or held power in this political transition stood to gain jobs and resources.[73] The many individuals involved in this system provided the PRI with an important base of national political support that burrowed its way into the lowest levels of social life. Informal political networks, associated with local political bosses, carried out violent acts against potential opposition to local governments or the interests of well-connected landowners. The PRI also garnered electoral support through populist initiatives directed at peasants living on communal farms and workers organized through state-sponsored unions. The ability of the government to deliver resources to politically important constituencies through these networks enabled the PRI to maintain tight control over Mexican society, with relatively limited use of the types of centralized authoritarian tactics that characterized governments in Brazil, Argentina, and Chile.

The PRI also dominated criminal organizations. In the 1960s and 1970s, Mexico produced a significant amount of marijuana for export and, with the advent of the modern cocaine trade in the 1980s, began to serve as a major transshipment point for cocaine into the United States. In exchange for protection from regional political leaders, criminals provided kickbacks to, and took orders from, high-ranking politicians and police. Criminal organizations, thus, operated as a branch of the political patronage networks that dominated Mexican political life up until the mid-1990s. At this point, the breakdown of PRI power and the growing power of traffickers associated with increases of the cocaine and heroin trades resulted in conflicts with state officials and a number of assassinations.

Significant detailed evidence exists of Mexican drug traffickers having very close relationships with powerful political officials. General Arevalo Gardoqui, a former defense secretary, Manuel Bartlett, a former interior minister, and General Gutierrez Rebollo, the former Mexican drug czar, all had involvement with traffickers.[74] Some data also indicates that high-level politicians took campaign financing from traffickers in the 1985–1997 period.[75]

The corruption of Mexican police is legendary. Ask almost any traveler and you will hear a horror story about how police demanded a bribe from them. Frequently, police take payment from traffickers in order to fulfill their bribe "quota" to higher-ranking officers.[76] Typically, when a trafficker would achieve some success, both state and federal police would visit and ask for a bribe. Over time, these relationships were regularized.[77]

Finally, as in the other countries examined in this chapter, Mexican criminals also maintain strong ties to local populations. Significant evidence exists of donations by traffickers to build "roads, churches, schools, and medical centers" in the areas where they operate.[78] In Mexico, though, traffickers focus these efforts not on building social support for protection against the state, as they do in Brazil, but, rather, they use these investments to build their own social position and to retain the support of state officials. Since Mexican society was dominated by the PRI and traffickers operated as part of PRI patronage networks, their contributions to local social initiatives operate as part of their contribution to the political system they already participate in. Like criminals in Colombia, Mexican traffickers want society to accept them. The donations they give to social groups do not provide protection so much as social acceptance that, over the long term, could help traffickers to normalize their position in society.[79]

Conclusion

This analysis suggests that drug traffickers in Brazil and other parts of Latin America operate through networks that bring them together with actors in civil society and the state. These connections provide traffickers with the protection and status necessary to undertake long-term criminal activities by undermining both state and social efforts to control trafficking. These networks have remarkable similarities to those observed in Rio's favelas, but the evidence in this chapter suggests that political and economic differences have significant effects on the structure of criminal networking in each of these countries.

In every state examined here, the particular political structure had a powerful and direct effect on criminal organization. In the case of Colombia, fifty years of civil war, coupled with an elite-dominated party system, has produced a political environment in which drug traffickers find themselves at different times allied with both state actors and guerrillas and has also created situations in which traffickers have formed their own militias in coalition with legitimate business- and landowners. In Jamaica, criminal organizing has been driven by the structure of clientelism in that country and the ways that political parties have historically worked with gunmen to control neighborhoods and protect their own political interests. This has produced strong ties between some criminals and politicians and has resulted in specific types of cleavages among criminal gangs. Finally, in Mexico the dominant role of the PRI in politics, society, and the economy forced criminals to also work directly with powerful regional and national politicians. In this case, criminals themselves became directly part of the overall political structure of the country.

The role of politics in forming criminal organizations in Brazilian cities is harder to discern because of the strong similarities between political structures in different cities. Nevertheless, some issues are apparent. In Rio, the need of politicians to gain access to closed communities controlled by traffickers and the need of traffickers to have the support of residents who live in those communities drive political-criminal ties. This results in trading between politicians, local civic leaders, and criminals. In São Paulo, Belo Horizonte, and Porto Alegre, the overall position of criminals is much weaker, since they do not dominate particular areas of the city. Although some higher-level traffickers clearly have political connections, in these places low-level criminals take advantage of general corruption trends in Brazilian police. The clearest example of politics affecting crime in Brazil is the case of Vitória. Here the penetration of the state government by criminal actors gave great power to a death squad and led to high levels of corruption.

Within Brazil, the economics of drug trafficking has a significant effect on the structure of crime and the way it penetrates the state. As two of the largest ports on the continent, São Paulo and Rio de Janeiro serve primarily as drug transshipment hubs from Latin America to Africa, Europe, and North America. These two cities suffered first from the increasing Andean drug trade, with spikes in both drug trafficking and murders in the 1980s and early 1990s. Over time, drug dealers began selling more drugs to local consumers. With the saturation of these retail markets in the later 1990s, traffickers started to look for more internal markets. This led to an increase in drug sales and violence in other cities in the south and southeast of Brazil. Belo Horizonte, Porto Alegre, and Vitória all suffered from this process, as displaced criminals and others eager to increase their profits expanded their operations. In Belo Horizonte and Porto Alegre, primarily local consumption markets developed. The relatively low-level drug dealers involved in this have not yet developed strong political connections. Vitória, on the other hand, with its excellent port facilities under the control of the state government, was a much more powerful target for criminals. This brought more intense criminal activity and government corruption.

Rio, São Paulo, and Vitória all display the characteristics of areas involved in the transshipment of drugs. In these cases, criminals need control of secure locations to store drugs prior to shipment. This entails proximity to good port facilities and an ability to hide or defend the product prior to putting it on a plane or ship. In Rio, traffickers accomplish this by building alliances with police and politicians that allow them to have partial control over some segments of urban territory. Jamaica experiences a similar pattern of illegal activity. In São Paulo, this protection emerges from the huge size and density of the city. As a result, political and law enforcement connections are important to the drug trade—but not as essential as they are in Rio. The particular politics of security in the nearby port city of Santos also play an important role in the dynamics of the drug trade here. In Vitória, a smaller city where traffickers would have difficulty hiding or protecting drugs from the state, traffickers built a direct alliance with powerful state leaders and effectively co-opted the state apparatus. This case bears something in common with Panama, a country with a population and narrow elite similar to that of the state of Espírito Santo, where General Manuel Noriega had strong relationships with Colombian traffickers. In both cases, outside intervention proved essential in ending the criminal-state alliance.

Other countries also provide evidence of the role of illegal economies in the structure of criminal networks. In a drug-producing country such as Colombia, criminals need extensive control of rural areas to grow and manufacture narcotics. In these cases, criminals will have a strong incentive to undertake actions to wrest large portions of rural territory from state control. Peru, Afghanistan, and Burma offer examples of similar production sites, where guerrillas have come to control large portions of the countryside. In these cases, drug traffickers develop alliances with guerrillas and state actors who control drug-producing areas. Mexico is both a producer of heroin and a reexporter of cocaine. The complex relationship between state officials and traffickers reflects the need of criminals to maintain some control over rural areas and to maintain access to the border area to move the drug to the United States.

The evidence in this chapter suggests that criminals operate in networks throughout Latin America. These networks have certain basic functional similarities, in that they bring together criminals with actors in both the state and civil society. Similarly, in all countries examined, criminals invest some resources in building social support for their activities by contributing to local organizations. At the same time, however, both political and economic factors cause these networks to differ across the region. A deeper understanding of politics in Latin American today can be arrived at if we move beyond the institutionalist frameworks that currently dominate the study of the region and look at the more complex and nuanced historical, structural, and networked models that provide insights not just into formal political competition but also into how criminal and other social activity is integrated into the political system.

SEVEN

Theorizing the Politics of Social Violence

In the introduction to this book, I asked two questions: why is there so much violence in Rio and what can be done to improve this situation? I have answered these questions by showing that crime and violence have a heavy and ongoing impact on Rio's favelas as a result of the ways that criminals, state officials, and civic actors maintain connections with one another to achieve group goals. In other words, the organization of criminal networks in Rio's favelas leads to ongoing conflict in the city because of the cross-institutional ties that criminals maintain. The structure of these networks undermines many of the typical approaches used to control violence, rendering increased social services or more hard-line policing impotent to rein in crime. Data from Vigário and Tubarão, however, show the efficacy of an alternative networked form of local organizing that can help control crime and violence in favelas over the medium term. Comparative evidence indicates that these conditions exist in other countries in the Americas and other cities in Brazil, although the type of violence and the structure of the networks differ, depending on local politics and the types of criminal activity that occur there. This chapter summarizes these findings and analyzes them in the context of writings on social networks, the state, and democratization in developing societies.

Summary of Findings

By using network structures to achieve group goals, criminals can effectively take on long-term illegal activities with minimal external opposition. These networks transform state power at the local level in such a way that many government policies actually reinforce criminal activities. Analysis from Vigário, Tubarão, and Santa Ana suggests several structural characteristics that these organizations share.

Components of Illegal Networks

Violence in Rio reflects the particular ways that the international markets in illegal drugs and arms have been inserted into the city's economic, social, and institutional environment. These dynamics create conditions that encourage interactions among state, civic, and criminal actors and directly lead to the city's high levels of violence.

At the heart of criminal networks in Rio's favelas are drug traffickers who, as skilled operators in illegal markets, raise funds that they distribute to residents, civic actors, and some public officials. The failure of the state to provide a minimal safety net or effective policing to residents creates conditions that discourage their political participation and lead to an environment in which criminals can play a potentially significant local political role. Traffickers provide some aid to poor residents, who are neither adequately served by the marketplace nor by the eviscerated state programs that survived the 1980s debt crisis. These same criminals also enforce order within favelas, using a political calculus designed to build their support among residents excluded by society as a whole.

These drug dealers, however, also provide important services to state and civic actors. As skilled purveyors of illegal violence, criminals can provide protection for civic groups initiating programs in favelas, can threaten the use of force that may help allied civic groups gain compliance with difficult decisions from residents, and can provide monopoly access to politicians seeking votes. As operators in black markets, these same criminals can pay for police protection, supplementing limited law enforcement incomes from a relatively poor state apparatus. Traffickers also can provide funds to certain favored civic groups that may want to offer services to residents but that may have difficulty finding those funds through state actors or in the competitive philanthropic marketplace.

Of course, criminals could not operate without the support of state officials. Police provide them with protection for a fee but also, in their collusion, help to build criminals' image in favelas as legitimate actors in the face of a criminally corrupt and violent state apparatus. Politicians provide traffickers with resources to support services to residents and, similarly, increase traffickers' prestige through their mutual association.

Finally, through their well-developed interpersonal and political skills, civic leaders also provide important contributions to the network, by mediating relations between criminals and numerous other actors. They help to mediate relations with residents and reduce the possibility that conflicts between criminals and residents could emerge. Civic leaders also confer a certain degree of their hard-won local legitimacy on traffickers, help traffickers to establish agreements with politicians, and file appropriate paperwork with bureaucrats.

Network Characteristics

The networks that bring these actors together are generally flexible and horizontally organized. In each community studied, police, politicians, and even particular traffickers could leave the network and new ones could come in without a great disruption to illegal activities. Tubarão, perhaps, offers the best example of this. Here, different politicians, police, and traffickers entered and left the illegal network in the years before I came to the community. Nevertheless, the broad framework of the network continued despite these changes. This flexibility enables the illegal network to operate, despite the fact that members may be arrested or transferred to other places. The ability to survive these types of organizational casualties is an important factor in any network that engages in activities not formally approved of by the state. This flexibility to bring in new groups and exclude old ones also helps the network to co-opt other potential opponents.

All the criminal networks examined in this book also are semiclandestine. Actors involved in the network make statements in private about their relationships but do not make those statements publicly. Instead, as we saw in Tubarão and Santa Ana, leaders associated with traffickers would make public statements denying their connections to traffickers so as to minimize the public appearance of impropriety. To communicate traffickers' support for politicians, AM leaders might put up a sign saying that they and the traffickers' lawyer supported a particular candidate without ever directly saying that the traffickers also offered their support. These efforts helped instill community discipline without the traffickers taking actions that would upset residents, decrease local support, or increase their risk of arrest by police. This secretiveness makes possible their indirect connection to legitimate civic and political actors. The structure of the network, with its combination of weak and strong ties, allows traffickers to communicate different types of information through different channels in such a way as to minimize their risk of arrest, while also communicating threats and promises of security to their intended audience.

Criminal networks take full advantage of weak and strong ties to regulate contacts, both inside and outside the community, by simultaneously building tight ties with a limited free flow of information within the community and by constructing a few very weak ties with outsiders. More often than not, these outside links run through one or two actors that serve as network hubs. In the communities I examined, the leader of the AM and possibly a lawyer acted as the main contacts between traffickers and outsiders. Network members saw most other groups that maintained contacts with outsiders as potential threats. This structure strengthened the network by limiting what outsiders knew of criminal activities but could weaken these networks if those contacts with the outside were simultaneously removed. As a result, traffickers often had to keep AM leaders in place, despite conflicts with them. This does not mean that traffickers would not bully or kill an AM leader. Nevertheless, taking this type of action is politically difficult and could expose traffickers to higher degrees of internal and external pressure. This occurred in Tubarão in the 1980s, when traffickers forced the leadership of the community out and local leaders responded by helping other criminals to take over.

In all of the cases studied, conflict plays an integral role in supporting and propagating illegal activities. When violence combines with connections into civil society and the state, the functioning of local-level governance is partially disrupted and altered. As a result, criminals and their allies play a significant role in deciding what happens in a particular neighborhood. When the state makes decisions about what types of project to build, officials make those decisions in consultation with civic leaders allied with drug dealers. When improvements occur within a community, they occur in such a way that trafficker power there increases. Thus, if the government builds housing projects in a favela, as occurred in Tubarão, those projects will often end up occupied by the relatives of traffickers, and traffickers' allies will make decisions about how to use newly available common space. Over the long term, this creates a system where criminals gain power and where it appears that the state is absent. The state, however, is present—it just works with civic actors who have an interest in criminals using its influence. Trafficker power, as a result, comes not from state absence, but, rather, from the way that the state is present.

Political Dynamics in Favelas

Interactions between favela leaders and politicians go beyond top-down patron-broker-client relations suggested in the classic writings on clientelism. Criminals often have difficulty interacting directly with politicians, outside business leaders, and police. In all three favelas, civic leaders mediated trafficker-politician relationships. This evidence also indicates that traffickers use similar types of mediation to deal with state bureaucrats and business owners. Traffickers rely on this mediation because their status as criminals makes it impossible for them to interact with law-abiding citizens and officials—and even makes it difficult for them to interact with corrupt officials who believe that they may be held accountable. Further, traffickers lack the cultural capital and social skills necessary to negotiate agreements with state officials, other outsiders, and some residents. Lawyers and experienced community leaders have often honed these skills through years of experience and education. Without their support, traffickers could not maintain relationships with noncriminal actors.

This mediation reveals some of the limitations of a neoclientelist model. Traffickers themselves are not brokers in a hierarchical clientelist relationship between politicians and favela residents. Traffickers need to operate through more complex networks because, unlike other elements of society, they cannot work directly with state actors. In all three cases, actual negotiations with politicians and outsiders are carried out by civic leaders and other respected residents. As a result of their position, as Tubarão showed, AM leaders may negotiate on the trafficker's behalf and not even communicate with traffickers about their negotiations, and traffickers, presumably through other mediators, may make deals with other politicians. However, in Vigário, where the network had weakened, traffickers had much less ability to pursue these goals.

So what exactly happens when politicians go to favelas? With control of the means of violence in favelas, criminals essentially agree to ensure that no other politicians will come into a favela during an election. The difference between the Tubarão and Santa Ana negotiations makes this dynamic clear. In Santa Ana, the AM evidently had a close relationship with the traffickers, and the traffickers agreed to the deal with the politicians. Only the politicians who paid for the dance floor came to the community and received votes. In Tubarão, on the other hand, the AM leader went out of his way to communicate to the politician that he was working with the traffickers, even though the traffickers probably had no involvement in the negotiations. The politician went along with the agreement, in part because he thought that the trafficker had guaranteed his access to the community. In the end, as we know, this was not the case. The traffickers made a deal with another politician and the Neo-Pentecostal group voted for a third politician. Thus, when criminals do not work closely with local leaders, it is difficult for them to actually guarantee anyone monopoly access to the community. Only through collusion between traffickers and civic leaders can community groups make effective arrangements to guarantee to politicians access to a favela. As both Tubarão and Santa Ana show, civic leaders intervene with residents to help reduce tensions between residents and traffickers.

Again, Vigário provides a counterpoint. During the 1998 elections, traffickers had an arrangement with a particular politician, and a resident set up relations with a second politician. As a result, traffickers had to use threats of violence to attempt to uphold their agreement with the first politician. Lacking an adequate network, the traffickers not only failed to get the signs for the other politician removed, but they alienated residents in the process.

The evidence presented here suggests that a two-tiered form of clientelism has emerged in Rio's favelas. Whereas before, local brokers, usually AM leaders, worked to obtain patronage directly for a community by bargaining with a politician, today traffickers have emerged as an integral component in these relationships. AM leaders bargain initially on behalf of the traffickers with politicians to bring resources to the community. Traffickers then agree to provide the politicians with monopoly access to the community during the election. These resources, however, are delivered initially into the hands of AM leaders and drug traffickers, who then redistribute those goods to residents. Since drug traffickers are armed, residents have relatively little negotiating power in dealing with them. As a result, traffickers skim off a substantial portion of resources to benefit them and their allies in the AM and pass along only what little is required to build support to community residents. In this new set of relationships, traffickers gain control of state resources and use them, as we saw with the building of dance floors in both Tubarão and Santa Ana, to distribute services to residents. In these arrangements, politicians fall in the eyes of residents as a result of their association with traffickers and due to the fact that it is ultimately the traffickers who gain control of the resources coming into the community and then choose how to redistribute those resources. Traffickers gain control of resources that they dole out to residents and they gain the legitimacy that might have, in another era, flowed to politicians. Residents win a few parties thrown by traffickers, and politicians achieve the hollow support of votes from residents who feel little attachment to them. By providing mediated guarantees to politicians, traffickers make sure that politicians do not build direct personal bonds with residents. Certainly traffickers maintain patronage ties to favela residents, but a broader network enables these ties and drains the legitimacy created by clientelism out of the political system. By networking with politicians and local civic leaders, traffickers build differentiated sets of political connections that bind residents closely to them and favela leaders but that create distant links with politicians.[1]

Networks and Local Political Legitimacy

Illegal networks, however, do much more than build political connections. Traffickers use networks to create legitimacy in the communities they operate in. Others have shown that traffickers make significant efforts to build support among the population they live and work with.[2] I have shown that by working *through* respected local leaders, traffickers improve their reputations and prestige in the community and, as was the case with the *festa junina* in Santa Ana, that they use those contacts to promote events that will generate more goodwill for them. In exchange, social leaders gain resources and some flexibility in dealing with the traffickers. In the case of Santa Ana, the AM president would undertake efforts that mildly interfered with some trafficker activities in order to defuse the resentment of residents against traffickers. In Tubarão, Bernardo interceded on a number of occasions to prevent traffickers from using violence to resolve differences with residents and local leaders. In Vigário, when traffickers had adequate connections, such as when the CdP collapsed, they were able to manipulate politics in the favela without using violence. When they had inadequate contacts, such as when they tried to change the content of the election posters, they had to use threats to achieve their goal, which alienated residents. At other times, however, traffickers worked through respected local leaders to minimize conflict with residents and, as mentioned earlier, to deliver services to increase resident support.

One could argue that since traffickers have a limited monopoly on the means of violence, this obviates the role of social support and legitimacy within illegal networks. In the cases I have examined and in other studies, ample evidence has demonstrated traffickers' use of violence against leaders who oppose them and, as a result, undermine local social ties.[3] Clearly, traffickers can force out the leadership of an AM or any other favela organization through threats of violence. The issue for effective traffickers, though, is that they often do not want to do this. They could kill a respected local leader, but this could decrease their local support and increase police pressure. In Tubarão, when an unstable trafficker pushed community leaders out in the 1980s, Bernardo brought in a new set of traffickers and rose to the presidency of the AM. As can be seen with the social mobilization in Vigário, when trafficker activities brought too much violence to Vigário, their local support declined dramatically and they had to accept the development of organizations that tried to reduce violence and drug sales. In this context, it is not surprising that despite his differences with the president of Ceuzinho's AM, Bernardo prevented the traffickers from murdering the Ceuzinho president after he helped establish the police occupation. Had this murder occurred, it would, with some certainty, have increased pressure on traffickers in the favela. Criminal leaders benefit by working through established social networks in favelas and by using respected leaders to defuse tensions with residents. At times, they will threaten or kill a civic leader, usually in an effort to install someone more amenable to them, but traffickers must take care when they do this. As Marcos Alvito puts it, in a slightly different context, compromising legitimate community leaders hurts traffickers by cutting off their ties to the media and the outside world.[4] This research has shown that if traffickers force local leaders out, they could break up the very elements of their network that help to produce some of the goodwill that protects them. By working with respected leaders, as all three cases show, drug traffickers appropriate existing social networks, work within the local norms, and accomplish difficult political aims, with less violence than they might otherwise need to use.

Traffickers use networks to build legitimacy because they sit on the frontier between state and society. On the one hand, they have a limited monopoly on the means of violence in favelas and have the ability to sell protection.[5] On the other hand, they do not have at their disposal a large legitimacy-building apparatus and face a state that, in part, builds its legitimacy by opposing their activities. As a result, traffickers must work through localized networks of trust and reciprocity to build the support necessary to prevent residents of favelas from allying themselves with other traffickers or the state. Although traffickers are not just another member of a poor community helping out a comrade or a traditional wealthy patron, the more deeply they work within existing narratives of respect, trust, and reciprocity, the more likely they will be to receive the protection of favela residents.

This book has shown that connections to local leaders help traffickers deliver services and minimize conflicts with residents. Through these networks, traffickers manage difficult negotiations with police. The result is that, more than just filling in space left by the government, illegal networks appropriate existing state and societal resources and power and use them to establish protected areas in which traffickers can engage in illegal activities. More than parallel "states" or "polities," drug trafficking in Rio represents an expression of transformed state and social power at the local level. This transformation has altered the operation of liberal democratic government in Rio de Janeiro.

Network Variation

Although the three favelas that I examine in this book have many similarities, they also differ in some critical ways. At a basic level, the location of the favela within the city and the geographic structure of the community affected the types of local criminal operations and the politics of the favela. Rio de Janeiro as a whole is inserted into international markets in particular ways that have led to the expansion of the wholesale and retail cocaine and arms trades in the city. All three communities are vigorous centers of drug trafficking, be it retailing near downtown or in the wealthy Zona Sul, as with Santa Ana and Tubarão, or with combinations of retail and wholesaling, as was the case with Vigário, located on the far northern edge of the city, close to important transportation arteries. Although the type of criminal activities taking place in these favelas differed, both Vigário and Tubarão bordered on favelas that, for long periods of time, were controlled by rival drug gangs. This resulted in extended trafficker conflicts that brought large numbers of casualties to each community. On the other hand, Santa Ana, located in a place where it was surrounded exclusively by favelas controlled by friendly gangs, experienced persistent police trafficker shoot-outs rather than full-scale gang warfare. The specific internal geography of the communities also contributed to the role and effects of crime, with Vigário's traffickers being notoriously violent, as a result, residents argued, of its hard-to-defend flat topography and wide-open street pattern.

The nature of illegal networks in each of the communities is also affected by the particular types of social organizations and pressures that operate on them. Some communities had histories of strong AMs, and in these cases traffickers had to find ways of working with those AM leaders. In other cases, AMs were weaker, and traffickers and AMs had different relations. Each community examined in the study was also affected by the types of civic groups and pressures from its neighbors. Residents and traffickers in some favelas had to contend with the demands of powerful neighbors—and the way those demands were lodged in the political system—while other favelas had politically weaker and more acquiescent neighbors.

Finally, the structure of state institutions and operations in these communities affects the dynamics of local criminal networks. State elites evinced more interest in some of the communities in this study than in others. In Tubarão, for example, the government spent considerable amounts of money providing services to residents through the AM. This resulted in centralized civic power, which traffickers co-opted to their own ends. Also, the practice of policing in a particular area had substantial effects on the nature of the criminal network and its political impacts. In Vigário, for instance, the entire police battalion responsible for the favela appeared to be involved in an extortion racket. In other places lower-ranking police managed corruption.

Jointly, these factors help explain some of the differences among the three favelas studied. All suffer from high levels of violence, but the nature of criminal-civic-political networking varies. Thus, Tubarão incorporates a much more powerful AM than the other two communities, as a result of its location, strong social pressures, and state interventions. On the other hand, the Vigário network seemed to rely much more directly on power concentrated in the hands of traffickers, who occasionally developed alliances with a more independent AM.

Solutions

The evidence in this book shows that countermobilizations that make efforts to protect human rights and restore effective democratic governance have both similarities to and differences from illegal networks. The data from both Tubarão and Vigário suggest a number of important factors in the structure and operation of networked efforts to control violence. First, as with illegal networks, countermobilizations are functionally differentiated. Their membership includes actors with specific skills from both state and society. Some members may raise money, while others may engage in street protest. Activists from the favela where the network is centered play a critical role, but these mobilizations also include civic groups from other parts of the city and actors within the state. In Vigário and Tubarão, organizations' contacts with the press and international civil society played essential roles in controlling violence. This combination of contacts helped decrease resident dependence on drug traffickers and pressured state officials to change police policy to control crime in both Vigário and Tubarão.

Second, like illegal networks, antiviolence mobilizations focused on promoting good governance under these circumstances must be horizontal and flexible. Neither the mobilizations against violence in Vigário nor the similar state-led intervention in Tubarão had a leader, and groups could enter or leave the network as they wished. The absence of a clear network head helped each organization survive difficult times. In both cases, police or traffickers forced at least one critical activist out of the community. Despite having actors exiled, these networks continued as a result of their horizontal and diffuse nature. Moreover, the remaining groups took up some of the slack. In a sense, these actors created a backup system for those forced to leave. This does not mean, however, that removing a particular member did not hurt antiviolence efforts.

The diffuse nature of these antiviolence mobilizations, coupled with the multiple avenues of access created by their dense and overlapping membership, facilitated recruitment. The flexibility of the membership commitment allowed groups that might be nervous about participating to become involved without taking on large personal or financial burdens before they knew exactly what participation required. The nonhierarchical nature of the mobilizations reinforced this by allowing new groups to enter through connections to any number of other member groups.

Third, unlike illegal networks, countermobilizations were associative, in the sense that they publicly brought groups more closely together. These organizations had denser and less-restricted links than criminal networks. Member groups met publicly in ways that produced greater overlapping connections. Sometimes groups would have open meetings to which members would invite outsiders. These connections improved learning among members, supported peer surveillance efforts, transferred and built trust, and created economic efficiencies that supported individual group activities, despite a lack of funds.

Both the Vigário and Tubarão countermobilizations were distinctly focused on one community. Little evidence exists in Rio of effective cross-community networking that reduced violence. The behavior of each network indicates a clear need to focus efforts around one community to build up the close relationships necessary to sustain activities. This characteristic makes broadening or replicating countermobilizations very difficult.

Finally, violence control efforts in Vigário and Tubarão developed as a result of crises in their respective communities. The massacre of residents not associated with trafficking by police initiated popular protests, which in Vigário led to the formation of internal civic groups capable of making demands of the government and in Tubarão resulted directly in state intervention. Similarly, the murder of Nelsinho in Santa Ana provoked one of the few effective efforts in that community to control violence. These events created ruptures within illegal networks and helped to mobilize residents and state actors to control violence. Further, evidence in each of these cases suggests that when police violate basic community notions about how police/criminal conflicts should take place, by killing a civilian, residents would take to the streets in ways that would provoke some type of effective response, either within or outside the favela.

Evidence from both Tubarão and Vigário suggests some significant limitations to these locally focused efforts to control violence. Although each community experienced a dramatic drop in bloodshed for a period of two to three years, both antiviolence mobilizations eventually dissipated and conflict intensified. The fundamental reasons for this are the basic structural, social, and institutional conditions that pervade Rio de Janeiro and that have created the violence that affects the city. Today, there are immense amounts of resources supporting the illegal markets that drive the drug trade. Conversely, there is a paucity of funds for projects to provide basic social assistance to reduce dependence on criminals. Traffickers operate within markets that provide them with, often, a better living than their noncriminal peers and enough of a surplus to provide assistance to residents. Further, while favelas are privileged sites of illicit wealth accumulation, funds to legitimately provide services to residents must come from the outside. Activists skilled at raising and using these funds are also generally outsiders who, although they may work in a favela for a time, almost always move on to other places. To make matters worse, the number of highly skilled NGO and state workers is very limited, and these workers appear to be attracted to the most prominent crises in the city. In both Tubarão and Vigário, the best NGO representatives and state officials moved on to other, often more prestigious, jobs, leaving the favelas they worked in with worse services and less-committed outside interlocutors. Just as outside workers eventually move on to other places, favela residents, who are often subject to threats from criminals or police if they are involved in these mobilizations, eventually tire of the intense social activism that is involved in maintaining collaborative intersectoral efforts to control violence. Finally, as political power shifts and bureaucrats rotate into new positions, state commitment to these projects often wanes, in part because of constant competition over limited funds, an apparent declining need in these communities as a result of the reductions in violence, and the fact that new political and bureaucratic officials often want to engage in their own projects rather than deepen those of their predecessors. Ultimately, as demobilization proceeds, one trafficker or another, working with available civic and state actors, is willing to take up the reins of a more powerful gang that is able to operate effectively in the vacuum created by the collapse of mobilization efforts.

Democracy and the State in Latin America Today

Political scientists working on democratization in the 1980s and early 1990s made a stark choice in favor of advocating a moderate transition to liberal democracy rather than, in the face of waning authoritarian power, pushing for a more radical shift toward social democracy. Writing of the difficult decision to pursue some sort of socializing reforms or limited political democracy, Guillermo O'Donnell and Philippe Schmitter note: "In this context, all we can do is reaffirm our earlier presumption that political democracy per se is a goal worthy of attainment, even at the expense of forgoing alternate paths that would seem to promise more immediate returns of socialization."[6] Given the torture and brutal murder of intellectuals, students, and political activists in such diverse countries as Chile, Argentina, Brazil, Peru, and Guatemala, this position in favor of moderate reforms and limited democracy made a tremendous amount of sense. Advocating a minimal definition, Adam Pzerworski noted that the purpose of democracy was "that people shall not be killed!"[7]

This approach was extremely successful. For the most part, Latin American governments no longer systematically hunt down, torture, and kill political opponents. Liberal democracy, in the context of the expansion of the international drug and arms trade and an overall weakening of the state at the international level, however, has brought new problems with it. The government may not systematically persecute opponents but rogue police officers do arbitrarily arrest, torture, abuse, and kill many citizens. Drug traffickers murder other traffickers and innocents who get in their way, and they bribe and kill police, judges, and government officials.

Colombia and Jamaica are two of the region's oldest democracies. Brazil has had a liberal democratic government for over a generation. Yet all three of these countries face growing violence at the hands of rogue state officials and criminals. Brazil, as Anthony Pereira has noted, actually experiences more violence under its current republic than it did under the dictatorship.[8] These countries suffer from tremendous wealth inequalities and play important roles in the international drug trade. One would think, nevertheless, that a well-organized state apparatus would at least minimize the social costs of trafficking and restrain police corruption and violence. This, however, has not occurred. Evidence throughout this book points to the fact that traffickers operate through networks that bring them into contact with other state, social, and criminal actors who enable them to undertake long-term criminal activities. Liberal democratic states have not dealt effectively with the challenges posed by these networks, because those networks are themselves part of the political regime. Connections among traffickers, civic actors, and state officials help create policies that benefit traffickers.

Rio de Janeiro shows the long-term impacts of trafficker–civil society–state engagement on the conduct of governance in Latin America today. With few resources available to them, the poor have hardly any effective connections into a state closely tied to powerful interests and subject to the demands of transnational financial institutions. In the face of declining state services, poor police training, and inadequate housing, the poor are forced to fend for themselves and thus depend on relationships with criminals to get by. It is through networks associated with those criminals that the poor often have their most direct access to state officials. To make matters worse, badly remunerated police build contacts with traffickers and even sell weapons and drugs themselves to pay their bills. This results in a comfortable position for criminals in favelas, as they grow to have an important local-level political role through their connections to state actors and civic leaders.

Evidence from each of the empirical chapters suggests that politicians, criminals, and civic leaders maintain close relations. Whereas most existing political models generally look at bilateral interactions between state and society, this book shows that criminals also engage in relations with state and civic actors. Since criminals have attributes of both state actors and civic actors, they have an ambiguous position within the polity. Unlike other social actors, criminals have many difficulties directly interacting with the state. As a result, they engage with the state through indirect networks involving social actors. Civic leaders no longer act as effective mediators between state and society and have trouble building the types of dense ties that some argue support democratic governance.[9] The result is the establishment of a set of networked connections between state and society that does little to protect rights or to create accountability between voters and state officials. Rather, some state actors gain an interest in the drug trade and undertake actions that provide the basis for more intense crime. These same state officials then use rising crime rates to justify more repressive policing.

This book broadly suggests that the state-society model of politics dominant in contemporary social science needs to be replaced with a networked model of politics, in which state and civic institutions are given less weight than the formal and informal ties that bring together like-minded state officials, civic actors, and, in some cases, criminals. Illegal network members depend on these connections to achieve their goals. Given the specific abilities of members to use illegal networks to intimidate opponents while avoiding arrest, the evidence in this book suggests that countermobilizations that bring together state and social actors concerned with reducing violence provide one of the few political strategies that help to control violence in places where criminals work closely with state actors and civic leaders.

Theorizing Violent Politics in Latin America

Throughout Latin America, in places as diverse as Colombia, Bolivia, Peru, Jamaica, Honduras, and Mexico, we see rising violence depriving the region's citizens of life and liberty. The specific forms of conflict, and the politics that contribute to it, vary from place to place. Colombia, a major cocaine producer locked in a forty-year civil war, experiences violence very differently from Mexico, a country transitioning from one-party dominant rule involved in drug export and transshipment mostly across its northern border. Criminal networks come to play significant roles in these places, but they always depend on contacts with state and civic actors for the continuation of their operations. Evidence from this book suggests that we can develop a deeper understanding of the persistent social violence in different countries throughout Latin America by focusing on the specific types of criminal organizations that emerge and the particular ways those groups interact with state and social actors.

The concept of "brown" areas, as opposed to "blue" or "green" areas, puts emphasis on the breakdown of state power and the rule of law and suggests that, in some ways, these places of deficit are basically similar. To understand the challenges facing Latin American polities today we need to move beyond this powerful metaphor to achieve a deeper understanding of how violence not only undermines democratic governance but also creates new forms of political order. This book shows that spaces suffering from persistent social violence are contingent and reflect specific and differentiated political arrangements that are structured by the way particular types of criminal operations network with state and civic actors. The problem is not just state failure or a breakdown of the rule of law but rather the forms of engagement that exist among different state actors and forms of local power holders and the way these connections lead to the deployment of state power in such a way that it undermines the rule of law and establishes a separate, localized, order. "Brown" areas are not just semiprivate domains (or, as some might suggest, parallel states) that interact with the national state as foreign countries with legislative representatives acting as ambassadors. There is an immense diversity among "brown" zones, the actors who have power within them, and the multiplex relationships they, and different actors in these zones, maintain with different levels of state actors. Rather than "brown" zones, then, if we look closely, the map of Latin America can be seen as a myriad of different types of spaces representing varying forms of local political orders that can be described by how criminals, state officials, and social actors network together. These particular forms of violent localized authority that exist across the region have some similarities but also are embedded in the social, political, and economic dynamics operating in a specific country. These localized orders are part and parcel of Latin America's political regimes even if they are not publicly acknowledged as such.

Through an examination of three favelas in Rio, as well as through an overview of conditions in other Brazilian cities and countries in Latin America, this book has looked inside these "brown" areas and identified factors that contribute to their nature and dynamics. More than areas where the lights have gone out on democracy, favelas and other places like them experience high levels of social violence and suffer from localized authoritarian dynamics derived from the structural conditions that exist there, local historical and social conditions, and the liberal democratic institutional structures operating in that place. Only by understanding the ways that these factors come together to support specific forms of violent governance can we understand the problems that exist there and the potential solutions to those problems.

O'Donnell's argument, notably made in 1993 long before this was on the radar of most other political scientists—that striking variations exist in the rule of law across national territory in Latin America's new democracies—is deeply insightful and provides us with an important heuristic device to understand some of the major challenges facing the region. Where this approach comes up short, however, is in its metaphorical implication that somehow "brown" areas, be they in the Northeast of Brazil, in the suburbs of Buenos Aires, on the Colombian frontier, or in downtown Rio, are fundamentally, similarly "brown." Once we begin unpacking the politics that exist inside these places, something that O'Donnell has correctly noted as sadly lacking in political science writing on the region, we find that violence in these places has a particular nature, is based on specific and varied structures, and operates in a national, regional, and local context. "Brown" areas are not uniform, they are not produced solely by state institutional weakness, and they do not interact with the national state, in the cases I have observed, as foreign dependent satellites. To this extent, the otherwise insightful concept of "brown" areas is misleading. Evidence from the three favelas studied, as well as from secondary sources on other parts of Latin America, suggests the dimensions of these variations. By using these variables, we can gain a greater understanding of the problems facing the region.

The concept of "brown" areas, with their embedded notion of foreignness to the other parts of the polity, readily lends itself to the argument that parallel states exist in these areas. This then offers imperfect insights into the problems faced in the region and, to make matters worse, suggests that the solution to the problems facing Latin America are stronger state institutions. While this might be partially true, an indiscriminate strengthening of the state will only lead to more problems, since state actors themselves participate in the political alliances that contribute to violence and undermine the rule of law. Similarly, evidence in this book suggests that civil society is an ambivalent force in democracy and can serve to strengthen popular government, as much as it can break down the rule of law and support nondemocratic political outcomes. Arbitrarily attempting to strengthen civic institutions or the government, without regard to the type of institutions that are created or the type of relationships those institutions establish, will do little to promote democracy in the region. A subtler, more nuanced, and more contextualized approach to the nature of violence in Latin America provides us with a much stronger basis for understanding and solving the problems facing the region.

Looking toward the Future

Democracy in Brazil is unequal and discriminatory. The wealthy can flee to walled communities and to condominiums in Miami and New York, but the poor remain exposed to both state and criminal violence at home. Without access to resources to protect themselves, move to safer places, or hire lawyers, they have little way of pressuring the state to control violence. The result is that state leaders put little effort into controlling the police, until pressure comes from sources both inside and outside the country. More often than not, this pressure reaches a critical mass only after a group of people not involved in criminal activities is killed by the police. Much of this violence is sustained as a result of connections among state leaders, civic actors, and criminals. The existing liberal model of democracy provides few mechanisms for the poor to demand change on their own, and they must live under conditions that, for many, compare unfavorably to circumstances for similarly situated people under the dictatorships of the 1960s and 1970s.

Although there has been some writing on the interactions among state actors, civic leaders, and criminals in Latin America, little effort has been made to explain how these interactions work. The purpose of this book has been to fill these gaps by providing an on-the-ground analysis of how these connections operate and the challenges they pose to democratic governance.

This book has shown how criminals, civic leaders, and state officials interact in Rio's favelas. The nature of their interactions suggests that the core political cleavages in Rio cannot be understood simply as confrontations between state and civic actors broadly described in the weak states literature. Rather, criminals have emerged as political actors who are effectively part of neither state nor society, yet share attributes of both. Consequently, they must operate in the political system through other state and social actors. This analysis suggests that to understand politics in Rio we need to understand not just how state and society deal with each other, but how cross-institutional networks interact that bring together state, social, and criminal actors. Social scientists need to begin to develop models of political systems that adequately explain the role that criminals and other persistently violent nonstate actors play in them.

Scholars of Latin America should take seriously the specific role of crime and criminal organizations in the region's politics, without falling into the trap of ascribing too much power to criminal organizations or, alternatively, suggesting that their actions are in some way exogenous to the political system. Criminals in many parts of Latin America today are political actors not because they operate in ways somehow parallel to the state, but rather because they are integral to the operation of the political regime. Our notion and model of politics must be expanded so that we can adequately perceive the nature of their participation and their relations with state and civic actors. Although parallel states may exist at times, as may have occurred with the Sendero Luminoso in Peru in the 1980s, these are uncommon phenomena that do not characterize most organized violent actors. To understand these trends we need to move away from top-down studies of political institutions toward bottom-up examinations of local political dynamics.

The ability of traffickers to gain access to state resources and power to support their activities and their use of local ties to build legitimacy and gain protection suggest that this problem is not ephemeral. State repression and social programs do little on their own to control networks' criminal activity and, since criminals can link into and gain control of social groups, may actually strengthen criminal networks. Any long-term solution to these problems must be addressed through competing networks that bring residents, civic leaders, and state actors together to collectively resolve drug trafficking and local violence. Ultimately, a more in-depth understanding of the political role of crime in Latin America and solutions to the social violence that countries throughout the developing world face can only be found through more intense micro-level research into the operations of criminal organizations and the impacts that they have on state institutions and social groups.

Rio 2005

In July 2005, I sat in the air-conditioned offices of a foreign NGO in downtown Rio talking with Elísio, a resident of Vigário Geral, who had been active in the commission that had pushed for reforms in the Casa da Paz and who has since remained active in local organizations. I had read in newspapers and learned through conversations with friends concerned with the community that terrible things had happened in Vigário since I had left the country that had made that favela more violent and, indeed, more like Santa Ana and Tubarão. My hour-long conversation with Elísio made this clear and, in many ways, tied together the issues that continue to haunt all three communities—and this book.

Since 1999, violence has increased substantially in Vigário. The rivalry between the Vigário and Parada de Lucas gangs that had led to intense conflicts prior to the 1993 massacre reignited after the city-managed Favela-Bairro program built a ramp that connected the favela to a nearby highway so that residents who wanted to drive in and out of the favela could do so without having to pass through Parada de Lucas. This link to the outside created a degree of operational flexibility for Vigário's traffickers that the Parada gang found threatening. As time went by, and memories of the 1993 massacre faded, tensions increased. In 2000, a near invasion was averted only after the BOPE occupied the favela at the behest of local NGOs. Even this tenuous peace, however, broke down in 2003 when Parada's traffickers finally invaded in force. Elísio recalled that day:

> They [the Parada gang] came in directly with the police. The [regular]
> police gave them support [deram chapa]. They came in the morning and got
> them [the Vigário traffickers] out of bed. The went to the house of [a woman]
> where they got her in bed and beat her and committed various horrors on her
> until she told them where the others were. Then they went from person to
> person grabbing them. They grabbed nine and took them by van to Parada.
> They tortured them there. They killed them. It was a trauma. They [Vigário's
> traffickers] went recruiting, calling young kids, and old people here [to
> defend the community]. . . . In 2003, those guys invaded but turned tail

[*fizeram peneira*]. They weren't able to defend themselves. Reinforcements from other Comando Vermelho communities came to expel them. . . . Now it's turned into a civil war. The residents here are revolted with the residents from there. It isn't just a conflict between bandits now.[1]

The 2003 war broke the fragile peace that had existed in the community and turned residents of the two communities on each other. No longer was the conflict a matter of business between criminals, but the old angers and resentments of residents of the two communities had returned to the fore. As in the past, Vigário's residents now could not depend on the police for protection against the predations of criminals.

These conditions worsened a little over a year later when Parada invaded and occupied the community for several days, terrorizing residents and forcing many to seek refuge in a nearby park. Elísio noted: "In 2004 they invaded again, only that this time they firmed up. The war started on the second of October, on the eve of an election, on a Saturday. They took the community and stayed there for seven days." Again the Parada traffickers came in with the support of police. Frightened residents fled for their lives and set up camp in a nearby park as they waited for Vigário's traffickers to retake the community. These efforts, however, failed, as a result of the heavy armaments the invading gang brought with them and the support they received from law enforcement. Elísio continued: "The Parada traffickers had come to the community with strategy and arms and even with the police helping. The police stayed on the other side of the train [tracks] so that no one could walk around the street armed to prevent an invasion. The [Parada] traffickers put .30-caliber machine guns on the bridge, on the off-ramp, near Moacir's [a strategically located bar], in front of the *boca*, and next to the health post to prevent an invasion. The [Vigário] traffickers didn't have money to pay for help. They tried three times to retake the community but they didn't succeed."[2] Angered at their precarious situation, the inability of the local gang to retake the favela, and the failure of the government to do anything to make their neighborhood safe, Vigário's residents eventually burned a city bus in a street near the favela. After the press reported this, the governor ordered the BOPE to retake the community. Only their intervention successfully repulsed the Parada gang, reestablished a precarious peace in the community, and allowed residents to return to their homes.[3]

The close relationship between the police and the traffickers in Parada seems to be at the heart of problems in Vigário today. Elísio was very explicit about the nature and depth of police trafficker collusion: "The Sixteenth [Battalion] was paid R$50,000 to help the traffickers from Parada take the community. That story was way up there. The commanding officer of the Sixteenth was changed. He was involved in almost everything."[4] A young Afro-Reggae activist confirmed this, noting that "the Sixteenth Battalion is very close with the trafficking from there, clearly. They don't do anything. Here they come to beat residents, speak badly to them, break into and tear apart their homes. Sometimes the Sixteenth comes here to do a patrol. Generally, they come in the day in a group of up to four, but sometimes they come at night and there is lots of shooting. They beat residents."[5] This corruption goes beyond simply the invasion and affects more mundane matters of day-to-day policing. Elísio noted: "The police have an arrangement [arrego] with the traffickers from there. They pay R$5,000 to the police post so that they won't do anything. The traffickers walk past the police and call them 'my employee.'"[6]

The growing power of local traffickers, greater police corruption, and higher levels of violence has had a detrimental effect on local civic networking. One of the major changes that has taken place in the community since 1999 is that traffickers have again begun to depose elected AM leaders in favor of a trusted close ally and longtime friend. As Elísio put it: "After they succeeded in throwing the Parada traffickers out of the community the traffickers from here wanted someone closer to them in front of the Associação. So they called back Patricio [who had held the post in 2001 after traffickers forced out Lorivaldo, but whom Seu Almeida later defeated in an election] to be president. He was a childhood friend. He negotiates with the majority and with the traffickers. He calls the police and sees how much it costs. He hires lawyers for the traffickers. When one of the traffickers is arrested he calls the police and negotiates their release and then he talks to the lawyer who goes there and gets the police."[7] The AM in Vigário, which had been notably independent of criminals in the late 1990s, then, has gone back to being very similar to the AMs in Tubarão and Santa Ana, where leaders had very close relations to traffickers. The AM no longer provides serious support for the other civic groups operating in the community or actively seeks out resources from independent state agencies. Rather, it operates as a mediating agent between the traffickers, the community, and representatives of the state.

To make matters worse, the ongoing violence in the community has made the operation of the existing NGOs very difficult. All of the violence associated with the multiple wars that have occurred in the community has made it more difficult for local groups to secure funding and develop new programs than in the 1990s. As Elísio noted: "All of this was very complicated. We had various months of gunfights. The traffickers invaded because the police closed a deal with them, but this takes away our ability to do our job and establish goals for the future because what are your goals? Education? Health? Just not having gunfire is already a big accomplishment."[8] To make matters worse, when traffickers do invade the community, the operations of the civic groups are at risk. In the 2004 invasion, the Parada traffickers attempted to seize the incorporation documents of the local AM in order to legally fuse it with the Parada AM and eliminate Vigário as an independent favela. During this same invasion, the GCAR was accused of having an alliance with the Vigário traffickers and working against the Parada traffickers.[9] This led to substantial threats against the leadership of the GCAR in Vigário. With the specter of the long-term ascendance of the Parada gang, this could have resulted in the end of GCAR operations in Vigário.

Despite all of these problems, Vigário may still be better off than most other nearby favelas. Both the GCAR and the MOGEC have survived and remain strong. They both have a solid presence in the community, provide many services to residents, have succeeded in bringing in resources to expand their physical infrastructure, and help residents with basic problems. Both organizations remain well connected into city and state government, and their leaders display a solid grasp of how to interact with politicians and donors from the nonprofit world. They retain the active support of many residents, and there is no indication that their work will end anytime soon. They are, however, no longer part of a vibrant local movement, interacting with many other like-minded organizations within the community. They now face a more difficult political environment in which traffickers have effectively reestablished themselves and in which there are fewer committed activists. Nevertheless, they continue their operations, work to make life a little better for community residents, and provide a model for serious NGO operations in Rio's favelas.

Santa Ana and Tubarão

All of the changes that have occurred in Vigário suggest that that community, an exception when I studied it, has returned to a large extent to the norms typical of other favelas in the city. Despite some minor shifts in leadership, neither Santa Ana nor Tubarão has changed much. Both continue, for the most part, along the path traveled by other Rio favelas.

By 2005, higher-ranking traffickers had forced Doca, the manager of criminal operations in Santa Ana, to leave the community. They thought he was "getting soft."[10] The new traffickers did not trust Josias, Doca's father, so they pushed him out of the AM—and out of the community he had lived in for much of his life. Ruizão, a quiet but energetic evangelical Christian who had long had an interest in civic activism, took over the AM. When I visited with him he had a long list of complaints about life in the favela. The most important of these was the murder of seventy-five people in the first four months of 2005 in Santa Ana and surrounding favelas by a death squad that had been formed within the local police battalion. The commander of the battalion had a high degree of notoriety as a leader who tolerated and even expected violence from his troops, and Ruizão believed that he had formed this death squad, with troops he had personally brought with him from his previous command, to send a message to criminals in the district he now over-saw. In one particularly horrifying story, Ruizão recounted how police murdered an adolescent who had recently entered the local drug gang:

> The boy had run into the police and turned and ran. The police shot but the boy was able to keep going. He had gotten to around my home and fell down there in a corner. As I was arriving a very tense policeman arrived and would not let me get near the body. . . . I was upset; residents tried to calm me down. I wanted to help the boy and wouldn't stop trying. The police officer, who was very nervous, became very angry. Eventually, residents thought he would shoot me. Finally I gave up, and when I turned my back he fired three shots into the air. Eventually after twenty, thirty minutes of the boy bleeding on the ground his parents arrived, and they were allowed to attend to him. The police eventually provided some first aid and threw him in their truck to take him to the hospital. His family took a taxi but they ended up arriving before the police. The police drove around for awhile to let the boy bleed some more. He hung on for two or three days in the hospital and [then] died.[11]

Ruizão had no idea what to do about the pervasive and continuing problem of po-lice abuse, and he indicated that the police would only change their behavior with a serious alteration in policing practice, either through a change in the leadership of the battalion or through the implementation of a type of specialized commu-nity police reform that the city government had begun to attempt in various other favelas. For him, however, all of this was painful, frustrating, and pretty much out of his hands.

During my visit with Ruizão, a young man, apparently in his twenties, wearing a baseball cap and a prominent wedding ring, appeared in the AM with a well-dressed woman. They immediately went into a back room for a conversation with Ruizão. When they returned, Ruizão introduced me to the young man who then left with the woman. Ruizão looked visibly drained by the meeting. The man was one of the new clique of traffickers who had ascended to power in Santa Ana, and the woman had a connection to the city government. She had established ties with the gang to implement a city educational program in the community. Both had come to Ruizão to ask for his support. Apparently, the local gang still actively worked to maintain contacts with the government and still needed the help of the AM for these activities. Since Ruizão did not have their full confidence, the traffickers had taken a more prominent role in directly mediating their relationships with the government and helping deliver services to residents.

As in many other favelas, Santa Ana's traffickers have, under police pressure, begun to diversify their operations. Increasingly, Ruizão noted, traffickers are less likely to play "Robin Hood" with residents. Today, the traffickers have imposed a tax on the delivery of propane gas tanks used to fuel stoves. They have, in other words, begun to earnestly diversify beyond drug trafficking into other illegal activities. None of this, however, should be taken to mean that traffickers do not continue to maintain relations with local police—just that the form and nature of those relations have changed in response to the evolving political climate in the city.

In 2002, Bernardo, the longtime president of the Tubarão AM, died in a car accident in the interior of Rio. Some believed that the police had murdered him in retaliation for his criticism of police violence in the year before his death, but reliable sources indicated that it appears that at the end of a long drive from Rio to an interior town where he was hoping to run for city council he had fallen asleep and simply allowed his car to drive off the mountain road that he had been traveling on.

Ricardo, Bernardo's very quiet and long-standing vice president, stepped aside in favor of Jussara, an evangelical who headed the local city-funded crèche and who had worked closely with Bernardo as AM treasurer. Jussara was always an amiable and well-respected woman in the community, who also, through her connection with Bernardo, understood the relationship between the AM and the traffickers.

The job of AM president in Tubarão is, if anything, more difficult than most, since the favela's high-powered neighbors create pressures few other favelas have to deal with. Bernardo had done an excellent job balancing different interests and dealing with the myriad tensions involved in managing relations among politicians, residents, traffickers, and police. Jussara, in other words, had very big shoes to fill.

To complicate matters further, Bernardo died while the government was still testing the community-oriented police reform program in Tubarão. At about the time of his death, the head of the policing program was transferred out of the community and assigned to a political job in Brasília. His replacements were not nearly as innovative. Jussara had to take over the reins of the community at this particularly tense moment.

With the consolidation of the control of trafficking under one gang for both Tubarão and Ceuzinho that occurred in the late 1990s, the principal problem facing Tubarão today is not violence associated with gang warfare. Rather, most conflict in this community stems from police efforts to extort money or arrest traffickers. Since all policing in these communities today is managed through a specific community policing command located inside the favela, violence levels depend very much on the skills and ideology of the special unit's commander. Since Bernardo's death in 2002, there have been two different police commanders. One had a good relationship with the community and focused on controlling crime within basic norms of good police practice and human rights. The other commander had a more militarist approach that resulted in police under his command murdering an innocent resident in 2004. Jussara recounted this murder to me in the following story:

> The police went to a house in the community and demanded that the residents give them a snack. [After] they made them a snack . . . they burnt holes in the curtain to look out at the street. They stayed there from three until seven, when they started to commit atrocities. At a certain moment, they saw two traffickers there and they started to shoot. They killed the two but they also hit a worker who fell. The worker was in agony. They tried to put him on a board to carry him, but it broke. He screamed for help for his father and mother and family not to let him die. So then they [the police] told him to shut up, [which] a resident heard. They began to drag him. He screamed and they beat him. Each time he screamed more quietly. Finally the police stopped and cut him with a knife and he died. You couldn't hear him anymore. . . . They went all the way to the bottom [of the hill], and they threw his body like a sack of garbage in that truck of theirs. The next day there was a trail of blood where he had been dragged.[12]

Unfortunately, these types of acts, whether committed by traffickers or by police, are all too common in Rio today. What makes this event all the more horrific is that it occurred under the auspices of an innovative police reform program. After extensive resident protests in the well-off neighborhood below, the state government conducted an investigation that led to the removal of the more militaristic commander and his replacement with his more community-oriented predecessor. Residents and community leaders have indicated that although their relations with police have markedly improved, they remain very wary of law enforcement.

In general, residents and other local leaders do not see Jussara as Bernardo's equal, in terms of political or management skills. At the same time, everyone seems to recognize that she has a tough act to follow. As a former Ceuzinho community leader put it, "Bernardo was a great community leader. He was experienced, he had an understanding and wisdom about the community. He had a base in the history of the community, and he was one of the most important community leaders here in the Zona Sul. He had *jeito* [ability]; he knew how to administer. Now we don't have that. We look for it, but its hard. No other leader like that has emerged. You can't substitute him. You have to applaud what he did."[13] Cédric, the local Baptist pastor, had a similar though slightly more critical take:

> Today its different. Now its just conversation with Jussara. There are no more leadership council meetings. That no longer exists. Bernardo was a dictator, very bossy. He was different, he put a lot in his pocket but had a capacity for thinking that was very elevated. He never went after a person, and discussions never became personal. He was very intelligent. Jussara doesn't have the same capacity to interact. They imposed her as president of Ceuzinho. . . . She was imposed by the parallel power. She doesn't have the same ability. With her, other local leaders have distanced themselves. With Bernardo, there was always conversation and politics. Now the other leaders don't want to be marionettes.[14]

No one really expects Jussara to do the job that Bernardo did, but people still see the gap between her performance and his in this difficult role. In general, this change has led to more open tensions in the community, although there is no indication that rates of violence have changed dramatically as a result of her shortcomings.

In the end, none of these communities have changed that much. Everything seems to return to some underlying norm of violence that exists in and varies across the city. The shifts that have occurred in Vigário seem to have made that community more like other Rio favelas. Visiting Vigário, Tubarão, and Santa Ana today, I am often filled with an immense sadness at the missed opportunities for change and at the continual violence that both metaphorically and literally grinds up the lives of so many residents of these communities. In each of these places, people worry about their and their families' safety every single day, violence is always poised to break out, and the civil and political authorities that operate in and around these communities contribute to the fear and crime that reinforce a now twenty-year-old cycle of violence. There is no indication that this will change anytime soon. Until political leaders in Rio, and in Brazil more broadly, as well as those concerned about these issues beyond Brazil's borders, recognize the complicity of the political system, of formally democratic institutions, of local and national leaders, of elements of civil society, of the trade in drugs and arms, and of the international economy more generally in the ongoing conflicts affecting this city, there will be no solution to the problems faced by the millions of Brazilians who live under these horrible conditions. Any answer to these problems and, indeed, any possibility of changing the story told in this book depends on recognizing the deep connections of life, politics, and violence in places like Santa Ana, Tubarão, and Vigário Geral, and the rest of the city, and Brazil, and the world.

NOTES

Preface

1. On the United States, see, for example, Abinger, *Five Points*; and Asbury, *The Gangs of New York*. On Brazil, see Holloway, *Policing Rio de Janeiro*.
2. Perlman, *The Myth of Marginality*; and Leeds and Leeds, *A Sociologia do Brasil Urbano*.
3. On tours of favelas, see *Irish Times*, "Please Don't Shoot the Tourist," 7 June 2004, 15.
4. For more on the imperfection of internal control in favelas, see Arias and Rodrigues, "The Myth of Personal Security."

Introduction

1. On business closings, see Penglase, "The Shutdown of Rio de Janeiro," 3–6.
2. Goldstein, *Laughter Out of Place*, 201. See also Alvito, "A Honra de Acarí," 156; and Holston and Caldeira, "Democracy, Law, and Violence," 266–69.
3. Pereira, "An Ugly Democracy," 217.
4. Alves Filho and Pernambuco, "No Front Inimigo," 24–37; Soares, *Meu Casaco de General*, 269; and Fernandes and Rodrigues, "Viva Rio," 11–12.
5. Colburn, "Fragile Democracies," 76–80; Kruijt and Koonings, "Introduction," 1–30; Pinheiro, "The Rule of Law," 1–3; and Vilas, "Participation, Inequality, and the Whereabouts of Democracy," 26–29.
6. Sives, "Changing Patrons," 83–85; Human Rights Watch/Americas, *Violência X Violência*; Manaut, "Containing Armed Groups," 139–42, 143, 148–52; Guillermoprieto, *The Heart That Bleeds*, 114–17; Gunst, *Born Fi' Dead*, 10–11; Young Pelton, "Kidnapped in the Gap," 64–72, 92–98; Pécaut, "From the Banality of Violence to Real Terror," 142–47, 149–52; and Bowden, *Killing Pablo*, 1–70.
7. Caldeira, "Crime and Individual Rights"; Huggins, *Political Policing*, 201–4; and Koonings, "Shadows of Violence," 232–33.
8. For some of these exceptions, see Griffith, "Transnational Crime in the Americas," 63–86; Serrano, "Transnational Crime in the Western Hemisphere," 85–152; Clawson and Lee, *The Andean Cocaine Industry*; Koonings and Kruijt, *Societies of Fear*; Bailey and Godson, *Organized Crime and Democratic Governability*, 139–42, 143, 148–52; and Guillermoprieto, *The Heart That Bleeds*.
9. On the history of favelas as an other to the city, see Perlman, *The Myth of Marginality*, 1–3, 12–17; and Zaluar and Alvito, "Introdução," 7–19.
10. Múcio Bezerra, "Entrevista: Roberto Kant," *O Globo*, 9 June 2002, 18.

11. Fernandes, *Private but Public*, 148–49. See also Fernandes and Rodrigues, "Viva Rio," 11–12.

12. Soares, *Meu Casaco de General*, 269.

13. Fernandes, *Private but Public*, 104–15.

14. Múcio Bezerra, "Entrevista: Roberto Kant," *O Globo*, 9 June 2002, 18.

15. Soares, *Meu Casaco de General*,269.

16. Perlman, *The Myth of Marginality*, 1–3, 12–17; and Zaluar and Alvito, "Introdução," 7–19.

17. See, for example, Zuenir Ventura, "O risco da 'Colombina,'" *O Globo*, 22 June 2002, B12.

18. Leeds, "Cocaine and Parallel Polities in the Brazilian Urban Periphery," 47–50, 73–78; Zaluar, *A Máquina e a Revolta*; Alvito, *As Cores de Acarí*, 149–54, 160–64; and Burgos, "Dos parques proletários ao Favela-Bairro," 34–45.

19. See Perlman, *The Myth of Marginality*, 1–3, 12–17; and Burgos, "Dos parques proletários ao Favela-Bairro," 35–43.

20. Burgos, "Dos parques proletários ao Favela-Bairro," 43.

21. Leeds, "Cocaine and Parallel Polities in the Brazilian Urban Periphery," 50.

22. Ibid., 73–76.

23. Alvito, *As Cores de Acarí*, 162–64.

24. Ibid., 59–78. A similar argument can be seen in Sives, "Changing Patrons," passim.

25. On types of clientelist ties, see Grindle, "Patrons and Clients in the Bureaucracy," 43–49. On patron-client relations in Rio, see Gay, *Popular Organization and Democracy in Rio de Janeiro*.

26. Grindle, "Patrons and Clients in the Bureaucracy," 53.

27. On clientelism, see also Auyero, *Poor People's Politics*, 81–118.

28. Tilly, "War Making and State Making as Organized Crime," 170–71.

29. Malkin, "Narcotrafficking, Migration, and Modernity in Rural Mexico," 101.

30. Mark Bowden's *Killing Pablo*, a book on the life of Pablo Escobar, offers some interesting insights into this. He suggests that Escobar might have been able to live out his days as a wealthy and powerful criminal without ever touching off significant law enforcement efforts to bring him to justice had he not tried to enter the political arena. It was only after he tried to become a public figure and was elected an alternate member of Congress that the state began to make extensive efforts to bring him to justice. So long as he accepted his low social status and worked through accepted contacts with state actors he could influence the political system. When he violated these status rules and demanded official acceptance of illegal activities, the state moved against him. See Bowden, *Killing Pablo*, 35–59.

31. By differentially equal, I mean that actors possess different levels of status in different spheres and that although neither actor has clearly higher status overall, in some spheres one actor has more status than the other actor, and vice versa. Recent work on clientelism has however shown some of the status ambiguities in recent clientelist methods. See Auyero, *Poor People's Politics*.

32. Huggins, *Political Policing*, 201–3. On urban neighborhoods and private security, see Caldeira, "Fortified Enclaves," 115, 119, 124–25.

33. O'Donnell, "On the State, Democratization, and Some Conceptual Problems," 1361, 1364. See also Agüero, "Conflicting Assessments of Democratization," 6.

34. Méndez, "Problems of Lawless Violence," 20–24; Zaverucha, "Military Justice in the State of Pernambuco," 43, 70–72; and Frühling, "Judicial Reform and Democratization in Latin America," 237–38, 254–55.

35. Méndez, O'Donnell, and Pinheiro, *The (Un)Rule of Law*; Frühling and Tulchin, *Crime and Violence in Latin America*; and Rotker, *Citizens of Fear*.

36. Goldstein, *Laughter Out of Place*, 200, 225.

37. Ibid., 211.

38. Ibid., 210.

39. Blok, *The Mafia of a Sicilian Village, 1860–1960*, 179; and Tilly, "Foreword," xxi.

40. Goldstein, *Laughter Out of Place*, 211.

41. On Sendero Luminoso, see Rosenberg, *Children of Cain*, 152.

42. O'Donnell, "Why the Rule of Law Matters," 41.

43. Davis, "Contemporary Challenges and Historical Reflections," 5–6; and Pereira, "Armed Forces, Coercive Monopolies, and Changing Patterns," 387–90.

44. On Colombia, see Romero, "Reform and Reaction," 178–80, 202–5. See also Thoumi, *Political Economy and Illegal Drugs in Colombia*.

45. Caldeira, *City of Walls*, 78–82, 256–335.

46. Payne, *Uncivil Societies*, 1, 46.

47. Huggins, "Urban Violence and Police Privatization," 123–26; and Huggins, "From Bureaucratic Consolidation," 213, 225–26.

48. Huggins, *Political Policing*, 201–3; Shearing, "Reinventing Policing," 285–87, 291; and Duffield, *Global Governance and the New Wars*, 166–67.

49. Reno, *Warlord Politics in African States*, 4–7, 15–73; and Nordstrom, *Shadows of War*, 34–39. See also Duffield, *Global Governance and the New Wars*, 136–87; Kaplan, "The Coming Anarchy"; and Kaldor, *New and Old Wars*, 82–97. An analysis of this process in Rio can be found in Huggins, "Urban Violence and Police Privatization," 123–26.

50. For examples on Mexico, see Bailey and Godson, "Conclusion," 218–23. For examples on Jamaica, see Gunst, *Born Fi' Dead*, 10–11; and Sives, "Changing Patrons," 66–89.

51. For perspectives on state–civil society relations, see Mitchell, "The Limits of the State," 78–88. On the role of criminal actors in the polity, see Shelley, "Transnational Organized Crime: The New Authoritarianism"; Bailey and Godson, *Organized Crime and Democratic Governability*; Godson, *Menace to Society*; and Williams and Vlassis, *Combating Transnational Crime*.

52. Blok, *The Mafia of a Sicilian Village, 1860–1960*, 179; and Tilly, "Foreword," xxi.

53. On Mexico, see Bailey and Godson, "Conclusion," 218–23.

54. Strange, *The Retreat of the State*, 3–15, 110–21; and Reno, *Warlord Politics in African States*, 4–7, 15–73. See also O'Donnell, "On the State, Democratization, and Some Conceptual Problems," 1362.

55. See Huggins, "Urban Violence and Police Privatization," 123–26; and Caldeira, *City of Walls*.

56. Campbell and Brenner, *Death Squads in Global Perspective*, 16–17.

57. On local level networking and democratic governance, see Huggins, "From Bureaucratic Consolidation to Structural Devolution," 228–30.

58. Keck and Sikkink, *Activists beyond Borders*, 8; Powell and Smith Doerr, "Networks and Economic Life," 296–305; and Williams, "Organizing Transnational Crime," 72–77.

59. Powell and Smith Doerr, "Networks and Economic Life," 323; Keck and Sikkink, *Activists beyond Borders*, 8–9; and Boissevain, *Friends of Friends*, 24–28, 181–86.

60. On the role of network connections in creating trust, see Granovetter, "The Strength of Weak Ties," 212–13; and Espinoza, "Networks of Informal Economy," 52. On types of network ties, see also Putnam, *Bowling Alone*, 22–23.

61. Moss Kanter, "The Future of Bureaucracy and Hierarchy in Organizational Theory," 68.

62. Podolny and Page, "Network Forms of Organization," 57–76; Uzzi, "The Sources and Consequences of Embeddedness for the Economic Performance of Organizations," 674–98; Putnam, *Bowling Alone*, 174; and Diani, "Simmel to Rokkan and Beyond," 291.

63. Granovetter, "The Strength of Weak Ties," 212–21; and Espinoza, "Networks of Informal Economy," 52.

64. Alves Filho and Pernambuco, "No Front Inimigo," 36–37. Referring to survey data from urban Brazilians on repressive responses to crime, see Caldeira, "Crime and Individual Rights," 204–6. See also Caldeira, *City of Walls*, 339–75. For a critique of these militarized approaches, see Leeds, "Cocaine and Parallel Polities in the Brazilian Urban Periphery," 77.

65. On these types of efforts, see Arias, "Faith in Our Neighbors."

66. Putnam, *Making Democracy Work*, 167–87.

67. Dowdney, *Children of the Drug Trade*, 70–71; and Costa, "Segurança no palanque," 36–37.

68. Leeds, "Cocaine and Parallel Polities in the Brazilian Urban Periphery," 77.

69. Ibid., 70–73.

Chapter One

1. Luis Ernesto Magalhães, "Em Plena Zona Sul, um país melhor que a Noruega," *O Globo*, <www.oglobo.com.br>, 17 July 2003.

2. Meade, *"Civilizing" Rio*, 84–85.

3. On vaccination efforts, see ibid., 90–101; and Murilo de Carvalho, *Os Bestializados*, 91–135. On policing, see Holloway, *Policing Rio de Janeiro*, 285–91. On improvements in the city in the late nineteenth century, see Needell, *A Tropical Belle Epoque*, 33–51.

4. For analysis of the theme of civilization in the context of urban popular classes in Rio de Janeiro, see Meade, *"Civilizing" Rio*, 18.

5. Zaluar and Alvito, "Introdução," 12.

6. For an analysis and critique of this perspective, see Leeds and Leeds, *A Sociologia do Brasil Urbano*, 86–143.

7. Holloway, "A Healthy Terror."

8. McCann, *Hello, Hello Brazil*, 100; Dávila, *Diploma of Whiteness*, 55–57; and Vianna, *The Mystery of Samba*, 77, 90–92. See also Williams, *Culture Wars in Brazil*.

9. McCann, *Hello, Hello Brazil*, 41–95.

10. Meade, *"Civilizing" Rio*, 71n; and Zaluar and Alvito, "Introdução," 8–9.

11. On police actions against *quilombos* in Rio, see Holloway, *Policing Rio de Janeiro*, 35, 109, 137; and Meade, *"Civilizing" Rio*, 71, 92. See also Leeds and Leeds, *A Sociologia do Brasil Urbano*, 191.

12. Cited in Zaluar and Alvito, "Introdução," 8.

13. Ibid., 8–13.

14. Meade, *"Civilizing" Rio*, 173–84.

15. Burgos, "Dos parques proletários ao Favela-Bairro," 26. See also Vianna, *The Mystery of Samba*, 77–79. The Vargas period was also a time of great controversy over the use and meaning of samba that led the government and some musicians explicitly to attack the types of sambas coming out of favelas; see Williams, *Culture Wars in Brazil*, 85–87.

16. Burgos, "Dos parques proletários ao Favela-Bairro," 27. See also French, *The Brazilian Workers' ABC*, 81–84.

17. Burgos, "Dos parques proletários ao Favela-Bairro," 27.

18. Ibid., 27–28.

19. Ibid., 28.

20. Carolina, 17 December 1998; Valéria, 15 December 1998; Denise, 25 November 1998; Jorge, 17 January 1999; Miguel, 25 November 1997; Luís, 9 October 1997; and Tomás, 10 June 1997.

21. Burgos, "Dos parques proletários ao Favela-Bairro," 28–31.

22. The other period of democratic rule in Brazil, the Old Republic, 1889–1930, had a very limited franchise.

23. Zaluar, *A Máquina e a Revolta*, 181–82.

24. Zaluar and Alvito, "Introdução," 14. For a detailed description of this concept, see Leeds and Leeds, *A Sociologia do Brasil Urbano*, 213–21.

25. Prior to 1960, the city of Rio de Janeiro was the capital of Brazil and, as such, was administratively organized as the *Distrito Federal* (Federal District). With the removal of the capital to Brasília, the city of Rio was designated the state of Guanabara until it was merged with and became the capital of the surrounding state of Rio in 1975.

26. Perlman, *The Myth of Marginality*, 205–7.

27. Zaluar and Alvito, "Introdução," 14–15; and Burgos, "Dos parques proletários ao Favela-Bairro," 34.

28. Leeds and Leeds, *A Sociologia do Brasil Urbano*, 235–38.

29. Perlman, *The Myth of Marginality*, 258–60.

30. Ibid., 206–9; and Leeds and Leeds, *A Sociologia do Brasil Urbano*, 235–47. According to Perlman, the firefighters in the area were under orders to refuse calls for help from the favela.

31. Burgos, "Dos parques proletários ao Favela-Bairro," 38.

32. Perlman, *The Myth of Marginality*, 205–7.

33. Ibid., 207; and Burgos, "Dos parques proletários ao Favela-Bairro," 38–39.

34. On the role of AMs, see Burgos, "Dos parques proletários ao Favela-Bairro," 35.

35. Santos, *Toward a New Common Sense.*

36. Holloway, *Policing Rio de Janeiro*, 272–91; and Leeds, "Cocaine and Parallel Polities in the Brazilian Urban Periphery," 63–66.

37. Dowdney, *Children of the Drug Trade*, 27–28. For a discussion of the transition from *bicheiros* to traffickers, see Barcellos, *Abusado*, 232–34. On trafficking during this period, see also Leeds, "Cocaine and Parallel Polities in the Brazilian Urban Periphery," 55–56.

38. Trajano Sento-Sé, *Brizolismo*, 220; and Gay, *Popular Organization and Democracy in Rio de Janeiro*, 21–22.

39. Gay, *Popular Organization and Democracy in Rio de Janeiro*, 25–34; and Trajano Sento-Sé, *Brizolismo*, 217–31.

40. Burgos, "Dos parques proletários ao Favela-Bairro," 41–43.

41. Gay, *Popular Organization and Democracy in Rio de Janeiro*, 31, 40–41.

42. Gay, "Popular Incorporation and the Prospects for Democracy," 452–54.

43. Leeds, "Cocaine and Parallel Polities in the Brazilian Urban Periphery," 74.

44. *Jornal do Brasil*, "Polícia Critica Politicos Que Soubem Morros," 12 August 1996, 1, 3.

45. Dowdney, *Children of the Drug Trade*, 60–62.

46. Leeds, "Cocaine and Parallel Polities in the Brazilian Urban Periphery," 63–66; and Dowdney, *Children of the Drug Trade*, 32.

47. On the development of gangs in Rio, see Leeds, "Cocaine and Parallel Polities in the Brazilian Urban Periphery," 52–56; and Dowdney, *Children of the Drug Trade*, 29–32. See also Amorim, *Comando Vermelho*.

48. Dowdney, *Children of the Drug Trade*, 29–32.

49. Leeds, "Cocaine and Parallel Polities in the Brazilian Urban Periphery," 55.

50. Barcellos, *Abusado*, 234.

51. Ibid., 232.

52. Burgos, "Dos parques proletários ao Favela-Bairro," 44; and Leeds, "Cocaine and Parallel Polities in the Brazilian Urban Periphery," 50.

53. Fernandes, *Private but Public*, 104–7.

54. For a more detailed discussion of this, see Arias, "Trouble en Route."

55. On port sizes, see <http://www.aapa-ports.org/pdf/Container_CSAmerica.PDF>.

56. Data provided in official police reports and organized by Centro de Estudos de Segurança e Cidadania. Available at <http://www.ucam.edu.br/cesec>.

57. Dowdney, *Children of the Drug Trade*, 46–51.

58. Ibid., 42–46.

59. For an example of this, see Barcellos, *Abusado*, 488–89.

60. For an example of this treatment, see Larry Rohter, "As Crime and Politics Collide in Rio, City Cowers in Fear," *New York Times*, 8 May 2003, A3. For a critique, see Dowdney, *Children of the Drug Trade*, 40–42.

61. Gay, *Lucia*, 31; and Monica Torres Maia, "White admite conhecer acusados de tráfico na FAB," *O Globo*, 19 May 1999, 10.

62. For an example of this, see *O Estado de São Paulo*, "Pinheiro Landim renuncia ao mandato dedeputado," <www.estadao.com.br>, 25 February 2003.

63. Dowdney, *Children of the Drug Trade*, 40–41.

64. On traffickers need of favelas for protection, see ibid., 56–60; and Centro de Defesa dos Direitos Humanos "Bento Rubião," *Favelas e as Organizações Comunitárias*, 55–58, 63. For an analysis of this issue in the United States, see Sanchez-Jankowski, *Islands in the Street*, 180–93.

65. Dowdney, *Children of the Drug Trade*, 63–69; and Leeds, "Cocaine and Parallel Polities in the Brazilian Urban Periphery," 61.

66. For more details on dispute resolution in favelas, see Arias and Rodrigues, "The Myth of Personal Security."

67. Perlman, "Marginality," 130–31.

68. Patterson, "Religious Activity and Political Participation," 1–2, 7; and Burdick, "What Is the Color of the Holy Spirit?," 110.

69. Goldstein, *Laughter Out of Place*, 215–25. She shows here that participation in these denominations varies considerably over time for some individuals.

70. For an overview of this dynamic, see Dowdney, *Children of the Drug Trade*, 53–54.

71. Centro de Defesa dos Direitos Humanos "Bento Rubião," *Favelas e as Organizações Comunitárias*, 55–58, 63.

72. Leeds, "Cocaine and Parallel Polities in the Brazilian Urban Periphery," 60–61; and Weffort, *America Astray*, 20.

73. Leeds, "Cocaína e poderes paralelos na periferia urbana brasileira: ameaça à democratização em nível local," 243; and Dowdney, *Children of the Drug Trade*, 53–54.

74. Centro de Defesa dos Direitos Humanos "Bento Rubião," *Favelas e as Organizações Comunitárias*, 56. For an example of this in the U.S. context, see Sanchez-Jankowski, *Islands in the Street*, 180–93.

75. For examples of this approach, see Antônio Werneck, Elenilce Botari, and Gustavo Paiva Goulart, "Beira-Mar negocia até míssil," *O Globo*, 19 June 2002, 14; Vera Araújo, "As novas granadas do tráfico," *O Globo*, 9 June 2002, 17; Vera Araújo, "Favelas proibidas aos PMs," *O Globo*, 23 June 2002, 20; Roberto Kant, "As favelas passaram de refúgios a feudos (Entrevista)," *O Globo*, 23 June 2002, 18; Marcos F. Moraes, "A nação invadida," *O Globo*, 14 June 2002, 7; Zuenir Ventura, "O risco da 'Colombina,'" *O Globo*, 22 June 2002, B12; Ignácio Cano, "O Estado nunca estve presente," *O Globo*, 23 June 2002, 23; Ana Cláudia Costa, "Uma avenida dominada por ladrões de carros e 'bondes' de traficantes," *O Globo*, 19 June 2002, 19; and Berliner and Lado, "Brazil," 239–60. For a good synopsis of this perspective, see Alves Filho and Pernambuco, "No Front Inimigo," 24–37. The cover of this edition of *Istoé* carries a picture of a young masked man wearing no shirt carrying a shotgun with a presidential sash in green and yellow hanging across his chest. See also Goldstein, *Laughter Out of Place*, 225.

76. Flávio Pessoa, "Negócios entre tráfico e polícia," *O Globo*, 20 June 2002, 15. In 2002, about us$167 and us$333, respectively.

77. Muniz, "Ser Policial é, sobretudo, uma Razão de Ser," 70–71.

78. A comprehensive account of the police under the dictatorship can be found in Huggins, *Political Policing*, 99–186. See also Chevigny, *The Edge of the Knife*, 152.

79. Observations of trial of Ivan Maginário, defendant in Vigário Geral massacre, 26

November 1997. Lawyers at the trial read statements about extensive corruption in the civil police into the record.

80. Centro de Defesa dos Direitos Humanos "Bento Rubião," *Favelas e as Organizações Comunitárias*, 50–55.

81. This privatization of security and citizenship is not unique to favelas. For more on how this occurs generally in Brazil, see Huggins, *Political Policing*, 201–3. On urban neighborhoods and private security, see Caldeira, "Fortified Enclaves," 115, 119, 124–25.

82. Carvalho et al., "Cultura Política e Cidadania," 4, 31–33.

Chapter Two

1. Keck and Sikkink, *Activists beyond Borders*, 8 (quote); Powell and Smith Doerr, "Networks and Economic Life," 381; Powell, "Neither Market nor Hierarchy," 295–336; and Williams, "Organizing Transnational Crime," 72–73.

2. Powell, "Neither Market nor Hierarchy," 323; Keck and Sikkink, *Activists beyond Borders*, 8–9; and Boissevain, *Friends of Friends*, 24–28, 181–86.

3. On network connections in creating trust, see Granovetter, "The Strength of Weak Ties," 212–13; and Espinoza, "Networks of Informal Economy," 52. On types of network ties, see also Putnam, *Bowling Alone*, 22–23; and Diani, "Social Mobilization and Social Capital," 142–43.

4. Williams, "Organizing Transnational Crime," 72–78.

5. Ibid., passim.

6. Keck and Sikkink, *Activists beyond Borders*, 16–29. See also Risse, "International Norms and Domestic Change," 537–51; and Putnam, *Making Democracy Work*, 174.

7. Keck and Sikkink, *Activists beyond Borders*, 19–37. On types of network ties, see also Putnam, *Bowling Alone*, 22–23; and Diani, "Social Mobilization and Social Capital," 142–43.

8. Shelley, "Transnational Organized Crime: The New Authoritarianism"; Bailey and Godson, *Organized Crime and Democratic Governability*; and Godson, *Menace to Society*.

9. Strange, *The Retreat of the State*, 91–99, 110.

10. Reno, *Warlord Politics in African States*, 4–7, 15–73; and Nordstrom, *Shadows of War*, 34–39. See also Duffield, *Global Governance and the New Wars*, 136–87; Kaplan, "The Coming Anarchy," 44–76; and Treverton, "International Organized Crime," 47–56.

11. Crandall, *Driven by Drugs*, 84–99; Gamarra, "Transnational Criminal Organization in Bolivia," 184–86; Blok, *The Mafia of a Sicilian Village, 1860–1960*, 179; and Tilly, "Foreword," xxi.

12. Paley, *Marketing Democracy*, 5–6.

13. Moss Kanter, "The Future of Bureaucracy and Hierarchy in Organizational Theory," 63–87.

14. See Migdal, "The State in Society," 16–17.

15. On the identification effect, which has much broader implications than those described here, see Trouillot, "The Anthropology of the State in the Age of Globalization," 132.

16. Reno, *Warlord Politics in African States*, 45–68. See also Singer, *Corporate Warriors*, 101–18.

17. On the role of corrupt state officials in producing end user licensing certificates for weapons sales, see Naylor, "The Rise of the Modern Arms Black Market," 216–17. See also Lee, "Transnational Organized Crime: An Overview," 13.

18. On privatization and corruption in Mexico, see Curzio, "Organized Crime and Political Campaign Finance in Mexico," 91–92.

19. On policy networks, see Teichman, *The Politics of Freeing Markets in Latin America*, 16–21. Teichman's book focuses on policy networks containing state and social groups but also suggests the importance of contacts and linkages within the state.

20. Keck and Sikkink, *Activists beyond Borders*, 2–5, 16–25, and 79–120.

21. On state society links in new democracies, see Hagopian, "Democracy and Political Representation," 100–102, 109–19, 126–28. On Rio, see Fernandes, *Private but Public*, 25–29, 104–7.

22. Leeds, "Cocaine and Parallel Polities in the Brazilian Urban Periphery," 76.

23. This is most visible in the case of Mexico. See Chevigny, *The Edge of the Knife*, 233–36; and Pimentel, "The Nexus of Organized Crime," 41–42.

24. An interesting example of this can be seen with the resignation of Pinheiro Landim as federal deputy from the state of Ceará over his intervention with a judge in a trafficker's habeas corpus petition. See *O Estado de São Paulo*, "Pinheiro Landim renúncia ao mandato deputado," <www.estadao.com.br>, 25 February 2003.

25. Oxhorn, *Organizing Civil Society*, 311–12; and Cohen and Arato, *Civil Society and Political Theory*, ix.

26. Gellner, "The Importance of Being Modular," 42; Hall, "In Search of Civil Society," 23; and Kurtz, "Free Markets and Democratic Consolidation in Chile," 295.

27. Evans, *Embedded Autonomy*, 12–13; and Kurtz, "Free Markets and Democratic Consolidation in Chile."

28. In the context of terrorism and Cypriot efforts for independence, this can be seen in the links between Greek Cypriot religious leaders and militants. Hoffman, *Inside Terrorism*, 56–61.

29. See Paley, *Marketing Democracy*, 210; and Segarra, "Redefining the Public/Private Mix," 489–90.

30. On Pablo Escobar's charitable work, see Bowden, *Killing Pablo*, 32.

31. On the relationship between criminals and local populations, see Sanchez-Jankowski, *Islands in the Streets*, 180–93; and Centro de Defesa dos Direitos Humanos "Bento Rubião," *Favelas e as Organizações Comunitárias*, 55–58, 63.

32. On social contacts in communication, see Kurtz, "Free Markets and Democratic Consolidation in Chile," 289–95; Wang, "Mutual Empowerment of State and Society," 232–46; and Migdal, "The State in Society." On state society interactions in Brazil, see Hagopian, "Traditional Politics," 37–65.

33. Podolny and Page, "Network Forms of Organization," 62–64; Uzzi, "The Sources and Consequences of Embeddedness for the Economic Performance of Organizations," 677–680, 682; and Putnam, *Making Democracy Work*, 174.

34. Lee, "Transnational Organized Crime: An Overview," 22–25.

35. Podolny and Page, "Network Forms of Organization," 62–64; Uzzi, "The Sources and Consequences of Embeddedness for the Economic Performance of Organizations," 677–80, 682; and Williams, "Organizing Transnational Crime," 75.

36. On this, see Gambetta, *The Sicilian Mafia*. He suggests that the Mafia acts as a firm that sells protection. Although he has some excellent insights into how the Mafia operates and into illegal markets, it is worth noting that groups contract the Mafia because they know they are "men of honor." People come into contact with the Mafia because of their social networks.

37. Powell, "Neither Market nor Hierarchy," 303–4. On networks enforcing social norms, see Putnam, *Making Democracy Work*, 171–72.

38. Brzezinsky, "Re-engineering the Drug Business," 28.

39. On this process of drug production moving to other areas, see Serrano, "Transnational Crime in the Western Hemisphere," 101–2.

40. Granovetter, "The Strength of Weak Ties" (on the role of networks in impoverished communities, see 212–13); and Espinoza, "Networks of Informal Economy," 52. On types of network ties, see also Putnam, *Bowling Alone*, 22–23.

41. On social movement mechanisms for reform, see Alvarez, "Politicizing Gender and Engendering Democracy," 241; Gay, *Popular Organization and Democracy in Rio de Janeiro*, 25–34; and Cardoso, "Popular Movements in the Context of the Consolidation of Democracy in Brazil," 291. On movement deactivation, see Tarrow, *Power in Movement*, 49–52.

42. Williams, "Organizing Transnational Crime," 77.

43. Shelley, "Transnational Organized Crime: The New Authoritarianism," 37–42.

44. Bailey and Godson, "Introduction," 10.

45. Holston and Caldeira, "Democracy, Law, and Violence," 282–89; and Goldstein, "In Our Own Hands."

46. O'Donnell, "On the State, Democratization, and Some Conceptual Problems," 1356–57.

47. Payne, *Uncivil Societies*; Caldeira, *City of Walls*; Huggins, "Urban Violence and Police Privatization," 123–26; and Huggins, "From Bureaucratic Consolidation to Structural Devolution," 213, 225–26.

48. Shelley, "Transnational Organized Crime: The New Authoritarianism," 33–37.

49. Yashar, "Indigenous Protest and Democracy in Latin America," 87–122, 99; Chalmers, Martin, and Piester, "Associative Networks," 552–53; and Fernandes, *Private but Public*, 25–29, 104–7.

50. Méndez, "Institutional Reform," 221–26; Zaverucha, "Military Justice in the State of Pernambuco," 72; Correa Sutil, "Judicial Reforms in Latin America," 255–71; and Frühling, "Judicial Reform and Democratization in Latin America," 237–62.

51. Pereira, "An Ugly Democracy," 234–35.

52. Hernando de Soto, "The Constituency of Terror," *New York Times*, 15 October 2001, 19. On the role of the state in extending guarantees to the poor, see Reis, "The State, the Market, and Democratic Citizenship," 122, 133–34.

53. For a discussion of social actors building ties to state agents to prevent policy implementation, see Migdal, "The State in Society," 16–17.

54. On this phenomenon in Brazil, see Alvarez, "Politicizing Gender and Engendering Democracy," 241; and Gay, *Popular Organization and Democracy in Rio de Janeiro*, 25–34.

55. Cardoso, "Popular Movements in the Context of the Consolidation of Democracy in Brazil," 291.

56. Alvarez, Dagnino, and Escobar, "Introduction," 18–19.

57. Kurtz, "Free Markets and Democratic Consolidation in Chile," 289–95; Wang, "Mutual Empowerment of State and Society," 232–46; and Migdal, "The State in Society."

58. Leeds, "Cocaine and Parallel Polities in the Brazilian Urban Periphery," 69–73.

59. Keck and Sikkink, *Activists beyond Borders*, 16–29; and Risse and Sikkink, "The Socialization of International Human Rights Norms into Domestic Practices," 17–35.

60. Alvarez, Dagnino, and Escobar, "Introduction," 22; and Putnam, *Making Democracy Work*, 174.

61. Sikkink, "The Latin American Human Rights Network," 70–71; Chevigny, *The Edge of the Knife*, 169, 264–73; and Hochstetler, "Democratizing Pressure from Below?," 169.

Chapter Three

1. Vilma, 6 December 1998.

2. Elizete, 6 January 1999.

3. Ludmila, 25 August 1998; Regina, 23 November 1998; and Denise, 25 November 1998.

4. Vilma, 6 December 1998.

5. Ludmila, 25 August 1998; Regina, 23 November 1998; and Denise, 25 November 1998.

6. Bernardo and members of government/NGO micro-credit program, 24 November 1998; community observations, 24 November 1998; and Denise, 3 December 1998.

7. Conversation with Denise, 25 November 1998.

8. Sacha, 19 October 1998; and Bernardo and others in the AM, 16 November 1998.

9. Denise, 25 November 1998 (quote); also Irimina and Carlos, 16 December 1998; and Carolina, 17 December 1998.

10. Sacha, 19 October 1998; and Jorge, 17 January 1999.

11. Jorge, 17 January 1999.

12. Ibid.

13. Elizete, 7 January 1999.

14. Jorge, 17 January 1999.

15. Observed meeting in samba *quadra* in Ceuzinho, 25 January 1999.

16. Bernardo, 6 October 1998; and Bernardo and Jussara, 7 October 1998.

17. Jorge, 17 January 1999.

18. Bernardo, 6 October 1998; and Bernardo and Jussara, 7 October 1998.

19. Bernardo and Alexandre, 5 November 1998.

20. Bernardo, 27 September 1998.

21. Bernardo, 30 September 1998.

22. Jorge, 17 January 1999.

23. Zinha and César, 7 October 1998.

24. Denise, 3 December 1998.

25. Jorge, 17 January 1999.

26. Centro de Defesa dos Direitos Humanos "Bento Rubião," *Favelas e as Organizações Comunitárias*, 55–58, 63; and Sanchez-Jankowski, *Islands in the Street*, 180–93.

27. Bernardo, 6 October 1998; and Bernardo and Jussara, 7 October 1998.

28. Observations of Tubarão and Ceuzinho, 16 April 1999; and Cristiano, 18 April 1999.

29. Cristiano and unknown resident, 18 April 1999.

30. Bernardo, AM worker, and prospective adolescent employee, 20 November 1998.

31. Alvito, *As Cores de Acarí*, 224.

32. Elizete and her husband, Wilson, 20 November 1998.

33. Alexandre and Jorge, 9 January 1999.

34. Elizete, 27 November 1998.

35. Bernardo and unknown residents who had their radios stolen, 5 October 1998.

36. Pedrinho, 2 August 2001.

37. Susana, 18 April 1999.

38. Alexandre and Jorge, 9 January 1999.

39. Elizete, 6 January 1998.

40. For a further discussion of this issue, see Arias and Rodrigues, "The Myth of Personal Security."

41. Elizete, 8 January 1999.

42. Observed meeting of the Ceuzinho AM, 25 January 1999.

43. Denise, 3 December 1998.

44. Observed Ceuzinho AM meeting, 9 January 1999; and Denise, 3 December 1998.

45. During the period of this study, Brazilian *real*/U.S. dollar exchange rates ranged from R$1.20 to US$1 and R$2 to US$1.

46. Evaldo, activist from community, in conversation with Jorge and me on city street, 17 January 1999.

47. Elizete, 27 November 1998.

48. Bernardo and a number of women associated with traffickers, 7 December 1998.

49. Bernardo and multiple other residents, 7 January 1999.

50. Elizete, 6 January 1999.

51. Roberto, Carlton, police lieutenant, and other police officers, 25 August 1998.

52. Ricardo and Claudia, 18 August 1998.

53. Carolina, 15 January 1999

54. Carolina, 17 December 1998.

55. Ricardo and Claudia, 18 August 1998; and observed meeting in AM and observed conversation between Bernardo and residents, 3 October 1998.

56. It was clear that this group was made up of traffickers, because I had seen many of them dealing cocaine at the entrance of the favela on other days.

57. Observations of Children's Party in community's main plaza, 13 October 1998.

58. Elizete, 6 January 1999.

59. Ibid.

60. Bernardo and Mario, 26 August 1998.

61. Bernardo and residents looking for work, 6 August 1998; Bernardo, Solomão, and Jussara, 11 August 1998; and Bernardo, Jussara, and representatives of political candidate, 26 August 1998.

62. Bernardo and Jussara, 7 October 1998.

63. Bernardo and a young politician, 21 October 1998.

64. Between US$12 and US$18 per month during the period of study.

65. Jussara and César, 13 August 1998; and Jussara, 20 October 1998.

66. Sérgio, August 1996.

67. Sacha, 19 October 1998; observations of activities outside of a Spiritist crèche, 20 November 1998; Sacha, 30 November 1998; Sister Elena, 25 November 1998; Sara and Bartolomé, 1 December 1998; and Carolina, 21 January 1999.

68. Bernardo and residents in AM, 3 October 1998.

69. Gay, *Popular Organization and Democracy in Rio de Janeiro*, 41–60; and Gay, "The Broker and the Thief."

70. Amália, 3 July 2001.

71. João, 21 June 2001.

72. Observations of meeting at Viva Rio, 17 July 2001.

73. Ibid.

74. Observations of meeting about opening of sports facility at Viva Rio headquarters, July 2001; and observations of inaugural ceremony for sports facility at Ceuzinho samba *quadra*, 11 August 2001.

75. Cédric, 10 July 2001.

76. João, 21 June 2002.

77. Elizete, 4 July 2001.

78. Conversation with Carolina, 23 July 2001.

79. Major Antunes, 7 July 2001.

80. Cédric, 10 July 2001.

81. Ibid.

82. Alexandre, 13 June 2002.

83. Observations of Tubarão leadership council meeting, 7 July 2001.

84. Between 1998 and 2000, Soares served as state sub-secretary for public security and was later promoted to a supervisory position above the state secretary for public security. Prior to the implementation of this program, Soares was fired by Garotinho and, threatened with death by Rio police, fled into exile in the United States. In 2003, Soares served as nation secretary for public security in the Lula administration and was subsequently forced from office amid accusations of nepotism.

85. On the role of networks in linking the poor to the state, see Chalmers, Martin, and Piester, "Associative Networks."

86. Major Costa, 11 August 2003.

Chapter Four

1. It is a common misunderstanding among Rio residents that fireworks signal the entry of narcotics and their availability for sale. Residents indicated that this was not the case, and, at any rate, it made no sense for the traffickers to announce the presence of new drugs in the favela, since that would provide the police with an opportunity to interdict the shipment.

2. Observed conversation of local trash collectors, 31 July 1997.

3. Martinha, 9 July 1997.

4. Soares et al., "Criminalidade urbana e violência," 173.

5. Joselino and Ricardo, 3 July 1997.

6. Observations of traffickers at entrance of favela, 21 June 2001.

7. Ignácio, Maria, and Fernanda, 4 June 1997.

8. Josias and Eusébio, 21 May 1997.

9. Bête, 2 June 1997. This statement is commonly seen in graffiti around Rio.

10. Camilla, 11 August 1997.

11. Josias and Manoel, 10 July 1997.

12. Bête, 23 July 1997.

13. Caldeira, "Crime and Individual Rights," 204–10. In this chapter, Caldeira argues that crime is seen as a social disease in Brazil that has been confronted with repression.

14. Josias, 13 May 1997; Ignácio, Maria, and Fernanda, 4 June 1997.

15. Ignácio, Maria, and Fernanda, 4 June 1997; and Sandra, 1 August 1997.

16. Josias and Eusébio, 21 May 1997.

17. Joselino, 3 July 1997.

18. Observed conversation of community leaders and residents in AM discussing violence as they worried about possible bloodshed during a large party the traffickers would host that night which they planned to attend, 4 July 1997.

19. Manoel, 23 May 1997.

20. Josias, 10 July 1997; and Josias and others in the AM headquarters, 28 July 1997.

21. Aninha, 11 December 1998.

22. Ignácio, Maria, and Fernanda, 4 June 1997; Ana, 4 June 1997; Joselino, 3 July 1997; and Ricardo, 12 August 1997.

23. Joselino, 20 January 1999.

24. Camilla, 23 February 1999.

25. Josias, Eusébio, and Clara, 5 August 1997.

26. For a discussion of personal relationships and trafficker power in favelas, see Alvito, "Um bicho-de-sete-cabeças," 200–202. See also Mafra, "Drogas e símbolos," 180.

27. Camilla, 11 August 1997.

28. This is the story related by residents. The police version says there was an exchange of fire. Sandrão, 9 September 1998; Camilla, 9 September 1998; Joselino, 23 October 1998; and Antônio, 23 October 1998.

29. Camilla, 11 August 1997.

30. Joselino, 23 October 1998.

31. Ibid.

32. Ata da Assembléia, 24 February 1973; and Seu Abelardo, 3 July 1997.

33. Joselino, 13 January 1999.

34. Perlman, *The Myth of Marginality*, 195–240; Gay, *Popular Democracy and Political Organization in Rio de Janeiro*; and Ata da Assembléia, 10 June 1972.

35. Ata da Assembléia, passim (recorded in field notes on 20 May to 26 May 1997).

36. Leonel Brizola was an important populist politician prior to the dictatorship. When elections again took place in the 1980s, he returned to political life and conducted his electoral campaigns along similar populist lines to those he had used prior to the dictatorship.

37. Quote from Manoel and other residents, 23 June 1997; Ignácio, Maria, and Fernanda, 4 June 1997; Tomás, 10 June 1997; and older woman from northeast, 22 June 1997.

38. Joselino, 13 January 1999.

39. Traditional political arrangements did not reemerge in Rio's favelas after the dictatorship because politicians decided to break the back of the FAFERJ—it had become too powerful during the transition to democracy. At the same time that politicians were undermining the power of the leaders of favelas, money flowing into Rio's favelas through the narcotics trade led to the rapid strengthening of drug gangs in the city. The drug dealers began to provide some of the social services that had previously been provided by AM leaders through their contacts with politicians. For more on this, see the last section of the introduction and chapter 1.

40. Camilla, 25 July 1997; Camilla, 14 August 1997.

41. Camilla, 25 July 1997.

42. Around us$1,000.

43. Camilla, 14 August 1997.

44. Camilla, 25 July 1997.

45. Josias and Jânio, 11 June 1997.

46. Observed meeting of leadership of social club, 26 May 1997.

47. Josias, 4 July 1997.

48. Camilla, 18 September 1998.

49. Josias and Jânio, 11 June 1997.

50. Ibid.

51. Of course, no one even considered asking the police to move the cars since relations between residents and the police were so bad.

52. Observed conversation between Josias, Jânio, Manoel, and Ciro, 4 July 1997.

53. Camilla, 18 August 1997.

54. Ibid.

55. Ibid.

56. Historically, the political leadership of Rio's favelas has had little direct power to make residents do anything. Santos's "Law of Pasargada" offers numerous examples of how one AM leader in the 1970s worked to convince residents to compromise in informal dispute resolutions that he led. Santos, *Toward a New Legal Common Sense*, 123–248.

57. Josias, 13 May 1997.

58. Observed conversation in AM, 11 June 1997.

59. Josias and Mateus, 13 August 1997.

60. Graça, 8 October 1997.

61. Josias, Clara, and Eusébio, 5 August 1997.

62. Observed conversation of Josias, Tânia, Manoel, and Ciro, 4 July 1997.

63. Josias and Nicolau, 18 August 1997.

64. Josias and residents fixing road, 11 June 1997; and Camilla and Michele, 14 August 1997.

65. Alvito has noted that a trafficker in another favela set up families with a number of different women in his community because it helped him expand his network of local support and safe houses. See Alvito, "Um bicho-de-sete-cabeças," 198–200.

66. Zaluar, *O Condomínio do Diabo*, 107.

67. Josias on various dates; and Joselino, 29 July 1997. For example, traffickers evicted one resident who robbed other residents.

68. Ignácio, Maria, and Fernanda, 4 June 1997.

69. Joselino, 23 October 1998.

70. Ingácio, Maria, and Fernanda, 4 June 1997.

71. Joselino, 26 October 1998.

72. Joselino and Ricardo, 3 October 1997.

73. Joselino, 3 July 1997.

74. Centro de Defesa dos Direitos Humanos "Bento Rubião," *Favelas e as Organizações Comunitárias*, 55–58, 63.

75. Observations in Santa Ana, 12 August 1997.

76. Camilla, 14 August 1997. At this time the Brazilian *real* was worth about us$1.20.

77. Josias and others in AM, 27 June 1997; and Josias and others in AM, 30 June 1997.

78. Josias and others, 28 July 1997.

79. Joselino, 14 August 1997.

80. Josias, Geraldo, and Eusébio, 14 August 1997; and Joselino, 15 August 1997.

81. Josias and other unknown residents, 5 August 1997.

82. Joselino, 27 May 1999; and Camilla, 27 May 1999.

83. Joselino, 13 January 1999.

84. Joselino, 14 June 2002.

85. Manoel, 11 December 1997.

86. Tomás and Gabó, 14 January 1998.

87. Joselino, 23 October 1998; this account was confirmed by Manoel, 18 September 1998.

88. Camilla, 14 August 1997.

89. Bête, 14 July 1997; and Bête, 16 July 1997.

90. Bête, Martinha, and Andrea, 4 June 1997.

91. Bête, 2 June 1997; and Josias and Mateus, 13 August 1997.

92. Martinha and Luisa, 14 July 1997; Josias, Manoel, and other residents, 15 July 1997; and Ciro, 1 August 1997.

93. Manoel, 6 August 1997.

94. Joselino, 23 October 1998.

95. Bête, 24 July 1997.

96. Eusébio, 21 May 1997; Josias and Ciro, 6 June 1997; Camilla, 11 August 1997; and Bête, 8 October 1997. The story of Nelsinho's murder was related by residents. A police version says there was an exchange of fire. Sandrão, 9 September 1998; Camilla, 9 September 1998; Antônio, 23 October 1998; and Joselino, 23 October 1998.

97. Camilla, 25 July 1997.

98. Scott, "Everyday Forms of Peasant Resistance," 5–6.

99. Bête, 26 July 1996.

Chapter Five

1. Leeds, "Cocaine and Parallel Polities in the Brazilian Urban Periphery," 65–66.

2. Luís, 9 October 1997; Roger, 17 October 1997; and Miguel, 25 November 1997.

3. Roger, 17 October 1997; and Miguel, 25 November 1997.

4. Almeida and an unknown older man, 18 June 1997; Cynthia, 16 September 1997; and Roger, 17 October 1997.

5. Charles, 20 October 1997.

6. Ibid.

7. Luís, 9 October 1997; Caio Ferraz, 28 August 1997; and Paula, 24 September 1997.

8. Cynthia, 18 June 1997; Caio Ferraz, 28 August 1997; Luís, 9 October 1997; Miguel, 25 November 1997; and Evanildo, 8 January 1998.

9. Pedro and Wesley, 7 October 1997.

10. Evanildo, 8 January 1998.

11. Caio Ferraz, 28 August 1997.

12. Charles, 20 October 1997.

13. Ibid.

14. Evanildo, 10 January 1998.

15. Luís, 9 October 1997; and Cynthia and Tânia, 9 October 1997.

16. Luís, 9 October 1997. These sentiments were echoed by Cynthia, 2 October 1997; and Dé, 8 January 1998.

17. Charles, 15 October 1997.

18. Pedro and Wesley, 7 October 1997.

19. Almeida and Marcos, statement made by Marcos, 24 November 1997; and Miguel, 25 November 1997.

20. A similar dissatisfaction with police occupation was observed by Alvito, "Um bicho-de-sete-cabaças," 188–89.

21. Evanildo, 10 January 1998.

22. Charles, 20 October 1997.

23. Ibid.

24. Jorginho and Eric, 29 September 1997.

25. Paula, 24 September 1997. "Seu" is an abbreviation of the honorific "senhor," used to refer to certain respected older residents. Vigário is the only favela that I worked in where this honorific was regularly attached to AM leaders.

26. Almeida, Mateus, and Daniel, 16 January 1998.

27. Miguel, 25 November 1997.

28. Ibid.

29. Almeida, Mateus, and Daniel, 16 January 1998.

30. Paula, 24 September 1997.

31. Patricia, 19 September 1997; Paula, 24 September 1997; and Miguel, 25 November 1997.

32. Paula, 24 September 1997.

33. Daniel and Joana, 7 January 1998.

34. Clarinha, 30 January 1998; Dona Renata, 29 January 1998; and Pedro, 17 October 1997.

35. Charles, 20 October 1997.

36. Ventura, *Cidade Partida*, 66–68.

37. Patricia, 19 September 1997; Paula, 24 September 1997; and Miguel, 25 November 1997.

38. Caio Ferraz, 28 August 1997. The acronym of Movimento Comunitário de Vigário Geral is "MCVG." Residents, however, chose not to use this acronym and instead use the more complex phonetic "Mocovide" because the letters "CV" fall in the middle of "MCVG." Some worried that having "CV," the acronym for the powerful drug faction Comando Vermelho, in the middle of their acronym would send the wrong message to outsiders.

39. Charles, 1 February 1998.

40. Dona Renata, 29 January 1998.

41. Charles, 1 February 1998.

42. Pedro and Wesley, 7 October 1997.

43. Pedro and Wesley, 28 May 1997; and Almeida and unknown resident, 5 December 1997.

44. Charles, 20 October 1997; Mateus, 7 January 1998; Daniel and Joana, 7 January 1998; Jorginho and Eric, 15 January 1998; Dona Renata, 29 January 1998; and Clarinha, 30 January 1998.

45. Pedro and Wesley, 7 October 1997.

46. Newspaper reporter for *Estado de São Paulo*, 18 September 1997.

47. In Portuguese, the word for the type of candy that the CdP distributed is *balas*, which is also the Portuguese word for "bullet." Thus the exchange program was called *balas por balas*.

48. Dé, 1 October 1997; and observed meeting at CdP, 30 January 1998.

49. Daniel and Joana, 7 January 1998.

50. Cynthia, 2 July 1997.

51. Charles, 18 September 1997.

52. Pedro and Wesley, 7 October 1997.

53. Roger, 17 October 1997.

54. Miguel, 25 November 1997.

55. Unnamed accountant, 22 September 1997.

56. Roberto, 29 January 1998.

57. Observed meeting at CdP, 30 January 1998.

58. Charles, 1 February 1998.

59. The situation got so bad that the employees of the Casa went several months without pay in late 1997. Clarinha, 30 January 1998; and Evanildo, 29 January 1998.

60. Cynthia and Tarsila, 10 October 1997.

61. Observed conversation in street, 7 January 1998.

62. Observations of public conversation in community, 22 January 1998.

63. Evanildo and Rúbia, 22 January 1998.

64. Ibid.

65. Charles, 1 February 1998.

66. Ibid.

67. Observed meeting at CdP, 30 January 1998.

68. Amnesty International, "Urgent Action Appeal."

69. O Dia reporter, 29 January 1998.

70. Personal email, Paul Sneed, U.S. resident in Rio, August 2000.

71. Miguel, 25 November 1997.

72. Mateus, 7 January 1998.

73. Roger, 17 October 1997.

74. Almeida and Tony Lloyd, 18 September 1997.

75. Observations of GCAR presentation at the offices of the Serviço Nacional de Aprendizagem Industrial (SENAI, National Service for Industrial Learning), 23 January 1998.

76. Observations of Community Forum meetings, 9 September 1997, 10 October 1997, and 26 November 1997.

77. Cynthia and Felipe, 30 October 1997.

78. Cynthia, 29 January 1998.

79. Cynthia, 16 September 1997.

80. Almeida and unknown residents, 29 October 1997; and Daniel at Community Forum meeting, 7 January 1998.

81. Rúbia, Evanildo, and other residents, 5 October 1998; and Clarinha, 2 December 1998.

82. Observations in community of prosecutor visit, 19 September 1997.

83. Observations in Vigário Geral and at Rio courthouse on the day of the trial of one of the police accused in the Vigário massacre, 27 November 1997; and Dé, 1 December 1997.

84. Observed meeting of CdP leadership, 30 September 1997; and observations of discussion between community leaders and representatives of micro-credit program in AM, 24 November 1998.

85. Jorginho and Eric, 29 September 1997.

86. Observations of community the day after a major flood, 9 January 1998.

87. For a detailed history of the relationship between the Casa da Paz and the civil society in Rio, see Ventura, *Cidade Partida*.

88. Roberto, 10 October 1997.

89. Clarinha, 30 January 1998; and Ventura, *Cidade Partida*, 66–68.

90. Almeida, Jorginho, Eric, and Vagner, 30 September 1997.

91. Sérgio, 22 January 1998.

92. Unknown resident massacre survivor, 14 February 1998.

93. Caio Ferraz, 28 August 1997.

94. Pedro and Wesley, 7 October 1997.

95. Roberto, 10 October 1997.

96. Pedro and Wesley, 7 October 1997; Roberto, 10 October 1997; and Charles, 15 October 1997.

97. Roberto, 10 October 1997.

98. Cynthia and Kleber, 6 January 1998.

99. Observation of visit of NGO workers to community, 2 October 1997; and Cynthia, 7 October 1997.

100. Cynthia, 22 September 1997; and Roberto, 10 October 1997.

101. Plaques displayed inside the GCAR headquarters in Vigário indicate a number of sources of their funding.

102. Sérgio, 22 January 1998.

103. Observed meeting organized by MSF to form MOGEC, 29 January 1998.

104. Jaime, 28 May 1997.

105. Observations of community the day after a major flood, 9 January 1998.

106. Comments by Jaime at observed meeting organized by MSF to form MOGEC, 29 January 1998.

107. Comments by Daniel at Community Forum meeting, 7 January 1998.

108. Ibid.

109. Observations of Community Forum meeting, 7 January 1998; and observation of protest about faulty public works, 10 January 1998.

110. Tânia, 9 October 1997; Cynthia and Tânia, 30 October 1997; and Ventura, *Cidade Partida*, 242.

111. Mateus and unknown municipal bureaucrat, 6 November 1997; observed meeting of CVS in GCAR headquarters, 2 December 1997; Mateus, 3 December 1997; observed meeting of CVS, 6 January 1998; observation of protest about faulty public works, 10 January 1998; Alexandre, 23 January 1998; and observed meeting at CdP of "commission" trying to reform the CdP, 30 January 1998.

112. Observations in various places in Vigário on day and night of major flood, 8 January 1998.

113. Observations of Community Forum meeting, 10 October 1997; and Almeida and state bureaucrats, 24 November 1997.

114. Almeida, Cynthia, and Lorivaldo, 2 October 1997; Pedro and Wesley, 7 October 1997; Almeida, Cynthia, and unknown resident, 17 November 1997; Almeida and state bureaucrats, 24 November 1997; and observations of community forum meeting, 7 January 1998.

115. Rúbia, Evanildo, and other residents, 5 October 1998.

116. In other favelas I visited during the election, I noticed that the signs of conservative party candidates had been altered to remove the name of the gubernatorial candidate.

117. Observations in various places in Vigário on day and night of major flood, 8 January

1998. Statements were made by an irritated man to outside NGO workers in the street about why one woman would not evacuate her home despite rising floodwaters.

118. Cynthia and unknown resident, 2 July 1997.

119. Granovetter, "The Strength of Weak Ties." On the role of networks in impoverished communities, see pp. 212–13; and Espinoza, "Networks of Informal Economy," 52.

120. Leeds, "Cocaine and Parallel Polities in the Brazilian Urban Periphery."

121. Caio Ferraz, 28 August 1997.

122. For observations of visit of Tony Lloyd, see Almeida and Tony Lloyd, 18 September 1997.

123. Observed meeting at CdP, comments by Charles, 30 January 1998.

124. Viva Rio worker, July 2001.

125. On reporting on favela violence, see Alvito, "Um bicho-de-sete-cabeças," 188.

Chapter Six

1. Huggins, "From Bureaucratic Consolidation to Structural Devolution," 213, 225–26. For a history of this group, see Guimarães, *A Chancela do Crime*.

2. Amnesty International, "Brazil: Espírito Santo State under Siege"; Amnesty International, "Brazil: Espírito Santo—Witnesses at Risk." See also Global Justice, "The Human Rights Crisis in Espírito Santo," July 2002, 7.

3. Interview with sub-secretary for public security for the state of Espírito Santo, 28 August 2003.

4. Interview with retired São Paulo PM colonel who served in the Federal Ministry of Justice, 26 August 2003; and interview with sub-secretary for public security for the state of Espírito Santo, 28 August 2003.

5. Global Justice, "The Human Rights Crisis in Espírito Santo," July 2002.

6. Interview with sub-secretary for public security for the state of Espírito Santo, 28 August 2003; and interview with retired São Paulo PM colonel who served in Federal Ministry of Justice, 26 August 2003.

7. Interview with sub-secretary for public security for the state of Espírito Santo, 28 August 2003.

8. Amnesty International, "Brazil: Espírito Santo—Witnesses at Risk."

9. Huggins, "From Bureaucratic Consolidation to Structural Devolution," 221–24.

10. Beato et al., "Criminalidade Violenta em Minas Gerais," 6.

11. Of the homicides in Belo Horizonte in 1998, 55 percent were drug connected; see Beato et al., "Conglomerados de homícidios e o tráfico de drogas em Belo Horizonte," 4, 12.

12. Interview with Minas Gerais Polícia Militar Battalion Deputy Commander in Belo Horizonte, 24 July 2003.

13. Interview with head of Belo Horizonte Homicide Investigations and member of Civil Police high command, 23 July 2003.

14. Interview with state human rights ombudsman and staff, 23 July 2003; and interview

with head of Belo Horizonte Homicide Investigations and member of Civil Police high command, 23 July 2003.

15. Interview with state human rights ombudsman and staff, 23 July 2003.

16. Ibid.

17. Interview with director of Municipal Human Rights Office for Belo Horizonte, 22 July 2003.

18. Ibid.

19. Interview with coordinator of crime studies program at UFMG, 23 July 2003.

20. Ibid.

21. Frühling, "Policía Comunitaria y Reforma Policial en América Latina," 18.

22. Ibid.

23. Beato, "Reinventando a polícia," 12–16.

24. Ibid., 16–20; and interview with researchers at CRISP (Centro de Estudos de Criminalidade e Segurança Pública, the Center for Crime and Public Safety Studies), UFMG, 22 July 2003.

25. Interview with Minas Gerais Polícia Militar Battalion Deputy Commander in Belo Horizonte, 24 July 2003; and interview with director of Municipal Human Rights Office for Belo Horizonte, 22 July 2003.

26. Leite, "O Programa Fica Vivo!" 71.

27. Data available at <crisp.ufmg.edu.br>.

28. Interview with Universidade Federal do Rio Grande do Sul (UFRGS) professor researching violence, 19 August 2003.

29. Interview with members of Brigada Militar who work in Porto Alegre office of the Secretaria Nacional de Segurança Pública, 19 August 2003.

30. Ibid.

31. Interview with Major Tiago, representative of Secretaria Nacional de Segurança Pública in Rio Grande do Sul, 19 August 2003.

32. Interview with UFRGS professor researching violence, 19 August 2003.

33. Interview with Lieutenant Colonel Higinio, 21 August 2003.

34. Interview with retired São Paulo PM colonel who served in Federal Ministry of Justice, 26 August 2003.

35. Interview with Delegado Gabriel, 25 August 2003; Larry Rohter, "Police Are Criticized in Wave of Gang Violence in Brazil," *New York Times*, 28 May 2006, 3. See also BBC, "Prison Gang with Mobile Phones," <news.bbc.co.uk>, 19 February 2001; and interview with retired São Paulo PM colonel who served in Federal Ministry of Justice, 26 August 2003.

36. On this issue, see especially Barcellos, *Rota 66*.

37. De Gois, *Segredos da Máfia*; and Cardoso, *A Mafia das Propinas*.

38. Zuenir Ventura, "O risco da 'Colombina,'" *O Globo*, 22 June 2002, B12.

39. Melo, "Drug Trade, Politics and the Economy," 86–87; and Clawson and Lee, *The Andean Cocaine Industry*, 24–25.

40. Pécaut, "From the Banality of Violence to Real Terror," 141.

41. Melo, "Drug Trade, Politics and the Economy," 84.

42. Pécaut, "From the Banality of Violence to Real Terror," 143.

43. Clawson and Lee, *The Andean Cocaine Industry*, 37–61.

44. Pécaut, "From the Banality of Violence to Real Terror," 144.

45. Bowden, *Killing Pablo*, 24, 51.

46. Melo, "Drug Trade, Politics and the Economy," 82–85.

47. Clawson and Lee, *The Andean Cocaine Industry*, 166–67. See also Thoumi, *Political Economy and Illegal Drugs in Colombia*, 141.

48. Melo, "Drug Trade, Politics and the Economy," 76–77; and Crandall, *Driven by Drugs*, 115–18.

49. Walker, "The Limits of Coercive Diplomacy," 145.

50. Thoumi, *Illegal Drugs, Economy, and Society in the Andes*, 96.

51. For a discussion of how traffickers use investment in legitimate businesses to advance their interests, see Clawson and Lee, *The Andean Cocaine Industry*, 165–66.

52. Guillermoprieto, *The Heart That Bleeds*, 232–33.

53. Romero, "Reform and Reaction," 184.

54. The first paramilitary group, *Muerte a los Sequestradores*, was formed in 1981 in an agreement between Medellín and Calí traffickers as a result of the kidnapping of the Ochoa brothers' sister by the M-19 guerrillas. See Chepesiuk, *The Bullet or the Bribe*, 69.

55. Crandall, *Driven by Drugs*, 84–89; and Romero, "Reform and Reaction," 182–83.

56. Manwaring, "Nonstate Actors in Colombia," 6.

57. Ibid., 8.

58. Ibid., 5.

59. Pécaut, "From the Banality of Violence to Real Terror," 144–45.

60. Clawson and Lee, *The Andean Cocaine Industry*, 165–67.

61. I would like to thank Mary Kaldor for this thought.

62. Sives, "Changing Patrons," 80–84.

63. Chevigny, *The Edge of the Knife*, 208.

64. Gunst, *Born Fi' Dead*, 111; and Stolzoff, *Wake the Town and Tell the People*, 99.

65. Small, *Ruthless*, 140–42.

66. Gunst, *Born Fi' Dead*, 10–13; and Small, *Ruthless*, 242–43.

67. Gunst, *Born Fi' Dead*, 118–20. See also Stolzoff, *Wake the Town and Tell the People*, 10–11.

68. Chevigny, *The Edge of the Knife*, 203–26.

69. Small, *Ruthless*, 1–12.

70. Ibid., 42.

71. Ibid., 141–42; and Sives, "Changing Patrons."

72. Small, *Ruthless*, 242.

73. Pimentel, "The Nexus of Organized Crime," 37.

74. Curzio, "Organized Crime and Political Campaign Finance in Mexico," 86; and Shelley, "Transnational Organized Crime: The New Authoritarianism," 44.

75. Curzio, "Organized Crime and Political Campaign Finance in Mexico," 100–102.

76. Chevigny, *The Edge of the Knife*, 234–36; and Pimentel, "The Nexus of Organized Crime," 44–50.

77. Pimentel, "The Nexus of Organized Crime," 44.

78. Ibid., 51.

79. Ibid., 44.

Chapter Seven

1. Arias, "Trouble en Route."

2. Malkin, "Narcotrafficking, Migration, and Modernity in Rural Mexico," 101–3, 105–20. On traffickers' efforts to build legitimacy, see Alvito, *As Cores de Acarí*, 149–64.

3. Leeds, "Cocaine and Parallel Polities in the Brazilian Urban Periphery," 70–73; and Mafra, "Drogas e símbolos," 281–82.

4. Alvito, *As Cores de Acarí*, 161–62, 224.

5. On protection, see Gambetta, *The Sicilian Mafia*, 15–33.

6. O'Donnell and Schmitter, *Transitions from Authoritarian Rule*, 13–14.

7. Quoted in Reis, "The State, the Market, and Democratic Citizenship," 121.

8. Pereira, "An Ugly Democracy," 217.

9. See Putnam, *Bowling Alone*; and Putnam, *Making Democracy Work*.

Epilogue

1. Elísio, 27 July 2005.

2. Ibid.

3. Ibid.

4. R$50,000 was equivalent to approximately US$20,000. Conversation in office in downtown Rio, 27 July 2005.

5. Valdo, 25 July 2005.

6. Elísio, 27 July 2005.

7. Ibid.

8. Ibid.

9. Ibid.; and Valdo, 25 July 2005.

10. Camilla, 14 July 2005.

11. Ruizão, 14 July 2005.

12. Jussara, 25 July 2005.

13. Alexandre, 4 July 2005.

14. Cédric, 4 July 2005.

BIBLIOGRAPHY

Books and Journal Articles

Abinger, Tyler. *Five Points: The 19th Century New York City Neighborhood That Invented Tap Dance, Stole Elections, and Became the World's Most Notorious Slum*. New York: Plume Books, 2002.

Agüero, Felipe. "Conflicting Assessments of Democratization: Exploring the Fault Lines." In Agüero and Stark, *Fault Lines of Democracy in Post-Transition Latin America*, 1–20.

Agüero, Felipe, and Jeffrey Stark, eds. *Fault Lines of Democracy in Post-Transition Latin America*. Miami: North-South Center Press, 1998.

Alvarez, Sonia. "Politicizing Gender and Engendering Democracy." In Stepan, *Democratizing Brazil: Problems of Transition and Consolidation*, 205–51.

Alvarez, Sonia, Evelina Dagnino, and Arturo Escobar. "Introduction: The Cultural and the Political in Latin American Social Movements." In *Cultures of Politics/Politics of Cultures*, edited by Sonia Alvarez, Evelina Dagnino, and Arturo Escobar, 1–32. Boulder: Westview, 1998.

Alves Filho, Francisco, and Marcos Pernambuco. "No Front Inimigo." *Istoé* (São Paulo), 19 June 2002, 24–37.

Alvito, Marcos. "Um bicho-de-sete-cabeças." In Zaluar and Alvito, *Um seculo de favela*, 181–208.

———. *As Cores de Acarí: Uma Favela Carioca*. Rio de Janeiro: Editora FGV, 2001.

———. "A Honra de Acarí." In Velho and Alvito, *Cidadania e Violência*, 147–64.

Amar, Paul E. "Reform in Rio: Reconsidering the Myths of Crime and Violence." *NACLA Report on the Americas* 37 (September/October 2002): 37–42.

Amnesty International. "Brazil: Espírito Santo State under Siege—Authorities Cannot Afford to Make Mistakes." Amnesty International, <www.amnesty.org>. 27 September 2003.

———. "Brazil: Espírito Santo—Witnesses at Risk." Amnesty International, <www.amnesty.org>. 26 November 2002.

———. "Urgent Action Appeal." Amnesty International, <www.amnesty.org>. 11 December 1998.

Amorim, Celso. *Comando Vermelho: A História Secreta do Crime Organizado*. Rio de Janeiro: Editora Record, 1993.

Andreas, Peter. "When Policies Collide: Market Reform, Market Prohibition, and the Narcotization of the Mexican Economy." In Friman and Andreas, *The Illicit Global Economy and State Power*, 125–42.

Arias, Enrique Desmond. "The Dynamics of Criminal Governance: Networks and Social Order in Rio de Janeiro." *Journal of Latin American Studies* 38, no. 2 (May 2006): 293–325.

———. "Faith in Our Neighbors: Networks and Social Order in Three Brazilian Favelas." *Latin American Politics and Society* 46 (Spring 2004): 1–38.

———. "Trouble en Route: Drug Trafficking and Clientelism in Rio de Janeiro." *Qualitative Sociology* 29, no. 4 (Fall 2006), forthcoming.

Arias, Enrique Desmond, and Corrine Davis Rodrigues. "The Myth of Personal Security: A Discursive Model of Local Level Legitimation in Rio's Favelas." *Latin American Politics and Society* 47 (Fall 2006), forthcoming.

Asbury, Herbert. *The Gangs of New York*. New York: Thunder's Mouth Press, 2001. Originally published by Alfred A. Knopf, 1927.

Astorga, Luis. "Organized Crime and the Organization of Crime." In Bailey and Godson, *Organized Crime and Democratic Governability: Mexico and the U.S.-Mexican Borderlands*, 58–82.

Auyero, Javier. *Poor People's Politics: Peronist Survival Networks and the Legacy of Evita*. Durham: Duke University Press, 2000.

Bailey, John, and Roy Godson. "Conclusion." In Bailey and Godson, *Organized Crime and Democratic Governability: Mexico and the U.S.-Mexican Borderlands*, 217–24.

———, eds. *Organized Crime and Democratic Governability: Mexico and the U.S.-Mexican Borderlands*. Pittsburgh: University of Pittsburgh Press, 2000.

Barcellos, Caco. *Abusado: O Dono do Morro Dona Marta*. Rio de Janeiro: Editora Record, 2003.

———. *Rota 66: A Polícia que Mata*. Rio de Janeiro: Editora Record, 2003.

BBC. "Prison Gang with Mobile Phones." <news.bbc.co.uk>. 19 February 2001.

Beato F., Claudio C. "Reinventando a polícia: a implementação de um programa de policiamento comunitário." Working paper, <http://www.crisp.ufmg.br>. 2001.

Beato F., Claudio C., Bráulio Figueredo Alves da Silva, Frederico Couto Marinho, Renato Martins Asunção, Ilka Afonso Reis, Maria Crisitina de Mattos Almeida. "Conglomerados de homícidios e o tráfico de drogas em Belo Horizonte de 1995 a 1999." CRISP Working Paper, electronic copy.

Beato F., Claudio C., Renato Asunção, Marcos A. C. Santos, Cel. Lucio Emílio Espírito Santo, Luis Flávio Sapori, Eduardo Batitucci, Paulo César C. Morais, Sérgio Luiz Félix da Silva. "Criminalidade Violenta em Minas Gerais—1966 a 1997." Paper presented at 22nd ANPOCS Conference (Caxambu), 1998, electronic copy.

Becker, David G. "Latin America: Beyond 'Democratic Consolidation.'" *Journal of Democracy* 10 (April 1999): 138–51.

Berliner, Maria Velez de, and Kristin Lado. "Brazil: Emerging Drug Superpower." *Transnational Organized Crime* 1 (Summer 1995): 239–60.

Blok, Anton. *The Mafia of a Sicilian Village, 1860–1960: A Study of Violent Peasant Entrepreneurs*. Prospect Heights, Ill.: Waveland Press, 1974.

Boissevain, James. *Friends of Friends: Networks, Manipulators, and Coalitions*. Oxford: Basil Blackwell, 1974.

Bourdieu, Pierre, and John Coleman, eds. *Social Theory for a Changing Society*. Boulder: Westview, 1991.

Bowden, Mark. *Killing Pablo: The Hunt for the World's Greatest Outlaw*. London: Penguin, 2001.

Bratton, Michael. "Peasant-State Relations in Postcolonial Africa: Patterns of Engagement and Disengagement." In Migdal, Kohli, and Shue, *State Power and Social Forces: Domination and Transformation in the Third World*, 231–54.

Brzezinsky, Mathew. "Re-engineering the Drug Business." *New York Times Magazine*, 23 June 2002, 24–29, 46, 54–55.

Burdick, John. "What Is the Color of the Holy Spirit? Pentecostalism and Black Identity in Brazil." *Latin American Research Review* 34, no. 2: 109–31.

Burgos, Marcelo Baumann. "Dos parques proletários ao Favela-Bairro: as políticas públicas nas favelas do Rio de Janeiro." In Zaluar and Alvito, *Um seculo de favela*, 25–60.

Caldeira, Teresa P. R. *City of Walls: Crime, Segregation, and Citizenship in São Paulo*. Berkeley: University of California Press, 2000.

———. "Crime and Individual Rights: Reframing the Question of Violence in Latin America." In Jelin and Hershberg, *Constructing Democracy: Human Rights, Citizenship, and Society in Latin America*, 197–214.

———. "Fortified Enclaves: The New Urban Segregation." In Holston, *Cities and Citizenship*, 114–38.

Campbell, Bruce, and Arthur Brenner. *Death Squads in Global Perspective: Murder and Deniability*. New York: St. Martin's, 2000.

Cardoso, Ruth Corrêa Leite. "Popular Movements in the Context of the Consolidation of Democracy in Brazil." In Escobar and Alvarez, *The Making of Social Movements in Latin America: Strategy, Identity, Democracy*, 291–302.

Cardoso, José Eduardo. *A Mafia das Propinas: Investigando a Corrupção em São Paulo*. São Paulo: Editora Fundação Perseu Abramo, 2000.

Carvalho, Maria Alice Rezende de, Zairo Borges Cheibub, Marcelo Baumann Burgos, and Marcelo Simas. "Cultura Política e Cidadania: Uma Proposta de Metodoloogia de Avaliação do Programa Favela-Bairro." Unpublished manuscript, available in IUPERJ Library (photocopy), 1998.

Centro de Defesa dos Direitos Humanos "Bento Rubião." *Favelas e as Organizações Comunitárias*. Petropolis, Brazil: Editora Vozes, 1993.

Chalmers, Douglas, Scott Martin, and Elizabeth Piester. "Associative Networks: New Structures of Representation for the Popular Sectors." In Chalmers et al., *The New Politics of Inequality in Latin America: Rethinking Participation and Representation*, 543–82.

Chalmers, Douglas, Carlos M. Vilas, Katherine Roberts Hite, Scott Martin, Kerianne Piester, and Monique Segarra, eds. *The New Politics of Inequality in Latin America: Rethinking Participation and Representation*. Oxford: Oxford University Press, 1997.

Chepesiuk, Ron. *The Bullet or the Bribe: Taking Down Colombia's Cali Drug Cartel*. Westport, Conn.: Praeger Publishers, 2003.

Chevigny, Paul. *The Edge of the Knife: Police Violence in the Americas*. New York: New Press, 1995.

Clawson, Patrick, and Rensselaer Lee III. *The Andean Cocaine Industry*. New York: St. Martin's Griffin, 1998.

Cohen, Jean, and Andrew Arato. *Civil Society and Political Theory*. Cambridge, Mass.: MIT Press, 1994.

Colburn, Forrest. "Fragile Democracies." *Current History*, February 2002, 76–80.

Correa Sutil, Jorge. "Judicial Reforms in Latin America." In Méndez, O'Donnell, and Pinheiro, *The (Un)Rule of Law and the Underprivileged in Latin America*, 255–77.

Costa, Florência. "Segurança no palanque." *Istoé* (São Paulo), 19 June 2003, 36–37.

Crandall, Russell. *Driven by Drugs: U.S. Policy toward Colombia*. Boulder: Lynne Rienner, 2002.

Curzio, Leonardo. "Organized Crime and Political Campaign Finance in Mexico." In Bailey and Godson, *Organized Crime and Democratic Governability: Mexico and the U.S.-Mexican Borderlands*, 83–102.

Dávila, Jerry. *Diploma of Whiteness: Race and Social Policy in Brazil, 1917–1945*. Durham: Duke University Press, 2003.

Davis, Diane. "Contemporary Challenges and Historical Reflections on the Study of Militaries, States, and Politics." In Davis and Pereira, *Irregular Armed Forces and Their Role in Politics and State Formation*, 3–34.

Davis, Diane, and Anthony Pereira, eds. *Irregular Armed Forces and Their Role in Politics and State Formation*. Cambridge: Cambridge University Press, 2003.

De Gois, Chico. *Segredos da Máfia: Os Bastidores do Escândol que Abalou São Paulo*. São Paulo: Publisher Brasil, 2000.

della Porta, Donatella, and Alberto Vanucci. *Corrupt Exchanges: Actors, Resources, and Mechanisms of Political Corruption*. New York: Aldine de Gruyter, 1999.

Diani, Mario. "Simmel to Rokkan and Beyond: Towards a Network Theory of (New) Social Movements." *European Journal of Social Research* 3, no. 4 (2000): 387–406.

———. "Social Mobilization and Social Capital: A Network Perspective on Movement Outcomes." *Mobilization* 2, no. 2 (1997).

Diniz, Eli. *Voto e Máquina Política: Patronagem e Clientelismo no Rio de Janeiro*. São Paulo: Editora Paz e Terra, 1982.

Domínguez, Jorge, ed. *The Future of Inter-American Relations*. New York: Routledge, 2000.

Domínguez, Jorge, and Abraham F. Lowenthal, eds. *Constructing Democratic Governance: Latin America and the Caribbean in the 1990s*. Baltimore: Johns Hopkins University Press, 1996.

Dowdney, Luke. *Children of the Drug Trade: A Case Study of Children in Organised Armed Violence in Rio de Janeiro*. Rio de Janeiro: 7Letras, 2003.

Duffield, Mark. *Global Governance and the New Wars: The Merging of Development and Security*. New York: St. Martin's, 2001.

Escobar, Arturo, and Sonia Alvarez, eds. *The Making of Social Movements in Latin America: Strategy, Identity, Democracy*. Boulder: Westview, 1989.

Espinoza, Vincente. "Networks of Informal Economy: Work and Community among Santiago's Urban Poor." Ph.D. diss., University of Toronto, 1992.

Evans, Peter. *Embedded Autonomy: States and Industrial Transformation*. Princeton: Princeton University Press, 1995.

Evans, Peter, Dietrich Rueschemeyer, and Theda Skocpol, eds. *Bringing the State Back In*. Cambridge: Harvard University Press, 1985.

Farer, Tom, ed. *Transnational Crime in the Americas*. New York: Routledge, 1999.

Fernandes, Rubem César. *Private but Public: The Third Sector in Latin America*. Washington, D.C.: Civicus Press, 1994.

Fernandes, Rubem César, and José Augusto de Souza Rodrigues. "Viva Rio: Sociedade Civil e Segurança no Rio de Janeiro." Photocopy, Congress of the Latin American Studies Association (Washington, D.C.), 1995.

French, John D. *The Brazilian Workers' ABC: Class Conflict and Alliances in Modern Saõ Paulo*. Chapel Hill: University of North Carolina Press, 1992.

Friman, H. Richard, and Peter Andreas, eds. *The Illicit Global Economy and State Power*. Lanham, Md.: Rowman and Littlefield, 1999.

Frühling, Hugo. "Judicial Reform and Democratization in Latin America." In Agüero and Stark, *Fault Lines of Democracy in Post-Transition Latin America*, 237–62.

———. "Policía Comunitaria y Reforma Policial en América Latina ¿Cúal es el impacto?" CESC Serie Documentos (Santiago), 2003.

Frühling, Hugo, and Joseph Tulchin, eds. *Crime and Violence in Latin America: Citizen Security, Democracy, and the State*. Washington, D.C.: Woodrow Wilson Center Press, 2003.

Gamarra, Eduardo. "Transnational Criminal Organization in Bolivia." In Farer, *Transnational Crime in the Americas*, 171–91.

Gambetta, Diego. *The Sicilian Mafia: The Business of Private Protection*. Cambridge: Harvard University Press, 1993.

Gay, Robert. "The Broker and the Thief: A Parable (Reflections on Popular Politics in Brazil)." *Luso-Brazilian Review* 36, no. 1 (1999): 49–70.

———. *Lucia: Testimonies of a Drug Dealer's Woman*. Philadelphia: Temple University Press, 2005.

———. "Popular Incorporation and the Prospects for Democracy: Some Implications of the Brazilian Case." *Theory and Society* 19 (1990): 447–63.

———. *Popular Organization and Democracy in Rio de Janeiro: A Tale of Two Favelas*. Philadelphia: Temple University Press, 1994.

Gellner, Ernest. "The Importance of Being Modular." In Hall, *Civil Society: Theory, History, Comparison*, 32–55.

Global Justice. "The Human Rights Crisis in Espírito Santo: Threats and Violence against Human Rights Defenders." Global Justice, <www.global.org.br>. July 2002.

Godson, Roy, ed. *Menace to Society*. New Brunswick, N.J.: Transaction Publishers, 2003.

Goldstein, Daniel. "'In Our Own Hands': Lynching, Justice, and the Law in Bolivia." *American Ethnologist* 30 (February 2003): 22–43.

Goldstein, Donna. *Laughter Out of Place: Race, Class, Violence, and Sexuality in a Rio Shantytown*. Berkeley: University of California Press, 2003.

Granovetter, Mark. "The Strength of Weak Ties: A Network Theory Revisited." *Sociological Theory* (1983): 201–33.

Griffith, Ivelaw. "Transnational Crime in the Americas: A Reality Check." In Domínguez, *The Future of Inter-American Relations*, 63–86.

Grindle, Merilee. "Patrons and Clients in the Bureaucracy: Career Networks in Mexico." *Latin American Research Review* 12, no. 1 (1977): 37–66.

Guillermoprieto, Alma. *The Heart That Bleeds: Latin America Now*. New York: Vintage Press, 1994.

Guimarães, Ewerton Montenegro. *A Chancela do Crime: A Verdadeira História do Esquadrão de Morte*. Rio de Janeiro: Ambito Cultural Edições, 1978.

Gunst, Laurie. *Born Fi' Dead: A Journey through the Jamaican Posse Underworld*. New York: Henry Holt, 1998.

Hagopian, Frances. "Democracy and Political Representation in Latin America in the 1990s: Pause, Reorganization, or Decline." In Agüero and Stark, *Fault Lines of Democracy in Post-Transition Latin America*, 99–143.

———. "Traditional Politics against State Transformation in Brazil." In Migdal, Kohli, and Shue, *State Power and Social Forces: Domination and Transformation in the Third World*, 37–64.

Hall, John, ed. *Civil Society: Theory, History, Comparison*. Cambridge: Policy Press, 1995.

———. "In Search of Civil Society." In Hall, *Civil Society: Theory, History, Comparison*, 1–31.

Hobsbawn, E. J. *Bandidos*. Rio de Janeiro: Forense-Universitário, 1969.

Hochstetler, Kathryn. "Democratizing Pressure from Below? Social Movements in the New Brazilian Democracy." In Kingstone and Power, *Democratic Brazil: Actors, Institutions, and Processes*, 167–84.

Hoffman, Bruce. *Inside Terrorism*. New York: Columbia University Press, 1998.

Holloway, Thomas. "'A Healthy Terror': Police Repression of *Capoeiras* in Nineteenth-Century Rio de Janeiro." *Hispanic American Historical Review* 69, no. 4: 637–76.

———. *Policing Rio de Janeiro: Repression and Resistance in a 19th Century City*. Stanford: Stanford University Press, 1993.

Holston, James, ed. *Cities and Citizenship*. Durham: Duke University Press, 1999.

Holston, James, and Teresa Caldeira. "Democracy, Law, and Violence: Disjunctions of Brazilian Citizenship." In Agüero and Stark, *Fault Lines of Democracy in Post-Transition Latin America*, 263–98.

Huggins, Martha. "From Bureaucratic Consolidation to Structural Devolution: Police Death Squads in Brazil." *Policing and Society* 7 (September 1997): 207–34.

———. *Political Policing: The United States and Latin America*. Durham: Duke University Press, 1998.

———. "Urban Violence and Police Privatization in Brazil: Blended Invisibility." *Social Justice* 27 (Fall 2000): 113–34.

Human Rights Watch/Americas. *Violência X Violência: Violações aos Direitos Humanos e a Criminalidade no Rio de Janeiro*. New York: Human Rights Watch Americas, 1997.

Jackson, Robert. *Quasi-States: Sovereignty, International Relations, and the Third World.* Cambridge: Cambridge University Press, 1990.

Jelin, Elisabeth, and Eric Hershberg, eds. *Constructing Democracy: Human Rights, Citizenship, and Society in Latin America.* Boulder: Westview, 1996.

Joyce, Elizabeth, and Carlos Malamud, eds. *Latin America and the Multinational Drug Trade.* New York: St. Martin's, 1998.

Junquiera, Eliane, and José Augusto Rogrigues. "Pasárgada Revisitada." *Sociologia Problemas e Práticas* 12 (October 1992): 9–18.

Kaldor, Mary. *New and Old Wars: Organized Violence in a Global Era.* Stanford: Stanford University Press, 1999.

Kaplan, Robert. "The Coming Anarchy: How Scarcity, Crime, Overpopulation, Tribalism, and Disease Are Rapidly Destroying the Social Fabric of Our Planet." *Atlantic Monthly*, 1 February 1994, 44–76.

Keck, Margaret, and Kathryn Sikkink. *Activists beyond Borders: Advocacy Networks in International Politics.* Ithaca: Cornell University Press, 1998.

Kingstone, Peter R., and Timothy J. Power, eds. *Democratic Brazil: Actors, Institutions, and Processes.* Pittsburgh: University of Pittsburgh Press, 2000.

Kohli, Atul, and Vivienne Shue. "State Power and Social Forces: On Political Tension and Accommodation in the Third World." In Migdal, Kohli, and Shue, *State Power and Social Forces: Domination and Transformation in the Third World*, 293–326.

Koonings, Kees. "Shadows of Violence and Political Transition in Brazil." In Koonings and Kruijt, *Societies of Fear: The Legacy of Civil War, Violence and Terror in Latin America*, 197–234.

Koonings, Kees, and Dirk Kruijt, eds. *Societies of Fear: The Legacy of Civil War, Violence and Terror in Latin America.* New York: Zed Books, 1999.

Kruijt, Dirk, and Kees Koonings. "Introduction: Violence and Fear in Latin America." In Koonings and Kruijt, *Societies of Fear: The Legacy of Civil War, Violence and Terror in Latin America*, 1–30.

Kurtz, Marcus J. "Free Markets and Democratic Consolidation in Chile: The National Politics of Rural Transformation." *Politics and Society* 27 (June 1999): 275–301.

Lee, Rensselaer III. "Transnational Organized Crime: An Overview." In Farer, *Transnational Crime in the Americas*, 1–38.

Leeds, Anthony, and Elizabeth Leeds. *A Sociologia do Brasil Urbano.* Rio de Janeiro: Zahar Editores, 1978.

Leeds, Elizabeth. "Cocaína e poderes paralelos na periferia urbana brasileira: ameaça à democratização em nível local." In Zaluar and Alvito, *Um seculo de favela*, 233–76.

———. "Cocaine and Parallel Polities in the Brazilian Urban Periphery: Constraints on Local Level Democratization." *Latin American Research Review* 31 (Fall 1996): 47–83.

Leite, Flávia Lana. "O Programa Fica Vivo!: Um analise sob a perspectiva de capital social." Unpublished thesis, Fudação João Pinheiro, <www.crisp.ufmg.br>. 2003.

Mafra, Clara. "Drogas e símbolos: redes de solidareidade em contextos de violência." In Zaluar and Alvito, *Um seculo de favela*, 277–98.

Malkin, Victoria. "Narcotrafficking, Migration, and Modernity in Rural Mexico." *Latin American Perspectives* 28 (July 2001): 101–28.

Manaut, Raúl Benítez. "Containing Armed Groups, Drug Trafficking, and Organized Crime in Mexico." In Bailey and Godson, *Organized Crime and Democratic Governability: Mexico and the U.S.-Mexican Borderlands*, 126–60.

Manwaring, Max G. "Nonstate Actors in Colombia: Threat and Response." Carlisle, Pa.: Strategic Studies Institute, 2002, electronic copy.

Marenin, Otwin, ed. *Policing Change, Changing Police: International Perspectives*. New York: Garland, 1996.

McCann, Bryan. *Hello, Hello Brazil: Popular Music in the Making of Modern Brazil*. Durham: Duke University Press, 2004.

Meade, Teresa A. *"Civilizing" Rio: Reform and Resistance in a Brazilian City, 1889–1930*. University Park: Pennsylvania State University Press, 1998.

Melo, Jorge Orlando. "Drug Trade, Politics and the Economy: The Colombian Experience." In Joyce and Malamud, *Latin America and the Multinational Drug Trade*, 63–96.

Méndez, Juan E. "Institutional Reform, Including Access to Justice." In Méndez, O'Donnell, and Pinheiro, *The (Un)Rule of Law and the Underprivileged in Latin America*, 221–26.

———. "Problems of Lawless Violence: Introduction." In Méndez, O'Donnell, and Pinheiro, *The (Un)Rule of Law and the Underprivileged in Latin America*, 19–24.

Méndez, Juan E., Guillermo O'Donnell, and Paulo Sérgio Pinheiro, eds. *The (Un)Rule of Law and the Underprivileged in Latin America*. Notre Dame: University of Notre Dame Press, 1999.

Migdal, Joel S. "The State in Society: An Approach to Struggles for Domination." In Migdal, Kohli, and Shue, *State Power and Social Forces: Domination and Transformation in the Third World*, 7–37.

———. *Strong Societies and Weak States: State-Society Relations and State Capabilities in the Third World*. Princeton: Princeton University Press, 1989.

Migdal, Joel S., Atul Kohli, and Vivienne Shue, eds. *State Power and Social Forces: Domination and Transformation in the Third World*. Cambridge: Cambridge University Press, 1994.

Mitchell, Timothy. "The Limits of the State: Beyond Statist Approaches and Their Critics." *American Political Science Review* 85 (March 1991): 77–96.

Montes, Maria Lucia Aparecida. "Violência, Cultura Popular, e Organizações Populares." In Velho and Alvito, *Cidadania e Violência*, 218–31.

Moss Kanter, Rosabeth. "The Future of Bureaucracy and Hierarchy in Organizational Theory: A Report from the Field." In Bourdieu and Coleman, *Social Theory for a Changing Society*, 63–87.

Muniz, Jacqueline de Oliveira. "Ser Policial é, sobretudo, uma Razão de Ser." Ph.D. diss., Instituto Universitário de Pesquisas do Rio de Janeiro, 1999.

Murilo de Carvalho, José. *Os Bestializados: o Rio de Janeiero e a República que não foi*. São Paulo: Companhia das Letras, 1987.

Naylor, R. Thomas. "From Cold War to Crime War: The Search for a New National Security Threat." *Transnational Organized Crime* 1 (Winter 1995): 37–56.

———. "The Rise of the Modern Arms Black Market and the Fall of Supply-Side Control." In Williams and Vlassis, *Combating Transnational Crime: Concepts, Activities, and Responses*, 209–36.

Needell, Jeffrey. *A Tropical Belle Epoque: Elite Culture and Society in Turn-of-the-Century Rio de Janeiro*. Cambridge: Cambridge University Press, 1987.

Nelson, Joan. *Access to Power: Politics and the Urban Poor in Developing Nations*. Princeton: Princeton University Press, 1979.

Nelson, Toni. "Political Economy and Drug Trafficking in Brazil." Unpublished manuscript, 1 March 2005.

Nordstrom, Carolyn. *Shadows of War: Violence, Power, and International Profiteering in the Twenty-first Century*. Berkeley: University of California Press, 2004.

O'Donnell, Guillermo. "Polyarchies and the (Un)Rule of Law in Latin America: A Partial Conclusion." In Méndez, O'Donnell, and Pinheiro, *The (Un)Rule of Law and the Underprivileged in Latin America*, 303–38.

———. "On the State, Democratization, and Some Conceptual Problems: A Latin American View with Glances at Some Postcommunist Countries." *World Development* 21 (August 1993): 1355–69.

———. "Why the Rule of Law Matters." *Journal of Democracy* 15, no. 4 (2004): 32–46.

O'Donnell, Guillermo, and Philippe C. Schmitter. *Transitions from Authoritarian Rule: Tentative Conclusions about Uncertain Democracies*. Baltimore: Johns Hopkins University Press, 1986.

Oxhorn, Philip. *Organizing Civil Society: The Popular Sectors and the Struggle for Democracy in Chile*. University Park: Pennsylvania State University Press, 1995.

Paley, Julia. *Marketing Democracy: Power and Social Movements in Post-Dictatorship Chile*. Berkeley: University of California Press, 2001.

Patterson, Eric. "Religious Activity and Political Participation: The Brazilian and Chilean Cases." *Latin American Politics and Society* 47 (Spring 2005): 1–29.

Payne, Leigh. *Uncivil Societies: The Armed Right Wing and Democracy in Latin America*. Baltimore: Johns Hopkins University Press, 2000.

Pécaut, Daniel. "From the Banality of Violence to Real Terror: The Case of Colombia." In Koonings and Kruijt, *Societies of Fear: The Legacy of Civil War, Violence and Terror in Latin America*, 141–68.

Pedrosa, Fernanda, et al. *A violência que occulta a favela: o dia-a-dia nas favelas do Rio*. Porto Alegre: LP&M Editores, 1990.

Penglase, R. Ben. "The Shutdown of Rio de Janeiro: The Poetics of Drug Trafficker Violence." *Anthropology Today* 21, no. 5: 3–6.

Pereira, Anthony W. "Armed Forces, Coercive Monopolies, and Changing Patterns of State Formation and Violence." In Davis and Pereira, *Irregular Armed Forces and Their Role in Politics and State Formation*, 387–407.

———. "An Ugly Democracy: State Violence and the Rule of Law in Postauthoritarian Brazil." In Kingstone and Power, *Democratic Brazil: Actors, Institutions, and Processes*, 217–35.

Perlman, Janice. "Marginality: From Myth to Reality in the Favelas of Rio de Janeiro,

1969–2002." In *Urban Informality: Transnational Perspectives from the Middle East, Latin America, and South Asia*, edited by Ananya Roy and Nezar AlSayyad, 105–46. New York: Lexington Books, 2004.

———. *The Myth of Marginality: Urban Poverty and Politics in Rio de Janeiro*. Berkeley: University of California Press, 1976.

Pimentel, Stanley. "The Nexus of Organized Crime and Politics in Mexico." In Bailey and Godson, *Organized Crime and Democratic Governability: Mexico and the U.S.-Mexican Borderlands*, 33–57.

Pinheiro, Paulo Sérgio. "Polícia e Consolidação Democrática: O Caso Brasileiro." In *São Paulo Sem Medo: Um Diagnostico da Violência Urbana*, edited by Paulo Sérgio Pinheiro et al., 13–17. Rio de Janeiro: Garamond, 1998.

———. "The Rule of Law and the Underprivileged in Latin America: Introduction." In Méndez, O'Donnell, and Pinheiro, *The (Un)Rule of Law and the Underprivileged in Latin America*, 1–23.

———. "State-Sponsored Violence in Brazil." In Chalmers et al., *The New Politics of Inequality in Latin America: Rethinking Participation and Representation*, 261–80.

Podolny, Joel M., and Karen L. Page. "Network Forms of Organization." *Annual Review of Sociology* 24 (1998): 57–76.

Portes, Alejandro, and Patricia Landolt. "The Downside of Social Capital." *American Prospect*, May–June 1996, 18–21, 94.

Portes, Alejandro, and Julia Sensenbrenner. "Embeddedness and Immigration: Notes on the Social Determinants of Economic Action." *American Journal of Sociology* 98 (May 1993): 1320–50.

Powell, Walter. "Neither Market nor Hierarchy: Network Forms of Organization." *Organizational Behavior* 12 (July 1990): 295–336.

Powell, Walter, and Laurel Smith Doerr. "Networks and Economic Life." In Smelser and Swedberg, *The Handbook of Economic Sociology*, 368–402.

Putnam, Robert D. *Bowling Alone: The Collapse and Revival of American Community*. New York: Simon and Schuster, 2000.

———. *Making Democracy Work: Civic Traditions in Modern Italy*. Princeton: Princeton University Press, 1993.

Raustiala, Kal. "Law, Liberalization, and International Narcotics Trafficking." *New York University Journal of International Law and Politics* 32 (Fall 1999): 89–145.

Reis, Fabio Wanderley. "The State, the Market, and Democratic Citizenship." In Jelin and Hershberg, *Constructing Democracy: Human Rights, Citizenship, and Society in Latin America*, 121–37.

Reno, William. *Warlord Politics and African States*. Boulder: Lynne Rienner, 1998.

Risse, Thomas. "International Norms and Domestic Change: Arguing and Communicative Behavior in the Human Rights Area." *Politics and Society* 27 (December 1999): 537–51.

Risse, Thomas, Stephen C. Ropp, and Kathryn Sikkink, eds. *The Power of Human Rights: International Norms and Domestic Change*. Cambridge: Cambridge University Press, 1999.

Risse, Thomas, and Kathryn Sikkink. "The Socialization of International Human Rights Norms into Domestic Practices: Introduction." In Risse, Ropp, and Sikkink, *The Power of Human Rights: International Norms and Domestic Change*, 1–35.

Romero, Mauricio. "Reform and Reaction: Paramilitary Groups in Contemporary Colombia." In Davis and Pereira, *Irregular Armed Forces and Their Role in Politics and State Formation*, 171–208.

Rosenberg, Tina. *Children of Cain: Violence and the Violent in Latin America*. New York: Penguin Books, 1991.

Rotker, Susana, ed. *Citizens of Fear: Urban Violence in Latin America*. New Brunswick, N.J.: Rutgers University Press, 2002.

Sanchez-Jankowski, Martin. *Islands in the Street: Gangs and American Urban Society*. Berkeley: University of California Press, 1991.

Santos, Boaventura de Sousa. *Toward a New Common Sense: Law, Science and Politics in the Paradigmatic Transition*. New York: Routledge, 1995.

Scott, James. "Everyday Forms of Peasant Resistance." In *Everyday Forms of Peasant Resistance in South-East Asia*, edited by James Scott and Benedict J. Tria Kerkvliet, 5–35. Totowa, N.J.: Frank Cass, 1986.

Segarra, Monique. "Redefining the Public/Private Mix: NGOs and the Emergency Social Investment Fund in Ecuador." In Chalmers et al., *The New Politics of Inequality in Latin America: Rethinking Participation and Representation*, 489–90.

Serrano, Monica. "Transnational Crime in the Western Hemisphere." In Domínguez, *The Future of Inter-American Relations*, 85–152.

Shearing, Clifford. "Reinventing Policing: Policing as Governance." In Marenin, *Policing Change, Changing Police: International Perspectives*, 285–307.

Shelley, Louise. "Transnational Organized Crime: The New Authoritarianism." In Friman and Andreas, *The Illicit Global Economy and State Power*, 25–51.

Sikkink, Kathryn. "The Latin American Human Rights Network." In Jelin and Hershberg, *Constructing Democracy: Human Rights, Citizenship, and Society in Latin America*, 59–84.

Singer, Peter W. *Corporate Warriors: The Rise of the Privatized Military Industry*. Ithaca: Cornell University Press, 2003.

Sives, Amanda. "Changing Patrons, from Politicians to Drug Don: Clientelism in Downtown Kingston, Jamaica." *Latin American Perspectives* 29 (September 2002): 66–89.

Small, Geoff. *Ruthless: The Global Rise of the Yardies*. London: Warner Books, 1995.

Smelser, N. J., and Richard Swedberg, eds. *The Handbook of Economic Sociology*. Princeton: Princeton University Press and New York: Russell Sage Foundation, 1994.

Soares, Luis Eduardo. *Meu Casaco de General: 500 Dias na Front da Segurança Pública no Rio de Janeiro*. São Paulo: Companhia das Letras, 2000.

Soares, Luis Eduardo, et al. "Criminalidade urbana e violência: o Rio de Janeiro no contexto internacional." In Soares et al., *Violência e Política no Rio de Janeiro*.

Soares, Luis Eduardo, João T. S. Sé, José A. S. Rodrigues, and L. Piquet Carneiro, eds. *Violência e Política no Rio de Janeiro*. Rio de Janeiro: Editora Relume Dumará: ISER, 1996.

Stepan, Alfred, ed. *Democratizing Brazil: Problems of Transition and Consolidation*. Oxford: Oxford University Press, 1989.

Stokes, Susan. *Cultures in Conflict: Social Movements and the State in Peru*. Chicago: University of Chicago Press, 1995.

Stolzoff, Norman. *Wake the Town and Tell the People: Dancehall Culture in Jamaica*. Durham: Duke University Press, 2000.

Strange, Susan. *The Retreat of the State: The Diffusion of Power in the World Economy*. Cambridge: Cambridge University Press, 1996.

Tarrow, Sydney. *Power in Movement: Social Movements and Contentious Politics*. Cambridge: Cambridge University Press, 1998.

Teichman, Judith. *The Politics of Freeing Markets in Latin America: Chile, Argentina, and Mexico*. Chapel Hill: University of North Carolina Press, 2001.

Thoumi, Francisco. *Illegal Drugs, Economy, and Society in the Andes*. Washington, D.C.: Woodrow Wilson Center Press, 2003.

———. *Political Economy and Illegal Drugs in Colombia*. Boulder: Lynne Rienner, 1995.

Tilly, Charles. "Foreword." In Blok, *The Mafia of a Sicilian Village, 1860–1960: A Study of Violent Peasant Entrepreneurs*.

———. "War Making and State Making as Organized Crime." In Evans, Rueschemeyer, and Skocpol, *Bringing the State Back In*, 169–91.

Trajano Sento-Sé, João. *Brizolismo*. Rio de Janeiro: Editora FGV, 1999.

Treverton, Gregory. "International Organized Crime, National Security, and the 'Market State.'" In Farer, *Transnational Crime in the Americas*, 39–56.

Trouillot, Michel-Rolph. "The Anthropology of the State in the Age of Globalization: Close Encounters of the Deceptive Kind." *Current Anthropology* 41 (February 2001): 125–38.

Uzzi, Brian. "The Sources and Consequences of Embeddedness for the Economic Performance of Organizations: The Network Effect." *American Sociological Review* 61 (August 1996): 674–98.

Velho, Gilberto, and Marcos Alvito, eds. *Cidadania e Violência*. Rio de Janeiro: Editora FGV, 1996.

Ventura, Zuenir. *Cidade Partida*. Rio de Janeiro: Cidade da Letras, 1994.

Vianna, Hermano. *The Mystery of Samba: Popular Music and National Identity in Brazil*. Translated by John Charles Chasteen. Chapel Hill: University of North Carolina Press, 1999.

Vilas, Carlos. "Participation, Inequality, and the Whereabouts of Democracy." In Chalmers et al., *The New Politics of Inequality in Latin America: Rethinking Participation and Representation*, 3–42.

Wang, Xu. "Mutual Empowerment of State and Society: Its Nature, Conditions, Mechanisms, and Limits." *Comparative Politics* 31 (January 1999): 231–49.

Walker, William O. "The Limits of Coercive Diplomacy: U.S. Drug Policy and Colombian State Stability, 1978–1997." In Friman and Andreas, *The Illicit Global Economy and State Power*, 143–71.

Weber, Max. *Economy and Society*. Berkeley: University of California Press, 1978.

Weffort, Francisco. "America Astray." Working Paper, Helen Kellogg Institute for International Studies, no. 162. Notre Dame: Helen Kellogg Institute for International Studies, 1991.

Williams, Daryle. *Culture Wars in Brazil: The First Vargas Regime, 1930–1935*. Durham: Duke University Press, 2001.

Williams, Phil. "Organizing Transnational Crime: Networks, Markets, and Hierarchies." In Williams and Vlassis, *Combating Transnational Crime: Concepts, Activities, and Responses*, 57–87.

Williams, Phil, and Dimitri Vlassis, eds. *Combating Transnational Crime: Concepts, Activities, and Responses*. London: Frank Cass, 2001.

Yashar, Deborah. "Indigenous Protest and Democracy in Latin America." In Domínguez and Lowenthal, *Constructing Democratic Governance: Latin America and the Caribbean in the 1990s*, 87–122.

Young Pelton, Robert. "Kidnapped in the Gap." *National Geographic Explorer*, June–July 2003, 64–72, 92–98.

Zaluar, Alba. *Condomínio do Diabo*. Rio de Janeiro: Editora Revan, 1994.

———. "Crime, medo, e política." In Zaluar and Alvito, *Um seculo de favela*, 209–32.

———. *A Máquina e a Revolta: as organizações populares e o significado da pobreza*. São Paulo: Editora Brasiliense, 1985.

Zaluar, Alba, and Marcos Alvito. "Introdução." In Zaluar and Alvito, *Um seculo de favela*, 7–24.

———, eds. *Um seculo de favela*. Rio de Janeiro: Editora FGV, 1998.

Zaverucha, Jorge. "Military Justice in the State of Pernambuco after the Brazilian Military Regime: An Authoritarian Legacy." *Latin American Research Review* 34, no. 2 (1999): 43–74.

Newspapers

O Estado de São Paulo
O Globo
Irish Times
Jornal do Brasil
New York Times

Private Documents

Ata da Assembléia (Book of Assembly), Santa Ana, 24 February 1973 (recorded in field notes on 20 May 1997).

Ata da Assembléia, Santa Ana, 10 June 1972 (recorded in field notes on 20 May 1997).

Paul Sneed. Personal e-mail. August 2000.

Interviews and Observations

TUBARÃO

Interviews

Alexandre, Ceuzinho AM president, and Jorge, former Ceuzinho AM president (who would later reassume the presidency). This conversation took place walking to and then in Ceuzinho after the three of us had witnessed a brutal beating of a man by traffickers after the end of a large AM meeting in the samba *quadra*. Both Alexandre and Jorge were visibly upset. 9 January 1999.

Alexandre, former president, leader of state program to provide services to residents, and former resident. Conversation took place on beach, where he then gave soccer classes to young residents. 13 June 2002.

Alexandre. This conversation took place in the offices of the large school near Ceuzinho and Tubarão. We discussed events in the communities between 2002 and 2005. 4 July 2005.

Amália, young Viva Rio lawyer working in Ceuzinho. Conversation took place in her office in the Baptist church where she provided legal advice to residents. 3 July 2001.

Bernardo, AM president and godfather of Alberto's son, and residents looking for work. Observed conversation that took place between Bernardo and several women who had come to the AM looking for work at a sandwich shop in a nearby neighborhood. Bernardo noted that the owner had requested someone with *boa aparência* (good appearance), a code word in Brazilian hiring practice that usually means someone who phenotypically appears to have a substantial amount of European heritage. Bernardo encouraged one particular woman to apply because of her *boa aparência*. 6 August 1998.

Bernardo; Salomão, evangelical Christian and member of leadership of AM; and Jussara, AM treasurer and director of city-run crèche in community. Observed conversation that took place in the AM on the day when AM leaders from other favelas came to talk with Bernardo about how to work with politicians. 11 August 1998.

Bernardo, Jussara, and representatives of political candidate. Bernardo conducted a detailed conversation about his demands of the politician. 26 August 1998.

Bernardo and Mario, a campaign manager for a politician. The conversation took place in AM and was very rapid. Both men eventually retired, along with the AM vice president, to a back room for a private conversation. 26 August 1998.

Bernardo. Bernardo made a statement to various men drinking beer in front of a bar just below the favela after the very brief visit of gubernatorial candidate Anthony Garotinho to the community—in which Bernardo was visibly snubbed by the candidate at the behest of then-candidate for lieutenant governor Benedita da Silva. 27 September 1998.

Bernardo. An observed phone conversation in which Bernardo spoke on the phone as the leaders of various other prominent favelas near Tubarão were in the AM discussing political matters. 30 September 1998.

Bernardo and residents in AM. An observed conversation after a campaign stop by the former hard-line head of public security for Rio de Janeiro. 3 October 1998.

Bernardo and unknown residents who had their radios stolen. Conversation took place in the AM on a busy sunny afternoon. Bernardo was attempting to convince the residents not to go to the traffickers to redress their grievances. 5 October 1998.

Bernardo. Observed statements in the AM during which he angrily said, in the presence of others, that he needed more help with his work and that he was tired of working with people who weren't "as smart as" himself. 6 October 1998.

Bernardo and Jussara. This was an observed conversation during which Bernardo angrily complained about demands the traffickers made of him in return for payments. Also during the conversation he made plans, with Jussara, for a party for local children. 7 October 1998.

Bernardo and a young politician. Observations of large public works inauguration that many residents and members of the press attended; pictures were taken of Bernardo and the up-and-coming politician. Residents harassed a mentally ill woman from the community during the event. 21 October 1998.

Bernardo and Alexandre, Ceuzinho AM president. An observed conversation that took place in the main section of the Tubarão AM and that started with a discussion of payments that had to be made to local garbage collectors by the Tubarão AM. The conversation shifted to Alexandre's desire to step down as Ceuzinho president. 5 November 1998.

Bernardo in conversation with others in the AM. Bernardo expressed dissatisfaction with traffickers making him a scapegoat for many problems in the favela. 16 November 1998.

Bernardo, AM worker, and prospective adolescent employee. Conversation took place in the AM and was concerned with the employment of the adolescent. 20 November 1998.

Bernardo and members of government/NGO-run micro-credit program. 24 November 1998.

Bernardo and a number of women who were associated with traffickers. Bernardo complained about politics in Rio and expressed his desire to run for office in a small town in the interior of the state. 7 December 1998.

Bernardo and multiple other residents. Bernardo complained about problems in the community. 7 January 1999.

Carolina, middle-aged evangelical, whose adolescent daughter was romantically involved with a drug trafficker (killed soon after this conversation took place). This conversation, which covered a wide variety of historical and contemporary issues, took place in her home with her daughter and a mentally ill woman she was caring for wandering in and out of the room. 17 December 1998.

Carolina. Conversation took place in Carolina's home in the weeks after her daughter had to flee the community after her trafficker boyfriend was killed by other traffickers. 15 January 1999.

Carolina. Conversation took place at her home about her efforts to effect changes in the community. 21 January 1999.

Carolina. Conversation in her home about the implementation of police reform program. 23 July 2001.

Cédric, Baptist minister in Ceuzinho, NGO worker, and resident of Ceuzinho. Conversation took place in Baptist church in Ceuzinho. 10 July 2001.

Cédric. This conversation took place in the large school near Ceuzinho and Tubarão. We discussed events in the communities between 2002 and 2005. 4 July 2005.

Cristiano, resident and former co-owner of sound system with head trafficker. Conversation took place late one night walking on main path in the favela on our way to a nightclub outside the favela after police had been seen by many making threatening statements about residents. At various points we met up with other residents with whom Cristiano had conversations. 18 April 1999.

Denise, long-time resident of Ceuzinho who operates the elevators in nearby school. This was the first part of a two-part historical interview about the favela that took place in public in front of the community school. 25 November 1998.

Denise. This was the second part of a two-part historical interview about the community that took place in public in front of the community school. 3 December 1998.

Elizete, former drug dealer, former prison inmate, and wife of low-level but well-connected drug dealer and former inmate, in her apartment. Conversation began in her apartment and continued in front of a bar near her apartment. 6 January 1999.

Elizete and her husband, Wilson, a minor but well-connected drug trafficker and former convict. Both are active in the favela's samba school, and the conversation focused on the school's poor showing in the yearly competitions as a result of the school not having financial support from a *bicheiro* (numbers game banker). 20 November 1998.

Elizete. This conversation took place in her apartment on a day in which there were low clouds and rain. The discussion was driven by different people we saw wandering around on the street outside her window. 27 November 1998.

Elizete. This conversation took place in her housing project apartment and on the roof of her building, with her husband and children intermittently present, while drinking beer and eating pirão (fish head gravy). 7 January 1999.

Elizete. Conversation took place on the roof of her apartment building drinking beer, while her husband and children flew kites on roof. 8 January 1999.

Elizete. This conversation took place while we drank beer at a bar on the street in front of her apartment. 4 July 2001.

Evaldo, activist from community. Conversation with me and Jorge on city street. 17 January 1999.

Irimina, a seventy-two-year-old resident, and Carlos, her caregiver. The conversation took place in her home and was a historical interview that covered a wide variety of subjects. 16 December 1998.

João, coordinator for human rights and public security in Viva Rio. Conversation took place on patio at Viva Rio office. 21 June 2001.

Jorge, former leader of Ceuzinho AM who would five months later again become president. This conversation, in which he was very critical of Bernardo, began at a large street fair late one Sunday afternoon and continued as we walked along Zona Sul beaches and ran into numerous acquaintances of his. 17 January 1999.

Jussara and César, AM employee. Conversation in AM during a time in which few people were there. 13 August 1998.

Jussara. Conversation took place in crèche, during which we discussed her life history and the operation of the crèche. 20 October 1998.

Jussara, now AM president. This conversation took place in the AM headquarters during the evening. Her assistant was present and would occasionally interject. The conversation covered events in the community between 2001 and 2005. 25 July 2005.

Ludmila, teacher in school near community. Ludmila is a personal friend who happened to work in the school as an art teacher engaging in an innovative curriculum in which she used art to help children deal with the violence facing them. The entire conversation took place in the school near the community. She is also the godmother of Elizete's youngest child. 25 August 1998.

Major Antunes, leader of police unit in Tubarão and Ceuzinho. Statement at Tubarão/Ceuzinho leadership council meeting. 7 July 2001.

Major Costa, leader of police detachment, sometime after Antunes left. Interview in community policing headquarters near Tubarão. 11 August 2003.

Pedrinho, ex-trafficker from Tubarão and member of evangelical church. This conversation took place in a restaurant for which he provided private security. We were introduced by an NGO worker trying to bring Christian groups in the favela together to help control violence. As a result of this association, Pedrinho was visibly concerned with not saying anything that could cause the NGO to pull out of the favela. 2 August 2001.

Regina, bar owner and resident. This conversation, which touched on a small number of basic issues, took place immediately after a meeting about micro-credit in front of the small bar that she and her husband owned. 23 November 1998.

Ricardo, AM vice president, and Claudia, wife of jailed trafficker and resident. This conversation took place on a sunny day on the steps of the AM and focused mainly on the complaints of Claudia about the treatment of her husband in jail and descriptions of her efforts to travel out to the jail with the wives of other inmates who were protesting prison conditions. 18 August 1998.

Roberto, AM receptionist; Carlton, owner of pirated cable system; police lieutenant; and other police officers. Observed conversation during which a group of police were in the confined dark space of the AM headquarters with their weapons drawn. 25 August 1998.

Sacha, daughter of founder of Spiritist crèche. This conversation took place in the subject's office at the crèche and ranged over a variety of issues related to the history of the community and the crèche. 19 October 1998.

Sacha. Conversation about thefts that had occurred in the Spiritist crèche building. She was visibly anxious talking about this. 30 November 1998.

Sara and Bartolomé, directors of city-run health clinic. Conversation took place in the office of the clinic and concerned the history of the clinic and its relation to the community. 1 December 1998.

Sérgio, Ceuzinho AM president. He made this statement in a boisterous tone at the door of the AM after complaining about a lack of city services. August 1996.

Sister Elena. Leader of a group of nuns working to provide services to Turbarão residents. A conversation about the role of the group of nuns living in the community and their history there. 25 November 1998.

Susana, resident and wife of jailed trafficker, and Cristiano, resident former business associate of drug traffickers. Conversation took place on main community path. 18 April 1999.

Valéria, longtime Tubarão resident. 15 December 1998.

Vilma, resident and evangelical Christian. This conversation took place on a rainy Sunday evening in the informant's home. The conversation was extensive, lasting several hours, and covered a wide variety of subjects. 6 December 1998.

Zinha, older resident, and César, resident and worker in AM. César, on Bernardo's orders, was introducing me to Zinha in the favela's main plaza as part of my efforts to conduct historical interviews. 7 October 1998.

Observations

Observed meeting in AM and conversation between Bernardo and other residents. These meetings occurred in the AM after candidate speech by a hard-line former police chief. Residents and Bernardo complained about police corruption. 3 October 1998.

Observations of children's party in community's main plaza. 13 October 1998.

Observations of activities outside of a Spiritist crèche building in favela. 20 November 1998.

Observed Ceuzinho AM meeting in samba *quadra*. During this meeting Bernardo discreetly made the case for his election as Ceuzinho AM president. Residents also seemed to gently criticize his efforts, although, later, residents reported that he was roundly rebuked. 9 January 1999.

Observed meeting in samba *quadra* in Ceuzinho. This meeting took place on a hot, humid night. Sacha, a leader of the Spiritist crèche; Alexandre, the AM Ceuzinho AM president; Bernardo; and other community activists were present. The conversation was free-ranging but usually was structured as a dialogue between the other attendees and Bernardo. 25 January 1999.

Observations of Tubarão and Ceuzinho late one Friday night when an under-attended *baile funk* was taking place in the local *praça*. 16 April 1999.

Observations of meeting about opening of sports facility at Viva Rio headquarters. July 2001.

Observations of Tubarão leadership council meeting. 7 July 2001.

Observations of meeting at Viva Rio. 17 July 2001.

Observations of inaugural ceremony for sports facility at Ceuzinho samba *quadra*. 11 August 2001.

SANTA ANA

Interviews

Ana, longtime resident and sister of Maria. Conversation took place in her home and focused on history and current events in the community. 4 June 1997.

Aninha, resident and mother of young boy who participated in social club. Conversation concerned violence in the community. 11 December 1998.

Antônio, AM officer and former AM president. 23 October 1998.

Bête, director of social club. Conversation took place in Bête's home as she prepared lunch and introduced me to the community. 26 July 1996.

Bête. Conversation in social club during children's activities about events that had taken place over the weekend. 2 June 1997.

Bête; Martinha, director of social club; and Andrea, older resident and director of social club. Observed conversation of directors of social club that discussed a variety of issues related to the club, including the decision not to participate in the *festa julina* that the traffickers were throwing the following month. 4 June 1997.

Bête. Conversation took place in social club. 14 July 1997.

Bête. Conversation took place in social club. 16 July 1997.

Bête. During this conversation, we discussed events that had occurred over the weekend, her life history, and participation in the Catholic Liberation Theology Movement. 23 July 1997.

Bête. Conversation in the social club that concerned the relationship between the social club and the rest of the community. 24 July 1997.

Bête. 8 October 1997.

Camilla, longtime resident and manager of Roman Catholic Church center in the favela. Conversation took place in the crèche kitchen. 25 July 1997.

Camilla. Conversation in the crèche kitchen of the church center. Covered violence in the favela and the experiences of her grown children. 11 August 1997.

Camilla. Conversation in the crèche kitchen. 14 August 1997.

Camilla and Michele, Santa Ana resident and worker in crèche. Conversation took place in crèche kitchen. 14 August 1997.

Camilla. Conversation in bleachers watching dance performance at a party at nearby sports facility. 18 August 1997.

Camilla. Conversation in the crèche kitchen, during which we discussed protests after the murder of a resident by police and other events that had taken place during my absence from the community. 9 September 1998.

Camilla. Conversation in the crèche kitchen, during which she criticized traffickers and discussed events in the community. 18 September 1998.

Camilla. Conversation during visit to community in crèche after extended absence. 23 February 1999.

Camilla. Conversation on a wide variety of subjects shortly before I left Brazil after a two-year stay. 27 May 1999.

Camilla. This conversation took place in the crèche and covered events in the community between 2003 and 2005. 14 July 2005.

Ciro, community garbage collector who had run a raffle in which I won a large bag of food. Conversation took place in the AM headquarters. 1 August 1997.

Eusébio, AM treasurer. 21 May 1997.

Graça, longtime resident and mother of Aninha. Conversation took place at a local bar while we drank soda. 8 October 1997.

Ignácio, retired police officer; Maria, his wife; and Fernanda, their adult daughter. This very long conversation concerned the history of the community and political relations within the community. Many of Ignácio's statements had to be translated through his wife and daughter because, at a very advanced age, he was hard to understand. 4 June 1997.

Joselino, middle-aged evangelical hardware store owner and longtime resident; and Ricardo, middle-aged evangelical hardware store employee. This conversation took place just outside the hardware store on the main street of the community and covered many issues about their lives, especially their sexual exploits, before entering their fundamentalist church. 3 July 1997.

Joselino. 29 July 1997.

Joselino. Comments reported in conversation. 14 August 1997.

Joselino. 15 August 1997.

Joselino and Ricardo. Conversation took place in front of Joselino's hardware store. 3 October 1997.

Joselino. Extended conversation about history, crime, and violence in the community. Conversation took place in front of his hardware store and concerned events in the community during my absence. 23 October 1998.

Joselino. Conversation in street in front of his store about violence in the favela. 26 October 1998.

Joselino. Extended conversation about violence in the favela and community history. 13 January 1999.

Joselino. Conversation took place after my long absence from the community and covered events that had taken place while I was not working in the community. 20 January 1999.

Joselino. Conversation on a wide variety of subjects shortly before I left Brazil after a two-year stay. 27 May 1999.

Joselino. Conversation on return visit to favela. This conversation took place for the most part on the roof of Joselino's home on a quiet and cloudy Sunday afternoon as the sun set. 14 June 2002.

Josias, AM president. Statements made in the AM while others were present in which he recounted experiences during a period when I was absent from the community. Made specific statements such as "running the AM is very tough" and "if you screw up you die" in the presence of Manoel. 13 May 1997.

Josias and Eusébio, AM treasurer. Observed extended conversation in AM about threats and harassment in the favela and possible efforts to kill an X-9 (police informant). 21 May 1997.

Josias and Ciro. Observed conversation in AM. 6 June 1997.

Josias and residents fixing road. Observed observation that took place on community's main street. 11 June 1997.

Josias and Jânio, secretary of AM. Conversation took place in the AM headquarters. 11 June 1997.

Josias and others. Observed conversation that took place in the AM headquarters. 27 June 1997.

Josias and others. Observed conversation that took place in the AM headquarters. 30 June 1997.

Josias, Tânia, Manoel, and Ciro. Statement made by Josias in front of a large group talking in AM headquarters on the day of the *festa julina*. 4 July 1997.

Josias. Conversation about violence in the favela and, more broadly, in Brazil. 10 July 1997.

Josias and Manoel, AM vice president. Conversation concerned violence and took place in the AM headquarters. 10 July 1997.

Josias, Manoel, and other residents. Conversation took place in the AM headquarters and concerned my donation of a bag of food to the social club. 15 July 1997.

Josias and others in the AM headquarters. Conversation concerned corruption in Brazil and touched specifically on potential corruption in soccer and on particular events in the community that were not fully described. Josias and I also had a separate conversation that day. 28 July 1997.

Josias; Eusébio; and Clara, Eusébio's wife. The conversation took place in the AM headquarters and concerned Clara's brother, who had recently fathered a child with a woman in another favela. They worried he would be brutally murdered by the trafficking gang run by Josias's son. 5 August 1997.

Josias and other unknown residents. Conversation took place in AM. Residents discussed the efforts of some to ask the traffickers for financial support. Residents, including Josias, passed judgment on these requests. 5 August 1997.

Josias and Mateus, man who organized *pagode* party. Observed conversation took place in the AM headquarters. 13 August 1997.

Josias; Geraldo, government health worker; and Eusébio. Conversation took place in AM headquarters. 14 August 1997.

Josias and Nicolau, a minor trafficker and father in his early twenties whom many in the favela were trying to convince to leave trafficking. He was later murdered by the police. Conversation took place in the AM. 18 August 1997.

Manoel. Conversation took place in the AM headquarters after a BOPE intervention during which I was publicly searched by police. 23 May 1997.

Manoel and other residents. Conversation took place in the AM headquarters. 23 June 1997.

Manoel. Conversation in AM headquarters about outside groups that have programs in the favela. 6 August 1997.

Manoel. Conversation on return visit to favela. 11 December 1997.

Manoel. This conversation took place on a return visit to the community in the AM head-quarters and covered a variety of issues, including clientelist politics in the run-up to the 1998 national elections. 18 September 1998.

Martinha, longtime Santa Ana resident and director of social club. Extended conversation about history and contemporary politics of community. 9 July 1997.

Martinha and Luisa, worker at social club. Conversation took place when I dropped off a bag of food at the AM. 14 July 1997.

Older woman from the northeast. 22 June 1997.

Ricardo, employee in Joselino's hardware store. Conversation took place on street in front of hardware store. During the conversation, he complained about police abuse of a fireman who lived in the community. 12 August 1997.

Ruizão, Santa Ana AM president (2005), resident, and evangelical Christian. The conversation took place in the mostly empty AM headquarters and covered changes in the community between 2003 and 2005. Our conversation was interrupted by the arrival of a trafficker accompanied by someone politically connected in Rio. After they left our conversation resumed. 14 July 2005.

Sandra, longtime resident. Conversation took place in the AM. We discussed Josias's life on a day in which many people visited the AM headquarters in preparation for a party to celebrate Josias's birthday that evening. 1 August 1997.

Sandrão, husband of Bête, though they would later divorce. Conversation took place on the roof of the social club and concerned Bête's effort to organize a protest after the police murdered a resident. 9 September 1998.

Seu Abelardo, elderly longtime resident and brother of former president of AM. Conversation took place in the street of the AM as he walked home. He talked about the history of the favela, particularly of the time when his brother had served as AM president. 3 July 1997.

Tomás, older evangelical barber from northeast. Conversation took place in his shop. 10 June 1997.

Tomás and Gabó, young adult evangelical and son of Tomás. Conversation took place on a return visit to Tomás's shop. 14 January 1998.

Observations

Observed meeting of leadership of social club. 26 May 1997.

Observed conversation in AM. 11 June 1997.

Observed conversation in the AM headquarters of community leaders and several residents. Those present discussed violence, as they worried about conflict occurring during a large party the traffickers would host that night, which they planned to attend. 4 July 1997.

Observed conversation among local trash collectors and directors of AM in headquarters of AM during calm period. 31 July 1997.

Observations in Santa Ana after traffickers ordered a shutdown of community businesses during period of mourning. 12 August 1997.

Observations of traffickers at entrance of favela. 21 June 2001.

Interviews

Alexandre, community sewer cleaner. This conversation concerned the role of the CVS in the community. 23 January 1998.

Almeida, AM president, and an unknown older man. This was an observed conversation that took place in the AM headquarters concerning the history of the community. 18 June 1997.

Almeida and Tony Lloyd, British foreign minister. This was an observed conversation that took place in the midst of many residents just outside the GCAR headquarters after Lloyd's visit. 18 September 1997.

Almeida; Jorginho, executive director of CdP; Eric, Jorginho's assistant; and Vagner, AM director. This observed meeting took place in an upstairs room of the AM headquarters. This conversation took place between the AM leadership and the CdP leadership in an effort on the part of the CdP leadership to repair damaged relations with the AM. 30 September 1997.

Almeida; Cynthia, AM receptionist; and Lorivaldo, vice president of AM, 1997–mid-1998, and later president. This conversation concerned AM efforts to fix water problems in a particular home. The conversation took place in the AM headquarters. 2 October 1997.

Almeida and unknown residents. This conversation took place in the AM headquarters and focused on his belief that Neo-Pentecostals would not participate in running the community. 29 October 1997.

Almeida, Cynthia, and unknown resident. This conversation took place in the AM headquarters and concerned one woman's troubles with water service. Almeida explained his efforts to ensure better water services to the community. 17 November 1997.

Almeida and state bureaucrats administering the water treatment program. This was an observed conversation that took place in the streets of the community near where repairs were being made to the community's water system. 24 November 1997.

Almeida and Marcos, elderly resident in impoverished part of community. Conversation took place in the street and concerned problems with the water and sewage systems in the community and the conditions of the water and sewage systems when Flavio Negão led the drug gang. 24 November 1997.

Almeida and unknown resident. I observed this conversation in the AM common room about high school completion courses. 5 December 1997.

Almeida; Mateus, outside activist and teacher; and Daniel, local activist. Conversation took place in the back room of the AM. Almeida showed them documentation that visibly surprised them concerning the role of the traffickers in the AM before he took office. 16 January 1998.

Caio Ferraz, former community activist living in exile in the United States. This conversation took place at Au Bon Pain in Cambridge, Massachusetts. It concerned the history of activism in the favela and Ferraz's view of politics there. 28 August 1997.

Charles, activist and artist. This conversation took place in the GCAR headquarters on the day Tony Lloyd, the British foreign minister, visited the favela. 18 September 1997.

Charles. This conversation took place in the GCAR headquarters and focused on the origins of the Vigário movement and the history of trafficking in Vigário, and about Flávio Negão, the head trafficker at the time of the massacre. 15 October 1997.

Charles. Conversation took place in a bar and concerned favela history before the massacre. 20 October 1997.

Charles. This was an extended conversation on the porch of his home on a warm summer day about violence in the community and the movement to stop it. His mother and fiancée were also present, and his mother offered comments during the conversation. 1 February 1998.

Clarinha, CdP leader and a relative of the seven people killed in the house that became the CdP. This conversation took place in the CdP prior to a reorganization meeting after she and other activists had forced Jorginho and Caio Ferraz to resign. The conversation concerned violence in the community prior to the massacre and about problems in the CdP. 30 January 1998.

Clarinha. 2 December 1998.

Cynthia. This conversation took place in the AM and concerned the reasons why she had moved out of community and her work in the AM. 18 June 1997.

Cynthia and unknown resident. This conversation took place in the AM and concerned general issues in the favela and problems of community. 2 July 1997.

Cynthia. Conversation took place in the AM and concerned the activities of past AM presidents, some of whom she had worked for as secretary and receptionist. 16 September 1997.

Cynthia. This conversation took place in the AM and concerned groups that provide support to the community. 22 September 1997.

Cynthia. This conversation took place in the AM headquarters and concerned the role of traffickers in controlling crime in the community and the relationship of traffickers in Vigário to traffickers in other communities. 2 October 1997.

Cynthia. This conversation took place in the AM and focused on NGOs operating in the community. 7 October 1997.

Cynthia and Tânia, resident and friend of Cynthia's. The conversation took place in the AM headquarters and focused on the role of traffickers in the community. 9 October 1997.

Cynthia and Tarsila, resident. Conversation took place in the AM headquarters. 10 October 1997.

Cynthia and Felipe, community trash collector. The conversation took place in the AM headquarters. They expressed concerns that the AM was weaker and poorer since the collapse of trafficker power. 30 October 1997.

Cynthia and Tânia. This was an observed conversation in the AM headquarters about efforts to bring resources to the community. 30 October 1997.

Cynthia and Kleber, relative of Caio Ferraz. This conversation took place in the AM and concerned the role of NGOs in Vigário. 6 January 1998.

Cynthia. This conversation took place in the AM headquarters and concerned conflicts over a home she co-owned with a relative of a trafficker. 29 January 1998.

Daniel, community resident and activist, and his mother, Joana. This conversation took

place in their home. We discussed the history of violence in the favela, especially during
the period between the massacre and the police occupation. 7 January 1998.

Dé, activist from outside the favela who worked in the CdP but who would later work for
the GCAR, and unknown resident in street. This conversation took place next to the
statues in the entry way to the CdP. 1 October 1997.

Dé. During this conversation, Dé recounted events from the trial of Arlindo Maginário
Filho. 1 December 1997.

Dé. The conversation took place in a plaza in a poor part of the community and concerned
why many refused to leave their homes despite the flooding of the river that ran next to
the community. 8 January 1998.

Dona Renata, Mãe de Santo (Afro-Brazilian religious leader) and longtime resident. This
conversation took place at her home and concerned the community and the history of
the movement against violence. 29 January 1998.

Elísio, former commission member and NGO activist. This conversation covered events in
Vigário from 2003 to 2005 and took place in the offices of a foreign NGO in downtown
Rio. 27 July 2005.

Evanildo, longtime resident and former activist. Conversation took place as we traveled
to a naval base to request permission from the officer there to build on a piece of land
controlled by the navy. It rained the entire day and Vigário flooded that evening.
8 January 1998.

Evanildo. Conversation took place in community restaurant and concerned many different
issues related to the history of the community in the years before the massacre. The
restaurant owner and a friend of the interviewer were present. 10 January 1998.

Evanildo and Rúbia, restaurant owner and resident. This conversation took place in Rúbia's
restaurant and concerned the collapse of the CdP's leadership. 22 January 1998.

Evanildo. This conversation took place on the day of a meeting of the "commission" to deal
with problems in CdP. 29 January 1998.

Jaime, outsider and director of MSF Program. This conversation took place in the MSF
headquarters. We discussed the broad mission of the MSF in the favela. 28 May 1997.

Jorginho, executive director of CdP, and Eric, his assistant. This conversation took place
in a local restaurant. We discussed the plans of the CdP to deal with outside organizations. 29 September 1997.

Jorginho and Eric. Conversation took place in street after successful effort by residents to
depose Jorginho and Caio Ferraz. 15 January 1998.

Luís, former AM president and railroad worker. This conversation took place in his home
and concerned the history and politics of the community. 17 October 1997.

Mateus, outside activist and leader of CVS, and unknown municipal bureaucrat. This conversation focused on getting land to build the CVS headquarters. 6 November 1997.

Mateus. This conversation concerned his work in the community. 3 December 1997.

Mateus. Conversation took place in the streets of the community and concerned the future
of an NGO that Mateus was attempting to start in the community and his criticisms of
the CdP and its leaders. 7 January 1998.

Miguel, former member of AM board and AM plumber. Conversation took place in the small dark living room of his home. No one else was present. During the conversation we principally discussed the history of the community and the politics surrounding the breakdown of trafficker control in the community. 25 November 1997.

Newspaper reporter for *Estado de São Paulo*. I conversed with her in the street outside the GCAR headquarters during the visit of Tony Lloyd, the British foreign minister, to the favela. 18 September 1997.

O Dia reporter. The reporter had been called to the community by residents working to undermine the CdP leadership. He attempted to interview me. I observed a conversation between him and residents and later saw the critical article he wrote. 29 January 1998.

Patricia, resident, friend of Cynthia's, and mother of two killed in the massacre. Conversation took place in the streets of the favela as we walked on a sunny afternoon when the prosecutor in the massacre trial, his assistants, many police, and activists walked through the favela retracing the steps of the killers in the massacre. 19 September 1997.

Paula, wife of deceased former AM president. This conversation took place in her home. A companion was present during the entire conversation. The conversation concerned the history of the favela, especially during the period when her husband, who had also been president of the FAFERJ, was president. 24 September 1997.

Pedro and Wesley, adolescent residents and GCAR activists. This conversation took place as Pedro and Wesley gave me a tour of the community on an early visit. 28 May 1997.

Pedro and Wesley. We met in one of the rooms in the GCAR center in Vigário. The conversation concerned favela history and the GCAR and teenagers and activists. 7 October 1997.

Pedro. Conversation took place in the GCAR headquarters. 17 October 1997.

Roberto, director of GCAR. Conversation took place in GCAR headquarters while Roberto waited to use a computer. 10 October 1997.

Roberto. Conversation took place in Roberto's car as he drove me home from Vigário Geral. A worker from the CdP who was disaffected with Ferraz was present for most of the trip, although it is not clear from my notes if she was present when these statements were made. 29 January 1998.

Roger, former AM president and store owner. Conversation took place in his home with his wife and some adult children going in and out of the room. The conversation concerned the history of the community and the recent movement to control violence. 9 October 1997.

Rúbia, Evanildo, and other residents working on political campaign. This conversation took place in Rúbia's restaurant and concerned the problems that she had running a political campaign in the community, her conflicts with the traffickers, and her worries about the future of Rio de Janeiro. 5 October 1998.

Sérgio, documentary filmmaker. This conversation took place in Sérgio's apartment in a very wealthy part of Rio and focused on his experiences attempting to make a documentary about Vigário. 22 January 1998.

Tânia. This conversation concerned efforts to set up a workers' cooperative in Vigário. 9 October 1997.

Unknown resident and massacre survivor. Statements made during meeting of commission to replace CdP leadership. 14 February 1998.

Unnamed accountant, not a resident of the community. Our meeting took place in the AM headquarters. 22 September 1997.

Valdo, Vigário resident and Afro-Reggae activist. This conversation began in the temporary offices that Afro-Reggae was maintaining in the AM headquarters while the GCAR center was being renovated and continued as Valdo and I walked around the community. 25 July 2005.

Viva Rio worker. Conversation took place on the patio of Viva Rio's headquarters. July 2001.

Observations

Observations of Community Forum meeting. 28 May 1997.

Observations of Community Forum meeting. 9 September 1997.

Observations in community of prosecutor visit. A large group of activists, police, and reporters wandered around behind the prosecutor as he toured the community. The head of the local BPM conspicuously put his arm around Seu Almeida during this tour. 19 September 1997.

Observed meeting of CdP leadership in large building under construction on main street in Vigário Geral. 30 September 1997.

Observation of visit of NGO workers to community. 2 October 1997.

Observations of Community Forum meeting. 10 October 1997.

Observations of Community Forum meeting. 26 November 1997.

Observations in Vigário Geral and at Rio courthouse on the day of the trial of one of the police accused in the Vigário massacre. 27 November 1997.

Observed meeting of CVS in GCAR headquarters. This was an organizational meeting. It was well attended and very formal. 2 December 1997.

Observed meeting of the CVS. 6 January 1998.

Observations of Community Forum meeting. 7 January 1998.

Observed conversation in street after Community Forum meeting. Many residents participated in this conversation. 7 January 1998.

Observations in various places in Vigário on day and night of major flood. 8 January 1998.

Observations of community the day after a major flood. 9 January 1998.

Observation of protest about faulty public works. This meeting occurred on a street corner of the favela near an opened sewer pipe. The protest seemed to be led by CVS activists. Many residents and activists attended. 10 January 1998.

Observations of public conversation in community. These conversations took place during efforts to remove Jorginho from the leadership of the CdP. 22 January 1998.

Observations of GCAR presentation at SENAI, government-run linked business group. 23 January 1998.

Observed meeting organized by MSF to form MOGEC. 29 January 1998.

Observed meeting at CdP of "commission" trying to reform the CdP. 30 January 1998.

Meeting of commission to replace CdP leadership. 14 February 1998.

Director of Municipal Human Rights Office for Belo Horizonte. 22 July 2003.

Researchers at CRISP, UFMG. 22 July 2003.

Coordinator of crime studies program at UFMG. 23 July 2003.

Head of Belo Horizonte Homicide Investigations and member of Civil Police high command. 23 July 2003.

State Human Rights Ombudsman and staff. 23 July 2003.

Minas Gerais Policia Militar Battalion Deputy Commander in Belo Horizonte. 24 July 2003.

Members of Brigada Militar who work in Porto Alegre office of the Secretaria Nacional de Segurança Pública. 19 August 2003.

Major Tiago, representative of Secretaria Nacional de Segurança Pública in Rio Grande do Sul. 19 August 2003.

Universidade Federal do Rio Grande do Sul professor researching violence. 19 August 2003.

Lieutenant Colonel Higinio, senior battalion commander in Porto Alegre for Brigada Militar. 21 August 2003.

Delegado Gabriel, high-ranking civil police officer in São Paulo and official at federal level during the Cardoso presidential administration. Conversation took place in his office. 25 August 2003.

Retired São Paulo PM colonel who served in Federal Ministry of Justice. 26 August 2003.

Sub-secretary for public security for the state of Espírito Santo. 28 August 2003.

Bolivia, 42, 140, 202

Boston, 88, 146

Brazil: and human rights and violence, 1–14, 200–201, 204–5, 214–15; history of violence and inequality in, 19–30; overview of politics, crime, and corruption in, 30–37; policing structures in, 35; criminal networks and political order in, 42–44, 52, 55; ties between population and state in, 92, 127; massacres in, 141; crime and violence in Brazilian cities other than Rio, 170–77; violence in Brazil compared with violence in other Latin American countries, 177–88, 202–5

Brazilian military, 14, 21, 25–28, 36, 170; involvement in drug trafficking, 33

Breda Rio, 156

Bribes, 5, 29, 37, 44, 52, 75–78, 82, 87, 91, 98–99, 103, 114, 117, 127, 130–32, 137, 140, 171, 178–80, 185, 197, 201

Brigada Militar, 175. *See also* Porto Alegre

British Council, 156

Brizola, Leonel, 27–29, 36, 63–65, 81, 106, 126, 139

Brokers, 16, 26, 47, 81, 192, 194. *See also* Clientelism

"Brown" zones, 7–8, 52, 55, 203–4

Bureaucrats: relations with favelas, 33–37, 43, 47, 59, 66, 108, 157, 162; role in networks, 159, 191, 192, 200; in Colombia, 180

Burma, 187

Businesses: forced closings of, 1, 13, 113; role of business leaders in support of 1964 coup, 21; links to criminals, 40, 54, 65, 67–68, 70–72, 170–73, 178–79, 183, 186, 192; relations with civic actors, 47, 50; complaints to police, 112

Caldeira, Teresa, 9, 11

Calí, Colombia, 178–79

Candelária massacre, 141

Canudos War, 22

Capitanias Donataria, 20

Cargo robberies, 31

Carnival, 19, 21, 62, 147

Casa da Paz (House of Peace, CdP): founding of, 141–42; efforts to reduce violence in Vigário Geral, 142–44; and exile of Caio Ferraz, 145–46; Jorginho as executive director of, 147–48; relationship to other organizations in community, 149–63; recent events in, 207

Castaño, Carlos, 179

Cayman Islands, 54

Centro do Valorização do Ser (Center for Personal Development, CVS), 142, 158

Chagas Freitas, Antônio de Padua, 27

Channel Islands, 54

Children: traffickers' relations to, 32, 67, 70, 77, 97, 112, 134, 183; social programs' services for, 89, 99–100, 119, 126, 143, 152, 161; efforts to protect, 117; massacre of street children, 141

Chile, 184, 200

Citizens and citizenship, 4, 7, 11–13, 30, 37, 44–46, 57–63, 128, 139, 192, 201–2

City officials, 80, 157

Civil society: interaction with criminals, 2–3, 6, 10–14, 38–55 passim, 62, 65, 71, 82–87, 107–14, 116–18, 128–29, 139, 169, 178–94 passim, 201–6, 214; role in controlling violence, 15–16, 58–60, 87–92, 96, 99, 140, 166, 174–75, 198, 201–6; role in democratic transition, 21; role in mediating relations between favelas and the state, 37, 83, 96

Clientelism: theoretical discussion of, 2–6, 30–31, 192–94; changing practices in Rio, 24, 27–31, 35, 38, 54, 192–94; in Jamaica, 54, 181–86; contacts between politicians and traffickers in Rio, 67–69, 78–85, 87, 94–95, 115–17, 123, 126–28, 135, 155–61, 192–94

Coca, 53, 54, 180

Cocaine: global trade in, 13, 50; in Rio and Brazil, 28–29, 81, 106, 132, 170, 196; in Peru, 53; in Colombia, 53, 177–80, 202; crack cocaine, 173; in Jamaica, 182–84; in Mexico, 187, 196

Coelho, Paulo, 64

130–33, 139, 169; in Brazilian cities other than Rio, 170–77, 185–87; in other parts of Latin America and the Caribbean, 177–87. *See also* Crime; Criminal organizations; Gangs; Illegal networks

Drug transshipment, 31, 53, 169, 181, 186

Duffield, Mark, 41

Duque de Caxias, municipality of, 131

Dutra, Olívio, 175

Elections: in Latin America, 11, 179–84; in Brazil and Rio, 14, 20, 27, 36, 44, 69, 78–85, 106, 115–16, 159–60, 171, 193–95, 208; of favela leaders, 33, 37, 136, 148

Elites, 20, 21, 57, 197

Employment. *See* Jobs

Espírito Santo, 170–71

Estado Novo, 21–23

European Union, 163

Evangelical, Pentecostal, and Protestant Christians and Christianity, 34, 66–67, 71, 79–80, 89, 115, 141, 163, 193, 210–12

Expulsion of favela residents by drug traffickers, 34, 111, 136

Extortion, 26, 36, 76, 90–91, 103, 114–19, 175, 178–79, 212–13. *See also* Bribes; Corruption; Police and policing

Fábio, Caio, 142

Facções, 32. *See also* Gangs

Favelas: conditions in, 1, 30–38, 60–62, 96–104, 130–32, 207–13; drug traffickers' operations in, 1–2, 30–32, 64–74, 107–14, 162–64, 192–94; approaches to studying, 3–14; efforts to control violence in, 14–16, 87–95, 135–64, 198–200; establishment of, 22–23; under Estado Novo, 23; vigilantism in, 24; and electrical service, 24, 27, 63–64, 105–6, 131–32, 139; development of internal political organizations in, 24–30; and residents' associations, 24–30, 33–35, 65–70, 90–91, 105, 107–18, 132–35, 142–44, 147–51, 208–13; and removal efforts, 25–26; growth of drug trafficking in, 28–30; and politicians, 33–35, 37–38,

78–81, 91–95, 115–16; policing in, 35–37, 74–78, 114–15, 120–22, 126–27, 130–32; and NGOs, 73, 83, 88–95, 119–21, 135–64, 208–10

Federação de Associações de Favelas do Estado de Guanabara (Federation of Favela Associations of the State of Guanabara, FAFEG), 25–26

Federação de Associações de Favelas do Estado de Rio de Janeiro (Federation of Favela Associations of the State of Rio de Janeiro, FAFERJ), 26–27

Federal government of Brazil, 14, 21–25, 89. *See also* Brazil; State

Fernandes, Rubem César, 3, 30, 127, 142, 163

Ferraz, Caio, 141–46, 152–55, 162–63

Festa, 107, 108, 110, 113, 117, 118, 195

Festivities, 66, 70–77, 109, 117–18; Christmas parties, 70–71; *festa junina*, 107, 118

Flexa Ribeiro, Carlos, 25

Flood of 1998, 152, 157, 158, 160

Florida gun shops, 183

Força Nacional de Segurança Pública, 22

Formal economic sector, 23, 30

Forros, 62, 70

Fuerzas Armadas Revolucionarias de Colombia (Revolutionary Armed Forces of Colombia, FARC), 8, 178–80

Fundação Lar Escola Francisco de Paula, 142, 148

Fundação Leão XIII, 24, 131

Funding. *See* Gangs: and funding of services in favelas; Nongovernmental organizations: and funding; State

Funk. See *Baile funks*

Gangs: international gangs, 1, 177–85; impact of on Rio, 1–2, 7–8; and funding of services in favelas, 12, 70, 107, 134, 179; and history of Rio, 20, 28–29, 65, 105, 130–40; organizational structure of, 31–32; and theory, 46; and war and conflict, 61, 63, 74–78, 82, 134–36, 208–10; and police, 74–78, 87–88, 114–15, 130–31, 139–41, 207–14; and festivities, 76–81,

in Colombia, 178, 180–81, 187. *See also* Cocaine; Gangs; Marijuana

Negão, Flavio, 134, 136, 140, 149, 153, 160

Negrão de Lima, Francisco, 25

Neoclientelism, 3, 4, 193

Neoliberalism, 42, 57, 86

Neo-Pentecostals, 34. *See also* Evangelical, Pentecostal, and Protestant Christians and Christianity

Networks: effects and functions of, 2, 10, 13–15, 52–57, 86–87, 194–96; and co-optation, 2, 15, 27–28, 31, 39, 51, 60, 83–87, 94, 118, 125, 161, 169, 187, 191, 197; and politics, 5–6, 27–30, 37–38, 78–81, 114–16, 159–60, 184–85; and weak and strong ties, 13, 47, 119, 191; and efforts to avoid arrest, 13–14, 31, 39, 47–48, 50–51, 59, 134, 169, 191, 202; and efforts to control violence, 14–16, 34, 57–60, 87–95, 119–24, 132, 140–65, 172–74, 198–200, 209; and hubs, 31, 118, 182; defined, 39–41; components of, 41–48, 189–91; structure of, 48–52, 191–92; and flexibility, 51, 82, 119, 191, 195, 198, 207; and variation, 196–97. *See also* Clientelism; Illegal networks; Norms

New Republic, 21, 30–31, 91. *See also* Brazil

Newspapers, 122, 207

New York, 205, 215

Niteroi, 153

Nongovernmental organizations (NGOs): role in sustaining conflict, 10, 15–16, 59–60; and efforts to control violence, 15–16, 33–34, 43–58, 61, 64, 88–92, 99, 105, 115, 119–23, 135, 137, 141–63, 207–10; and limitations of violence control efforts, 15–16, 92–94, 122, 130, 163–67, 199–200, 209–10; and workers, 15–16, 209–10; and funding, 119, 156, 161, 163, 174, 209. *See also* Civil society; Social movements and mobilizations

Nordstrom, Carolyn, 41

Noriega, Manuel, 187

Norms: and criminality, 3, 32–33, 41, 44, 47, 50, 59, 71–73, 98, 112–13, 117, 121, 196;

international norms, 6, 12, 21, 44, 86, 213; and politics, 6, 46; and networks, 13, 40–41, 44, 46–47, 60, 69, 98; and communities, 24, 26, 33, 71–73, 98, 104, 112–13, 117, 121, 196; and policing, 213. *See also* Networks

Northeastern Brazil, 62, 100, 132, 204

O'Donnell, Guillermo, 7, 52–53, 55, 200, 203–4

Ofícios (official memos), 71

O Globo, 18–19

Old Republic, 20, 21, 22

Onda Azul, 148, 163

Operação Rio, 14

Operation Cease Fire, 88–90, 146. *See also* Police and policing

Paley, Julia, 42

Panama, 187

Parada de Lucas, 130–33, 138–40, 147–48, 154, 164, 207–10'

Parallel powers and states, 1, 3–5, 8, 53, 86, 203, 204, 206, 214

Paramilitary attitudes and behaviors in law enforcement, 35, 175

Paramilitary organizations, 9, 46, 178–81

Parques proletários, 23, 131

Partido dos Trabalhadores (Workers' Party, PT), 22, 36, 175. *See also* Da Silva, Benedita; Da Silva, Luiz Inácio Lula; Soares, Luiz Eduardo

Partido Revolucionario Institucional (Institutional Revolutionary Party, PRI), 184–86

Patrons and patronage, 5, 30, 34, 69, 85, 156, 192, 194, 196. *See also* Clientelism

Payne, Leigh, 9

Peasants, 11

Pécaut, Daniel, 178

Peer surveillance, 50, 199. *See also* Networks

Penitentiaries, 28, 176. *See also* Prisons

Pentecostals and Pentecostalism, 34, 79–80, 193. *See also* Evangelical, Pentecostal, and Protestant Christians and Christianity

People's National Party (PNP), 181, 182. *See also* Jamaica

Pereira, Anthony, 9, 201

Perlman, Janice, 19, 25, 215

Peru, 1, 11, 53–54, 187, 200, 202, 206

Plata o plomo, 178. *See also* Colombia; Corruption

Police and policing: and violence, 1, 3–4, 7, 9, 16, 22, 26–29, 34–37, 57, 61, 75–114 passim, 121–24, 126–28, 130, 135–56 passim, 161–76 passim, 182–86, 189, 197–213 passim; and repression, 1, 4, 9, 12, 19–20, 26, 31, 33–34, 37, 87, 128, 144, 202; and policies, 1, 4, 15, 22, 31, 36, 57, 72, 82, 87–90, 92–93, 95, 101, 104, 115, 118, 123, 130, 135, 142–48, 159, 166, 168, 173–75, 189–90, 195, 197–201; and race, 1, 19–21, 26, 176; and illegal networks, 3, 7–8, 12, 15–16, 35–37, 43–58 passim, 62, 64, 71–72, 74–78, 82, 87, 94–95, 98–99, 104–5, 110, 114–28 passim, 132, 137–40, 164, 170–72, 176, 178–79, 183–86, 190–92, 195–96, 200–201, 207–9, 212; and corruption, 5, 7–8, 15–16, 20, 26, 29, 35–38, 44, 47–48, 50–52, 54, 57–58, 62–64, 74–78, 82, 84–85, 87–88, 90, 98–99, 104, 114–16, 118–21, 126–28, 130, 132, 137, 140, 145, 153, 164, 170–73, 176, 178–79, 183–85, 190–92, 195–96, 201, 207–9, 213; and reform, 7, 15, 21, 27, 57–60, 66, 82–84, 87–94, 123, 130, 135, 140–76 passim, 190, 195–99, 201, 205, 213; and authoritarian legacies, 9; and private security, 9, 45; and training, 11, 57; and "War on Drugs," 12; and massacres, 16, 130, 137–41, 151, 199; history of, 19–22, 23; and favelas, 23, 29, 112, 133; and Belo Horizonte, 24, 31, 170, 172, 173, 174, 176, 186; and favela leadership, 34, 37, 65, 71, 83–84, 91, 108, 110, 149; and leadership, 37, 84, 89–91, 93–94, 117, 127, 130, 139, 172–73, 196–97, 201, 205, 207–9, 213; and civic networks, 57–60; and arrests, 71, 114–15, 117, 191; and informants, 71, 134; and domestic abuse, 72–73; and conflict resolution, 72–73, 111, 158; and NGOs, 88, 89, 95, 118, 119, 120, 121, 122, 145, 146, 147, 151, 152, 153, 156, 161, 165, 167, 208, 209; and Boston reform program, 88, 146; conflict among police, 94; and elite units, 101; and *baile funks*, 164; in Espírito Santo, 170–72, 186; in Porto Alegre, 175–76; in Colombia, 178–79; in Jamaica, 181–84; in Mexico, 184–85

Polícia Civil (Civil Police, PC), 35–36, 108, 126, 173

Polícia Federal, 171

Polícia Militar (Military Police, PM), 35, 61, 63, 68, 75–77, 87–88, 90, 93, 97, 101, 108, 126–27, 130, 137, 139, 146, 173–75

Polícia mineira (vigilante groups), 24, 65

Policy networks, 41

Political cleavages, 205

Political coalitions, 65

Political networks, 38, 57, 169, 184

Political order, 7, 55, 82, 87, 186

Political prisoners, 28

Political systems, 7, 11–12, 41, 53, 205

Politicians, 4–5, 12–14, 21–38 passim, 43–54 passim, 62–67, 69, 74, 78–82, 85–87, 95, 98–99, 104–6, 114–18, 123–28, 131, 136–37, 140, 159, 165–66, 170, 178–79, 180, 182–86, 190–94, 201, 210, 212. *See also* Clientelism

Popular housing: history of, 19, 22–24

Populism, 24, 27, 184

Porto Alegre, 31, 170, 174, 176, 186

Ports and port facilities, 31, 53, 169, 171, 181–82, 186–87

Portuguese colonial government, 19–20

Poverty, 3, 18–19, 22, 53, 61, 169

Powell, Walter, 39

Praia do Pinto favela, 25

Prisons, 7, 28, 41, 66, 70, 79, 89, 108; prison gangs, 31–32, 65, 176–77; prison uprisings, 176. *See also* Jails

Private and informal protection, 1, 2, 12, 14, 33, 34, 37, 46, 54, 57–58, 68, 70, 78, 80, 104, 116, 122, 164, 169, 176–90 passim, 194, 196, 202, 206, 208

Private military contractors, 10

transition to democracy, 21, 27–28, 38; and theory, 51, 58, 122–23, 129, 165; and efforts to fix sewer, 159; and guerrillas, 178. *See also* Uncivil movements

Social networks. *See* Illegal networks; Networks

Society: and authoritarianism, 7, 58; and Latin America, 17; and engagement with criminals, 41–44, 47, 60, 95–96, 116–17, 128–29, 180, 185–86, 192–93, 205; in Colombia, 180; in Mexico, 185–86. *See also* Civil society; Social movements and mobilizations; Uncivil movements

Society-at-large, 5, 117

Soviet Union, 178

State: and globalization, 1, 11–12, 39, 41–43, 57, 190, 200; and corruption, 1–9, 28, 57, 63, 75–76, 112, 115, 139, 185; and violence, 2, 4–5, 7, 9–10, 25–27, 41, 55, 57, 85, 99–104, 130, 132–33, 140; in Brazil, 3–5, 20–28, 30, 37, 53; and authoritarianism, 7, 25–27; weakness and failure of, 7, 37, 42–43, 87, 201, 203–6; and criminal networks, 11–13, 31, 37–64 passim, 74–87, 95–96, 98, 110, 114–18, 126, 128–29, 138–40, 169, 171, 177, 186–203 passim; role in favelas, 14, 19, 22–38 passim, 61, 64, 67, 74–80, 83, 101, 112, 117, 122, 125–26, 128, 192, 210; contact with violence control networks, 14–16, 57–59, 88–92, 121, 141–43, 145, 150–51, 158, 161, 164–67, 174, 198–99; role in favela removal, 25–27, 63, 106; contact with NGOs in violence control networks, 34, 43, 58–59, 88–92, 142–52 passim, 158, 161–65, 198, 209–10; state government of Rio, 36, 63–64, 88–90, 92, 94, 133, 159, 164, 169, 210, 213; state-society frontier, 40, 196; contact with civil society, 45–46, 48, 88–92, 96; in Peru, 53–54; in Colombia, 53–54, 177–81; in Jamaica, 53–54, 181–84; in Cayman Islands, 54; in Channel Islands, 54; in Hong Kong, 54; state bureaucrats, 65, 85–86, 192; role in favela reform efforts, 88–95; and weakness of

violence control networks, 93–95; role in provision of services in favelas, 106, 131, 152, 209; role in building schools in favelas, 133, 139; and criminal networks in Espírito Santo, 171–72, 186–87; contact with violence control networks in Minas Gerais, 173–74; and criminal networks in Colombia, 178, 180–81, 187; and criminal networks in Jamaica, 182–83; and criminal networks in Mexico, 184–85, 187; and criminal networks in Panama, 187. *See also* Illegal networks; Parallel powers and states

State penetration, 54

State secretary for public security, 164

State-society frontier, 10, 40, 47, 174, 190, 196, 198, 201, 214

Status hierarchies, 5

Strange, Susan, 41

Strong ties. *See* Networks

Structural adjustment, 11, 44, 203

Suburbs, 19, 77, 131, 204

Suffrage, 24

Supremo Tribunal de Justiça, 147

Terrorism, 9, 35

Theft, 63, 72, 76, 106, 122. *See also* Crime

Topography, 138, 197

Torture, 102, 200

Tourists, 31, 92, 124, 182, 215

Training, 20, 90, 121, 125, 155

Transition: from authoritarian rule, 1, 9, 27–30, 36, 57, 81, 200; from one-party dominant rule in Mexico, 184, 202

Transnational advocacy networks, 40, 58

Trash collection and collectors, 33, 103, 109, 119, 150

Trash slide: destruction of homes in, 62

Trust: and networks, 13, 39–40, 48, 50–51, 98, 137, 162, 196, 199; and relations between gangs, 32; and relations in favelas, 84, 89–90, 101, 118, 120, 124–25, 196, 209–10; and relations between favela residents and police, 90, 101–2, 145; and relations between favela residents and outside groups, 118, 120, 124, 162. *See also* Favelas; Networks; Police and policing

Uncivil movements, 9

Universidade Federal de Minas Gerais (UFMG), 173–74

United States, 12, 145–46, 153–55, 179, 182, 215

Vargas, Getúlio, 21, 23

Veloso, Caetano, 155, 156

Ventura, Zuenir, 142

Vigário Geral favela, 1, 16, 92, 101, 103, 115, 122, 129–67, 174, 189, 193, 195–99, 207–10, 214–15

Vigilantes. See *Polícia mineira*

Violence control efforts, 2, 12, 14–16, 57, 59–60, 82, 84, 88, 90, 121, 123, 129, 131, 154, 165–66, 189, 199–200, 202, 205; role of crisis in, 60, 123, 141, 142, 178

Vitória, 31, 170–72, 186–87

Viva Rio, 88–94, 142, 163, 175

War Ministry, 22

War on Drugs, 4

Water spigots, 24, 105, 131. *See also* Associações de Moradores; Clientelism

Weak ties. *See* Networks

West Africa, 42

Williams, Phil, xvi, 39, 40

Women, 32, 34, 71, 73, 80, 102, 105, 120–21, 157

World Bank, 43

Zaluar, Alba, 19

Zona Sul, ix, x, 18–19, 23–24, 29, 31, 35, 62, 64, 66, 71, 95, 104, 124, 142, 146, 196, 214